EDUCATION AND FEMALE EMANCIPATION: THE WELSH EXPERIENCE, 1847–1914

EDUCATION
AND
FEMALE EMANCIPATION:
the Welsh experience, 1847–1914

W. GARETH EVANS

CARDIFF
UNIVERSITY OF WALES PRESS
1990

British Library Cataloguing in Publication Data

Evans, W. Gareth
  Education and female emancipation: the Welsh experience
  1. Wales. Women. Education, history
  I. Title
  376.9429

ISBN 0-7083-1079-6

Typeset and printed at the Alden Press,
Oxford London and Northampton

Er cof am fy rhieni
Robert John a Mary Evans

Patriots, republicans, friends of the people and all who deeply care for the welfare of the Principality, all admit that it is only by making the foundations of education strong and deep — so strong and deep that it will reach not one sex only, but both — that the full measure of national prosperity, of national happiness and usefulness, and of national growth can be attained.

Frances E. Hoggan, *Education for Girls in Wales* (1882)

Contents

page

Preface   ix

Acknowledgements   xiii

1   The Place of Girls and Women in the Educational History of Wales   1

2   The Historical Context   11

3   Limited Schooling, 1840–1880   44

4   Teacher Training and Higher Education, 1840–1880   80

5   Promotion of Educational Reform in the 1880s   110

6   Intermediate and Secondary Education for Girls, 1889–1914   153

7   Teacher Training for Women in Wales, 1880–1914   185

8   Women in the University Colleges of Wales, 1880–1914   208

9   Conclusion   254

Appendix A   264

Appendix B   265

Notes   270

Bibliography   306

Index   323

Preface

In 1985, one of the four excellent packs of resource material accompanying the television series *The Dragon Has Two Tongues* highlighted aspects of Welsh women's history. It was promoted 'in response to the series' failure to grasp the opportunity to restore to visibility more than half the population of Wales.' Attention was given to the varied aspects of the Welsh woman's social and economic condition throughout history. The thirty-eighth, of the forty themes examined, focused briefly on women's education. The many perspectives to Welsh women's history identified, albeit briefly, both emphasize the current interests of feminist historians and concentrate the mind wonderfully on this vast unknown and unresearched territory.

In this study of the educational history of Victorian, Edwardian and pre-war Wales, the focus has been on locating the female and her education within the social, religious, political and cultural context of society. It has been shown that the educational experience of women varied according to social class; therefore this study presents an educational history of girls and women as social beings rather than in institutional isolation.

The book also attempts to put the female back into the record of the educational history of a most significant era for the Principality from which she had been virtually excluded. Girls and women did not live in society in isolation, and, to avoid a new bias or reverse discrimination, I have shown that women's history in Victorian, Edwardian and pre-war Wales has to be integrated into the discipline of history as a whole. This study, though focusing primarily on one of the sexes, has been concerned with a Welsh past encompassing both sexes. The exclusion of the educational experience of boys and men would have led to the writing of little more than ghetto history.

Researched partly during the latter half of the United Nations' 'Decade for Women' (1975–85) which aimed to eliminate all obstacles in the way of women enjoying equal status with men, the study also shows the relevance of the historical perspective for the feminist and women's struggle today. It provides meaningful examples, and a broad historical perspective, that should prove valuable in a balanced approach to such current educational issues as inequalities between the sexes, gender stereotyping and sexism in the curriculum. A century after the formation of 'The Association for Promoting the Education of Girls in Wales', the exploration of the history of girls and women remains relevant in the quest for a deeper understanding of the educational issues and problems of contemporary Wales.

This book is based not only on the insights of previous historical research, but also on a wide range of primary and secondary sources, manuscript and printed materials. Various government reports have proved invaluable. They include the reports of Parliamentary and Departmental Committees and Royal Commissions, Committee of Council minutes, and HMI reports. Hansard and census returns were used extensively. Charity Commission reports and endowment and institutional files deposited at the Public Record Office have also been of vital importance.

While much research was carried out in the archives of central government, the theme could not be examined fully without reference to the extensive source materials at the level of local government. The minutes and reports of the Joint Education Committees of Wales and Monmouthshire, the minutes of county council, county governing bodies and local education authorities were also drawn upon. The reports of the Central Welsh Board have been essential in evaluating the development of the intermediate schools.

Institutions figure prominently in this study and a wide range of minutes, calendars, reports, magazines and varied manuscript and printed sources relating to schools, training-colleges, and university colleges, have been consulted in numerous archives. The minutes of the University of Wales Court and Senate, and the Guild of Graduates have proved useful. The publications of the 'Cymmrodorion Section of the National Eisteddfod', the contributions of Eisteddfod essayists, and the minutes and publications of 'The Association for Promoting the Education of Girls in Wales' have been invaluable source material.

The wider setting of the theme in its cultural and social context could not be structured without reference to the extensive evidence of English and Welsh newspapers and periodicals. In particular, *The Cambrian News* and *Baner ac Amserau Cymru* have proved to be a rich vein, primarily because of the especial interest of Sir John Gibson, Thomas Gee and J.H. Griffith 'Y Gohebydd" in the role of women. Ieuan

Gwynedd's *Y Gymraes*, Cranogwen's *Y Frythones* and Ceridwen Peris's *Y Gymraes* have also proved valuable. Advertisements in newspapers and trade directories have been a major source for unravelling the fortunes of the private schools of Victorian Wales.

The papers of such key individuals as Ieuan Gwynedd, R.J. Derfel, Thomas Gee, Lewis Edwards, T. Charles Edwards, Samuel Holland, Hugh Owen, Lord Aberdare, Lord Rendel, A.C. Humphreys-Owen, Isambard Owen, J. Viriamu Jones, H.R. Reichel, T. Francis Roberts and T.E. Ellis have been consulted with a varying success, and reveal that the advancement of female education received much support from enlightened men. Pioneering women have also left archival material of varying utility. The papers of Frances Power Cobbe deposited in the National Library of Wales were a disappointing source, and any substantial collection of papers of Lady Verney and Miss Carpenter have proved too elusive for the present writer. More success has been gained with the papers of Lady Llanover, Lady Charlotte Guest, Mrs Rose Mary Crawshay, Dr Frances Hoggan, Lady Aberdare, Miss Elizabeth P. Hughes, and the recently deposited Dilys Glynne Jones collection at UCNW Bangor.

Acknowledgements

My debts in the writing of this book are many. Indeed, some of them extend over a quarter of a century when I was fortunate in being introduced to the methodology of historical research by two masters of the historian's craft, the late Professor David Williams and Emeritus Professor Gwyn A. Williams. On my return to Aberystwyth, I have profited greatly from Professor J. Roger Webster's advice and encouragement. I am grateful too, for help from colleagues and friends, Dr Peter Ellis Jones and Mr Gareth Williams, and also for the typing skills of Mrs Lynne Richards.

The work could not have been accomplished without the generous assistance and limitless patience of the staff of numerous libraries, record offices, colleges and schools mentioned in the book. In particular, I am greatly indebted to the staff of the National Library of Wales, the Worshipful Company of Drapers, the staff of the library of the University College of North Wales, Bangor, and the late Mr John Davies, librarian of Trinity College, Carmarthen. I should like to thank Hughes Hall, Cambridge and also Miss Dilys E. Glynne. Mrs Onfel Thomas, Builth Wells was most helpful in allowing access to her late husband's papers concerning Dr Frances Hoggan. My wife's patience and support were invaluable throughout the years of research and writing.

I acknowledge with gratitude the advice given by Mr John Rhys, Director of the University of Wales Press, and also by Professor J. Gwynn Williams, Chairman, regarding the format of the book. I particularly wish to thank Ms Liz Powell for her invaluable guidance and the care and professionalism with which she has seen the work into print.

W. GARETH EVANS
University College of Wales, Aberystwyth

1

The Place of Girls and Women in the Educational History of Wales

Until comparatively recently, historical writing in Britain gave little attention to the experience of women. Though constituting half the population, they have been invisible in our history books. Juliet Gardiner has called for the 'rescue of women' who have been traditionally 'hidden' from history.[1] The male bias in historical writing has been highlighted in such works as Dale Spender's *Invisible Women* (1982) and Sheila Rowbotham's *Hidden from History* (1973). Lord Asa Briggs has referred to 'the long neglected study of women's history'.[2] In numerous general studies of Victorian Britain, only peripheral attention has been given to the changing role of women in society, and even less to the education of girls and women.

In Wales, also, there has been an increasing awareness of the neglect of women's history. In 1980, Professor Deirdre Beddoe focused attention on 'the sex imbalance' and 'the missing Welsh women' in the Principality's histories. Indeed, she maintains that:

> The history of women in Wales has yet to be written. Our female forbears remain hidden from history as securely and as invisibly as Indian women in old-style purdah. . . . An extra-terrestrial visitor to the planet, landing in Wales and seeking to find who the Welsh people are, would turn to the bulky corpus of historical writing. She would come away bewildered at how the Welsh managed to procreate themselves. They were all men! . . . In the past, the history of Wales — like the history of England, the United States, France, Germany etc. — simply omitted women. History was neither about them nor for them.[3]

Professor Beddoe noted further in 1981 that of the 12,500 theses accepted for higher degrees of the University of Wales in the period 1905–80, only seven dealt with an aspect of 'women in Wales', and only three were concerned with the history of women in Wales.[4]

With the possible exception of Madam Bevan and Lady Llanover, women have hardly figured at all in accounts of Welsh educational history. Significantly, the female is conspicuous by her absence from

that brief but excellent volume published over two decades ago—
Pioneers of Welsh Education (1963).

Much research remains to be accomplished. In 1981, Theodore
Zeldin argued that women's history is still in 'a comparatively early
phase and is absorbed by the need to collect information'.[5] Likewise in
Wales, whilst 'the history of omission'[6] is slowly being rectified, it was
accurately stated in *Llafur* in 1982 that the historical study of women
in the Principality 'had hardly started'.[7] At *Llafur*'s 1983 Easter Conference which focused on the theme of 'Working Class Women: the Welsh
Experience Past and Present', recent research findings were highlighted
and the need for many further studies to correct a hitherto male-
orientated tunnel vision of Welsh history.[8]

During the 1970s and 1980s, research in women's history has grown
at a rapid pace both in Britain and the USA. Such works as Robin
Morgan (ed.) *The International Women's Movement Anthology: Sisterhood is Global* (1985); R. Bridenthal and C. Koong (eds.), *Becoming
Visible, Women in European History* (1977); Martha Vicinus (ed.),
Suffer and Be Still: Women in the Victorian Age (1972); Patricia Branca,
Women in Europe Since 1750 (1973); Olive Banks, *Faces of Feminism*
(1981); Leonore Davidoff and Catherine Hall, *Family Fortunes: Men
and Women of the English Middle Class 1780 to 1850* (1987) and Susan
Bassnett, *Elizabeth I: A Feminist Perspective* (1988), epitomize the
wide-ranging nature of recent research.

In Wales also, Professor Deirdre Beddoe's *Welsh Convict Women*
(1979) and *Discovering Women's History* (1983), Angela John's *By the
Sweat of their Brow: Workers at Victorian Coal-mines* (1980), and
Llafur (1981–4), a journal of Welsh labour history, have explored the
much neglected role of women in the industrial and social history of the
Principality in the eighteenth and nineteenth centuries. Significantly,
one of the themes examined, albeit briefly, in a highly successful television series in 1985—*The Dragon Has Two Tongues*—was the
woman's historical experience. The theme was further examined in
Professor Gwyn A. Williams's *When Was Wales?* (1985). In January
1986, for the first time in its distinguished history, *Y Traethodydd*
focused exclusively on a feminine theme—women and literature—
'Merched a Llenyddiaeth'.[9] Filling the historical vacuum is seen as
relevant, both to the perpetuation of a Welsh identity, and to the
woman's struggle today.[10]

Such work as *Merched Llên Cymru o 1850 i 1914* (1935) by Iorwen
Myfanwy Jones, offers useful literary perspectives on femininity, which
are also evident in two scholarly articles by Principal R. Tudur Jones

in *Coroni'r Fam Frenhines* (1976) and *Ysgrifau Beirniadol XI* (1979).[11] In particular, the impact of the perception of the female as 'the Angel in the House' is examined with reference to Welsh literature. Recent studies in Welsh legal history — D. Jenkins and M. Owen, *The Welsh Law of Women*[12] — have also given some attention to the position of women in medieval society.

The interest in women's history has been generated by numerous social changes that have affected historical perception. The emergence of an international feminist movement in the 1960s, inspired by a commitment to justice and equality, has been a powerful influence. History has been viewed as a reservoir of evidence concerning women's subjection, exploitation and quest for emancipation which is of direct relevance to current feminist concerns. The historical record is seen as an instrument to infuse greater awareness of the inequalities experienced by girls and women both in the past and today. The past and present are seen as interlocked, with the past informing the present and the present providing meaningful explorations into the past. Currently, there is much interest in seeing feminist issues, including educational inequalities, in a historical context. The great increase in feminist publications in Britain and abroad, which give the historical perspective significant attention, is epitomized in the growth of Virago's turnover from £30,000 in 1977 to £1 million in 1984.[13]

A number of studies of women's history, not necessarily all written by feminists, have been motivated by Marxism, and these are preoccupied with class as well as sexual exploitation. Their work reflects the growth of working-class history attested by such journals as *History Workshop* and *Llafur* which are committed to women's history as well as labour history. They have made a significant contribution to broadening the perspectives of both British and Welsh history through studies of working-class women. Women's involvement in nineteenth-century campaigns against enclosures in Wales, as well as the Rebecca and Chartist movements, are now being recognized.[14] In particular, these studies highlight the dangers of ignoring the influence of social class on the female experience.[15]

The widening compass of social history has also focused attention on hitherto neglected themes such as the family, marriage, motherhood, domesticity, the doctrine of separate spheres and Social Darwinism. These are now being increasingly explored and are of profound importance for studies of women in history.

In spite of the attention given to women in books and courses in higher education, women's history has yet to gain academic respectability. It has been viewed as 'a ghetto subject', 'a trivial history' and even as 'uterine history'.[16] It met with the same distrust in some quarters as Black Studies.[17] In 1986, when a high powered delegation pleaded the cause of historical studies in the House of Lords, Professor Sir Geoffrey Elton equated women's history with non-history. Many critics regard some recent studies as distorting the historical record through pursuing a quest for a separate feminist past in order to restore women to history.[18] The sex imbalance in historical studies needs to be corrected through examining the female experience within a specific cultural context, rather than endeavouring to view the history of women as though they were a separate species. Men as well as women were affected by oppression. A balanced interpretation of the woman's past requires the examination of the whole of society at a particular time. The history of women and men together, needs to be interpreted from new perspectives. The exploration of a whole society and culture is thus necessary for a valid study of the provision of secondary and higher education for girls and women in nineteenth and twentieth-century Wales.

Amongst recent studies in education from a feminist viewpoint, Margaret Bryant's *The Unexpected Revolution* (1979) is of particular importance.[19] Though her concentration on the education of middle-class girls and women has been criticized, her work has highlighted the weakness of earlier studies of girls' education which failed to examine the relationships between education and a range of social, economic, political, religious and cultural determinants in Victorian Britain. As well as pinpointing the middle-class nature of the quest for access to secondary and higher education, Bryant also analyses the changing economic pressures that forced middle-class women into the labour market. She also contends that '. . . the most unexpected revolution occurred within a surprisingly short period in the mid-nineteenth century, at a time, when all educational institutions were ripe for reform and expansion'. She sees the education of girls as an aspect of educational reform *in toto*, involving boys as well as girls, rather than a pure struggle between the sexes. The campaign for girls' education was supported by influential middle-class men as well as women.

Sheila Fletcher's *Feminists and Bureaucrats* (1980)[20] underlines the significance of the attention given to girls' education in the inquiries of the Taunton Committee that ensured that the Endowed Schools Commission, created by the Endowed Schools Act of 1869, also sought ways of creating and developing girls' schools. Such a movement was greatly influenced by civil servants such as Lord Lyttleton, and Joshua Fitch, HMI. Joan M. Burstyn's *Victorian Education and the Ideal of Woman-*

hood (1980) shows the profound influence on education of the domestic ideal of womanhood as articulated by the middle class, which insisted on separate spheres for men and women with, of course, men retaining ultimate supremacy. Carol Dyhouse's *Girls Growing up in late Victorian and Edwardian England* (1981) takes the argument further by showing the influence of Social Darwinistic ideas that seemed to support the division of the sexes and strengthen the impact of the domestic ideal on attitudes to girls' education and the sexual division of labour.[21]

June Purvis's writings in 1981 and 1982 highlight the impact of the prevailing feminine–domestic ideology on attitudes to, and the provision of, girls' education.[22] The notion of separate spheres for men and women in a partriarchal society is further illustrated in her work. Feminine ideology was equated in the Victorian age with a domestic role involving wifehood and motherhood. Purvis chastises educational historians for not giving sufficient attention to the sexual divisions of society. She discusses those men who helped the female cause and she looks at those middle-class women who were opposed to higher education for their own sex. She also prompts researchers to consider further the influence of the State on the content of girls' education.

Much progress has been made in unravelling numerous aspects of the educational history of Wales, but education has yet to be integrated within the mainstream of Welsh historical studies.[23] Indeed, but for a few exceptions, most of the studies in Welsh educational history have been the histories of institutions divorced from the overall social context.

The struggle for the education of girls and women in Victorian and Edwardian Wales remains a neglected topic. The task facing the historian of women's education in the 1980s is similar to that perceived in 1883 by Dr Frances Hoggan, one of the great pioneers of female education in Wales, as '. . . starting afresh on what may be called educationally virgin soil'.[24]

Educational developments do not occur in a social and political vacuum, and the fortunes of girls' and women's education in nineteeth and twentieth-century Wales are only really meaningful with reference to the broad, social context and a whole complexity of interrelationships. Here, a range of factors proved to be constraints and impediments to progress as well as agents of change. Prevailing perceptions of femininity and the family, together with the force of tradition, conservatism and prejudice, were major barriers to educational change. So also were the impact of Mosaic and Pauline religion, Social Darwinism, the law, and medical opposition to girls' higher education. The interrelationship of social class structure and education was particularly evident, with the provision of secondary and higher education perceived primarily in terms of the needs of the middle class. For working-class girls, elementary schooling with a particular domestic orientation was deemed essential. Its influence on attitudes to female education in the secondary sector was considerable.

In pinpointing the determinants of developments in the provision and content of secondary and higher education for girls and women in the Victorian era in Wales, the influence of key individuals, both male and female, groups and societies such as the Cymmrodorion and National Eisteddfod, religious, economic and demographic factors as well as impersonal trends need to be assessed. The changing concept of womanhood and the wider quest for emancipation were instrumental in ushering change and development in the educational sphere. As well as showing the crucial impact of educational developments in England on events in Wales, the differences between the circumstances of the two countries also need to be noted. In particular, the relationship between the quest for female secondary and higher education and the Liberal Nonconformist struggle in Victorian Wales was decisive.

Key events in the growth and development of female education include the role of official educational inquiries and the ensuing reports — Blue Books, Pakington, Newcastle, Taunton, Aberdare and Cross. The influence of the State on the development of female education through the reform of educational endowments and the agency of the Endowed Schools Commission and Charity Commission in the 1870s and 1880s, had a decisive impact on the varying fortunes of girls' secondary education at Dolgellau, Beaumaris, Llandaff, Denbigh, Pengam, Haverfordwest and Monmouth. The Welsh Intermediate Education Act 1889 was significant for girls' education as was the long and often acrimonious quest for legislation over the previous decade.

The educational debate is only meaningful with reference to the contemporary religious and political conflicts. The evaluation of the nature of the system of intermediate schools focuses attention on such key issues as co-education, curriculum content and differentiation, dual schools, status of women headteachers, and female representation on governing bodies.

The promulgation of a range of educational ideas exerted a significant impact on the fortunes of secondary and higher education for girls and women. A large number of treatises were published over four decades, from the 1850s to the 1890s. As well as the work of essayists in numerous eisteddfodau, they included the work of such perceptive thinkers as the socialist, R.J. Derfel, and the redoubtable Huwco Meirion and the Reverend Rhys Gwesyn Jones in the 1850s and 1860s. The response of Ieuan Gwynedd in *Y Gymraes* to the strictures against Welsh womanhood in the Blue Books was of particular significance. The journal made a key contribution to the female cause in Victorian Wales, as did its worthy successor — *Y Frythones*. Hitherto completely neglected sources of enlightened educational thought in the 1870s and 1880s exist in the writings of Dr Frances Hoggan, Dr Sophie Bryant, Dilys Glynne Jones and Elizabeth P. Hughes. They exerted a profound impact on the fortunes of girls' intermediate education and women's higher education in Wales, particularly through the agency of the much underestimated Association for Promoting the Education of Girls in Wales, in existence from 1886 to 1901, and the influential Cymmrodorion Society.

The reformers of secondary and higher education in the 1850s and 60s, and even in the 1870s, espoused a male-orientated perception of the educational needs of Wales, as is evident from B.T. Williams's *The Desirableness of a University for Wales* (1853), the proposed Gnoll College 1857, Dr Thomas Nicholas's *Middle and High Schools and a University for Wales* (1863), the University of Wales Movement in the 1860s and 70s, and the eventual opening of the University College of Wales, Aberystwyth in 1872 with twenty-six male students. The advocacy of greater educational opportunity in the 1870s by the Revd. D.L. Lloyd's *The Missing Link in Education in Wales* (1876), Bishop Joshua Hughes' *A Plea for Higher Education in Wales* (1876) and 'The North Wales, Scholarship Association (1879–94) needs to be reassessed from the novel standpoint of female education.

The foundation and development of key establishments of secondary and higher education in Victorian Wales, such as the endowed Howell Schools at Llandaff and Denbigh and the Dr Williams' School at Dolgellau was of major significance. Judge Falconer's critique of the orientation of Howell's School Llandaff in 1860 was of educational and sociological importance. The involvement of the Charity Commission in the dispute at Howell's School, Denbigh during 1863 to 1865, offers insights into the management and organization of a major Victorian school. Though located outside the Principality, the reorganized Welsh School at Ashford figured prominently in the Welsh educational debates of the 1880s and 90s. The Welsh Intermediate Education Act of 1889 had considerable impact on existing endowed girls schools, particularly from the standpoint of institutional independence and assimilation. The successful intervention in the House of Lords by

Bishop A.G. Edwards on behalf of Howell's School, Denbigh was motivated by denominational considerations. The controversy that afflicted the Dr Williams' School at Dolgellau also had considerable significance for female education, as did the transformation of the Swansea High School for Girls from a girls' public day-school into an intermediate school.

The much-neglected private and non-endowed girls' schools played a more significant role in the educational history of Victorian Wales than has hitherto been recognized. The establishment of a Diocesan High School for Girls at Carmarthen was one of a number of successful private educational ventures.

The quest for equal education opportunities for girls was strongly moulded by the concept of imitation of male-orientated academic education. The dawn of the Victorian age in Wales was, paradoxically, the era of masculine supremacy in education. For many years, the girls of Wales were to remain the victims of educational inequality and its concomitant emphasis on 'feminine' domestic accomplishments. However, by the late nineteenth century, there emerged a new perception of girls' secondary education. Curriculum development in the girls' schools of Victorian Wales highlights social accomplishments, curricular identity and differentiation.

The pupil-teacher system and teacher training were important in the provision of post-elementary and higher education for women throughout the second half of the nineteenth century. Until the establishment of Swansea Training College in 1872, Welsh women attended training-colleges in England. The Victorian teacher training-colleges were orientated towards infusing their women students with the perceptions and principles of femininity and domesticity. Future elementary school teachers were trained to promote amongst working-class girls a domestic ideology and sex-role stereotyping, which provide modern feminist writers with much historical ammunition. Swansea Training College's development reflected the overall context of late Victorian teacher training. The quest for expansion, the forging of links with the universities in the 1880s as well as the establishment of three 'day training departments' attached to the university colleges in the early 1890s were significant trends, as were the opening of a 'South Wales and Monmouthshire Training School of Cookery and Domestic Arts' in 1891 and the conversion of St Mary's Training College, Bangor into an exclusively women's establishment.

The role of the three university colleges in women's education was crucial. The opportunities at Aberystwyth in the 1870s were limited, and the controversy surrounding Dr Joseph Parry had significant implications. There was a hitherto unrecorded atttempt to convert the University College of Wales into an educational establishment for women in the years 1882–4. At the University Colleges of Aberystwyth, Cardiff and Bangor, the 1880s were significant for women's higher education from the standpoint of students' admission and enrolment, the opening of halls of residence, and the quest for female representation on governing bodies. The female presence was consolidated in the 1890s as is evident from the Univesity of Wales Charter, the erection of new halls of residence, the development of the day training departments, and varied student activities. But also, the 'Bangor College Scandal' (1892–4), generated by a complex situation focusing on the female presence at the college, placed the survival of the University College of North Wales in some jeopardy.

The progress and condition of female education in Wales at the turn of the nineteenth and twentieth centuries, underlines the interrelationship between trends towards women's emancipation and greater educational opportunity. The winding up of the influential 'Association for Promoting the Education of Girls in Wales' in 1901 was a significant landmark in the development of female education.[25]

During the years leading up to the First World War, the gradual change in attitudes to women's role in society, and coterminously to their education, was a continuing phenomenon. Major issues relating to the provision of State secondary education for girls at that period were: enrolment, fees, free places, co-education, matters of health and welfare as well as sexist and socio-economic inequalities. The curricular issues included differentiation and bifurcation, the place of domestic subjects, and also the concept of a balanced liberal education embodying a utilitarian or technical element as well as academic subjects. In this study, the policies of the Central Welsh Board and Board of Education (Welsh Department) will be assessed anew, from the perspective of girls' intermediate and secondary education. The second, successful defence of the independence of Howell's School Denbigh in the House of Lords in 1910 by Bishop A.G. Edwards in the name of freedom and diversity of type in schools, also merits a critical evaluation.

In the field of teacher training in Wales the female presence was consolidated, and local education authority involvement in teacher training at Swansea, Bangor Normal and in the new training-college for women opened at Barry in 1914 was a significant development. Questions of supply and demand exerted a profound impact on the training of women teachers in Wales. An examination of the machinery of the University Senate and Court, as well as the institutional history of each of the university colleges, highlights the position of women in the University of Wales. Enrolment, student affairs and hostels were important issues.

The years 1847–1914 were a significant period in the history of female education in Wales. Dr R.D. Roberts's perceptive observation a century ago was not inappropriate:

> It is almost incredible that we are now in 1884 arguing whether more than half the nation are to have the privileges of citizens, to be allowed to educate themselves as completely as they please and to be free to engage in any occupation for which they have a mind. In years to come people will wonder how it could ever have been.[26]

As well as endeavouring to promote an understanding of human activity in the past, this book attempts to highlight the major issues of the debate and show their relevance for a balanced evaluation of current problems relating to the education of girls and women.

2

The Historical Context

(i) *Impediments confronting women in the struggle for equality in education*

The study of the education of girls and women in nineteenth-century Wales is only meaningful with reference to the broad social, political, economic and cultural context. Here, there were numerous conditioning factors which included vital agents of change as well as major impediments and obstacles to change.

Perceptions of femininity in Victorian Wales

The most significant recent studies of the education of girls and women in nineteenth-century England have shown the impact of the prevailing middle-class female ideology. The middle-class ideal of womanhood also had considerable significance in Welsh society. It was essentially a domestic ideal embodying the notion of separate spheres for men and women.[1] The home, and her family, were the female's sphere of interest, whilst the male's was the public sphere of the workplace. By the end of the century, the ideal of 'the perfect wife and mother' was being slowly transformed to accommodate the 'new woman' who sought education, employment, legal and political rights. This ideology also spread to the working class, who increasingly espoused its tenets during the course of the century.

In a class-divided society, the feminine–domestic ideology was, however, to have differing socio-economic and educational implications. The middle-class pioneers of higher education who were criticized for breaking the link between femininity and domesticity, insisted that they were doing no more than educating women to be more competent wives and mothers. Elementary education came to be seen as a vehicle of social and cultural control. It was not only perceived as a means of improving the working-class family by inculcating the skills of efficient wives and mothers but also as a means of training domestic servants for middle-class households. Victorian educational institutions for both middle and working-class girls were thus directly influenced by the prevailing feminine–domestic ideology.

In Victorian Britain, the woman was expected to be the perfect wife and mother.[2] Indeed, in European societies in general, 'the growing restriction of women to the home' was one of the trends of the nineteenth century which affected both the middle and working classes. 'The mother became the repository and guardian of society's morality . . . Bourgeois mothers had the time and standard of living to aspire to such a role, and gradually the middle class ideology of motherhood became the norm for the working class.'[3] Though the law confirmed the male's pre-eminence in a patriarchal society, the mother's femininity, authority, and indeed angelicity were deemed to be the essential characteristics of the ideal Victorian home. The ideal mother was enthroned in the home, and came to be seen as the crucial educative and disciplining agent in the family. This was also the prevalent view in Wales.[4]

The Victorian paragon appeared regularly in the Welsh press and periodicals. A typical example was 'Y Dylanwad Benywaidd' in *Y Dysgedydd* in 1850 which emphasized the mother's exalted and strategic position as the source of moral influence in the home.[5] Likewise, in 1857, the woman's responsibilities within her home were underlined in a letter published in *Baner ac Amserau Cymru*.[6]

The wisdom of women departing from this role was questioned. For example, in 1859 it was argued that they should not aspire to careers in medicine, business, public life or politics.[7] This view persisted throughout the century.

In 1886, the angelic concept of the mother and her importance in the family was being voiced in verse in *Y Frythones*.[8] Similarly, in 1893, in an enlightened article recognizing the importance of education for the female, her especial duties and responsibilities within the family unit were also underlined.[9] This perception was propagated by contemporary literature — poetry, prose and sermons — and was to remain influential until the early twentieth century.

In the 1850s and 1860s this image of femininity was reiterated in verse and prose both in England and Wales. 'Woman worship' is evident in English literature of the mid-Victorian period in the works of Ruskin, Tennyson, Patmore, Kingsley and George Eliot. The female was portrayed as virtuous, a divine guide, the inspirer of man and the angel in the house whose duty was the moral elevation of man. Accordingly, her domestic emancipation and quest for equal educational and professional opportunities were equated with coarsening the female's nature and weakening her moral influence. Ruskin's *Of Queen's Gardens* (1865) was particularly influential. It emphasized that the sexes were complementary opposites. The woman's sphere was the home, and her education was seen in terms of improving the effectiveness of her domestic role.[10] From the 1830s, *Y Fam Cartref: Neu Egwyddorion y Ddyledswydd Famaidd yn Cael eu Hegluro*, a Welsh translation of an American work by T.S.C. Abbott, had voiced the need to recognize the mother's authority and the crucial importance of her influence over her offspring. It was a manifesto enthroning the mother as sovereign in the home.[11] It was the mother's duty and responsibility to ensure that her offspring became morally upright and thereby were a beneficial influence on society at large.[12] Ieuan Gwynedd's *Y Gymraes*, Thomas Gee's *Baner ac Amserau Cymru*, denominational journals and literary work in National Eisteddfod competitions in the 1850s and 1860s, portrayed motherhood as the ideal form of womanhood.[13]

The 'angelic concept' of motherhood was evident in Victorian thought and literature. At the Denbigh National Eisteddfod in 1860, when the bards were invited to respond in verse to the theme of 'the ideal woman' — 'Y Ferch Rinweddol', she was portrayed as 'the angel in the home'.[14]

The mores of domesticity were romanticized and consolidated through such journals of the Victorian era as *Y Gymraes* (1850–51) and *Y Frythones* (1879–91). Towards the end of the century, O.M. Edwards's *Cartrefi Cymru* epitomized the influence of the concept of family in Victorian thought. Likewise *Y Gymraes* in 1898 emphasized the impact of the homes, and especially the mothers of Wales on the nation's character.[15]

Evangelical Christianity was a contributory influence. It stressed the importance of the family and of relationships and attitudes within the family unit. It taught respect for the mother and stressed the sanctity of marriage.[16] It preached discipline in the home and opposition to changing the female's domestic role.[17] A mother's love and influence were portrayed in and through religious terms and analogies; a mother's influence was equated with godliness.[18] Motherhood was being constantly portrayed as the woman's noblest function, an angelic role.[19]

In Victorian Wales, the family was the most important unit in the community and its influence was strengthened by perceptions of its sanctity. The influential Dr Lewis Edwards, Principal of Bala Theological College for over four decades, underlined the formative influence of the female within the family unit.[20]

It has been suggested that the political and social tensions of the 1840s — the years of Chartism and Rebecca in Wales, and revolutions in Europe — had the effect of strengthening and consolidating the family unit as a haven from the world.[21] The reality of the woman's role in Victorian Wales, however, differed markedly from the literary ideal. Recent studies have revealed the large numbers of Welsh women involved in work outside the home — 25 to 30 per cent — in the Victorian years, and thereby, have corrected an over-romanticized view of the domestic-orientated Welsh female.[22] The harsh realities of life for working-class women in Victorian Wales, not only in heavy industry, but also in agriculture, have now been underlined anew.

But it is also evident that increasingly in the second half of the century, not only in middle-class but also in working-class homes, paid labour outside the home came to be seen as unfeminine. In the coal and iron producing districts, the sexual division of labour became more evident, with the female becoming the guardian angel of the home. Criticisms of working conditions in factories and mines led to legislation which introduced restrictions on the employment of women. A woman who worked, came to be seen as 'an affront against nature, and the protective instincts of man'.[23] The employment of married women became associated with the disintegration of home life. A typical rejoinder appeared in 1874, emphasizing the doctrine of 'separate spheres' and the domestic role of the female.[24] Census returns indicate a declining trend in women's employment in Wales after 1871.[25]

The growth of the cult of domesticity and the consolidation of the woman's position in the home acted as a constraint on the growth and development of female education. Though the inculcation of moral values and the formative influence of the mother during the child's early years were an integral part of the domestic ideal, initially, only a few saw formal schooling as a necessary medium for increasing the effectiveness of the female at home. In the middle of the century, the emphasis on the importance of the mother strengthened the voluntary principle of education voiced by such litterati as Ieuan Gwynedd. It was argued that parents, rather than the State, should mould their children. Indeed, until well into the twentieth century, the domestic orientation of the female role was to have a restrictive and indeed detrimental effect on attitudes to girls' education. Overall, schooling appeared less important for the girl than for the boy.

Attention to social accomplishments at the expense of a domestic-orientated education was regularly criticized in the mid-nineteenth century.[26] The prevailing domestic perception was underlined in 1863 in an article contrasting the differing responsibilities, and thereby the differing educational needs, of males and females.[27]

On the eve of the Welsh Intermediate Education Act, John Gibson, one of the most perceptive observers of the Welsh social scene felt that the prevalence of the traditional marriage role for women adversely affected the fortunes of their education:

> It is tacitly understood that the business of women is marriage . . . The absence of definite purpose in reference to the future of girls, enfeebles all that is done in reference to their education. Women are the toys, the pets, or the sport of men, instead of being their equals and companions.[28]

Although the prevailing feminine ideology acted as a barrier to equal educational opportunity for girls and women in Victorian Wales, its impact was not entirely negative. There was also a growing awareness of the advantages of education which gradually came to be seen as a means of increasing the effectiveness of the female within the family unit. In particular, it was seen as a vital instrument for disciplining and indoctrinating the future working-class wife and mother with such virtues as sobriety, thrift, cleanliness and orderliness.[29] Though most commentators in the Welsh press and periodicals, such as R.J. Derfel in 1854, did not distinguish between elementary and secondary education, and were undoubtedly thinking primarily in terms of the former, higher education was also seen as making a positive contribution towards strengthening the female role within the family unit.[30]

When laying the foundation stone of Dr Williams' School in 1876, Samuel Holland MP, though a staunch advocate of widening the female's sphere of employment, noted that men often married badly educated wives. They were consequently driven to public houses for the comfort which they failed to find at home. Education would enable women 'to be better wives and better able to make the home comfortable'.[31]

Thus the education of girls and women came to be viewed as a means of strenghtening the female's influence in society at large. while still maintaining the status quo of male supremacy in the workplace. The presumed relationship between education and moral reform became an important conditioning factor of the cause of female education in mid-Victorian Wales. The connection between immorality and inadequate education, voiced in the *Blue Books* (1847), proved to be a catalyst for the ensuing debate of the 1850s and 1860s highlighted in particular in the columns of *Baner ac Anserau Cymru*. The educated woman was in a powerful position to exercise moral influence over her husband and family, and came to be seen as an effective agent in the struggle against sexual immorality and drunkeness, and an instrument of moral improvement.[32]

The Temperance Movement recognized the importance of the educated woman as a reformist agent in society. The formation of The North Wales Women's Temperance Movement in 1892 epitomized female involvement in social reform. Women in late Victorian Wales saw the need to imbue the community with an awareness of the detrimental effects of drink.

In a speech at Liverpool in 1881, Lewis Morris, who was at the time involved in the inquiries of the Aberdare Committee, emphasized the importance of female education. He recognized the deficiencies in the provision of girls' education, and attributed much of the malaise of contemporary society to this neglect: 'When I think of the ignorance in which the female half of the human race has been contentedly left so long, I do not wonder at the immorality, the vice, the crime, the blood guiltiness and the pestilences which afflict humanity'.[33] Likewise, at Swansea Training College in 1900, D. Lleufer Thomas put forward his view of the relationship between female education and social reform:

> As educated women, you can do much for the welfare and happiness of your own sex — and indirectly of mine — by quiet unobtrusive talk with mothers and housewives as to the laws of health, the elements of sanitary science . . . how to make the home sweet and cheerful for the husbands and sons on returning from work.[34]

Through their crucial position in the homes of Wales, educated mothers were being regarded as powerful agents in a crusade for moral reformation.

Tradition, conservatism and prejudice

Educational change was subject to the dictates of tradition and downright prejudice. Throughout the ages, the female had been given little attention by educational theorists and practitioners. In William Boyd's *The History of Western Education*, there are only a few paragraphs needed to summarize ideas about the education of girls. In the perspective of West European educational thought, with the notable exception of Plato, the female was ignored or regarded as subservient to the male.[35]

In her study of the female experience in nineteenth-century Europe, *Women in Europe since 1750* (1978), Patricia Branca maintains that tradition was the strongest obstacle faced by the feminist cause.[36] M.E. Bryant's emphasis on 'the immense weight of convention' in her study of England, is relevant also in the context of Wales. In both countries, 'the majority of women did not know they were in prison nor desired to be free'.[37]

In 1861, the irrational prejudice against educating women was epitomized in a winning entry at the Conwy National Eisteddfod where it was argued that some mothers equated girls' education with the promotion of vanity and laziness.[38] In the 1860s, the few women who were involved in preaching and public speaking, were subject to criticism, although it was occasionally admitted that the female's ability and influence on society had not been given due recognition.[39] In 1864, an anonymous female writer in *Y Beirniad* epitomized the educational conservatism that still existed in Wales: it was futile to educate a child for an unattainable position in society; in particular, she had no desire to see a woman in a university; the BA would be an unfeminine appendix to her name.[40]

The prevalence in many circles of a narrow perception of the female's educational needs was a significant impediment to change. R.J. Derfel referred to contempt for learned women in 1850, claiming that 'The blue stocking was ostracised by young men'.[41] There was a widespread feeling that women did not require general education, and that it could not be of much benefit for them. Such attitudes were criticized by Lewis Edwards in 1859 when he underlined the need for a broader perception of girls' educational needs: mere reading and writing were not sufficient.[42]

At the Denbigh National Eisteddfod in 1860, one of the joint winners of the essay competition on 'Addysg Merched' (Women's Education) noted the traditional prejudice against it.[43] Another competitor — Miss Roberts, Llansannan — criticized the attitude of many at the time who failed to see the value of education for the woman, and who believed that through education, a woman would lose the feminine attributes of tenderness and sympathy.[44]

Families were more willing to make sacrifices for the education of their sons rather than their daughters.[45] Though such attitudes gradually dissipated during the Victorian age in Wales, their impact was still felt by the architects of intermediate education in the 1890s.[46] At the opening of the new hall of residence for women students in Bangor in 1888, Revd H. Price Hughes thought it relevant to tell his audience that it was a delusion to think that an educated woman was a 'blue stocking'.[47]

The conservative attitudes of women themselves was a significant impediment. In 1870, Thomas Gee maintained that women's awareness of their rights was a recent phenomenon.[48] In 1873, in resposne to a letter from J.H. Griffith, 'Y Gohebydd' — a staunch supporter of both femininism and educational causes — *Baner ac Amserau Cymru* referred to a lecture delivered six or seven years earlier in Cincinnati, USA by Miss Anna Dickenson. Examining the condition of women, she had attributed their lack of opportunities in education and employment to the conservatism of society. Thomas Gee claimed that prejudice against the female was even stronger on this side of the Atlantic.[49] Recounting that Miss Dickenson had called for the removal of 'the barricades of women disabilities', the writer noted that there was no provision for educating women at Oxbridge or Dublin '. . . as if they did not exist',[50] whilst the findings of the Taunton Committee had shown that in the endowed schools, girls were virtually non-existent.[51] The revelations of the Taunton Committee — fourteen endowed schools for girls in England and Wales and 820 for boys, £277,000 endowments for boys and £3,000 endowments for girls — were deployed in the Welsh press as a prime illustration of female disabilities, prejudice and traditional attitudes towards the education of girls.

Though attitudes were changing, there was still much prejudice against women in the 1870s.[52] Objectors to the extension of the parliamentary franchise to women in the early 1870s had argued that it would destroy women's femininity, contravene the laws of nature, and ignore a fundamental difference between the sexes.[53] In 1872, readers of *Baner ac Amserau Cymru* were told that one of the most popular sessions at the British Association Conference at Brighton was a discussion of a paper on 'Female Education' by a Miss Shirreff which had underlined that centuries of prejudice against women would only disappear gradually.[54] Again, in 1883, in a perceptive letter to the same paper, prejudice was seen to be the major obstacle to the educational development of the female. It was wrongly assumed that education dissipated the female's especial characteristics.[55] Even in 1893, whilst welcoming the positive developments in the education of girls in Wales and changes in attitudes to the female, Revd J.M. Morgan, Kirkdale, recalled the traditional attitudes to the education of the female and noted the persistence of much conservatism regarding her social role. Women had suffered educational neglect for too long.[56] In her award winning essay on 'The Education of Girls in Wales' at the Swansea National Eisteddfod in 1891, Miss Winter, Headmistress of Swansea High School for Girls noted that:

> . . . for many years, even for generations, girls had been denied the benefit of that liberal education so long enjoyed by their brothers, and although many girls are now allowed to prosecute their studies to a point before

undreamt of, the old prejudices yet remain in some of the remoter parts of the Principality.[57]

In 1894, with the provisions of the Welsh Intermediate Education Act being actively implemented, John Gibson was arguing that there was still lingering prejudice towards the education of girls. He was afraid that the county governing bodies' anxiety to establish five or six intermediate schools in thinly populated Merioneth might cause injustice to girls, and especially to Dr Williams' School. He concurred with an observation by one of the Assistant Charity Commissioners to Miss Fewings, headmistress of Dr Williams', that 'a battle had still to be fought in Wales in order to get people to think girls need education as well as boys'.[58]

Readers of *The Cambrian News* were informed in 1896 that petitions from over 2,000 people had been sent calling for university degrees to be thrown open to women at Cambridge. The opposition and prejudice of Professor Alfred Marshall were particularly condemned:

> We have no hesitation in saying however, that the folly and prejudice behind those who seek to with-hold Cambridge degrees from women are unquestionably beyond parallel, and show how little education is able to do, even for Professors, in the way of broadening the mind and keeping away fads, prejudices and groundless fears.[59]

John Gibson, appointed editor of *The Cambrian News* in 1873, was one of Victorian Wales's staunchest feminist supporters. For over a quarter of a century, his vigorous editorials and perceptive volume *The Emancipation of Women* (1891) highlighted the prevalence of the forces of tradition, conservatism and prejudice in the Principality. In 1885, whilst recognizing that much had been accomplished during the previous twenty years to place women on a more equal footing with men, he argued that: 'Women are still either slaves or are legally, socially and politically non-existent. Here and there, a few women smart under the ban of inferiority, but as a rule, they scarcely realize the nature or extent of their bondage and many actually rejoice in their enslaved condition'. In his view, 'Women's inferior position was the result of centuries of wrong'.[60] In a letter in 1887, he was critical of the subservience of women: 'The progress of women is hindered more by women than by men . . . A large number of women in Wales think that to possess all the privileges and responsibilities of men would be ruin to them'.[61] In 1898, he was still arguing that women were 'the victims of unjust law, priest-made religion, ignorant custom and ancient prejudice'.[62]

At the end of the century, Miss Edmunds Bangor, an astute observer of the Welsh scene, recognized that women's sphere of activity had been extended greatly, but only after a considerable struggle. Nevertheless, tradition and prejudice still exerted considerable force and perpetuated the domestic ideal of womanhood.[63]

Perceptions of the Victorian woman's intellectual abilities

Attitudes towards the education of the Victorian female were coloured by misconceptions concerning her intellectual abilities. Many assumed that, compared with men, women were intellectually inferior. In a radical treatise in the 1850s — *Yr Angenrheidrwydd o roddi Addysg Gyffredinol i ferched Ieuainc* — R.J. Derfel highlighted the deep-rooted misconceptions concerning the female's mental capacity which had arrested the development of educational provision.[64] Furthermore he argued that women themselves assumed that education was intended to be a male preserve.[65]

The widely held belief that women were intellectually inferior was also reflected in *Yr Athrawes o Ddifrif — Lloffion o Hanes Bywyd a Marwolaeth Mrs Edmunds Bangor* (1859). A teacher trained at the British and Foreign School Society's Borough Road College in 1847, she rejected such misconceptions.[66] At the Denbigh National Eisteddfod in 1860, one of the joint prizewinners in the essay competition on 'Addysg Merched' argued that parents had doubted whether their daughters had the mental capacity for education.[67]

The 1860s witnessed debate and controversy in England concerning women's equal intellectual standing with men. In the mid-nineteenth century, the view was held by many that, because a woman's brain was smaller in cubic content, she was unable to reason as well as a man could, and was therefore mentally and physically inferior to man. Miss Frances Cobbe's paper to the Social Science Congress in London on the education of women, and the justice of their cause to compete with men for academic degrees, and Miss Emily Davies's pleas on behalf of female doctors, were noted in a prize-winning essay at the Caernarfon National Eisteddfod in 1862.[68] However, the author, though advocating a fairer and more equal treatment of the female, rejected any claims to intellectual equality.

An article in *Y Beirniad* in 1871 recognized that, on average, the female brain was smaller than the male's.[69] However, it was not accepted that this had adverse intellectual consequences. The writer claimed that phrenology suggested that the female possessed qualities which had a crucial effect on mental development and powers, temperament and sensitiveness. Furthermore, it was maintained that the elementary school system had revealed that girls were just as able as boys. On the basis of innate ability, it was claimed that the female was just as suited for education as the male. It was unequal opportunity rather than inferior intellectual endowment that accounted for their comparatively fewer achievements in literature, art, science and moral philosophy.[70]

In 1873, in an article — 'Dyfodol ein Merched' — generated, in particular, by Jacob Bright's Bill and the opening of Swansea Training College, an increasingly important role for the female in the teaching profession was foreseen.[71] Reference was made to the American experience, in an attempt to explode prevailing myths about female intellectual ability:

> . . . In the USA, where children of both sexes are often sent to the same schools, and for a time pursue the same studies, the females are found to have equal power of comprehension and memory with the boys.[72]

During the 1880s, in addresses and in the press, Welsh people were being informed that the female possessed the intellectual prowess to pursue higher education. In 1883, in his inaugural address at the opening of University College of South Wales at Cardiff, Lord Aberdare stressed that the College was not being influenced by traditional misconceptions about women's abilities:

> Women have not been slow to profit by the opportunities thus offered them. The number of scholarships and exhibitions won by them . . . afford pretty clear indications that assumption of intellectual superiority by men will, like many other long accepted doctrines, be speedily tested by the stern logic of facts.[73]

The debate concerning the female's intellectual prowess focused especially on the alleged mental strain experienced by women pursuing courses of higher education. This aspect was particularly evident in the 1870s and 1880s, though this fear had been expressed in earlier years. In 1852, Matthew Arnold had reported a 'serious amount of ill health' amongst female pupil-teachers and warned school managers of the need for precautions.[74] In HMI reports of the 1870s, concern was expressed that the health of female students in teacher training-colleges should not be damaged. At Swansea in 1875, it was reported that 'the students have been overworked, the health of 5 students broke down about June after an examination in science subjects and during the preparation for the half-yearly examination held by the training school authorities'.[75] Following a specch by Miss Dilys Davies on 'Higher Education for Girls' at the 1886 National Eisteddfod, attention was given to the alleged strain experienced by women pursuing courses of higher education. Speakers, who included Principal Reichel, recognized that though the intellectual powers of women were equal to those of men, the physical powers were different. They were prone to overwork themselves and more likely to suffer breakdowns under acute examination conditions.[76]

During 1887, at a meeting of the Association for Promoting the Education of Girls in Wales, Dr Sophie Bryant argued that experience showed that 'the educated woman did not fail in health.'[77] At the influential Shrewsbury Conference in January 1888, it was stated that the commonest objection to the equal provision of intermediate education for girls was the danger to their health. Miss Dilys Davies argued forcefully that

> . . . those actually engaged in teaching as well as those having a personal acquaintance with the mental work of girls and women were agreed that the dire results apprehended did not exist. The health of girls and women engaged in mental work would be found on due examination to compare most favourably with that of women who spent their lives in the pursuit of pleasures.[78]

In her analysis of the main objections voiced against the higher education of girls, Miss Winter noted in 1891 that 'it was at first asserted that woman's intellectual capacity was less than that of man — her brain weighed less and she was mentally incapable of sustained and systematic study'.[79] She felt that the academic achievements of such women as Miss Fawcett had disproved this allegation. Likewise, with detailed references to investigations conducted in England in 1887 and correspondence in learned journals, she found unsubstantiated the criticisms that intellectual study had an adverse effect on a female's health: 'As large a proportion of the women who have had a University education enjoy good health now as did so at the time they entered College . . . that any serious alarm as to the effect of University education on the health of women is groundless is clearly shown . . .'[80]

At the opening of Bangor Intermediate School for Girls in 1897, Dr Isambard Owen referred to the health hazard that was alleged to be associated with girls' higher education. He acknowledged that cramming could affect the physical health both of girls and boys. However, he was not convinced that 'education properly conveyed and supervised' had an adverse effect on girls.[81]

During the Victorian era, medical opinion gave respectability to the arguments linking female higher education and overstrain and physiological damage. It was maintained that there was an inherent conflict between the demands of motherhood and intellectual study. Brainwork and examinations were regarded as a danger to a woman's health. The female body was subject to the competing demands of academic study and menstruation.[82] Such influential figures as Dr Henry Maudsley, University College London, argued in 1874 that 'intellectual strain' particularly during puberty would have an adverse effect on the normal development of menstruation and the reproductive system.[83] Likewise, in the 1880s, a number of specialists in gynaecology and obstetrics, including Professor John Thorburn, Owen's College Manchester and R.L. Tait, President of the British Gynaecological Society, drew attention to the physiological dangers to the female of the pursuit of higher education.[84] Dr Withers Moore's presidential address to the British Medical Association at Brighton in 1886, which underlined the dangers of higher education to women's health, was widely circulated and exerted much influence on the deliberations concerning the Higher Education of Girls at the Cymmrodorion Section of the National Eisteddfod 1886. Such women as Dr Sophie Bryant, Miss Emily Pfeiffer and Mrs H. Sidgwick, were equally vigorous in rejecting any suggestions that higher education might harm women's health and especially their reproductive capacity.[85]

The conservatism and anti-feminist attitudes of the British Medical Association were much in evidence in the nineteenth century.[86] Although the main theatre of the struggle for the advocates of medical education for women was outside Wales, the involvement of Frances E. Hoggan, in particular, was to have a crucial impact on the educational debate in Wales in the 1870s and 1880s. The opposition she had faced in her quest for medical education made her even more determined that the obstacles on the way to secondary and higher education for girls and women in Wales be removed.

Even in 1879, the opposition to the admission of women to the medical profession was still being voiced in *The Lancet* and conveyed to a wider readership in west Wales: 'Women have deserted their legitimate province as nurses and ministering attendants on the sick, and with unfeminine feeling, desire to obtrude into the domain of men as practitioners of art which in its training and following often overpower even masculine sensibilities'.[87]

The debate concerning the female's intellectual calibre, and the propriety of higher education, was moulded by Social-Darwinistic ideas which exerted a considerable influence on social and political thought by the end of the Victorian era.[88] In particular, attention was given to the importance of motherhood and especially the educated mother in

the process of evolution. In general, Social Darwinism with its acknowledgement of separate sex roles, consolidated traditional attitudes to the
education of women. Women were seen as physiologically different and
medically weaker than men. It was argued that too much academic
education would have an adverse effect on women.

In the 1860s and 1870s, the initial impact of the theory of evolution
and its emphasis on differing sexual roles appeared to strengthen the
traditional ideal of womanhood and the accompanying economic
division of labour.[89] Such influential exponents as Herbert Spencer had
many followers who had considerable reservations about the wisdom of
providing intellectual education for females at a secondary and higher
level. They feared that the overstrain and fatigue and the ensuing
physiological damage would have an adverse effect on the role of the
woman for motherhood. For them, the proper place for women was at
home, performing their traditional role as housewives and mothers.[90]

By the 1880s, the medical opposition to girls' intellectual education
was being expressed in characteristic Darwinistic phraseology. Dr
Withers Moore's address in 1886 maintained that it was '. . . not good
for the human race, considered as progressive, that women should be
freed from the restaints which law and custom have imposed upon
them, and should receive an education intended to prepare them for the
exercise of brain power in competition with men'.[91]

The leaders of the female education movement in Wales, who were
well aware of Social Darwinistic thought, were to argue their case in
terms of strengthening and improving the role of the woman both in the
home and in her contribution to society at large. By the turn of the
century, the Social Darwinistic debate had generated a school of
thought, which together with ideas about the decline of the British
Empire and the physical deterioration of the population, recognized the
importance of a differentiated curriculum for effective fulfilment of the
woman's role as housewife and mother in the process of evolution. As
well as an intellectual education which came to predominate in the late
Victorian secondary schools, it was deemed important for girls to
receive domestic and technical training if they were to make their
especial contribution towards furthering the progress of the race.[92]

(ii)   *Agents of educational change in Victorian Wales*

The quest for emancipation

The changed educational fortunes of girls and women in Victorian
Wales was part of the wider quest for female emancipation both within
and outside the Principality. The struggle for the woman's cause was

fought on many fronts, and the educational campaign occurred simultaneously with the appearance of numerous publications in the Welsh press advocating the political, legal, economic and social emancipation of women.[93]

Victorian Wales witnessed pleas for the enhancement of the female's influence. Thomas Gee, 'S.R.', 'Y Gohebydd', Frances Hoggan, John Gibson and others associated educational disadvantages with the injustice, disabilities and even oppression faced by women in many spheres of life: 'The emancipation of Women strikes down to the roots of our social, religious and political life'.[94] And again in 1890, Gibson argued that 'the sphere of women must widen until there are no limitations except those which nature has fixed. The sphere of woman is not to be limited by law'.[95]

Dr Hoggan gained prominence not only through her educational campaign in the 1870s and 1880s, but also for her pamphlet in 1884, advocating changes in the legal position of women.[96] Also, she was one of the twelve British medical women registered in 1885, who signed the suffragist letter to the House of Lords.[97] In 1893, in an editorial — 'Women and Freedom' — John Gibson rejoiced that women were gaining freedom on a wide front:

> We are not dissatisfied with the rate of progress women are making, politically, socially and industrially. Opposition and prejudice are crumbling down in every direction under the impact of the 1870 Education Act and other educational changes which have given to women the same sort of training that is given to men.[98]

Various legal restraints reflected and embodied the female's inferior status in Victorian Wales. The cause of educational and social reform was impeded by archaic law. Women's exclusion from the franchise, the unfairness of the divorce and property laws, the arrangements for the custody and guardianship of children, their exclusion from holy orders, and until well on in the century from the privileges of Oxford and Cambridge universities, as well as professional and trade disabilities, became issues of much debate. In 1873 the woman's path to a fair and equal opportunity was seen to be blocked not only by tradition but by legal 'barricades'.[99]

In the early 1870s, when four unsuccessful attempts by Jacob Bright to extend the vote to property-owning women were made, the columns of *Baner ac Amserau Cymru* gave considerable attention to the restrictions on women and the quest for emancipation. Unsurprisingly, the obituary to J.S. Mill in 1873 noted his influential work *On the Subjection of Women* (1869).[100] Throughout the decade, attempts to extend the parliamentary franchise to women were vigorously supported by *Baner ac Amserau Cymru*. In 1870, Gee thought that Jacob Bright's Bill to give the vote to those women who enjoyed the same property rights as men who benefited under the terms of the 1867 Reform Act — leaseholders or ratepayers in boroughs, £12 leaseholders and property owners in counties — did not go far enough, as only a comparatively small number of women would benefit.[101] Attempts in 1869–70 by Russell Gurney MP and Robert Raikes MP, to safeguard married women's property rights were also welcomed. The existing law was condemned in *Baner ac Amserau Cymru* for its servile treament of married women.[102] The formation of a women's suffrage society, publication of the monthly *Women's Suffrage Journal* by Miss Lydia E. Becker and petitions to Parliament were welcomed.[103] Women's right to vote in school board elections and become members was seen as an important step forward for the woman's cause. It underlined the injustice of their exclusion from the parliamentary franchise: educational justice for women was seen as the concomitant of political enfranchisement.[104] Such women as Mrs Garrett Anderson and Miss Emily Davies on the London School Board and Mrs Crawshay, vice-chair of the Merthyr Tudful School Board, were seen as exemplifying women's effective and worthwhile participation in public affairs.[105]

However, even in 1886, it remained a difficult task to convince many that women should be freed from wide-ranging restraints.[106] The fact that the newly formed Association for Promoting the Education of Girls in Wales found it necessary to publicly advocate, 'the claims of girls to be educated as men are educated', was viewed in 1887 as clear evidence of the subjection of women.[107] Women's lack of educational opportunities epitomized the need to change their inferior position in social, commercial and political life.

> Every business thrown open to woman, every social and political prejudice regarding women that is overthrown, every political privilege that is secured for women, every new responsibility that is imposed upon women will make their complete education easier. Marriage ought not to be more to women than to men . . . Women are the toys, the pets, or the sport of men, instead of being their equals and companions. There can be no real education of women until they are free as men are free, and responsible as men are responsible.[108]

Though not without much controversy, women were becoming more prominent in Welsh public life in the 1870s and 1880s. Sarah Jane Rees (Cranogwen) was a well known preacher and lecturer, whilst Rosina Davies became an evangelist. In 1887, three women were sent by the

Calvinistic Methodists to serve as missionaries in India's 'Bryniau Cassia'.

The Mosaic and Pauline elements in the Christian legacy had exerted a significant influence on attitudes to the female's social condition. On the basis of the scriptural account in Genesis of the creation of Eve from Adam's rib, Christianity could be used to justify the social inferiority of women. It could be maintained that the female's position in the world was necessarily inferior to that of men because it was part of the order of divine providence that it should be. Woman was created late to be a helpmeet to man, but subsequently lured man to his Fall. She came to be seen as having brought a curse upon the earth which was still supposed to exist. Male authority over the female could be traced back to the Fall.[109] Later, the Epistles of Paul confirmed, and even asserted anew, the subjection of women. Opposition to female participation in preaching and public speaking was voiced in scriptural terms, with particular evocation of Paul's teachings.[110]

On the eve of the Aberdare Committee's inquiry into intermediate and higher education, it was claimed by John Gibson that women exerted less influence in Wales than in England because religion was 'more dogmatic and fuller of negatives than in England'.[111] Another well known commentator viewed some aspects of the feminist movement in 1882 as 'reform against nature' and an attack on the Pauline teachings.[112] In 1891, Gibson still attributed much of the social injustice experienced by women to the influence of Mosaic and Pauline religion:

> Women have suffered many centuries of injustice of the writings of Moses and Paul, and whenever women seriously determine to be free they will find their last and strongest enemies entrenched behind religious barricades, and pleading the Pentateuch and the Epistles of Paul in support of their position as determined opponents of justice to women . . . The friend of women was Jesus Christ and it is high time for women to revolt against Mosaic and Pauline religion and to insist upon the religion of Jesus which contains no hint that women are either to be silent in churches or to be subject to their husbands.[113]

He was advocating emancipation on a broad front. Winning the parliamentary franchise came to be seen as an essential step on the road towards female emancipation. Gibson warned that the effects of generations of political injustice and personal degradation could not be erased by the mere removal of political inequality.[114] It was essential that women were made the legal equals of men:

> The admission of woman to the political franchise will not by any means

complete the work of her emancipation, but by placing power in her hands will be rather, only the first step towards enabling her to work out her own political, social, commercial, and educational salvation, by breaking down those barriers and restraints which men through many ages, have built up around her on the shallow pretext of defending and protecting her.[115]

Only when all legal barriers had been removed would the female be able to go her own way and take her own position in society.

Individuals, social structure and economic pressures

In her study of educational developments in nineteenth-century England, Margaret Bryant suggested in 1979 that earlier writers might have over-emphasized the part played by such leaders as Emily Davies, Frances Buss and Elizabeth Garrett.[116] Whilst this is a salutary remainder of the dangers of over-personalizing such complex developments, the fortunes of girls' secondary and higher education in Wales could hardly be satisfactorily explained without an appreciation of the considerable impact on strong-willed individuals, both male and female. Their foresight, determination and sacrifice, proved to be of crucial importance. Such personalities as Ieuan Gwynedd and Lady Llanover in the 1850s, John Griffith 'Y Gohebydd' in the 1870s, Frances Hoggan, Dilys Davies and Elizabeth P. Hughes and John Gibson in the 1880s and 1890s exerted a profound influence on the quest for secondary and higher education for girls and women.

The progress of female education in Victorian Wales was also activated and constrained by internal factors. Momentum came from within educational institutions themselves. The headmistresses of the Howell Schools, Dr Williams' and Swansea High School, as well as Miss Carpenter at UCW Aberystwyth, Lady Aberdare in Cardiff and the British and Foreign Schools Society's establishment of a teachers' training-college at Swansea, were to influence the nature and ethos of female education in Wales.

The social class factor also forms a crucial element in the backdrop to this Victorian educational movement. The quest for secondary and higher education for girls and women was primarily a middle-class movement.[117] Bryant (1979) emphasizes the 'middle class' complexion of the educational movement in England,[118] whilst Deem (1978) notes that between 1870 and 1901 'middle class girls did fare better than their working class sisters'.[119]

In Wales, although their numbers increased more rapidly from the 1860s with the growth in number of professional people, the middle class was still relatively small.[120] Nevertheless, the momentum for secondary and higher education for girls and women came from the ranks of the middle class and its objectives were conceived primarily in terms of middle-class needs.[121] Only the ablest of working-class pupils would be given the opportunity of entering the intermediate schools in the 1890s. For the majority of girls in Victorian Wales, educational oportunity meant no more than elementary education. Entry to the Howell Schools or Dr Williams' was hardly contemplated by the majority of families, nor indeed advocated by the leaders of the educational movement in Wales. They perceived the purpose of schooling the majority of Welsh girls in terms of improving the effectiveness of their domestic role rather than being an instrument for their social mobility.[122]

In a recent study, Rosemary Deem (1978) stresses that the ideology of the sexual division of labour influenced elementary education throughout the Victorian era.[123] Her thesis is well substantiated. During the age of the Revised Code, needlework, cookery and domestic economy were given greater prominence in the girls' elementary school curriculum.[124] By the end of the century, the education of working-class girls was more sex-specific than in earlier years.[125] As well as educating their pupils to be good wives and mothers, the schools were greatly influenced by the predominant role of domestic service for women in employment in Victorian Britain.[126] The Committee of Council and HMI endeavoured to ensure that there was a 'domestic' orientation to the education of girls.[127] For the middle classes, domestic work was synonymous with the lower echelons of a stratified society. Therefore, in the quest for intermediate and higher education which included equal opportunity, advocates of female education were conscious of the need to prove the intellectual mettle of girls. A higher premium was placed on academic rather than domestic subjects. In 1891, Miss Winter, headmistress of Swansea High School for Girls, emphasized the need for girls to pursue an academic education:

> Let your girls use their minds, let their natural tastes be developed, let their reasons be directed and their intellects trained . . . A girl with such training will not when she grows up to womanhood leave you dinnerless or neglect to sew on your buttons; she will give you a well ordered household and will also really be your companion, the help-meet given you by God.[128]

The curricular debate in intermediate schools could not be immune from the association of girls' education in the elementary and post-elementary schools with 'domestic' subjects.

Social class divisions remained important. Extensions of the franchise, reform of the property laws, and the provision of secondary and higher education were conceived primarily in middle-class terms. During the House of Commons debate on the second reading of Forsyth's Bill in 1876 to enfranchise women, it was stressed that there was no substance in the argument of those who saw the granting of the franchise as a prelude to a great revolution. The vote would only be given to those women who owned property (about 1:7) and paid rates (about 13 per cent). Likewise in education, Lord Aberdare in 1875 saw social class determining educational opportunity. The educational needs of the working classes were to be promoted through elementary schools, whilst an attempt was made 'to supply the middle class education by the means of the University College of Wales'.[129]

In 1880, on the eve of the appointment of the Aberdare Committee, John Gibson maintained that as a consequence of the 1870 Education Act and the establishment of board schools, 'the girls of the poor are now far better off as regards education than the girls of the middle classes'.[130] Whilst grammar schools were available for middle-class boys, there was scant provision for middle-class girls other than in private schools. His concern was for the establishment of schools for the daughters of the middle classes. The Welsh Intermediate Education Act 1889 was perceived in terms of providing opportunities 'for the women of the middle classes in Wales similar to that begun for the women of the industrial classes in 1870'.[131] The middle-class orientation of the developing intermediate schools in the 1890s was welcomed as the embodiment of the philosophy of the Aberdare Report.

The demand for improved education for middle-class girls and women in both England and Wales was influenced by social and economic factors. Bryant (1979) has underlined the impact of demographic trends on the emergence of the movement in England. The growth in population in nineteenth-century England and Wales was characterized by more women than men of marriageable age. There was a 16.8 per cent increase in the number of single women over fifteen years of age in the period 1851–71, with numbers increasing from 2,765,000 to 3,228,700.[132] More significantly, with large numbers of young men emigrating, there was a 72.7 per cent increase of surplus single women.[133] For many middle-class families during the nineteenth century, the unmarried daughters could be a financial burden.[134] Thus, with surplus women in the population, and marriage unlikely for many middle-class women, the provision of improved educational facilities for middle-class girls and women came to be seen as a means of enabling them to live independently.[135]

In Wales, advocates of the educational campaign were aware of the significance of this trend. In 1875, whilst supporting the women's quest for the same medical qualifications as men, and for free entry into the labour market, J.H. Griffith 'Y Gohebydd', emphasized 'that there were thousands of women without any male relations and had to support themselves'.[136]

In the 1870s, Mrs Rose Mary Crawshay of Merthyr, a philanthropist and reformer, was concerned about the preponderance of women over men in England and Wales. She told the Social Science Congress in 1874 that there were 900,000 more women than men in Great Britain for whom marriage was consequently impossible.[137] In a paper read at a British Association meeting at Bristol in 1875 she claimed that women were not sufficiently well educated to maintain themselves, and that 'remaining single means in some cases starvation'.[138] She began a scheme to find employment for 'needy gentlewomen'. She was particularly concerned about the daughters of professional men who were not sufficiently educated to be governesses or competent enough to run businesses alone.

Likewise in 1884, John Gibson highlighted the precarious position of the single woman. In an editorial advocating the extension of the 'Women's Sphere and Influence' he observed that 'the best thing that could happen to every woman, perhaps, was that she should be married. But many did not. There was exceedingly limited range of occupations before her and hemmed in and restricted by law, custom, training and fashion, her life is indeed far from enviable'.[139] Education was seen as a crucial instrument enabling the female to earn a livelihood and enjoy an independent status:

> The great aim of women should be to give girls early training in handicrafts and to fight for freedom to work in any part of the great field of labour which men claim as their own, to the loss and degradation of women . . . 'The angel of humanity' humbug is very nauseating out of the mouths of men who must know that the inability of women to earn a living drives them to prostitution or pauperism.[140]

Recent studies of female education in nineteenth-century England, advocate caution in over-emphasizing the orthodox view that the educational developments were in response to the labour requirements of an industrial society.[141] In essence, the provision of secondary and higher education for girls and women was concerned with the needs of the middle classes, whilst the overwhelming majority of jobs spawned by industrialization were filled by the elementary educated working classes.[142] The extent of the availability of new job opportunities for educated middle-class women should not be exaggerated.[143] Dyhouse argues that in the Victorian era, there was clear recognition of the doctrine of 'separate spheres' and 'division of labour' rather than a determined attempt to reject it or change the socio-economic situation.[144]

Developments in Wales also substantiate these conclusions. In 1887, Principal Viriamu Jones, a staunch advocate of women's higher education, warned that careers for women were limited.[145] Likewise, John Gibson, in a lengthy editorial following a meeting of The Association for Promoting the Education of Girls in Wales, acknowledged that in contrast to boys, the choice of occupation for girls was extremely limited. Even if intermediate schools were established 'there would be something wanting ... to give their whole training point and definiteness, and that something is a career for girls as wide and as general as the career open to boys'.[146]

Whilst individual women had made significant progress for two decades in widening the sphere in which their sisters could function, marriage was still regarded as their foremost vocation. An analysis of the census returns shows that housewives and domestic servants dominated the 'occupation' tables for women throughout the Victorian era in Wales.[147] In 1881 and 1891, during two crucial decades for higher education in Wales, over half the occupied females were in domestic service. Large numbers of Welsh women were also involved in agriculture, working in the fields and pastures. But equally significantly, the occupied women amongst whom wives were not included, constituted only 26.5 per cent in 1881 and 28.7 per cent in 1891 of all females aged ten years and over.[148] Whilst many Welsh women were thus engaged in paid labour, the overwhelming majority were unpaid wives and mothers. The employment participation rate for women in Wales was considerably lower than in England.[149]

The concentration of women's employment into a limited range of occupations dominated by domestic service reveals the lack of alternative occupations in the Principality.[150] Throughout these decades, only a very small proportion of women were found in professional occupations; however, they showed an increase from 2.1 per cent in 1851 to 9.1 per cent in 1911: a figure of 3,144 women in professional employment in 1861 grew to 9,568 in 1871 and 11,681 in 1891. Whilst teachers predominated, there were also increasing numbers of women employed in nursing, in local government service, the post office, banks and insurance companies. Trends evident throughout the Victorian era were confirmed by the 1901 census returns for Wales and Monmouthshire (Table 2.1). Many Welsh women moved to England where the

Table 2.1
Occupation of Females in Wales and Monmouthshire, 1901

Domestic indoor service	76,040
Laundry and washing service	6,007
Teaching	10,713
Nurses and midwives	2,015
Civil Service & telegraph/telephone service	1,577
Local government	1,132
Commercial bank & insurance clerks	834

Source: *Census, Wales and Monmouthshire 1901*, Summary Volume, pp. 228–9.

pattern of female employment revealed similar trends. Whilst domestic service predominated, there was also an increase in the proportion of women engaged in various professional occupations, as is evident from census returns for England and Wales (Table 2.2).

From the standpoint of the overall employment opportunties for women, the pull of the professions should not be over-emphasized. However, there was a growing awareness of the opportunities available for young women who had pursued courses of intermediate and higher education. The availability of 'new' occupations for women was an important economic argument advanced to justify the provision of education for girls in Wales, particularly from the 1870s. J.H. Griffith, 'Y Gohebydd', drew attention to the new job opportunities available for women in post offices, medicine and particularly in teaching. He contended that Welsh parents and their daughters had given inadequate attention to the attractive salaries available in these spheres.[151] In

Table 2.2
Occupations of females in England and Wales, 1881–1911

	1881	1891	1901	1911
Local government	3,017	5,165	10,426	19,437
National government (incl. Post Office & Civil Service)	4,353	9,875	16,074	25,463
Law clerks	100	166	367	2,159
Medical: doctors	25	101	212	477
Nurses/midwives and ancillary staff	{ 2,646 { 35,239	{53,057 { 887	{ 3,055 {64,214	{ 6,602 {77,060
Teaching	122,846	144,393	171,670	182,298
Domestic service	1,230,406	1,386,167	1,285,072	1,271,990
Commercial/business clerks	5,989	17,859	55,784	117,047

Source: *Census 1911*, Vol. x, p. 540.

particular, new job opportunities for educated women were highlighted. Women employed as clerks in post offices in London and elsewhere were executing their duties competently without any degradation of their sex. They were performing a far more useful social role than being idle at home. A large Welsh readership was informed of attitudes in London where the employment of women was not regarded as undignified.[152] It was prophesied that there would also be increasing opportunities for women in medicine and there would be many female doctors within twenty years.

An increase in the number of female schoolteachers was also foreseen. With the growth in the number of schools, particualrly for infants, and the comparatively high wages available to men in other spheres, school boards would have to employ women, particularly in infants' schools and in rural areas. A virtual guarantee of employment would thus be provided for large numbers of women.

Similarly, the establishment of a high-class girls' school at Dolgellau was also advocated for economic reasons.[153] Samuel Holland MP, the chief instigator of Dolgellau's quest for the Dr Williams' monies, emphasized the economic benefits of such education:

> It would give a great many girls the opportunity of showing what they could do in other lines beyond that of village seammistresses at 8/- or 10/- a week. Posts would not only be open for them in this part of the country but also in England, for in London the post offices and telegraph offices were filled with females and such a school would enable girls to make themselves proficient enough to earn a livelihood this way.[154]

He maintained that female labour was rising in value in the labour market and educated persons found employment sooner than those poorly educated.

The decisions taken with respect to the location of educational institutions at Aberystwyth in 1872, Swansea in 1873 and Dolgellau in 1874 were seen as vital for the well-being of the nation, otherwise Wales would be left 'behind in the race'.[155] In 1874 John Gibson was urging the authorities at UCW, Aberystwyth to admit women — for sound economic reasons:

> The best means of opening up new sources of profitable employment to women is to fit them by education and training for the employment they seek, . . . it is quite evident that whatever facilities are offered in the way of work they will be useless unless special training has been attended to. Indeed there can be no doubt that the first step towards improving the position of that large section of women in the middle classes . . . is to give them a higher class education.[156]

In similar vein, 'Y Gohebydd' urged UCW to follow the example of University College, Bristol and admit women students. New employment opportunities made this essential.[157]

During the 1880s, a decade that witnessed the Inquiry and Report of the Aberdare Committee, and a vigorous quest for intermediate and higher education, the educational condition of girls was given increasing attention in Welsh society. The relationship between educational needs and the growing job opportunities for women was being recognized.[158] At a meeting of the Association for Promoting the Education of Girls in Wales at Aberystwyth in 1887, Gibson emphasized the need for society to appreciate the economic importance of educating girls.[159] On the eve of the Welsh Intermediate Education Bill becoming law, T.E. Ellis MP was stressing the need for girls to be given the same educational oppportunities as boys so as to qualify for posts in the teaching profession and postal and telegraph offices.[160] In 1895, on the occasion of the laying of the foundation stone of Alexandra Hall in Aberystwyth, Principal T. Francis Roberts expressed the hope that more women would take advantage of the opportunities now available for those who had received higher education. He noted that women were rapidly entering many professions including medicine and especially teaching.[161]

English influences, Cymmrodorion, National Eisteddfod and Liberal–Nonconformist politics

Continuously in the 1850s and 1860s, the case for improved education for girls had been built up in England.[162] The institutions established for middle-class girls in England, as well as the education and experience gained by a small group of women who later turned their attention to Wales, proved of seminal importance. To a very great extent, educational developments in the Principality were to be influenced by the models already existing in England. Such campaigners as Miss E.P. Hughes, Mrs Dilys Glynne Jones and Dr Sophie Bryant, second headmistress of the North London Collegiate School, were themselves moulded by their experience in middle-class English educational establishments and their association with such pioneers as Miss Buss, Miss Beale and Miss Emily Davies.

Recently, attention has focused on the important role of Frances Power Cobbe in the history of female education in England. Her paper on university degrees for women at a meeting of the National Association for the Promotion of Social Science in 1860 has been viewed by Josephine Kamm as 'the first shot in the campaign'.[163] Though she resided at Hengwrt, Dolgellau, from the late 1870s and wrote extensively to the press, there is no evidence that she exerted any direct influence on Welsh education during its formative period.[164]

Nevertheless, developments relating to the education of girls and women in Wales did not occur in isolation, and the wider UK dimension needs to be borne in mind. In 1884, Miss E.P. Hughes accurately interpreted the situation in maintaining that 'it is undesirable and impossible to discuss the Higher Education of Girls in Wales and ignore the wider question of the higher educaiton of women, and the still wider one of higher education itself'.[165] In Wales, as in England, the Taunton Report, and the ensuing activity of the Endowed Schools Commssion in the 1870s, were important factors in the advancement of secondary education for girls. The report's basic educational philosophy had a significant impact on the Aberdare Committee's Inquiry and Report, and thereby on the pattern of intermediate education. Also, the London-based Girls' Public School Day Company extended its activities to Wales in the 1870s.

In the early 1870s, the Welsh press carried reports of significant educational developments in England. The impressive presence of Miss Garrett Anderson and Miss Emily Davies on the London School Board, Miss Beecher on the Manchester School Board and Miss Temple at Exeter were cited as evidence of a significant change in attitudes. The admission of women to examinations at Cambridge in 1869 was credited to the influence of Miss Emily Davies. By 1873, Oxford, London and Edinburgh had established examinations for women. These were indicative of a significant change in attitudes regarding the woman's rights and position in society.[166] The medical achievement of Miss Jex-Blake at Edinburgh, the opening of a female medical college in London, and the growth in the numbers of female teachers in both England and the USA, indicated the changing attitudes towards education and employment, whose significance ought not to be lost on women in Wales.

On the occasion of the initial moves at Dolgellau to establish a girls' high school, 'Y Gohebydd', who himself had been interested in female education ever since he heard Miss Anna Dickenson lecturing on the USA, took the opportunity to inform his wide readership of considerable developments outside Wales.[167] In 1872, 'Milton House College for Girls' was established at Gravesend, and in November 1871, the National Union for Improving the Education of Women of all Classes was formed. Female education was also discussed at the Social Science Association in Leeds in 1871 and at numerous Social Science and

Society of Arts meetings which had underlined the urgency of improvements and remodelling. 'Y Gohebydd' noted in particular that the Social Science Association inspired the establishment of a number of high-class girls' schools. He suggested that the National Eisteddfod could follow the Social Sciences Association by staging a discussion on the education of girls in Wales: it could initiate a development of vital importance for the nation's well-being.[168]

The establishment of the North London Collegiate School, the provision of lectures to women by university teachers in Lancashire and Yorkshire towns, the work of Bedford College for Ladies, and the moves by Professor Holloway to establish a 'University for Ladies', and the admission of a number of 'lady students' to the Department of Fine Art at University College London and South Kensington School of Art, were seen as further evidence of major educational change taking place in attitudes to, and provision of education for women.[169] The establishment of the Oxford and Cambridge Local Examinations had inspired greater thought about the educational needs of girls. It was essential that Wales responded in a constructive manner to these developments and provide educational opportunities comparable to those of the Scots and English.[170]

In 1875, the parliamentary debate on Cowper-Temple's Bill to allow women to sit degree examinations in medicine at Scottish universities did not go unnoticed in the Welsh press. Readers were informed of the activities of Miss Jex-Blake since 1869, and of the restrictions of the 1858 Medical Act.[171] By 1890, an editorial on 'The Education of Women' in *The North Wales Observer and Express* noted that Wales was beginning to feel the effects of changes that had been occurring for some years in England.[172] It was an accurate diagnosis, but there were, nevertheless, significant forces at work within the Principality itself.

The influence of Welsh exiles in London, and in particular their association with the Honourable Society of Cymmrodorion and the National Eisteddfod proved of considerable importance in advancing the fortunes of girls' intermediate education and higher education in the 1870s and 1880s. Indeed, from the 1860s, there were numerous literary competitions at Eisteddfodau which focused on various aspects of femininity. This reflected public interest, and the publications helped to mould public opinion.[173]

Though John Gibson was highly critical in *The Cambrian News* of the attitudes of some London Welshmen towards the University College of Wales in the 1870s and 1880s, the positive contribution of the London Welsh to the educational health of Victorian Wales is well recorded. It has been argued that they 'represented the more progressive element of the Welsh community', and that in London 'they were subject to influence which never obtained in a country predominantly rural'.[174]

The impact of the Cymmrodorion Society, particularly the Cymmrodorion Section meetings of the National Eisteddfod, was a very important determinant of change. The Third Cymmrodorion Society was formed in 1873 and successfully introduced its 'Cymmrodorion Section' of the National Eisteddfod at the Caernarfon National Eisteddfod in August 1880 when papers by Hugh Owen *On the Intermediate Education in Ireland and Secondary Education in Wales* and Mrs Peter of Bala on *Higher Education of Girls* were heard. The intention was to provide a platform for the discussion of key issues of the day and initiate a variety of reforms. In this respect, it was following the well-recorded path of the Social Science Section suggested in 1861 by Hugh Owen at the Aberdare National Eisteddfod, and begun at the Caernarfon National Edisteddfod of 1862. The following year at Swansea, Dr Thomas Nicholas read an influential paper on *Higher Education in Wales*.[175]

It was Hugh Owen, almost two decades later, who suggested to the Council of the Cymmrodorion Society the desirability of holding meetings to be called the 'Cymmrodorion Section of the National Eisteddfod' annually during the National Eisteddfod week. During the vital period in the 1880s and 1890s, it provided an influential platform for the cause of female education. Members of the Honourable Society of Cymmrodorion included some of the leading advocates of educational reform in late Victorian Wales — Sir Hugh Owen, John Griffith 'Y Gohebydd', T. Marchant Williams, Lord Aberdare, Lewis Morris, Isambard Owen and Sir John Williams. During the 1880s they were to be supportive of such leading protagonists of the cause of female education in Wales as Dr Frances Hoggan, Mrs Dilys Glynne Jones, Miss E.P. Hughes and Mrs Verney, and the newly formed Association for Promoting the Education of Girls in Wales.

Attention was first given to education by the Cymmrodorion Society on 26 February, 1877 when a paper was read by T. Marchant Williams — *The Educational Wants of Wales*.[176] In the following two decades, intermediate education, technical education, the Univesity of Wales and the place of the Welsh language in education, figured prominently in the deliberations and publications of the Cymmrodorion Society.[177] Advocacy was also given to the educational needs of girls and women in Wales. The Cymmrodorion Society was well represented in the inquiry and deliberations of the Aberdare Committee through Lord

Aberdare himself, John Rhys and Lewis Morris, whilst Hugh Owen and B.T. Williams submitted evidence. Its sympathetic advocacy of female education exerted a vital influence on the events of the following decade. At the annual dinner of the society at the Freemasons' Tavern on 9 November 1881, one of the guests was Dr Frances Hoggan, who at the time was the first and only woman invited to a Cymmrodorion dinner.[178] She appealed for support to establish a scholarship fund for women at University College, Cardiff.

Various Section meetings between 1882 and 1888 were allocated to discuss female education, and these, together with the publication of papers, undoubtedly exerted an important influence on public opinion. In 1882, at the Denbigh National Eisteddfod, Miss Dilys Davies's paper on *A Model School for Girls* and Dr Hoggan's contribution on *The Co-education of Women* were heard. In 1883, at the Cardiff National Eisteddfod, there were addresses from Dr Hoggan on *The Past and Future of the Education of Girls* and from Miss E.P. Hughes on *The Future of Welsh Education with special reference to the education of Girls*. At the Aberdare National Eisteddfod in 1885, Dr Bryant gave an address on *University Local Examinations in Wales*, whilst the following year at Caernarfon, there were important contributions from Isambard Owen on *Race and Nationality* and from Miss Dilys Davies on *The Education of Girls*. The meeting of 1886 proved crucial in the formation of the Association for Promoting the Education of Girls in Wales. Even more prominence was given to this association and to the educational needs of girls, at the London National Eisteddfod in 1887, particularly in contributions from Miss Dilys Davies and Miss E.P. Hughes, and at the Shrewsbury Conference in January 1888.

In an address in 1888 referring to the work of the Cymmrodorion Society, Dr Isambard Owen emphasized the considerable success of the Cymmrodorion Section of the National Eisteddfod. It had spawned the National Eisteddfod Society, the Society for Utilizing the Welsh Language and the Association for Promoting the Education of Girls in Wales.[179] On the occasion of the National Eisteddfod visit to Bangor in 1890, the importance of the various ancillary societies was underlined in *Tarian y Gweithiwr* where they and their members were seen as Wales's hope for the future.[180]

It has been argued that because of significant differences in the prevailing conditions in the two countries, it would be misleading to discuss the development of Welsh education simply in terms of that of England.[181] In 1884, Miss E.P. Hughes wrote 'in England, the chief work has been to enable women to share the educational advantages of men, but in Wales, we have to create a higher education system for both sexes'.[182] In the 1880s Wales lacked effective secondary schools for either sex, and the female educational campaign was, in significant ways, an integral part of the quest for increased educational opportunity for both sexes. The pressing need to reform and extend boys' education was a conditioning factor. It provided stimulus and debate for the female campaign, rather than conflict between the sexes. Women were admitted to the newly established university colleges in Wales in the 1880s on equal terms with men, and though at times special pleading was necessary to safeguard female interests, as witnessed by the formation of the Association for Promoting the Education of Girls in Wales in 1886, one detects no bitter opposition to the provision of secondary schooling for middle-class girls. On the eve of the Welsh Intermediate Education Act, public opinion was favourable to the provision of greater educational opportunities for females.[183]

The Liberal–Nonconformist struggle for equality in nineteenth-century Wales, in which education figured prominently, was also a significant conditioning factor. The Aberdare Report and the Welsh Intermediate Education Act were not only significant landmarks in that struggle, but also recognized the claims for equal educational treatment of girls and women. However, it would be a gross exaggeration to claim that female issues dominated the educational debate. On the eve of the Aberdare Inquiry, the education of girls and women was not a major issue to Nonconformists who were more concerned with freeing endowments from Anglican control and obtaining State finance for UCW Aberystwyth and intermediate schools.[184] Conflicts over the Intermediate Education bills in the 1880s were concerned primarily with questions of finance, representation, constitution of governing bodies and religion.[185] When Rendel's Intermediate Education Bill was before Parliament in 1889, the Nonconformists' major concern for the inclusion within the terms of the legislation of the Ashford and Howell endowments was to ensure equality and justice for Nonconformists rather than for women. They claimed that the endowments had been misused to the detriment of Nonconformity.[186] It would also be a misinterpretation of the period to ignore the positive contributions of Anglicans to the female educational cause at this time.[187]

Though difficult to quantify, and perhaps overemphasized at times, it is undeniable that there was considerable enthusiasm for, and interest in education in general in Wales. In particular, the Aberdare Report recognized 'the desire among the Welsh people for a better education'.[188] Concern over the nature of the existing grammar schools became evident from the 1860s, and though many placed a higher premium on the education of boys, attitudes were gradually changing, and the female cause was undoubtedly stimulated thereby. In 1876, attention was drawn to the greater advantages enjoyed by boys with their access to the endowed schools.[189] By 1893, it was being accurately claimed that the attention given to the needs of girls was a key feature of the education movement in Wales.[190]

Significantly, greater effort and participation in the cause of educational and social reform by women themselves was also advocated.[191] The publication of the Blue Books in 1847 played an important part in the growth of Nonconformist radical opinion in Victorian Wales. Their impact on attitudes to the female condition was considerable. In particular, the criticisms of Welsh women in the report generated a vigorous response from Ieuan Gwynedd and others, thus asserting the claims of women and laying the foundations for their later educational and social advancement.[192]

From the heroic efforts of Ieuan Gwynedd's *Y Gymraes* in 1850 to Thomas Gee's *Baner ac Amserau Cymru*, Cranogwen's *Y Frythones*, John Gibson's *Cambrian News* and Ceridwen Peris's *Y Gymraes* in 1896, Wales was to be well served by journals and newspapers that aroused enthusiasm, moulded public opinion and provided a valuable forum for the cause of female emancipation. Referring specifically in 1895 to *Y Gymraes* and *Y Frythones* during the laying of the foundation stone of Alexandra Hall, Aberystwyth, Principal T. Francis Roberts drew attention to the important role of Welsh journals in advancing the female cause before the formation of any general organization. He also recognized the support of *The Cambrian News* under the editorship of John Gibson:

Any reference to the movement especially in Aberystwyth would be incomplete and ungrateful if it did not refer to the efforts for the advancement of women made by the able newspaper published in the town. Whether they agreed or disagreed with the principles or criticism of that paper they could not refrain from admiring the work it had done for the advancement of women.[193]

(iii)   *The turn of the century: towards emancipation and greater educational opportunity*

By the dawn of the twentieth century, much had been done, especially in the previous two decades, to emancipate women. In various spheres, they now enjoyed greater freedom and justice. After a long struggle, the married women's property law had been reformed. Since 1882, women were able to retain ownership of property after marriage. In laws ruling such matters as the custody and guardianship of children, the estates of husbands who died intestate, sexual offences and marital relations, various obstacles had been removed. Women had acquired rights of citizenship to the extent that they could vote and be members of county, district and parish councils. They could also be members of boards of guardians and school boards. They had successfully revolted against the old notion of 'women's sphere', and their circle was rapidly widening. They had gained entrance into such professions as medicine, and were gradually forcing their way into a variety of occupations, trades and business. Though there were still restrictions in the older universities, the University of Wales Charter (1893) gave women equality with men. In secondary and higher education, facilities for women had undergone enormous change, and they had proved their intellectual equality with men.[194]

Educational change was seen as both an agent of, and a symptom of female emancipation.[195] But bondage and inequality had far from dissipated.[196] Women were still subject to various legal and social restrictions and, in particular, they were still denied the parliamentary franchise. Many women, themselves, were opposed to change and in regular editorials in *The Cambrian News*, John Gibson was highly critical of those women who were not in earnest concerning the franchise.[197] Not only were law and custom a hindrance, but also there was irrational prejudice against giving the franchise to women.[198] The divorce laws remained unfair to women and were an indication of their inferior status. A man could divorce on the grounds of his wife's adultery, but to divorce an adulterous husband a women had also to prove cruelty. In addition, the marriage laws were unfair to women because they merged a woman's identity with that of her husband: marriage was not a mutal contract between two perfectly equal individuals.[199] Likewise, the bastardy laws were unjust to women: they favoured men, through placing the burden of illegitimacy on women. In holy orders, the legal profession, public life and Oxford and Cambridge universities, women's sphere of action was limited or hindered by social custom, prejudice or the law. In spite of many important changes in the late Victorian era in the direction of greater freedom and justice, the laws of the land still treated women as the inferiors of men.

The female's precise role in society remained an issue of controversy. Though women, in increasing numbers, were taking up a variety of posts, there were still supporters of the traditional view that the sphere of women was marriage and motherhood. There was still divergence of opinion regarding women's participation in public affairs and their suitability for some occupations. These issues were highlighted in journals such as *Y Gymraes*.[200] By 1894, *Y Tyst*, which had previously voiced doubts, was approving women's participation in public life. By then, scores of women had been elected members of public bodies. On public platform and in the world of music, Edith Wynne and Mary Davies were well-known names.[201] John Gibson saw the main debate as being not over women's sphere, but whether or not women should be fully emancipated. Nothing less than perfect equality would be acceptable. He regarded every restriction imposed upon the freedom of women but not imposed on the freedom of men as 'an act of tyranny and injustice to women'.[202] In 1902 he wrote that women 'are still looked on by men as mere chattels, as sexual toys; as potential mothers; as subsidiary aids to man's exclusive regard for himself'.[203]

Student debates at UCW Aberystwyth echoed the debate in society at large regarding the position of women. Women's suffrage attracted much attention, there being a strong feeling that it ought to be secured in the name of justice. The woman's social and economic position was also discussed, and her exclusion from any profession condemned. In 1896, in a debate on 'the Education of Women', the growth of higher education was regarded as having improved the position of middle-class women through providing a range of new job opportunities. Elsewhere also, there was a realization by 1902 that significant changes had occurred in the education of girls and women in Wales:

> The girls of Wales now possess a system of education extending from the Elementary School to the University. . . . It is a matter of sincere congratulations however, to observe the remarkable change which has taken place in the position of the whole question of the education of girls in Wales since the Association for Promoting the Education of Girls in Wales commenced its labours.[204]

3

Limited Schooling, 1840–1880

(i) *Working-class girls in elementary schools*

The growing educational debate, 1840–1847

In the educational history of Wales, the 1840s were to be years of considerable significance. There were developments which left a major impact on the provision and attitudes to education during the rest of the Victorian era.

Elementary education was the main focus of attention.[1] Though the voluntary societies were to play a crucial role in the mid-Victorian years, the provision of parliamentary grants led to greater State involvement. Parliamentary debate, a commission of inquiry, legislation and inspection by HMI — hallmarks of the 1840s State machinery — were to affect the educational scene in Wales. For many, the extent and nature of the State's involvement became highly controversial issues.

It was a period of political and social turmoil in many West European countries, and the provision of education for the 'lower classes' came to be viewed within those parameters. In Wales, the Chartist disturbances and the Rebecca Riots dominated the debate concerning the social role of education. It was argued that if there had been a system of efficient schools, 'the Chartist rising at Newport and the Rebecca disturbances . . . would not have taken place; the people would have redressed their grievances by constitutional means instead of violence'.[2]

In the 1840s, it became increasingly evident in a country experiencing the turmoil of rapid industrialization and population growth, that the quantity and quality of schooling was inadequate. In 1840, a *Report on Elementary Education in the Mining Districts of South Wales* by Seymour Tremenheere, HMI, which focused on the Merthyr Tudful district and neighbouring areas of Monmouthshire, revealed a lack of schooling among the working classes who were subject to the dictates of the labour market. There was 'lamentable deficiency of the means of elementary instruction in a great portion of that district'.[3] Children were employed at an early age, and women also worked. Parents showed little enthusiasm for sending their children to school.[4]

In suggesting benefits that would accrue from a better system of schooling, Tremenheere advanced a thesis that was to characterize attitudes to the education of girls for much of the nineteenth century. He saw the need for 'an adequate provision for the industrial training of female children with reference to the careful and proper discharge of domestic duties'.[5]

Such recommendations were to be reiterated in 1843 with the publication of the *Second Report of the Children's Employment Commission* which highlighted the defects in the intellectual, moral and religious culture afforded to working-class children. It was concluded that the evidence of witnesses indicated that in south Wales 'school education . . . is quite inadequate to the wants of the people'.[6] Shortly, more was to be heard of the relationship between education, and especially the education of girls, and morality.

It is undeniable that, in spite of much voluntary effort, there was an educational vacuum in Wales in the mid-1840s. There was also a demand for better schools. The State, voluntary societies and private individuals saw the need for action. But, unfortunately, elementary education could not be divorced from religious rivalry and differing views regarding the educational role of the State.

In 1843, Hugh Owen, who was later to play a crucial role in the provision of secondary and higher education in Wales, addressed his *Letter to the Welsh People* embodying proposals for an efficient educational system based on the establishment of a network of British schools. Following the appointment of the Revd John Phillips as the British Society's agent in north Wales, there was considerable educational activity there during the years 1844–7. Later, in 1846, when William Williams, MP for Coventry, raised the question of the educational condition of Wales in Parliament on 10 March, it was an opportune moment. Already there was concern, and a realization that more and better elementary schools were needed.

Women, however, though helping locally, had not been prominent amongst the leaders of this male-dominated educational movement of the 1840s. It was intended that both sexes would atttend the elementary schools being contemplated, and accepted that females, as well as males, would be teachers. However, the new training-colleges opened at Brecon in 1846 and Carmarthen in 1848 were exclusively male institutions.

In Wales, by 1847, elementary education was the subject of much interest. Though attention did focus on the advantages of education for the individual as well as a means of ameliorating poverty, reducing crimes and propagating religious belief, the main issues of concern for the advocates of elementary education were the trend towards government involvement and control, the position of Nonconformists, the nature of religious education, and support for the voluntary principle.

As yet, no especial attention was being given to the education of girls in Wales. Tremenheere had already identified issues which were later to play an important role in the debate concerning female education. Yet for many, the woman's sphere of influence was seen not as the world of learning but as the stable family unit which she would imbue with a Christian morality and the beauty of her character. In 1845, her role was delineated in such terms by Revd Lewis Edwards. It is unlikely that anything more advanced than elementary schooling was being contemplated for the majority of the girls of Wales at this time. However, ironically, one of the most remarkable women in Victorian Wales, Lady Llanover, was instrumental in 1847 in establishing one of the most successful experiments in higher education—the exclusively male dominated, Llandovery College.[7]

For girls, however, there were no endowed secondary schools, training-colleges or institutes of higher education in Wales. The very limited educational opportunities were about to be highlighted by the publication of the results of the government's inquiry in November 1847.

The Blue Books and their aftermath: perspectives on education and femininity, 1847–1849

The publication of the *Reports of the Commissioners of Inquiry into the State of Education in Wales* — the so-called Blue Books — in November 1847, was to prove a traumatic event both for education and the reputation of women in Wales. The suitability of the commissioners, their *modus operandi*, the objectivity of witnesses and the conclusions of the inquiry have been the subject of much debate.[8] Undoubtedly, there was much misrepresentation of the actual conditions in the schools of Wales, but it is undeniable that the quality of education left much to be desired.

Though the accuracy of the statistical data in the reports of 1847 has been questioned, it is clear that a much higher proportion of boys than girls were at school. R.R.W. Lingen reported that in Carmarthenshire and Pembrokeshire, the female population's 'educational destitution is

Table 3.1
Percentage of Scholars in the Population of Each Sex

		Carmarthenshire	Glamorgan	Pembrokeshire
5–10 years:	Male	31.8	48.1	44.5
	Female	21.3	39.0	27.4
10–15 years:	Male	27.1	19.9	36.7
	Female	14.7	23.4	22.1

Source: *Reports of the Commissioners of Inquiry into the State of Education in Wales*, (1848 edition), pp. 92, 227, 213.

comparatively greater than that of the other sex'.[9] In Glamorgan, where there were far more dame schools, there was 'greater equality between the male and female scholars'.[10]

Furthermore, because of the impact of socio-economic factors which were to influence the progress of girls' education in Wales even into the twentieth century, those at school appeared to be less well educated than boys:

> In my district, not only in amount of schooling, but in attainment, they are decidedly worse off than boys. The reason for this inferiority is, that, money being the sole motive for acquiring the little education that exists, that inducement is much less strong with respect to females than with regard to males, for men are supposed to be more in need of arithmetic and writing for their advancement in life.[11]

As well as reporting on the educational condition of Wales in 1847, the Commissioners offered highly controversial perspectives on femininity, which were to exert considerable influence on the fortunes of female education in the Principality. Welsh women were portrayed as being immoral as well as ignorant. Indeed, their poor education and low moral standards were seen as interrelated.

The education of girls of ten to fifteen was particularly neglected in Anglesey — 'a fact which should be compared with the prevalence of incontinence in that county', ran the report. Indeed, H. Vaughan Johnson regarded it as the besetting vice of north Wales. He quoted the evidence of the Revd J.W. Trevor, chaplain to the Bishop of Bangor:

> It is difficult, as it is mortifying to describe in proper terms the disgraceful state of the common people in Wales in the intercourse of the sexes; but it is important that the truth should be known . . . the moral principles of the Welsh people are totally corrupt and abandoned in this respect; that no restraints or penalties of law can cure or even check the evil, until the appliances of better education and more general civilization, they are taught to regard their present custom with a sense of shame and decency.[13]

In his report on Brecknock, Cardigan and Radnor, Jelinger C. Symons quoted the evidence of the Revd H.L. Davies, Troed-yr-Aur: 'Morals are generally at a low ebb, but want of chastity is the giant sin of Wales. I believe that the best remedy for the want of morals and of education, is that of the establishment of good schools'.[15] The commissioner noted:

> the alleged want of chastity in the women. If this be so, it is sufficient to account for all other immoralities, for each generation will derive its moral tone in a great degree from the influence imparted by the mothers who reared them. Where these influences are corrupted at their very source, it is vain to expect virtue in the offspring.[15]

Likewise, in the mining and manufacturing districts of south-east Wales, R.W. Lingen referred to the evidence of Revd John Griffith, Vicar of Aberdare, who commented that 'Nothing can be lower, I would say more degrading, than the character in which women stand relative to men . . . Promiscuous intercourse is most common, is thought of as nothing, and the women do not lose caste by it'.[16]

The publication of the report generated a storm of protest in Wales. Nonconformists, in particular, reacted sharply to the allegations, refuting both the exaggerated picture of educational conditions and especially the slur cast upon the moral condition of Wales. A determined effort followed later in the 1850s and 1860s to assert the true virtues of Welsh womanhood. But immediately, in March 1848, *Yr Amserau* thundered against the reports. The women of Wales were urged to respond to the unjustified slur on their character through a national petition to the Queen demanding the immediate abolition of the Committee of Council. The proposal was welcomed by Ieuan Gwynedd who was about to become the staunchest defender of the women of Wales. Likewise, *Remarks on the Reports of the Commissioners of Enquiry into the State of Education in Wales* (1848) by Jane Williams (Ysgafell), and Sir Thomas Phillips's, *Wales: The Language, Social Condition, Moral Character and Religious Opinions of the People* (1849) condemned the Commissioners and their findings and endeavoured to correct the erroneous impression of the character of the Welsh people.

But undoubtedly, the most rigorous and persistent critic of the Blue Books was the Revd Evan Jones — Ieuan Gwynedd. He was already well known in the Welsh press for his support of the Voluntaryist cause. The reports made him more hostile to the principle of state education which became his main educational battle during the years 1848–50, and an issue of major debate throughout Wales.[17] But he also rebutted the slight cast by the Commissioners on Welsh Nonconformists in general, and females in particular. In 1849, in *Facts, Figures and Statements in Illustration of the Dissent and Morality of Wales*, he argued that the allegations regarding unchastity were 'greatly and invidiously exaggerated'.[18] He saw the reports as a deliberate Anglican ploy to disparage the Welsh in order to justify an Anglican State programme of education — 'a grand movement for church extension'.[19] Statements to the commissioners on illegitimacy were said to be grossly exaggerated. Almost all the cases of illegitimacy arose from a breach of promise: 'The daughters of Cambria need not blush when their reputation is measured with that of their Anglo-Saxon Sisters'.[20]

In particular, he rejected the view in the 1847 reports that the prevalence of Nonconformity and immorality were interrelated. But Ieuan Gwynedd also widened the debate. In 1849, he was writing about the influence of women on a nation's character — *Dylanwad Merched ar Nodwedd Cymru*.[21] Noting Napoleon Bonaparte's observation that France needed good mothers, he argued that there was a direct relationship between the characteristics of a nation and those of its constituent families. The mother's role was formative. But as yet, the women of Wales were in an inferior social position. Throughout the ages, their potential had been undervalued. The limited nature of their education attested to their social inferiority.

With the 1840s drawing to a close, issues which exerted a crucial influence on the provision of education for girls in Victorian Wales had been identified. The social status, role and education of the female required a major reassessment and moral uplift. To this end, plans were being made in 1848–9 to promote the female cause in Wales through the publication of a monthly journal, and Ieuan Gwynedd was being canvassed for the editorship. In January 1850, the first edition of *Y Gymraes* was published. It was intended to be a monthly journal, costing two pence, for the enlightenment of the women of Wales. From the first issue it was evident that Ieuan Gwynedd was concerned about the educational neglect of Welsh girls, and that he wanted to promote the benefit that families and in particular the young child, would gain from the education of the mother. The main objective of *Y Gymraes* was the female's moral, religious and social elevation.

The publication of *Y Gymraes* was welcomed, and its discussions of woman's low and inferior social status, lack of educational opportunity, and the interrelationship of female education and moral reform underlined. However, owing to lack of finance, insufficient support amongst Welsh women, and Ieuan Gwynedd's ill health, *Y Gymraes* was shortlived. By January 1852 it had been forced to merge with *Y Tywysydd*. Under the editorship of Revd David Rees, Llanelli, it was published until 1870, but no especial attention was given to the female.

There have been criticisms in recent editions of *Llafur* of the conservative nature of the underlying philosophy of *Y Gymraes* and the selective picture given of the life of Welsh women in the mid-nineteenth century. The woman's role was seen only in terms of her home and family. She was to be the romanticized 'Angle in the House'.[22] Significantly, Coventry Patmore's highly influential poem bearing that title appeared in 1854.[23] Much vagueness characterizes the educational sections of *Y Gymraes*. Whilst more education is deemed worthwhile for all women, the implications are not defined in socio-economic terms, though it may be deduced that there was particular concern about the working classes. Nor is any clear attention given to the institutional agents of educational enlightenment outside the home. Ieuan Gwynedd's precise views on different levels of education — elementary, secondary, higher — are not spelled out, though undoubtedly he would have welcomed most educational opportunities for girls.

Nevertheless, *Y Gymraes* was important in the long quest for the proper recognition and improved status of the woman in Welsh society. It had defined the female's formative social role and the importance of her education. In February 1852, the month of his untimely death, Ieuan Gwynedd was reiterating his view of the instrumental role of the mother in the home and in society at large. His much-lamented death was followed by a national campaign to raise subscriptions for a monument which was later erected on his grave at Groes Wen.[24]

The social and educational cause of the Victorian female was about to be championed with even greater vigour in Wales in the 1850s and 1860s. Robert Jones Derfel (1824–1905) though resident in Manchester, for most of his life, became one of the most original thinkers and writers of Victorian Wales. He espoused both national and socialist sentiments.[25] In 1864, a selection of many of his early writings, *Traethodau ac Areithiau* was published. He pleaded for the establishment of a university in Wales, a national library, village libraries, a national museum, a school of arts and crafts and an observatory. But also, the volume included an ariticle calling for the education of girls — 'Yr Angenrheidrwydd o roddi Addysg Gyffredinol i Ferched Ieuainc' — which had been published originally in *Y Traethodydd* in 1854.[26] This provides a valuable perception both of femininity and education by a radical Welsh thinker of the period.

Another voice speaking out during the 1850s in the cause of female education was Hugh Evan Thomas, 'Huwco Meirion', (1830–89). A native of Bala, he became a well-known independent minister at Birkenhead from 1853, until he emigrated to the USA in 1867, to become minister of a church at Pittsburgh. He was also a successful poet and frequent contributor to the press on both sides of the Atlantic.[27]

In the 1850s, education was being increasingly seen as a vital asset enabling both working-class and middle-class women to become better wives and mothers, and effective 'Angels in the House'. Modern feminist writers such as Carol Dyhouse, who have detected similar trends throughout English society in the 1850s, view such pleas for female education as conservative rather than socially revolutionary in nature.[28] The doctrine of separate spheres and the division of labour were not being challenged. In Emily Shirreff's *Intellectual Education and its Influence on the Character and Happiness of Women* (1858) the education of middle-class girls was justified in terms of strengthening and refining their influence as guardians of the home.

With growing awareness of the weaknesses in Wales's system of education, the need to improve the female's educational condition became even more evident. Though much of the literature of the period is vague on precise details, it is clear that the provision of greater educational opportunities for girls was being conceived in terms of elementary education. The 'new deal' being advocated by HMIs was viewed in terms of effective elementary education for the working classes — *y gwerin*. In an editorial, welcoming the opening of the Bangor Normal College in 1858, Gee viewed its role within this socio-economic context. The new training-college merited financial support towards its building fund to enable it to fulfil its educational and social role effectively.

Female education was by no means the main educational issue of the day, for attention was also focused in Wales on the provision of elementary education, and in particular, questions of state control and unsectarian education in an age of voluntary activity were given especial consideration.[29] The columns of *Baner Cymru* revealed Thomas Gee's staunch support for greater provision of unsectarian education, and the voluntary principle. Education needed to be seen as a priority. Within this social and educational context, female education was also given attention. Again, education was seen as enabling the mother and housewife to fulfil her domestic duties more effectively. Thomas Gee criticized existing educational agencies for insufficient attention to the duties and responsibilities of the mother.

The exclusively male orientation of Bangor Normal College elicited no comment. However, through the establishment of the pupil-teacher system and training-colleges in England, an important extension of educational opportunity into the post-elementary and 'higher' sectors was now also available for Welsh girls.

For both sexes in the elementary schools, there was curricular emphasis on the basic skills of literacy and numeracy. The duration of schooling was comparatively brief for both boys and girls. In 1859, only 38 per cent of the 10,971 boys and 8,882 girls in average attendance in 193 Church of England schools in Wales had been in school for two or more years. With the provision of domestic subjects for girls, a degree of curricular differentiation advocated by the Education Department and HMIs was already evident. During the 1850s, sewing, needlework and domestic economy were recommended in HMI reports as important elements in the education of girls who were destined to be 'servants and poor men's wives'.[30] Gender stereotyping was to be a key feature of the curriculum for working-class girls in Victorian Wales.

The most detailed survey of education in Wales during the 1850s occurred in 1859, when John Jenkins, an Assistant Commissioner for the Newcastle Commission investigated 'the state of Popular Education in the Welsh Specimen Districts in the Poor Law Unions of Corwen, Dolgellau, Bala, Ffestiniog, Neath and Merthyr Tydfil in North and South Wales'. It was concluded that insufficient attention was given in the elementary schools to the especial requirements of the female.

The need for the provision of an efficient national system of elementary education was increasingly acknowledged during the 1860s in the Welsh press and by essayists in National Eisteddfod competitions who pinpointed the interrelationship of educational and social thought. There was growing awareness of the inadequacy of the existing provision. Under the Revised Code, the grant to an elementary school could be withheld altogether 'if the girls in the school be not taught plain needlework as part of the ordinary course of instruction'.[31] Mixed schools were to increase in number in the 1860s, primarily because of financial reasons. Both the merits and disadvantages were voiced by HMI.[33]

Though it would thus be an exaggeration to maintain that the provision of elementary education for girls was a major issue in the 1860s, it did, nevertheless, attract attention, and it was acknowledged that it had been given a lower priority than boys' education.[33] Objections to female education were still being voiced. Charges of masculinity and selfishness were still being levied against learned women, though such critics were becoming fewer in number.

In 1864, the Registrar-General's figures were published showing that in spite of the extension of education, literacy rates in Wales were far from satisfactory. In south Wales, an average of 64 per cent of males and 43 per cent of females were able to write their names. In north Wales, the corresponding figures were 64 per cent of men and 48 per cent of women. The Children's Employment Commission 1861–7 revealed the early employment of large numbers of girls and young women in tinplate works and ironworks, on pit banks and coke heaps, and drew attention to the evils of their early withdrawal from school. In industrial Wales in general, educational opportunities were very limited for both sexes, though the important role of the works' schools in the provision of elementary education has been underestimated.[34] However, by 1870, large numbers of working-class families in Dowlais had benefited from the educational scheme established by Sir John and Lady Charlotte Guest, which provided not only elementary education, but also an element of 'higher' education in adult day and evening schools. Dr Leslie Wynne Evans has shown the key role played by Lady Charlotte Guest (later Schreiber) in the establishment and operation of a successful educational scheme which was 'the most comprehensive and practical ever to be attempted' during the nineteenth century. The schools grew in number and influence between 1828 and 1892, when they were taken over by the Merthyr Tudful School Board.

Lady Charlotte, who mastered the Welsh language sufficiently well to publish a complete translation of the *Mabinogion* in 1864 was undoubtedly one of the most remarkable women of Victorian Wales. She showed particular interest in the female population of Dowlais, and at one time, between seventy and eighty young women attended evening schools. Significantly they were taught sewing and embroidery as well as reading and writing, and exhibitions of their embroidery were arranged.[35] What this cultured philanothropist was providing, therefore, was the opportunity for working-class girls to perform the woman's traditional role that much more effectively.

The reality of the educational and social condition of girls and women in Wales on the eve of the Forster Education Act was revealed by the Taunton Report which noted that the Howell schools were the only two endowed schools offering secondary education for girls in the Principality. Also of importance for the educational historian is the erstwhile neglected *Report on the Employment of Children, Young Persons, and Women in Agriculture* (1870). This showed that the educational opportunities available in Wales were very lmited.[36] Girls, as well as boys, were subject to the dictates of early employment. Almost half the total labouring population in agriculture were females. The signatories of the section on Wales—H.S. Tremenheere and E.C. Tufnell—concluded that 'elementary education in Wales appears, excepting in a few localities, to be making but slow progress'.[37] It was commonplace for girls as well as boys to enter farm service between the ages of nine and thirteen years 'to the detriment of their opportunities for education'.[38]

Like their predecessors in 1847, Tremenheere and Tufnell provided a disparaging portrayal of Welsh womanhood. Attention was given to 'the laxity of morals amongst the female peasantry of Wales'.[39] This immorality was attributed, in particular, to overcrowding in cottages. But the typical woman in rural Wales was also perceived as most unrefined and poorly educated — a view which was, of course, informed by the orthodox Victorian conception of culture. Moreover, the report blamed 'the obstacle to Welsh civilization which is created by the prevalance of the Welsh language'.[40] The compilers of the report called for a more effective provision of elementary education in rural Wales: more schools, more trained teachers and a period of compulsory education were seen as essential for improving the well-being of womanhood.[41] It was noted that whilst the employment of females in field work was declining, work as 'domestic servants' was much in evidence. This trend would strengthen the sex-role stereotyping that characterized the elementary school curriculum and influence the debate concerning the intermediate school curriculum in the 1890s.

Socio-economic realities dictated that for the majority of girls in Wales, only elementary education would be available in the 1860s. Social mobility was not an issue of the day, and much attention focused on the importance for the well-being of society of a disciplined, working class. To maintain this structure, the female's role was still being seen primarily in terms of the family and its responsibilities. She needed more education, but of a domestic rather than intellectual nature to equip her for her role as wife and mother. The family remained the vital social institution and the cult of the home, and the virtues of family life, stability and discipline, were constantly emphasized.

In the 1860s, therefore, female education in Wales is only explicable within the parameters of the broader social context. Concern for the nation's moral condition was a vital determinant within that backdrop. In September 1863, Dr Thomas Rees read a paper on 'The Alleged Unchastity of Wales' at one of the Social Science Meetings of the National Eisteddfod in Swansea.[42] Pre-marital intercourse rather than adultery and systematic prostitution was deemed to be the real moral problem of the Principality. Thomas Gee also examined the country's moral condition, noting, in particular, the social malaise indicated by immorality and prostitution in industrial south Wales, and the moral dangers facing young women who migrated to England in search of work. He argued that both home and school were instrumental in moulding the female's moral character. In 1863, a Committee of Council report evoked the Blue Books in its criticism of moral standards in the Principality. However, as well as illegitimacy, drink and inadequate education figured in the social analysis.

Concern for the nation's moral well-being also figured prominently in one of the most well-known Welsh lectures of the decade. Revd Rhys Gwesyn Jones delivered the lecture *Caru, Priodi a Byw* on over a hundred occasions before its publication in 1866.[43] By 1904, the printed version had reached its fifth edition. The main focus was on enunciating general principles of guidance for courtship, marriage and happy family life. Education was seen as vital to a stable family life. Girls and young women of all social backgrounds required effective instruction in the principles of domestic economy. It was recommended that institutions should be established in all districts to provide short-term courses for young women already in employment. A well-managed home would keep the husband away from the pleasures of the tavern, and women could exercise a powerful influence on behalf of sobriety.

Though her precise role outside the home was a matter of debate in the 1860s, it was clear that the female's participation in various spheres of society was increasing. By the end of the decade, the deliberations concerning the proposed legislation affecting the property rights of married women introduced by Russell Gurney MP, were indicative of the changing status of the female in society. Opponents of the measure were taken to task for their hostility to the principles of justice and equity. Such trends exerted a profound impact on considerations of education in general, and female education in particular, in Wales.

(ii)   *Middle-class schooling for girls: private and endowed schools*

Private schools in the 1850s and 1860s

The provision of institutions of secondary and higher education for girls was not a major issue in Wales in the 1850s. As in England, grammar schools and universities were the province of the middle and upper classes. In Wales, however, the middle class were comparatively few in number in the 1850s and an important momentum for education-al improvement was thereby lacking: 'The country was divided into two classes, small farmers and large landowners, without any intermediate class to fill up the great distance between them'.[44]

For both sexes, the Blue Books showed that schooling was most prevalent between the ages of five and ten years when, in 1847, 10,187 boys and 7,970 girls were at school. In the ten to fifteen age group, 6,413 boys and 5,068 girls in north Wales received schooling of an average duration of sixteen months.

It is difficult to evaluate the precise nature and quality of the education of Welsh girls between ten and fifteen years at this time. Though girls had attended Llanrwst Grammar School following its reopening in 1828, and though their admission to Lewis School Gelligaer had been mooted in 1836, the endowed grammar schools of Wales were exclusively male establishments at the end of the 1840s. It is also abundantly clear that sound learning had long since disappeared from them: 'the tendency is to degrade grammar schools into elementary schools of inadequate extent and inefficient character'.[45]

For boys and young men, secondary education of a varied quality was also available in a wide range of non-endowed private schools and academies. Of importance were establishments run by Nonconformist ministers, particularly Unitarians and Independents. But females were conspicuous by their absence in the 1840s from such successful instititutions as Adpar Academy, Rhydowen School Pontsian, Eben Fardd's School at Clynnog, and Ffrwdfâl Academy, in Carmarthenshire.[46]

The Blue Books suggest that girls in the ten to fifteen age group, whose education only continued for a short duration, received little more than elementary schooling. Its quality was dependent on the varying standard of the local voluntary or private venture school, where most of the teachers were untrained. In north Wales, 94.2 per cent of female teachers were said to be in this category. The Blue Books have only limited value for the study of girls' secondary education. Precise details about specific schools and home tuition are not provided. Though other sources are limited, further information may be elicited from trade directories and newspaper advertisements. Entries in such directories as *Pigot's*, *Robson's*, *Slater's* and *Hunt's* have only a limited value because they do not differentiate clearly between those schools offering elementary and 'secondary' education.[47] They do show that there were private schools catering for females in most urban centres in Wales in the 1840s. Whilst some were exclusively for day pupils, others also admitted boarders. Being non-endowed private ventures, their fortunes varied considerably. Whilst some functioned for only a brief span of time, others were more endurable. At Wrexham, Miss Sadler's

'School for Young Ladies' had a continuous history from the 1830s until the proprietor's death in 1870. There were a number of other well-established schools in north and mid-Wales in the 1840s and 1850s.[48] In south Wales also, there were ladies' boarding and day-schools in most towns.[49] It is extremely difficult to ascertain the precise nature of the schooling provided in these institutions. Their designation as 'Establishments for Young Ladies' suggests that they aimed to provide more than mere elementary education. Though the quality of the instruction varied, social accomplishments and elementary work were more likely than a rigorous academic curriculum.

Middle-class schooling for girls in Victorian Wales was initially dominated by the emphasis on accomplishments in the curriculum. Gradually, and particularly during the 1880s and 1890s, more attention was given to academic subjects. The 'accomplishments' curriculum usually included the study of music, art and modern languages as well as the grammar, literature, composition and elocution which constituted an 'English education'. Some attention would also be given to dancing or calisthenics and needlework. The domination of an 'accomplishments' curriculum for much of the Victorian era epitomized the prevalent middle-class notions of culture and womanhood. The economic changes of the late eighteenth and early nineteenth centuries had divorced the home from the workplace. In a patriarchical society, conscious of complementary sex differences and different educational abilities, the home was deemed the proper sphere of the middle-class 'lady' and an accomplishments education the most appropriate.

In the 1850s it is also clear that a number of middle-class families with sufficient financial resources sent their daughters to boarding-schools in England. Also, a number of families employed governesses. The 1851 census returns show that there were 466 governesses in Wales, but the precise nature of the work and the sex and age of their charges are not easily ascertained.[50] Newspaper advertisements and *Slater's Directory* 1850 and 1858–9 indicate that there were non-endowed private establishments in most of the main centres of population.

A consciousness of social class and the place of social accomplishments were evident in this sector of education. An advertisement for Mrs Maingay's School, Tenby in 1855 states that 'none but the daughters of gentlemen were admitted'. French was taught by 'a resident Parisian lady'.[51] At The Young Ladies Boarding School, Red-Hill Mansion Beaumaris, 'masters of talent attend the school and the French and Italian languages are taught by a resident French Governess'.[52] But it is also evident that at least some of the schools offered more than mere accomplishments. At Wynnstay House, Wrexham, in 1858, pupils were taught arithmetic, English, history, Latin and the classics, Scripture, geography, French, German, needlework and music. Some girls entered for the College of Preceptors examinations.

By 1859 some critical attention was given to the education received by the daughters of farmers and other sufficiently prosperous to attend boarding-schools in England. Schools at Chester, Bristol, London and elsewhere, advertised in newspapers circulating in Wales. Typical was Long Ashton School near Bristol where 'a limited number of young laides' were offered 'every requisitive of a finished English education with superior advantages for the acquirement of music, singing and modern languages'.[53] In particular, criticism was being voiced of their over-emphasis on accomplishments.[54] In a long editorial in December 1859, Thomas Gee condemned the attention given 'to the study of inessentials' — embroidery, literature, French, accomplishments — and the neglect of those aspects of knowledge, essential for effective fulfilment of the role of wife and mother.[55]

Other than the Taunton Report, sources are meagre for the 1860s, with newspapers, advertisements and *Slater's Directory* of 1868 being the most useful. Advertisements for boys' schools were more predominant in the Welsh press. Significantly the Welsh press also carried advertisements for girls' schools in England.[56] Precise numbers of schools offering girls more than mere elementary education are not easily quantitifed from these sources. However, it is evident that there were private girls' schools in most urban centres, and some were well established.[57]

The appeal for clientele was couched in terms explicable in the context of prevalent middle-class ideology. Their aims were social rather than academic. There was little attempt at cultivating scholarly attitudes or providing intellectual rigour. Some 'ladies schools' were content with the 'finishing school image' whilst others claimed to provide 'all branches' of useful and modern acquirements and 'a thorough English education with every other accomplishment a Lady may require'.[58]

Volume VIII of the Taunton Report gives the only detailed insight into private schools in Victorian Wales. Here, H.M. Bompas's general report on the state of middle-class education in Glamorgan, Flintshire, Denbighshire, Monmouthshire, Herefordshire, Chester and Shrewsbury, provides valuable information. In the four Welsh counties, there were as many as seventy-two private schools providing education for approximately 1,800 girls. In an unspecified number, the education was both 'elementary' and 'secondary'.

Overall, girls' schools tended to be small in comparison with boys' schools. This was attributed to the larger number of women who desired to teach, and to their preference for a small establishment. Teacher–pupil ratios were very satisfactory, particularly in the more expensive schools.[59]

The constraints on the development of girls' secondary education were noted. In Cardiff, though there were one or two boarding-schools in the healthy suburbs, the close proximity of Bath or Clifton attracted the daughters of the upper middle class, and consequently had an adverse effect on 'upper-class schools', in the Welsh town. The economic circumstances of the small farmers who constituted a large proportion of the agricultural community in Glamorgan, 'many of whom have to work harder and live more sparingly than ordinary labourers', did not enable them to contemplate more than elementary schooling for their children. Those with larger farms experienced considerable difficulty in attracting adequate labour because of the high wages available in the mining district. Consequently, they were virtually obliged, at times, to keep their children at home to work on the farm.

As a whole, the schools for girls were assessed as being in a less satisfactory condition than those for boys. To a considerable extent, this was the consequence of women 'without having any taste or aptitude for teaching' opening schools simply for profit, and often being less than energetic in the work. The lack of opportunity for university education, the absence of a system of examination and certification of teaching competence, and the frequent change of female staff on account of marriage were also determinants both of the condition of girls' schools and also of the efficacy of governesses.[60] But Bompas's judgement was that the major obstacle to the provision of satisfactory education for girls was the preference given to the acquisition of elementary facts from such works as *Magnall's Questions* and the teaching of accomplishments, rather than intellectual development.[61] It was suggested that this reflected society's differing roles for the male and female. For the girl, marriage and home-making rather than a career in business or in a profession provided no incentive to pursue an academic, intellectual education.[62]

At a time when socio-economic background exerted a profound influence on educational opportunity, and where there were significant gradations within the middle-class community, it was inevitable that middle-class girls' schools varied in terms of fees, clientele and emphasis, from cheap schools offering only elementary education to an accomplishments-orientated, expensive finishing school such as the one at Chester which was patronized by Welsh parents who desired 'to send their daughters to school out of Wales to finish their education; that they may lose their Welsh accents and habits'.[63] Indeed, as elsewhere, the ethos of the middle-class girls' schools was English rather than Welsh.

Fees at private boarding schools — few of which had satisfactory buildings — ranged from under twenty-five guineas to over forty guineas. Day pupils might pay up to four guineas per annum. It was customary for extra payments to be made for accomplishments. At Swansea, one school charged fifty guineas per annum for boarders. Signifcantly, only the daughters of merchants, manufacturers and professional men were to be found in the more expensive schools in the town.[64] The daughters of 'the upper class of tradesmen' were ususally attending only the cheaper schools. Sometimes, some schools deliberately attempted to attract an up-market professional clientele, through excluding the daughters of these tradesmen.[65]

Private schools for girls were more widely available in urban than in rural areas. Farmers who experienced difficulty in finding a convenient school for their daughters, recoursed to hiring governesses for home tuition. However, low salaries and poor conditions of service made such work unattractive to well-educated women. Consequently, the governesses were 'often very unfit for their work, being very imperfectly educated themselves'.[66] They tended to be the daughters of tradesmen or farmers who found such duties preferable to domestic service.

The irregularity in attendance and short duration of girls' schooling were underlined in the Taunton Report as causing considerable difficulties for mistresses. Because of the expense, it was not uncommon for many middle-class girls to be educated at home until they were about fourteen to sixteen years of age, and then spend one or two 'quarters' being taught accomplishments.[67] The expensive nature of girls' secondary education in comparison with boys', was particularly emphasized in the report. In addition to the basic fee, between ten pounds and twelve guineas on average would have to be paid for such essential 'extras' as music, dancing, French and other accomplishments. This expense had the adverse effect of dissuading some parents from sending their daughters to a private secondary school at an early age. It also led to bargaining between parents and mistresses, and quite often, fees quoted in prospectuses were reduced.[68]

The schools' neglect of a rigorous, intellectual education can be shown by reference to the subjects taught. Latin was only taught in three schools, whilst neither Euclid, advanced mathematics nor a science such as chemistry or botany were taught systematically anywhere. In a few schools, elementary scientific facts were taught ineffectively. Few of the mistresses had the knowledge to teach these subjects, and Bompas was constantly told that these were regarded as unnecessary and irrelevant elements in girls' education.[69] Arithmetic, English grammar, history and geography were taught, but often very imperfectly. More emphasis on constitutional history was recommended.[70] The schools' emphasis was on accomplishments, particularly instrumental music:

> In many cases, farmers' daughters who know hardly any history or even spelling, and who have only 6 or 9 months in which to finish their education, learn music and that though there may be no instrument at their homes on which they can practice. In the higher class schools, a great deal of time is usually devoted to it, from 1 to 2 hours a day being spent thus, and sometimes even more, if singing be also learned.[71]

Bompas disapproved of such emphasis, because it was expensive in terms of equipment and time; it provided little opportunity for intellectual development and caused the exclusion of more worthwhile subjects from the curriculum.

French was also prominent, and in the more expensive schools it was usual to have a resident Frenchwoman and to designate French as the pupils' medium of communication on certain days in the week. Unsurprisingly, the Welsh language was conspicuous by its absence from these schools. Bompas, like the Welsh community at large, saw the language as a barrier to progress.

> It would appear that it is beginning in some parts to be considered unfashionable for girls to know Welsh, and this feeling is likely to make the language die out rapidly, at least among the middle classes . . . The Welsh language interferes with education.[72]

Drawing, dancing, needlework and deportment were prominent subjects of instruction, but cooking and other household duties were not taught.[73] Their neglect was attributed to the lack of suitable facilities and equipment, and the teachers' limited knowledge.

The subjects taught were viewed by witnesses and the assistant commissioner as an embodiment of the prevailing conception of female education and the woman's role in society rather than the consequence of a belief in girls' inferior mental capacity.[74] Indeed, contrary to the view of many, and anticipating much later research, it was suggested by Bompas that: 'girls . . . arrive much earlier at a full development of their minds and are able to study from 15–17 years with a mature power of thought and appreciation of the value of knowledge which boys do not attain till 17 or 18'.[75] It was evident that there was a desire amongst mistresses for some increase in the more solid parts of education. The assistant commissioner suggested that the introduction of examinations into private girls' schools would provide motivation for pursuing a more academic course of studies. Examination success would provide as much stimulus as did the prevalent display of acquirements.

The opening of the Howell endowed schools at Denbigh and Llandaff

In 1858, the foundations were being laid for one of the most significant experiments in female education in Victorian Wales. Schools were being erected for The Howell Foundation at Denbigh and Llandaff. Significantly, it was the religious implications that were of especial concern to Thomas Gee: Anglican control of the governing bodies of endowed grammar schools was causing resentment in Nonconformist ranks.

Thomas Howell, a native of Monmouthshire and one of the members of the Drapers' Company of the City of London, had died in Seville, Spain in 1540. In his will, he left to the Drapers' Company, a sum of money for providing yearly marriage portions for four orphan maidens of his own kindred, or, in default of such, for other maidens.[76] In 1559, a suit was instituted in the Court of Chancery by certain orphans of Wales on behalf of themselves and other kinsmen of the said Thomas Howell, against the company. They alleged that the defendants who had received the legacy, had purchased with part of it, lands and tenements of the yearly rent of £105, but had disposed of the residue to their own uses. The Drapers' Company were directed by the Court of Chancery to pay the income — £84 yearly — to the four orphans whose connections with the founder were to be ascertained by the Bishop of Llandaff, of whose diocese Thomas Howell was a native.

By the early nineteenth century, when the charity was investigated by the Charity Commission, the rental of the trust property had increased to over £2,000 per annum. Following the commissioners' inquiry, a suit was made against the Drapers' Company in the Court of Chancery in 1838. It was contended by the Attorney General that the company were bound to apply the whole of the income to the purposes of the charity. A Chancery scheme for the future conduct of the charity was deemed necessary. The Attorney General's application was heard by Lord Langdale, the Master of the Rolls, on 3 May 1843. He decreed that the whole of the rents derived from lands purchased were intended to be applied for the charity's purposes. It was referred to the Master of the Rolls in chambers to formulate a scheme for regulating the future conduct of the charity. Eventually, in 1845, it was decided that it would be best to extend the scope of the charity, so as to cater for the education of female orphans in Wales. But his Lordship considered that this was beyond the scope of his powers and required legislation.

Accordingly, an act of Parliament was passed in 1852 which provided that the Court of Chancery might extend the charity for the establishment, maintenance and benefit of schools in Wales for the instruction of girls, and also, maintaining, clothing and providing marriage portions for the orphan inmates educated in these schools. Preference was to be given to the Diocese in Llandaff, both as to the priority and size of the foundations to be established. The Bishop of Llandaff was to be 'ex officio' a governor of the school. Not more than one school was to be established beyond the limits of the diocese. In pursuance of the Act, a Scheme was established by the Court of Chancery in 1853, and by this Scheme, as amended by the Court in 1859, and again in 1865, the charity was regulated when the Welsh Intermediate Education Act came into operation.[77]

The precise location of the schools was left to the Attorney-General Department. In the autumn 1852, John Fearon — a solicitor in the department — inspected possible sites in south and north Wales. Six possible sites had been suggested: Llandaff, Swansea, Usk and Abergavenny in south Wales and Rhuthun and Denbigh in north Wales.[78] Abergavenny and Usk were rejected because of the belief that in view of their rural catchment area, there would not be enough day pupils. Swansea was regarded with great enthusiasm, but following the exertion of considerable influence by Bishop Ollivant and Sir Thomas Phillips, a former Mayor of Newport, Llandaff was chosen. Petitions in favour, from the Archdeacons of Llandaff and Monmouth were heard in the House of Lords. Arguments voiced in support of Llandaff included its central position in the diocese, accessbility by rail, attractive site, proximity to the cathedral, and its convenience for day pupils in the growing urban centre of Cardiff.[79]

In north Wales, Denbigh was chosen in 1852 primarily because of the availability of an attractive and not over-expensive site, and the interest shown by the local landed gentry, though its rural setting was viewed as a disadvantage from the standpoint of the enrolment of sufficient day pupils.[80]

By the Scheme of 1853, the Drapers' Company were authorized to purchase out of accumulated income, ten acres of land at Llandaff and likewise at Denbigh, and to spend such sums as the Court of Chancery should approve in erecting a school at each location. Orphan maidens of the blood of Thomas Howell were to have a preferential right of admission. Each school was to be managed by fifteen governors resident within fourteen miles thereof, to be appointed from time to time by the Drapers' Company with the bishop of the diocese as an ex-officio governor. The pupils were to be well versed in the catechism of the Church of England. It was also stipulated that the schools were to be open to the children of all religious denominations and in the case of a written request from parents to governors, pupils could be exempted from learning the catechism.[81]

Various representations had been made to the Attorney-General concerning the organization and curriculum of the schools. Lady Charlotte Guest had emphasized the need for 'a broad and elevated curriculum', rather than the establishment of a further two 'female industrial schools' which would be little better than orphanages for pauper apprentices.[82] The Scheme's curricular provisions showed that it was not intended to establish two charity schools offering mere elementary education. There was to be a wide curriculum with the pupils taught 'the principles of the Christian religion, reading, writing, arithmetic, English grammar, geography, biography, history, elements of astronomy, garden botany, music, French, drawing, together with such subjects as the Governors' should decide.[83] Every girl was to be taught needlework and 'to cut and make up her own clothes'.[84] Also, 'domestic cookery' was to be taught to those girls on the foundation 'as the chief matron shall appoint'. With 'pay boarders' as well as 'day pupils' to be recruited, the establishment of two orphanages was not contemplated. The school was intended to cater for the daughters of the middle classes. The Howell schools illustrate key aspects of research into mid-nineteenth century female education by recent feminist writers such as June Purvis, Carol Dyhouse, and Joyce Senders Pedersen.[85] The schools were not established and controlled by committed feminists but rather by men who were unlikely to radicalize the prevailing concept of femininity. They were committed to the middle-class ideology of the 'perfect wife' rather than to the establishment of academically rigorous institutions bent on the rejection of the concept of separate roles and the swamping of the professions with learned women. Howell's schools at Llandaff and Denbigh were intended to provide more than mere social accomplishments. First and foremost, they were to educate cultivated middle-class wives, mothers and governesses. Shortly, the proposed curriculum and clientele were to be highlighted in a vigorous critique of the schools' orientation.[86]

The Drapers' Company were not pleased that they had not been consulted over the selection of sites for the two schools. Their grievances were exacerbated when Fearon chose Decimus Burton as architect for the scheme. His work was already evident at Kew, Harrow School and the Athenaeum.[87] Between 1855 and 1857, land was bought at Llandaff and Denbigh, and plans submitted by Burton. Clashes with the Drapers' Company caused his resignation, and consequently the Company's own surveyor — Herbert Williams — prepared new plans for the Denbigh School and modified those for Llandaff in 1857. In March 1858, building tenders were invited, and within a comparatively short time, the Gothic edifices were erected. The Denbigh school buildings with extras, furniture and architect's fees, cost £18,980 and those at Llandaff £22,650.[88] The Denbigh School was opened in May 1860 and the Llandaff School in August 1860.

With the Howell schools ready to admit their first pupils, Judge Thomas Falconer, in a lengthy and widely published pamphlet headed *The Mystery of Improvidence* voiced major criticisms of the whole scheme, and the activities of the Drapers' Company, the Court of Chancery and Parliament in connection with the Howell charity. The great expenditure involved in erecting the schools was severely criticized.[89] In his opinion, the money had been deployed in a most misguided manner through the establishment of two 'gigantic and costly buildings'.[90] As many as thirty or forty Howell schools could have been established. Similarly, the wording in the Act that only one school was to be erected outside the diocese had been interpreted to justify the establishment of a similarly costly edifice in north Wales: 'The express words of the Act of Parliament appear to have been interpreted so as to sanction the most irrational conclusions, and the most reckless waste of the Charity funds'.[91] He was also critical of the scheme for ignoring Thomas Howell's links with the county of Monmouth.[92]

The control exercised by the Church of England over the charity was another criticism voiced by Falconer. There was no Nonconformist amongst the governors, and the provision for the admission of a non-Anglican pupil could only be regarded as nominal since the charity was virtually under the surveillance of the Bishop of Llandaff.[93] This, he maintained, was contrary to the spirit of the trust.

But as well as legal niceties, Judge Falconer's critique embodied a perception of girls' education and social needs that was at variance with the intended aims of the newly established schools. In his opinion, there had been 'wasteful expenditure' through a narrow and mischievous scheme which was 'a great public calamity' to the counties of Monmouth and Glamorgan.[94]

Falconer, well aware of poverty in the industrial areas, recognized the need to provide schooling for girls in the diocese of Llandaff, but his perception of the clientele was different. He maintained that there were many female orphans in the diocese, particularly in the accident-prone mining districts: 'Nowhere are schools for the education of females more needed'.[95] With an annual income of £2,000 and at a time when the accumulated funds of the charity amounted to over £40,000, exclusive of interest, he saw the opportunity of enlightening and reforming large numbers of the working-class populace. Under the proposed Scheme, they would be sacrificed for the sake of a privileged few.

Falconer argued that education could be a powerful instrument of moral and social reform: '. . . It is through a really efficient and improved system of education of the poorer classes that the vices sought to be dealt with by institutions now so popular with magistrates, for the moral training of adults must be checked'.[96]

Falconer proposed that the Drapers' Company be removed from the trusteeship, a new scheme obtained for the administration of the charity, and the buildings at Llandaff and Denbigh sold as quickly as possible. If the latter sale were not feasible, the building at Llandaff should be converted into an institution for the deaf and dumb, open to the whole of Wales. Falconer regarded the sale of the building at Denbigh as essential in order to restore the moiety or half-share of the annual income of the charity to the counties of Glamorgan and Monmouth. The money could be deployed with other income to endow girls' schools. The Llandaff building could also be used to provide Glamorgan with a much needed county hospital, and indeed '. . . it might have served as a County Lunatic Asylum but that the new buildings for that purpose are determined on'.[97]

Thomas Falconer's critique, published originally in January 1860, entered its second edition in March. Unsurprisingly, it was rejected by the school governors.[98] Predictably, Falconer's criticisms, particularly of Anglican control and unjustifiable waste of resources through their concentration in only two establishments, were quoted approvingly, and his pamphlet reviewed favourably in the Welsh press.[99] Such criticisms would be reiterated regularly in Victorian Wales. Even in 1957, an echo of Falconer's criticism was to be heard in *Monmouthshire Schools and Education to 1860* by E.T. Davies: '. . . a Monmouthshire man founded a charity . . . which ultimately developed into an educational scheme in which Monmouthshire has not shared'.[100]

The Taunton Commission

By the early 1860s, the education of the middle classes was a major issue in England.[101] In 1864, the government appointed a Royal Commission under the chairmanship of Henry, Baron Taunton:

> . . . to enquire into the education given in schools not comprised within the scope of the Newcastle and Clarendon Reports, and also to consider and report what measures, if any, are required for the improvement of such education, having regard to all endowments applicable or which can rightly be made applicable thereto.[102]

Girls were not specifically mentioned in the terms of reference defining the inquiry. It is not unlikely that unless the Schools Inquiry Commissioners had been pressurized by a handful of the leaders of the feminist movement in England, they would have confined their attention exclusively to boys' schools. However, following the submission of a strong memorial presented by Miss Bostock and Miss Emily Davies urging consideration of the claims of girls and women, a wider interpretation was secured. Assistant Commissioners were then instructed to report upon girls' schools, and it was also agreed to take evidence from women.[103]

The main recommendations of the Taunton Commission with regard to female education were less original than is sometimes assumed. The need for adequate endowments, external examinations and inspection, the desirability of teacher training, and a change in parental attitude towards the education of girls and their employment, had already been voiced by the advocates of female education. Now, however, in 1868, they were given the sanction and approval of a Royal Commission which recognized the importance of female education and the educated mother. In the history of female education in the nineteenth century, the Taunton Report was a significant landmark. The State's concern with the provision of suitable secondary education for girls was now acknowledged, and this was to prove to be an important determinant of change. The Taunton Report had been concerned with the educational requirements of the middle classes, not of the community as a whole. This was appreciated by Thomas Gee who had earlier noted the differing educational needs of the lower orders and middle classes.[104]

Ever since 1853, the Charity Commissioners had been responsible for the reform of endowed grammar schools. However, they could only initiate reform at the request of school trustees. In 1868, the Schools' Inquiry Commission was to recommend the establishment of a central authority, be it the Charity Commission with new powers, or a new body to initiate schemes.

The Endowed Schools Act became law in 1869. One of the clauses was concerned with girls' education: '. . . In framing schemes under this Act, provision shall be made as far as conveniently may be, for extending to girls the benefits of endowments'. The virtual monopolization of post-elementary educational endowments by boys was criticized.[105] Together with the provision in the legislation for the establishment of an Endowed Schools Commission that would take the initiative in reorganizing endowments, this was an important step for the development of girls' secondary education in both England and Wales. In 1898, Alice Zimmern saw it as 'the Magna Carta of girls' education, the first acknowledgement by the State of their claim to a liberal education'.[106] Though it may be argued that the measures taken under the new legislation to extend endowments for the benefit of girls were far from adequate, it is undeniable that during the years that followed, the implementation of the Endowed Schools Act was an important phase in the history of girls' secondary education in Wales.

As well as highlighting the condition of private schools it was revealed that in Wales, the Howell schools were the only two endowed secondary schools for girls. This contrasted sharply with the provision for boys, for whom there were sixteen classical schools — establishments with Latin and Greek in their regular course — with a total of 706 pupils, together with eight semi-classical schools which taught Latin, but not Greek, as a regular part of the curriculum to 255 pupils. There were also another 169 pupils who were educated in four non-classical schools.

Though Volume xx of the Taunton Report (Wales and Monmouthshire) was not published until February 1870, Assistant Commissioner H.M. Bompas actually visited the Llandaff and Denbigh schools in 1865 and 1866. His reports focused mainly on the condition of the schools at that time, whilst the returns from trustees and masters referred primarily to the latter half of 1864.[107] The Drapers' Company failed to respond to the request for information. It was noted that the schools were located in 'very handsome buildings' which '. . . contain every requisite for high class schools. The schoolrooms are large and commodious, and fitted with every convenience. The other arrangements of the buildings are exceedingly good and a large playground and garden is attached to each'.[108] In 1868, their gross annual income from the Howell charity amounted to £5,435. Though there was no resident French governness, and the teacher–pupil ratio was less favourable than usual in expensive ladies' schools, Bompas concluded that the two schools were providing 'a high class' education and that the accomplishments — French, music, drawing — were being carefully taught '. . . and to have as much time and attention bestowed on them as desirable for any ladies'.[109]

It was noted that the two schools were administered in accordance with the scheme sanctioned by the Court of Chancery in 1853, and amended in 1859 and 1865. It was clear from the 1865 Scheme that the Anglican influence was prominent. The headmistress and assistants were to be members of the Church of England, the church catechism taught (Clause 39) and the diocesan bishop or inspector of schools to be present for the annual examination. However, the schools were to be open to children of all religious tenets, and exemption from learning the catechism and attendance at church was to be allowed.[110]

It was Bompas's judgement that the Howell schools exemplified the effective utilization of endowments. Free education was provided for fifty-five orphans, whilst another sixty girls, whose fathers were gentlemen or members of the professional classes paid only for board and clothing. The fees charged on day pupils were lower than the going rate.[111] The assistant commissioner waxed eloquently regarding the sociological role of the Howell schools in mid-Victorian society. It was observed that the wants of the lower middle class were not being met by the schools. At Llandaff, the social class background of some of the initial intake of day pupils had caused some concern. In the original scheme, it was stipulated that day pupils could be admitted on payment of a maximum of sixpence a week. Some of the governors had thus concluded that the school was intended for the lower middle class and consequently the initial intake had included the daughters of small farmers and labourers. However, an application was made to the Court of Chancery in 1865, and the maximum fee for day pupils was raised to £2 a quarter.[112] There was no doubt about the school clientele: '. . . the school is intended for gentle-women, and the governors will not, except in the absence of any other candidate, elect one who is not such by birth'.[113] At Denbigh, the situation had been different and '. . . pupils have from the beginning been confined to rather a higher class than was at first the case at Llandaff'.[114] Bompas viewed this change as sensible, because the buildings and the education were better suited to the daughters of the higher rather than the lower middle class.[115]

His judgement reflected the Victorian belief that through educating the lower orders beyond their station in life, education could foment social discontent. He noted that some people were advocating the deployment of endowment funds to found scholarships for the educational benefit of those classes who would otherwise be restricted to elementary education. Bompas was not in favour of such educational and social engineering. Referring to Llandaff, he commented:

Where, as at that school, the education includes all the accomplishments, and the mode of living includes all the comforts of a high class school, such girls are often rendered dissatisfied with their homes and unfit for the mode of life to which their family circumstances necessarily call them.[116]

If such scholarships were to be established, it would be necessary to avoid the social problems that could accrue from a mismatch between educational qualifications and employment opportunities. The economic aspirations of the better educated lower classes would have to be met.[117]

The remarks of Assistant Commissioner Bompas on the socio-economic background of the pupils and his support for the higher fee for day pupils introduced by the amendment to the Scheme in 1865, would have met the approval of the governors of Llandaff School, and the headmistress Miss Emily Baldwin. There had been a reluctance to admit day pupils, because it was anticipated that the low fee would attract an unsuitable clientele.[118] At Llandaff, there were twenty-five day pupils, some of whom travelled three miles, and sixty boarders. Thirty of the boarders were receiving accommodation, food and clothing free, whilst the others paid an annual sum of £20 for board, lodging and washing. All the boarders were exempt from tuition fees.[119] It was recommended that the governors should reconsider the subjects taught and in particular allocate less time for music. Bompas, aware of the influence that the school would have elsewhere in education circles, wanted to ensure that the education would be 'of the very highest possible class' and, significantly, recommended that '. . . the introduction of some more solid subjects of study in its place would be an advantage'.[120] Latin and Euclid were mooted as suitable for inclusion. During the 1860s, 160 girls passed through the school. The increasing number of applications from orphans and pay boarders attested to the growing reputation of the school under Miss Baldwin, particularly after 1865.[121]

At Denbigh, there were twenty-five orphans and thirty pay boarders, and following the recent modifications of the scheme, it was not intended to admit day pupils. It was suggested that this should be at a moderate charge, as was intended in the scheme. Bompas advised that in order to ensure the selection of the most deserving candidates for admission, more thorough investigations might be conducted into their circumstances. But the assistant commissioner's major criticism of the selection procedure focused on the preference given by the local governors to girls born in Wales or descended from Welsh parents.[122] It was maintained that this was an improper practice which was in no way sanctioned by the Howell scheme.

It was also noted that in contrast to Llandaff, the early years of the Denbigh School had been seriously blighted by problems involving lack of rapport between the headteacher and staff. They emanated from 'the unfitness of the late headmistress for her position'. Here the *Taunton Report* was referring to one of the most unfortunate episodes in the school's history.

The school opened in May 1860, with Mrs Elizabeth Booth, who had experience in residental schools in England and Tasmania, as 'chief matron' or headmistress. Within a short time, the relationship between her and the assistant teachers or 'governesses' and pupils became very unsatisfactory. Several inquiries were instigated by the local governors, who in 1863 contacted the Charity Commission. They maintained that Mrs Booth's removal was essential 'for the well-being and efficiency of the school'.[123]

In April and May 1865, an inquiry was held at Denbigh before Charity Commissioner Hare that lasted nine days in all. Evidence by pupils and staff was highly critical of Mrs Booth and there was also 'an imputation of improper intimacy' between her and the school doctor. It was alleged that she was in the habit of taking children to her mother to be beaten and one one occasion beat a girl with a book called *What is Christianity*. She was said to have ignored the illness of one pupil who later died at the school.[124] Assistant Commissioner Hare's Report found that several of the complaints made at different times by the local governors were substantiated. It was concluded that Mrs Booth was '. . . unable to direct the studies of the school and is without the qualities essential to gain and preserve the affection of the pupils and secure the respect and obedience of the Governesses and Assistants'.[125] Having failed to inspire love, or command respect, she attempted to 'govern through fear'. It was recommended that she be removed from office and awarded a pension not exceeding £50 per annum for life.[126]

Hare also took the opportunity of recommending changes to improve the school's image and efficiency as an institution of middle-class female education and 'relieve it as far as possible from a pauper character'. More day pupils should be admitted according to a scale of fees regulated by the local governors with the approval of the Drapers' Company. The curriculum should include all subjects taught in 'ladies' colleges now established in London'. If necessary, such subjects as Latin and mathematics could be taught by masters. The school's work should be subject to assessment by university local examiners. On their recommendation, scholarships, tenable at 'any superior ladies college in London or elsewhere', should be awarded to the most successful pupils.[127]

There was no hint in the Taunton Report of the criticisms of the school being orchestrated at the time by Thomas Gee at Denbigh and elsewhere in Welsh newspapers.[128] He condemned the subservience of Howell's schools to Anglican control, and called for the admission of a larger number of girls from a wider cross-section of the community.[129]

The revelations of the Taunton Report were important at a time when increasing attention focused on the inadequate provision of girls' secondary education. Commenting on a public meeting held at Dolgellau in 1874 to consider establishing a girls' high school, 'Y Gohebydd' quite accurately viewed the evidence of the Taunton Commission as having contributed to the changing attitudes regarding female education.

(iii)   *Reforms and proposals towards meeting 'the educational wants' of girls in the 1870s*

The provision of an effective network of elementary schools for the working class was the main concern of enlightened educationists and politicians. Forster's Education Act 1870 and the establishment of School Boards were to dominate the educational developments of the decade. In Wales, especial importance was given to the need for unsectarian education.[130] The legislation of 1870 generated discussion of wider aspects of education. It was acknowledged that the economic well-being of the nation depended on an effective provision of education for all classes, with secondary and higher education also available for some.[131]

It would be a gross misinterpretation of the decade's educational history to view the provision of secondary and higher education for girls as the major priority. The Endowed School's Commission, and the leading supporters of the new University College at Aberystwyth, were primarily concerned with the establishment of unsectarian educational institutions for a middle-class, male clientele. Thomas Gee underlined the Taunton Report's revelations of the widespread opposition to denominational education.[132]

One of the most significant educational treatises of the decade was concerned with the secondary and higher education needs of boys and young men. Revd D. Lewis Lloyd's *The Missing Link in Education in Wales* (1875) was to exert considerable impact on public opinion.[133] It focused attention on the need to connect the elementary schools and the grammar schools (the 'missing link' in the educational machinery) and thereby open the door of educational opportunity to the able working class. He advocated the creation of a fund, probably through voluntary subscriptions, and establishment of a scheme of scholarships or bursaries worth at least £25 per annum each, tenable at any first-grade school in England or Wales. He referred to the scholarship scheme of Liverpool Council of Education.[134] Significantly, the focus throughout the manifesto was male-orientated, and there was no reference to the educational needs of girls. Elsewhere, however, the need to provide for the educational needs of women as well as men was being recognized. In February 1877, at a meeting of the Cymmrodorion Society at the Freemasons Tavern in London, with Mark Pattison in the chair, T. Marchant Williams (an inspector of schools for the London School Board), delivered a paper — *The Educational Wants of Wales*. It was to be the first significant contribution by the Cymmrodorion Society (re-established in 1873) to the quest for the reform of intermediate and higher education.[135] In a wide-ranging survey of elementary schools, private adventure schools, endowed grammar schools, four training-colleges and the University College of Wales, he underlined the considerable improvement in the educational condition of Wales since 1847. However, he acknowledged that the education of women required immediate attention.[136] Whilst welcoming the establishment of the Dr Williams' School at Dolgellau, he voiced strong criticism of the short-sighted action of the people of Caernarfon in rejecting the offer made to them. It was '. . . a remarkable instance of the apathetic attitude of the Welsh mind towards the question of the Education of Women . . . it has brought much discredit upon the nation'.[137] He urged the Council of University College of Wales to adopt a course of 'decisive and energetic action' regarding female education and showed his support for extending the educational opportunities of middle-class girls: '. . . I hope to see the day when efficient middle-class girls' schools shall stud the whole country'.[138]

In north Wales, at Rhianfa, Menai Bridge, the home of Captain Verney was to be the location of a significant educational speech on 18 October 1879 by Hugh Owen. Earlier in the year, at the annual meeting of Bangor Normal College, he had mooted the idea of scholarships being established linking elementary and higher grade schools. Now, in the home of the Verneys, who were to be staunch supporters of female education in Wales, Hugh Owen outlined his scholarship scheme. The invited audience included the headmasters and headmistresses of elementary schools in Anglesey and others interested in public education.[139] He delineated the details of a scheme which eventually adopted the title of 'The North Wales Scholarship Association'.[140]

It was intended that up to ten per cent of the 50,548 pupils in average attendance at day schools in north Wales be candidates for awards, and that girls as well as boys would be beneficiaries.[141] In his speech Hugh Owen said that '. . . with respect to girls who may gain scholarships, it is earnestly hoped that arrangements may be made for their admission into the Howell's Charity School for Girls in Denbigh; the Dolgelley Endowed School for Girls; or the Anglesey or Caernarvonshire Endowed School of the future for Girls'.[142] At this time, Captain Verney was supporting the establishment of a new girls' school at Menai Bridge.

At a time when there were already scholarship associations in various parts of England, the foundations were being laid in 1879–80 for a scheme that was to play a significant role for almost a decade and a half in extending educational opportunity for girls as well as boys of 'exceptional merit in Wales'. Also in 1879, Wales saw the publication of a worthy successor to *Y Gymraes* in *Y Frythones*. The appointment of a female editor — Sarah Jane Rees ('Cranogwen') was another significant landmark in the changing conception of femininity in Victorian Wales.[143] A monthly journal, it appeared regularly for the next twelve years and it proved to be a valuable forum for the discussion of a wide range of topical issues, including the education of women, its editor being a staunch supporter of female education.[144] Recently, it has been criticized for its conservative, middle-class orientation and conception of femininity, and neglect of the problems of working-class women.[145]

The Endowed Schools' Act 1869, and the establishment of the Endowed Schools Commission which functioned until 1874, initiated a period of reform of school endowments which was continued thereafter by the Charity Commission.[146] Under Section 12 of the 1869 Act, the Commissioners were empowered to utilize endowments of the old grammar schools to establish schools for girls.[147] Though there was much opposition from existing boys' schools and also from certain localities such as Anglesey in 1871–2 and again in 1878 over the proposal to reorganize the David Hughes' charity at Beaumaris which included provision for girls, approximately ninety girls' schools were established under the Endowed Schools Act in England and Wales.

The Endowed Schools' Commissioners of 1869–74 and the Charity Commission thereafter, undertook important investigations of educational charities in England and Wales. In Wales, thirteen schemes were introduced between 1868 and 1874 but only six were successful, primarily because of religious opposition.[148] The attempts at the reform of endowments in Wales in the 1870s had not been primarily concerned with the provision of girls' education. The main obstacle facing the commissioners was the religious division in the Welsh community and the associated question of control of the schools. Eleven schemes were introduced between 1874 and 1880 and the Charity Commission were successful with nine.

Following the Aberdare Report of 1881, and anticipating legislation for intermediate education, the Charity Commission were comparatively inactive in Wales in the 1880s. But by 1889, tired of waiting for a Welsh Intermediate Education Bill, they had published schemes for the reorganization of Abergavenny Grammar School, Jones' School Monmouth, and Tasker's School, Haverfordwest. Henceforth, girls were to benefit from these substantial endowments as well as boys.

Though it would be a misinterpretation of the work of the commissioners in Wales to maintain that the educational interests of girls were the main focus of attention, the decisions taken were of importance for the future pattern of girls' education in the Principality. The inquiries also exerted an impact on public opinion.

In Wales, though the proposed reforms of the David Hughes charity and Howell's charity proved unsuccessful, the establishment of the Dr Williams' School at Dolgellau in 1878, and the changes introduced in the case of the Tasker's charity at Haverfordwest, Jones' charity at Monmouth, and Lewis School at Pengam, were to have a significant positive impact on girls' secondary education in Wales. In Anglesey, in 1871, opposition focused primarily on the proposal to remove the David Hughes charity from the county and to merge with the Friars' endowment to establish a large boys school for both counties located at Bangor. The conversion of the Beaumaris school into an institution for girls was viewed as a doubtful sop. In 1878, plans for reorganization foundered primarily on the proposal to locate a first-grade school for boys at Holyhead, though there was also little real enthusiasm to convert the existing grammar school at Beaumaris into a girls' school.

The Drapers' Company and the Howell schools' governors remained unshakeable in their opposition to proposed changes in the composition of exclusively Anglican governing bodies and the religious complexion of the schools. They insisted that the Howell charity had always been tied to the Church of England. It was to remain a running sore for Nonconformist advocates of girls' secondary education in Wales for another two decades.

The establishment of the Dr Williams' School at Dolgellau in 1878 as an undenominational girls' school owed a great deal to the reforming zeal of the Endowed Schools' Commissioners. The 1875 Scheme giving Charity Commission approval to the school involved the transfer to a

Welsh secondary school of endowments previously applied to elementary education under the terms of Daniel Williams' bequest in 1711.[149] On 21 July 1874, the Dr Williams' trustees decided

> . . . to recommend Dolgelly to the Endowed Schools Commissioner as the most desirable site after Caernarvon for the proposed Girls' school, provided there be adequate local co-operation. The Trustees have reason to believe that at Dolgelly the conditions of the Commissioners as to a building and a playground will be complied with.[150]

Samuel Holland's role proved decisive. It appears that he now acted on the suggestion of W.R. Davies, a Dolgellau solicitor, who wrote to him advocating that the town should attempt to secure the school following its rejection by Caernarfon.[151]

By 1878, the building was completed. Samuel Holland had paid £500 for the two acres of land and altogether subscribed over £800 to the building fund. He had played a key role in the location of the school at Dolgellau and was to be chairman of the governors till his death in 1892.[152] The school opened on 1 February 1878 and was to be an important institution until its closure in 1975.

It is difficult to judge the quality of private girls' schools in Wales in the 1870s. Though the condition of private schools for girls varied considerably, they were not regarded as meeting the educational needs of a country subject both to economic transformation and changing perceptions of femininity.[153] The schools were weakened by their quest for maximum profit with the minimum of labour and outlay, and their lack of permanence (often due to change of proprietors or staff because of marriage).[154] Attention to accomplishments, and a really cultivated education, were still much in evidence. The schools were aiming to turn out refined middle-class ladies rather than implementing a new definition of femininity.[155] But some of the schools were also providing more attention to preparing certain pupils for external examinations.

Some parents opted out of this uneven provision of education through hiring private tutors and governesses. Evidence is very scanty regarding precise numbers and the quality of their teaching. However, in Anglesey in 1871, there were approximately eighteen governesses working with private families.[156] Other parents continued the trend of sending their daughters to schools in England. In 1875, readers of the *North Wales Chronicle* were informed that at Eccleshall, Staffordshire, 'Stanley House' was

> . . . conducted by Mrs Smith, assisted by good Masters and English and Foreign Governesses . . . The object is to afford parents an opportunity of giving their daughters a sound and accomplished education at a moderate

expense; at the same time strict attention is paid to the health and happiness of the pupils.[157]

'Thorncliffe House', Chester, advertised that it prepared for 'competitive exams'. Elsewhere in the Welsh press, there were similar advertisements from schools in Chester, Liverpool, Taunton, Bristol, Stroud, Gloucester, Malvern and Bath. At the end of the decade, it was estimated that there were more than a hundred girls from Anglesey attending schools in England.[159]

Information about specific private girls' schools in Wales is very sparse. Newspaper advertisements and trade directories are the most valuable sources.[160] At Wrexham, the largest town in north Wales, there were a number of private schools offering secondary education to a middle-class clientele.[161] Being in a competitive situation, they made considerable use of the columns of *The Wrexham Advertiser* and *North Wales Guardian* to advertise both their educational wares and their pupils' achievements in Oxford and Cambridge locals and Royal College of Preceptors examinations. Detailed reports of prize days were also published.[162] Along the north Wales coast, there were a number of establishments catering for a fee-paying, middle-class clientele, and endeavouring to offer varying amounts of academic studies and accomplishments.[163] In the Conwy Valley, at Salisbury House, Llanrwst, the Misses Mathews and Standring were advertising a 'Good Middle-Class School for Young Ladies' that provided a 'sound English education with accomplishments'.[164] Likewise, in other centres such as Bangor, Conwy, Caernarfon, Menai Bridge and Llangefni, there were ladies' day and boarding schools.[165] At Towyn, Rhianfa School was conducted successfully for many years, and by the end of the decade was controlled by Mrs Peter, widow of Reverend Professor John Peter of Bala, who was shortly to testify to the Aberdare Inquiry. Pupils were prepared for College of Preceptors and university local examinations.

The main towns of mid and south-west Wales offered similar educational opportunities for girls. Some were more established and more prestigious than others. At Haverfordwest, Hill House College for Young Ladies had been established for sixty years by 1875 and had accommodation for fifty boarders.[166]

In most instances, the numbers of boarders were not large because of the limited space available. But schools were also at pains to emphasize their exclusivity through focusing on the limited numbers that could be admitted. At Aberystwyth, in Miss Trubshaw's School for Young Ladies at Caerleon House, there was a resident French governess, and pupils were prepared for the Oxford and Cambridge local examinations in 1878. Likewise at The Ladies' Collegiate School in North Parade, where assistance was given by 'masters and a staff of qualified English and foreign teachers', pupils were prepared for the universities' local examinations, Civil Service and training-college preliminary examinations. However, the presence of a croquet lawn indicates that social accomplishments were also taught. The principal appeared to be aware of the need for a balanced education for she devoted 'her whole time and individual attention to the intellectual, moral and physical training of the pupils'.[167]

At Swansea, there were numerous private schools for girls, such as Glyn Cerrig School, Mumbles, which offered tuition for university locals and other public examinations. The 'English and French Establishment for Young Ladies', boasted '... unusual advantages for the acquirement of the French language which is constantly spoken ... Many of the Ladies educated are now filling first-class positions as Principals of Schools and as Governesses'.[168] Mrs Rose Jones (une Parisienne Diplome) conducted a 'Finishing Establishment for Young Ladies' in 1879. Reverend B.J. Binns HMI, was amongst the school referees. It advertised a course of study providing '... thorough instruction in the English and French languages, with other branches of a solid education including the Pianoforte Singing, Drawing, Dancing and Calisthenics Dancing class every Wednesday afternoon'.[169] Throughout the 1870s, the social accomplishments in particular were well catered for in Swansea.

At Cardiff, Windsor Place, Crockherbtown was still open 'for a limited number of Young Ladies'[170] as was Miss Stephenson's Somerset Villa in Roath. At Harrow House, Dumfries Place, the Misses Marks' Boarding School for Young Ladies had 'competent English and Foreign Governesses' and also 'the comforts and attention of home'. There were other similar establishments in Cardiff, but more prestigious was Heath House Boarding and Day School for Young Ladies at nearby Cowbridge. It was founded by Miss Annie Llewellyn, one of the first orphans at Howell's Llandaff. In 1870 she received £50 from the governors to open a school at Cowbridge.[171] Elsewhere, in south-east Wales, girls could attend such establishments as Penarth Ladies' School or 'Ladies' School, Abergavenny' where there was '... a sound, comprehensive and religious education ... The Boarders ... a limited number — have all the comforts of home, with a most liberal diet'.[172]

In May 1876, the St David's Diocesan Ladies' School was opened at Mount Pleasant, Brecon. It was intended for the daughters of clergymen, professional men and of 'the agricultural and commercial classes generally'.[173] By 1878, however, it was evident that the school was not a success. There were already at Brecon two well-established girls' schools — Boughrood House, Struet, conducted by Miss Buck, and Misses King's Ladies' Boarding and Day School at Bulwark. On 29 August 1878 the question of girls' secondary education was raised at the annual meeting of the St David's Diocesan Board of Education at Abergwili. The Bishop's wife, Frances Jones, was particularly interested in the matter and was to play an important part in the transfer of the school to Carmarthen.[174] The town's central position in the diocese, and the ease of access it enjoyed by rail, were seen as advantages.[175]

On 17 October 1879, at the annual meeting of the Diocesan Board of Education, a Provisional Council was appointed to implement the scheme. It included the Bishop, Viscount Emlyn and Principal Harper, but significantly, there was no woman member. It was decided that the name 'The Carmarthen High School for Girls' would be adopted for the establishment.[176] A prospectus was circulated throughout the five counties comprising the diocese, announcing the opening of the school in January 1880. It was intended to educate 'girls of the middle class and lower higher class, something on a similar footing to what existed at Llandaff and Denbigh'.[177] In contrast to all other private non-endowed girls' schools in Wales, it was to enjoy a long, continuous history of over eighty years until its final closure in 1964.

4

Teacher Training and Higher Education, 1840–1880

(i) Pupil-teachers and teacher training 1850–1880: the female experience

During the 1850s and 1860s there was increasing financial aid from the State in support of voluntary elementary schools. There was no policy of establishing institutions of secondary or higher education as such; indeed, there were no state elementary schools until the legislation of 1870. However, a semblance of secondary and higher education became available for Welsh girls through the establishment of pupil-teacherships and training-colleges which extended educational opportunity. Nevertheless, it must be noted that these colleges were an integral part of the elementary system of education and prospective female teachers were infused with its underlying philosophy and assumptions.

Pupil-teachers in the 1850s and 1860s

Official attitudes to female pupil-teachers were governed by these perceptions of elementary education. For a small, yet increasing number of females in the 1850s and 1860s, it may be argued that this was a form of secondary or higher education between the ages of thirteen and eighteen years which was followed in some instances by a period at a teacher training-college. It has been suggested that the success of the pupil-teacher system in the mid-Victorian era was one reason for the delay in establishing a state system of secondary education.[1]

The pupil-teacher system was introduced by Sir James Kay-Shuttleworth in 1846 to provide elementary schools with more effective teachers. It involved a five-year apprenticeship for promising male and female pupils from thirteen to eighteen years of age. As well as teaching for a stipulated period of each day, they themselves were also receiving instruction, usually from a master or mistress at the school where they were apprenticed, and were paid on a scale rising from £10 in the first year to £20 in the fifth. They were examined each year on an official

Table 4.1
Pupil-teachers in Wales in the 1850s

Year	Male	Female
1850	143	43
1851	199	76
1852	230	94
1853	246	104
1854	247	116
1855	244	111
1859	484	258

Source: Minutes of the Committee of Council on Education, 1850–59.

syllabus, and duly graded. At eighteen years, though they were not obliged to continue as teachers, they could compete for Queen's Scholarships which were tenable at teacher training-colleges. Pupil-teachers could also take up teaching posts at eighteen years, without further training at a teaching college. The Committee of Council Minutes reveal the increase in the numbers of pupil-teachers in Wales in the 1850s (Table 4.1). At this time, pupil-teachers were mainly working class.[2] The salary received by female pupil-teachers compared more than favourably with what could be earned by their working-class peers in other employment. Young men, however, could earn higher income elsewhere.[3]

During these years, official perceptions of the role of female pupil-teachers became evident. The importance of cookery and domestic management in their course of instruction was emphasized.[4] There was no intention that the education of female pupil-teachers should become academic or intellectually orientated. Concern was expressed by some observers that the five-year apprenticeship was too rigorous, particularly for girls: 'the duties of pupil-teachers alone, without any positive infirmity, unfits a girl for discharging them without great risk'.[5]

In a letter to the Reverend H. Longueville Jones HMI, instructions were given by the Committee of Council relating to the apprenticeship of pupil-teachers in mixed schools. Unless the master was present, a pupil-teacher should not be allowed to teach girls.[6] Where part of the instruction was to be given by a master, both his age and character needed careful consideration: 'It is extremely doubtful whether such an apprentice ought, in any case, to be recommended where the master is young or unmarried. It certainly ought not be to recommended if he is both young and unmarried'.[7]

For the pupil-teacher system and training colleges, the Revised Code that came into operation in 1862 had considerable significance. A new mode of payment was introduced. Under Article 81, they were henceforth to be paid out of the grants to the schools and to receive such wages as they could induce the managers to pay them. The stipends paid annually to pupil-teachers were abolished, and the grants which headteachers received for instructing them were cancelled. There was now to be no extra subsidy for maintaining a pupil-teacher. Grants were to be paid to school managers in proportion to the number, regularity and proficiency of their pupils. School managers would have to maintain a minimum of pupil-teachers — one for every forty pupils after the first fifty. Teachers' salaries were to be dependent on the 'payment by results' system. There was much criticism of these changes in both England and Wales.

There was a decline in the number of pupil-teachers and this continued until 1867. In England and Wales, there were 13,849 pupil-teachers in 1863, but only 11,519 in 1867.[8] By 1865, the Reverend J. Bowstead HMI, having inspected schools in south Wales and the border counties noted that 'the number of Pupil-teachers in my district has fallen off very considerably within the last two years. In the case of girls, this is simply a question of economy with the patrons of schools, most of whom seem disposed to reduce their teaching staff to the minimum prescribed by the Revised Code'.[9] Schools with under ninety pupils were not able to engage even one pupil-teacher. This had a considerable impact on recruitment of pupil-tachers in the small schools of rural Wales.[10] However, the loss of male pupil-teachers was the main problem: during a period of rising wages, they were attracted to other employment.[11] The uncertainty surrounding the renumeration of pupil-teachers had considerable influence on recruitment. There was now no fixed scale of payment, and wages of pupil-teachers depended on the agreement entered into with school managers. There was also dislike of the regulation and inspection introduced via the Code.[12] Female pupil-teachers were more readily available because their profession was as remunerative to them as any other. Again, details regarding the number of pupil-teachers in Wales may be collated from Committee of Council Minutes (Table 4.2).

In February 1867, William Corry, Vice-President of the Education Department, endeavoured to arrest the decline which was also having an adverse effect on training-college enrolment. 'Corry's Minute' enabled special grants to be paid to schools which produced pupil-teachers for the colleges that year. There was an increase in the number of pupil-teachers for the first time since 1863. It is clear that in spite of

Table 4.2
Pupil-teachers in Wales in the 1860s

Year	Male	Female	TOTAL
1860	514	244	758
1862	495	286	781
1863	440	260	700
1864	362	254	616
1865	315	248	563
1866	306	241	541
1867	325	278	603
1868	406	343	749
1869	463	391	854

Source: Minutes of Committee of Council on Education, 1860–69.

the adverse effect of the Revised Code on total recruitment, the enrolment of female pupil-teachers was much less affected than males. Throughout the decade, the pupil-teacher system provided an important medium of post-elementary education for young women in Wales.

The domestic orientation of their work continued to be emphasized. Competency in needlework was particularly stressed:

> Female pupil-teachers, before admission to apprenticeship must produce a written attestation from the schoolmistress and managers that they possess reasonable competency as sempstress: and at the annual examinations must bring specimens of plain needlework to the inspector, together with a statement from the school-mistress specifying whether they have been receiving practical instruction in any other kind of domestic industry.[13]

Modern feminist writers perceive female pupil-teachers' instruction of working-class girls in domestic subjects as maintaining the sexual divisions between girls and boys in the classroom and in society at large.[14]

Female student-teachers and teachers

Unsurprisingly, attitudes to female students in the teacher training-colleges also reflected the prevailing perceptions of female education in the elementary schools. Gender considerations were to be important in the training of women as elementary school teachers in the Victorian era.

The 1840s and 1850s saw the establishment of voluntary controlled training-colleges. In Wales, the South Wales and Monmouthshire College opened at Carmarthen in 1848, only admitted male students, as did the training-college opened at Brecon in 1846 but moved to

Swansea in 1849 and closed in 1851. Similarly, in north Wales, the training-college at Caernarfon, opened in 1856, and the Bangor Normal College, opened in 1858, were also exclusively male colleges. By then, the absence of a female training-college in Wales was regretted.[15] Even in 1848, Revd H. Longueville Jones HMI, had noted the need for such an institution:

> It is a hope entertained, by many of the warmest promoters of education in Wales that measures will be adopted for instituting a Training School for Mistresses somewhere within the twelve counties, and I should conceive the town of Aberystwyth to be well calculated by its special circumstances and central position for such a purpose.[16]

In 1856, a project for a training-school for women was mooted by the Caernarfon School Committee. Miss Kenrick, the mistress of the girls' National School was 'to train three young women for the office of National School mistress'. For a brief period in 1857, a house was taken over for this purpose but 'the females in training proved too much for her and she resigned'.[17] The trust deed of Bangor Normal College referred specifically to the training of 'masters or teachers conducted upon the principles of the British and Foreign School Society'.[18] There was to be no training-college for women teachers in Wales prior to 1872.

Consequently, female students from Wales attended training-colleges in England. By 1858, there were twelve Church of England training-colleges for schoolmistresses only, and four training-colleges for males and females including the well-known undenominational Borough Road College. There were 818 students in the female colleges, 752 in the fifteen male colleges and 496 in the colleges for both sexes.[19] Lack of sources makes it impossible to ascertain the precise number of Welsh women who were enrolled in these colleges but it is clear that they were present at such colleges as Borough Road, Warrington, Whitelands and Cheltenham in the 1850s. Between 1844 and 1858, 166 students from Wales attended Borough Road College.[20]

The admission registers of Cheltenham College show the presence of a few Welsh students virtually every year from the 1850s to the end of the century.[21] During 1850–51, the Monmouthshire Diocesan Board who had founded four exhibitions for male student-teachers at Carmarthen training-college, were proposing to establish another four for women students, presumably in England.[22] The importance of adequate attention to domestic subjects during their training—needlework and domestic economy—was regularly voiced.[23]

Prevailing attitudes to the education of women were also highlighted by the concern that the course of study and particularly the examinations were too severe for the delicate constitution of women students![24]

In the teacher training-colleges, the decline in the number of students following the introduction of the Revised Code was one of the significant developments of the 1860s. The colleges at Bangor, Caernarfon and Carmarthen were all affected. In 1867, training-colleges for men were only two-thirds full.[25] Women's colleges were less adversely affected, and there was less anxiety concerning the supply of female candidates for admission. In 1869, the local management committee of Carmarthen College considered the feasibility of its conversion into a women's college because of the shortage of male students. However, at a time when there were vacancies in the existing training-colleges for women, such a change was eventually deemed inopportune.[26]

For those Welsh women in training-colleges in England, the courses of instruction embodied the philosophy enunciated during the previous decade.[27] At Cheltenham where the enrolment varied from fifty-eight to sixty women students, there was an average of between three and five students every year from Wales. They studied the subjects taught in elementary schools.[28] Significantly, in contrast to colleges for male students, 'none of the subjects intended for the general refinement of the students' mind was included'.[29] The four books of Euclid, algebra, Latin, physical science, mechanics and mathematics did not figure in their course of study: 'The syllabus for female colleges resembled that for male colleges, but the subjects were fewer and easier'. To some extent, this sexist approach reflected the concern voiced regarding the effect of academic study on the health of women students.[30]

In mid-nineteenth century Wales, following the revelations of the Blue Books of 1847, teaching did not enjoy a very high esteem. Gradually, with the establishment of training-colleges, a teaching career came to be seen as a more attractive proposition with regard to both salary and security. In 1855, the average salaries of teachers in Church of England schools in Wales were as follows:

Schoolmistress:	Certificated	—	£61 4*s.* 11*d.*
	Uncertificated	—	£31 3*s.* 8*d.*
Schoolmasters:	Certificated	—	£76 9*s.* 2*d.*
	Uncertificated	—	£50 5*s.* 0*d.*

The number of certificated female teachers remained low during the 1850s, though there was a twenty-five per cent increase and even a 380 per cent increase in certificated male teachers. There were, in addition, uncertificated female and male teachers in the elementary schools. These were pupil-teachers who had completed their apprenticeship and

Table 4.3
Certificated teachers in Wales during the 1850s

Year	Females	Males
1851	18	51
1853	20	69
1854	21	92
1855	22	110
1856	35	141
1859	63	245

Source: Minutes of Committee of Council on Education, 1850–59.

under a Committee Council Minute 1852 were designated assistant teachers. In 1859, there were thirteen male and six females in this category.

It is clear that at the end of the 1850s, elementary school teaching in Wales was not yet dominated by women. Comparatively few Welsh women were receiving post-elementary or para-secondary education through the pupil-teacher and training-college agencies. In an obituary to Lady Rhys, formerly Elspeth Hughes Davies, who died in 1911, it was recalled that her departure from Llanberis in 1859/60 to train as a teacher in London was a very unusual event.[31] In 1859, Dr Lewis Edwards suggested that Welsh women were reluctant to become teachers in British schools because of a fundamental inferiority complex. The tendency of many in Welsh society to place a high premium on learning English was associated with the belief that English teachers in Welsh schools would be an advantage for children.[32]

Not all the former female pupil-teachers or college-trained teachers from Wales worked in the Principality's schools. In 1856, Revd H. Longueville Jones HMI, drew attention to the scarcity of qualified male and female teachers in Wales: 'There is a tide of teaching power setting out from Wales, not flowing into it. All the young teachers have a tendency to go and try their fortunes in England, while few English teachers like to come into Wales'.[33]

The demand for trained schoolmistresses still exceeded supply.[34] A number of female pupil-teachers and certificated teachers were lost to the profession at this time because of marriage. In 1859, Assistant Commissioner John Jenkins was told that 'A good mistress, like any other good servant, is difficult to find, and the higher their qualifications, having due regard to good looks the most likely they are to marry early and well'.[35] In particular, educated pupil-teachers were seen as marriageable assets, and their loss was viewed as a major cause of the

Table 4.4
Certificated teachers in Wales during the 1860s

Year	Females	Males
1860	84	268
1862	109	327
1863	112	383
1864	144	419
1865	159	441
1866	161	467
1867	182	484
1868	212	535
1868	230	546

Source: Minutes of the Committee of Council on Education, 1860–69.

disproportion between the supply and the demand of schoolmistresses: '. . . Yes, chiefly from the pupil-teachers generally marrying, being cultivated so much above their class'.[36]

Others were lost to the profession because of their diffidence in taking the qualifying examinations. The need for female teachers in the mixed elementary schools of Wales was to be reiterated often during the 1850s.[37] Not only was the teaching of needlework, and industrial training essential, but the general influence exerted by female teachers on young girls was regarded as considerable. For female teachers, mostly from a working-class background, in elementary schools, just as for middle-class women in private schools, teaching was perceived as a natural extension of femininity because of the supposed link between femininity and domesticity. The number of certificated female teachers in Wales almost trebled during the 1860s whilst the number of certificated male teachers doubled (Table 4.4). However, there was still a problem in meeting the demand for teachers.[38]

Whilst it would be wrong to assume that all these women teachers were born in Wales, it is undeniable that an increasing number of Welsh women were entering training-colleges in England prior to a career in teaching. In 1867, it was noted that 'the increased employment of mistresses over masters was going on uniformly, though slowly, throughout England and Wales'.[39] Between 1863 and 1867, the proportion of female teachers increased from 45 to 47.6 per cent in England and Wales. The respective merits of male and female teachers were discussed throughout the decade.[40] In 1869, Revd B.J. Binns HMI expressed approval that of the thirty-six separate girls' schools in Glamorgan, thirty-four were under certificated mistresses:

The advantages of such institutions are obvious. In addition to industrial training, girls acquire habits of order and neatness, together with an improved tone and quiet demeanour when taught by a mistress, which more than compensate for any intellectual sharpness or proficiency to which they may attain in a mixed school, and a visit to such a one as the girls' school at Rhymney would speedily convince those who felt any doubt on the subject, that a course of education similar to that received by the female scholars there, can hardly fail of producing the most beneficial effects upon the next generation.[41]

By the end of the 1860s, for reasons of economy in particular, the appointment of mistresses to take charge of mixed schools in rural areas was being increasingly advocated: '. . . a good mistress is preferable to an inferior master, and further, a good mistress may be had for the salary paid to an inferior master'.[42] It was suggested that Wales had not yet really appreciated the feasibility of such appointments, partly at least because of its male-dominated teacher training institutions at Carmarthen, Caernarfon and Bangor.[43] Young women who became pupil-teachers and entered training-colleges, were key agents in inculcating the daughters of their own working class with those fundamental principles and skills of femininity and domesticity deemed appropriate for their station in life as wives and mothers, or as domestic servants in middle-class households. Critical modern feminists see them as endeavouring to perpetuate 'the sexual division of society'.[44]

The foundation of Swansea Training College

In February 1872, with the opening of the Swansea Training College, teacher training for women became available for the first time within the Principality. In *The Cambrian* it was suggested that 'The British and Foreign Schools Society have taken what may seem to some a bold, but what we have little doubt time will show to be also a prudent step in establishing a Training College'.[45] The previous year, on 8 May 1871, the British Society decided to open a training-college for women in the north of England and in Wales.[46] There was growing demand for qualified women teachers and the society was concerned that although there were three training-colleges in Wales for men, there was no institution for training mistresses. With the establishment of school boards, and the growth in the number of schools, it was anticipated that the existing training-colleges would be unable to meet the demand for teachers. Already, there were difficulties in providing suitable school-mistresses for Welsh schools.[47] There was a scarcity of Welsh-speaking applicants for teacher training. Though the Welsh language was only one factor mentioned by Alfred Bourne, the British Society's Secretary in 1871, it was stated by L.L. Dillwyn, MP in 1875, that the college was established '. . . as a meams of promoting education in Wales by supplying teachers conversant with the Welsh Language'.[48] The distance from Wales to London, as well as the expense, caused a dearth in the numbers of pupil-teachers seeking admission to Stockwell College for Schoolmistresses. There were also increasing difficulties in securing accommodation for Welsh pupil-teachers there, because of the growing pressure on this training-college to cater for schools in England.[49] Dr B.L. Davies has underlined the crucial role played in the decision of 1871 by Hugh Owen. He exerted influence in support of establishing a training-college in Wales and was to be regarded 'as one of the founders of the Swansea Training College'.[50]

Having decided that such a training-college was needed, a number of possible locations—Shrewsbury, Brecon, Aberystwyth and Swansea—were considered. The lack of suitable premises narrowed down the final choice between Aberystwyth and Swansea. Swansea, rather than Aberystwyth, was finally selected because of the availability of suitable premises, and because of its geographical advantages: 'Swansea appeared to be a suitable place, central for South Wales, easy access by railway and steamboat from North Wales and the West of England'.[51] In 1871, at a time when the date of opening of a University College was still undecided, Hugh Owen was asked by the British and Foreign Schools Society whether the buildings at Aberystwyth, earmarked as the location of a Welsh University College could be sold or let for temporary occupation 'for the purposes of a Female Training School'.[52] Alfred Bourne inspected the buildings at Aberystwyth and considered them 'in many respects suitable for the proposed Training College'.[53] However, the Provisional Committee eventually decided that it was inexpedient to enter into any arrangement for letting a portion of the building to the British Society in view of the possibility of it being sold.[54] After addressing both a 'semi-private' meeting in Queen Street British School, and public meetings called by the society in the Guildhall on 3 and 10 November 1871 concerning the feasibility of opening a training-college for schoolmistresses, Alfred Bourne was satisfied that local support for the proposed college would be forthcoming. Strong support was voiced for more thoroughly educated schoolmistresses. Though most of the local participants in these meetings were men, Mrs Crawshay of Cyfarthfa was also prominent amongst those who pledged support.[55]

It was emphasized by Mr Bourne that the training-college was intended as a temporary experiment because it was not thought that the demand for teachers would continue to rise. Its continuance on a permanent basis would be dependent on adequate local funding. The 'religious problem', which, significantly, was raised at the public meeting, would be overcome through pursuing a deliberate unsectarian policy. Students would be admitted without reference to sectarian differences and would be allowed to choose their own places of worship. The catechism would be excluded from the course of study in a religious, but undenominational, institution.[56]

The college was to be located in those premises at 13 Nelson Terrace used by the earlier, ill-fated Normal College for male students from 1849 to 1851, after its transfer from Brecon. Following its closure, it was converted by the Principal, Dr Evan Davies, into a boys' secondary school which remained in the building until his retirement in 1867. After being vacant for four years, the premises were now rented by the British and Foreign School Society for the purpose of an experiment in female education. By 27 December 1871, a 'New Training College for Wales' was being advertised, and applications and donations were being invited.[57] In January 1872, the premises were taken on lease by the society, and on 5 February 1872, the Swansea Training College commenced its work with thirty-eight students in residence. The society spent £800 on the initial establishment of the college.[58]

The British and Foreign Schools Society accepted responsibility for operating the college over three years. It was to be managed by the General Committee of the British Society, through a sub-committee of local representatives meeting at the college. Alfred Bourne, in London, acted as the college's principal, and David Williams, the British Society's agent for south Wales as the all important vice-principal. Bourne accepted the post of principal of an institution which was unlikely to function for more than a few years. It was clearly intended that the new college would be modelled on the existing British Society's colleges at Borough Road and Stockwell.

The amount of the annual grant received from the Education Department would be dependent on student members and success in examinations. It was hoped that £300 per annum would be subscribed in Wales towards its operating costs.[59] During the official opening ceremony on 28 March 1872, attended by people mainly from Swansea and south-west Wales, the contemporary debate on the respective merits of secular and unsectarian religious teaching was alluded to, and significantly, it was also suggested that there would be an increased demand for mistresses, not only because of the increase in schools following the 1870 Education Act, but also because it would be found that in rural areas, teaching in elementary schools could be conducted much more economically and quite as efficiently by female as by male teachers. There was a dearth of qualified mistresses in Wales.[60]

With the local committee recognizing that the demand for trained teachers was unlikely to subside, a resolution was passed on 25 April 1873 at the first annual meeting, affirming the importance of ensuring that the college became 'a permanent institution' and appointing a committee to raise funds with a view of purchasing and renovating the premises. Furthermore, on 17 November 1873, a meeting described as 'very large and influential' was held at the Albert Hall to enlist support to make the training-college permanent.[61]

It was recognized that a sum of £3,000 would be needed to purchase the lease and renovate the premises. Though reports concerning the college were widely circulated, and deputations sent to various conferences, fund raising was very slow. By November 1874, readers of the Welsh press were being informed that there was 'a crisis in the history of Swansea Training College'.[62] The college's future was reviewed at a crucial conference on 13 November 1874 under the chairmanship of Lord Aberdare.[63] Bourne reported that the college was in good working order and free from debt, because the costs had been met by the British Society. Again, it was emphasized that no regard was paid to sectarianism and that the society had intended to support the college for a period of three years which had now expired. However, it had already incurred an outlay of £2,500 in establishing and supporting the establishment. A sum of £3,000 would be required to purchase and alter the premises, and an annual sum of £350 to enable the college to function effectively.

It was evident that in spite of the acknowledged unsectarian nature of the Swansea institution, the comparatively lukewarm response to the college's financial appeal was attributed to the religious problem. It was maintained that the committee had failed because of its composition of eleven Nonconformists and a majority of seventeen Anglicans making it unrepresentative of the different denominations. Lord Aberdare also deprecated those who viewed educational developments from the standpoint of denominational rather than national advantage. He emphasized that the college was conducted on principles which agreed with the religious condition of the Principality. In *The Cambrian*, the editor interpreted the problem as basically religious: 'The difficulty that steps in is the bugbear of all educational movements — sectarianism'.[64]

It was evident that the meeting was unanimously in favour of the college remaining open, and a majority favoured its management by the British Society.[65] A Provisional Committee, consisting primarily of the membership of the Building Committee, was now appointed to raise

funds and prepare a scheme of management for the college's administration from Christmas 1875 in accordance with the principles of the
British Society.[66] The decision to continue with Wales's only, and much
needed, unsectarian institution, that had already trained sixty teachers,
was welcomed by Thomas Gee, who now called on Wales to respond
generously to its financial needs.[67]

This decision, together with the opening of the University College of
Wales at Aberystwyth, and the imminence of a decision concerning a
girls' high school at Dolgellau, were seen as prime evidence of Wales's
education awakening.[68] Wales's educational, economic and international well-being were at stake. The decision to establish a 'Chair for Celtic
Languages and Literature' at Aberdeen University epitomized further
the value placed on education in Scotland. It was maintained that
unless Wales provided her own effective training for schoolmistresses,
the alternative was importing Scottish and Irish teachers: '. . . importio
athrawesau i'n Board Schools o Ysgotland a'r Iwerddon'.[69]

During 1874, fund raising continued, and by the third annual
meeting, on 9 April 1875, subscriptions of £1,593.11s. were reported. No
financial contribution could be expected from the Education Department because their grants were confined to seventy-five per cent of the
annual cost of maintenance. The campaign contrasted the thirty-seven
training colleges in England—fifteen for men and twenty-two for
women, with accommodation respectively for 1,264 male and 1,628
female students—and the position in Wales. The three colleges for
male students could accommodate 169 students whilst 'the College at
Swansea is the only one in the Principality for preparing young women
for the work of a teacher. Surely, one such institution can be established
and maintained'.[70]

A constitution was also framed stipulating that 'the institution' was
to be conducted according to the regulations of the British and Foreign
Schools Society. Women of all religious persuasions were to be
admitted and the management was to be vested in a committee of
forty-two members including six nominated by the British Society. The
college would be financed by Education Department grants, fees and
public subscriptions. Its full name under the constitution was designated as 'Training College for Educating Mistresses for Elementary
Schools in the Principality and elsewhere' and briefly as 'Swansea
Training College'.

On 9 April 1875, at the third annual meeting, when the management
was faced with a shortfall of £1,400 for the purchase of the freehold, it
was decided to acquire the premises on a long lease of seventy-seven

Table 4.5
Enrolment and Attendance at Swansea Training College

Year	Admitted	Left through ill-health	Left after 1 year	Training of 2 years
1872	38	3	10	—
1873	29	3	—	25
1874	29	1	1	26
1875	28	1	—	27
1876	28	1	—	27
1877	28	1	—	26
1878	27	—	—	28
1879	28	1	—	27

Source: Swansea Training College Reports.

years. Over the following twelve months, the Nelson Terrace premises were renovated, and a new wing — with a lecture hall, committee room, teachers' room and nineteen students' bedrooms — was opened in 1876 at a cost of £1,900.[71]

The constitution was also adopted and the British and Foreign Schools Society handed over the management of the college to a local, undenominational committee.[72] Alfred Bourne, whose guidance had been invaluable, resigned the principalship and was succeeded by David Williams who held the office until 1891. He had acted as vice-principal during the years 1872–5. Previously, as agent for the British and Foreign Schools Society in south Wales since 1863, he had been instrumental in starting nearly 200 British schools. An initial experiment in higher edcuation for women had now become a permanent institution under local management at Swansea.

During the 1870s, satisfactory enrolment of women at the college attested to the demand for teachers (Table 4.5). From 1874, the numbers seeking admission increased steadily and were far in excess of the accommodation available.[73] During the first seven years there were 357 candidates for admission and of the 242 who passed, 207 were admitted. The college authorities' confidence in 1877 appeared not misplaced:

> Grave fears were at one time entertained that the proportion of Welsh Primary Teachers seeking entrance into English Training Colleges would be so great as to make it a difficult, if not impossible, matter to fill Swansea College. Time has proved the groundlessness of such activities and shown the foresight and liberality of the British Society in establishing the College.[74]

Schoolmistresses trained at Swansea had little difficulty in obtaining posts in the 1870s. By the end of the decade, 199 young women trained at Swansea had taken up teaching appointments in England and Wales, and another fifty-six were in training.[75] Both English and Welsh students attended the college. In 1878, the homes of thirty-eight were in Wales and sixteen in England. Significantly, twenty-one came from Glamorgan but only two from north Wales. Teaching posts were also obtained in both England and Wales. By 1876, out of eighty-nine appointments, forty-one were in south Wales, eleven in north Wales and thirty-one in England.[76]

Throughout the decade, the unsectarian nature of the college had been emphasized, and undoubtedly, this was a key factor in its success in gaining the confidence of the public. Of the 264 admitted in the 1870s, eighty-three were Anglicans, forty-nine Calvinistic Methodists, forty-six Independents, forty-three Baptists, twenty-nine Wesleyans, seven Unitarians, three Presbyterians and four of other Christian connections.[77]

The funds at the college's disposal were only barely adequate. The financing of its operations, and upkeep of the buildings, was a considerable challenge and worry particularly in such times as 1876–7 when the depressed state of industries in the area increased the anxiety.[78] As well as the essential grants from the Education Department and the Science and Art Department, annual subscriptions and donations were important, particularly after withdrawal of direct support from the British Society. As well as emphasizing the college's unique female complement and the attractions of schoolteaching for women, appeals for financial support and the structure of the curriculum reflected prevailing perceptions of the college's role as an agency to promote 'habits of order, industry and economy, and in the principles of religion and morality'.[79]

The course of studies included school management as well as reading, grammar, arithmetic, writing, Scripture, geography, history, callisthenics, animal physiology, drawing, needlework, domestic economy. Botany was also available from 1877 and French was added to the curriculum in 1879. The health of students received careful attention and the Victorian concern about the possible dangers to women's health from the rigours of academic study was evident in the college reports.[80]

Teacher training and Welsh women in the 1870s

Welsh women also continued to attend training-colleges in England during a decade of growing demand for teachers.[81] There also, as in Swansea, colleges were instructed to ensure that female students' health

Table 4.6
Pupil-teachers in Wales during the 1870s

Year	Male	Female
1872	719	622
1873	854	759
1874	855	904
1875	768	814
1876	615	709
1877	919	1,061

Source: Minutes of Committee of Council on Education.

was not adversely affected.[82] Encouraged to advocate physical fitness, training-colleges were being told that schoolmistresses should embody religious and moral culture, possess intellectual proficiency in the subjects that they would be teaching, as well as aptitude to teach which involved the understanding of child nature.[83]

The importance of 'industrial and domestic training' for female teachers was stressed throughout the decade.[84] The attention given to needlework and domestic economy and the call for more systematic attention to cookery, epitomized not only the Education Department's influence over the training-colleges' courses of study and certification of teachers, but also the role of the schoolmistress and the female in Victorian society.[85]

By 1876, sixty per cent of the teachers in elementary schools in England and Wales were women. The demand for qualified teachers in Wales exceeded supply, particularly in the years immediately after the 1870 Education Act.[86] Whilst average salaries for mistresses were £57 in 1871 and £81 in 1895, students from Swansea were being appointed to teaching posts at salaries of between £60 and £80 per annum in 1875.[87] The number of female pupil-teachers also increased steadily during the 1870s. In 1877 the length of apprenticeship was reduced, with pupil-teaching commencing at fourteen years of age rather than thirteen years (Table 4.6).[88]

For an increasing number of young Welsh women, pupil-teaching and teacher training provided an important medium of post-elementary or higher education in the 1870s.[89] As women teachers, they were deemed especially qualified to ensure adequate attention to the essential feminine element — needlework, domestic economy — of a basically working-class programme of elementary education which was given increasing importance throughout the decade. In 1877, every girl presented for examination in 'specific subjects' had to include domestic economy as one of them, and to encourage more systematic teaching, needlework, which had been an obligatory subject for girls ever since the Code was introduced in 1862, now became a 'specific grant-earning subject' under the New Code:

> Important as it is that sound mental training should be the chief aim and object of all attempts at education, the probable future occupation of the children ought not to be lost sight of entirely . . . Domestic matters will form the principal matter for thought in the daily life of almost all the girls in our elementary schools . . . It would be good for the girls to learn to be useful in the state of life to which it has pleased God to call them.[90]

(ii) *Women and higher education in Wales 1850–1880: limited opportunities*

General orientation

The most significant ideas mooted in the sphere of higher education were concerned primarily with the education of middle-class boys and the establishment of a University of Wales. In the petition of 'The Association of Welsh Clergy in the West Riding' in 1852; in B.T. Williams's pamphlet in 1853 — *The Desirableness of a University for Wales* — and in the deliberations of Hugh Owen and such leading Nonconformists as Lewis Edwards, Henry Rees and S.R. in London in April 1854, the provision of university education for the female sex was not contemplated.

Such existing academies as the Presbyterian College at Carmarthen, the Methodist College at Bala, and the Anglican seminary at Lampeter, were valuable institutions of higher education, but exclusively male establishments. It was not until 1891 that the Bala College, with the missionary field in mind, began to consider the possibility of admitting women. Similarly, the publication in 1857 of an 87-page prospectus for the establishment of a scientific college at Gnoll Castle near Neath, exemplified the exclusively male perception of higher education.[91] Here, the intention was to establish 'A National Institution adapted to the wants of the Age'. In particular, following the example of continental countries aware of the value of scientific education for the development of national resources, it was intended that science should figure prominently in the education of 'the rising manufacturing and mercantile class'. Candidates for admission, who were to be limited in number to 200, were to be between sixteen and eighteen years, would pursue a three-year course in mathematics, mechanics, physics, chemistry, natural history, human history and design. Fees in the region of £70 per term or £200 per annum were anticipated. Rt. Revd Connop Thirlwall,

Bishop of St David's, H.A. Bruce MP, H.H. Vivian MP, and C.R. Mansel Talbot MP, supported a venture which, if implemented, would have been remarkable for the age. But significantly, though the project was being conceived in national terms, the female sex were not included within the ambit of a scientific education:

> Gnoll College is not intended simply to meet the wants of South Wales. Its objects are National in the broadest sense and with an appreciation of the desire for the systematic training of young men in practical science.[92]

Indeed, the absence of the female dimension was viewed as one important advantage of the proposed location: '. . . the college will be at a sufficient distance from the temptations and allurements of large cities, while every manly and becoming recreation will be available'.[93] Though teaching staff were appointed, the project never materialized, primarily because of the high fees, and unforeseen difficulties concerning the Gnoll estate's management.[94]

The quest for a University of Wales, which was one of the most significant projects of the educational history of the 1860s was also conceived solely in terms of the needs of men. At the request of the Committee of the National Eisteddfod at Swansea in 1863, Dr Thomas Nicholas read a paper entitled *Middle and High Schools and a University for Wales*.[95] He diagnosed a lack of educational provision for the middle and higher classes at the levels both of secondary and higher education. As well as contrasting Wales's meagre educational provision with high schools and universities in England, Scotland and Ireland, he also gave detailed information about university institutions in continental countries: 'Wales alone is destitute of what all other lands have been careful to possess.'[96] He argued that in such an important manufacturing and industrial country as Wales, there was need for institutions of higher education to educate young men:

> How few men from the Principality, which ought to be a nursery of mechanical and scientific genius, as she is a nursery of poets, rise to distinction in these lines. Do we raise men to fill the posts of honour which our own hands are creating?[97]

He voiced concern at the need for middle-class boys to be 'sent to England for education at great expense and social discomfort'.[98]

In his detailed proposals, he called for the provision of both secondary and higher education — the establishment of high schools and a University in Wales. He favoured a network of 'middle schools', founded on the 'proprietary' or 'limited liability' principle 'where sound, useful education shall be given, at charges commensurate with the means of parents in that rank of life'.[99] For the sons of wealthy, professional and aristocratic families, he favoured two 'high schools' — one in north Wales and the other in south Wales.[100] Young men educated in such 'high schools' would be awarded degrees by a University of Wales, which he conceived on the lines of London University as a degree-awarding body rather than as a teaching institution:[101] 'Hundreds of our sons would then quit our schools thoroughly equipped for careers of distinction, instead of the dozens which do so now; the intellectual power of the country would be indefinitely recruited'.[102]

Dr Nicholas called for the establishment of a committee 'from among known friends of education' to ensure that action was taken urgently. In November 1863, in a leading article — 'Prifysgol Cymru' — Thomas Gee expressed support. Referring to developments in Ireland and Scotland, he called for the establishments of two colleges — in the north and south — as well as high schools. But it was clear that the issue was only being considered from the standpoint of male education.[103] In December 1863, a provisional committee was formed to advance the cause of university education. With Dr Nicholas as secretary, the all-male membership which included Gee, Hugh Owen, William Williams MP, Revd Owen Thomas, Morgan Lloyd and G. Osborne Morgan, showed its concern for the educational neglect of young Welshmen in an era of increasing demand for educated talent.[104] The committee viewed its role in exclusively male terms.[105] Equality of educational opportunity was a male concept. At the Llandudno National Eisteddfod in August 1864, Dr Nicholas's paper to the Social Science Section on 'Education of the Middle Classes' again focused solely on the needs of men. He called, not only for the establishment of a university in Wales, but also for the formation of companies to found schools, thus enabling parents who had sons to become shareholders and governors of the institutions where their children were educated.[106]

By April 1867, the possibility of acquiring a building at Aberystwyth for use as a national university was being considered. The real concern was to ensure that its student intake and staff were unsectarian. A female dimension was not an issue.[107] In August 1868, with the Castle Hotel at Aberystwyth having been bought for £10,000, the then secretary of the Provisional Committee, Revd David Charles, in unmistakenly male terms, delineated the purposes of the proposed unsectarian establishment.[108] An 1868 'Outline of Plan' confirmed the male orientation of the venture: 'It is proposed to establish in Wales a First-Class College with University privileges, whose advantages shall be open to young men of all classes and all denominations without distinction'.[109] Likewise in 1871, a 'Memorial from the Committee of the Proposed University College of Wales' to the Treasury seeking financial support, noted that since Wales did not possess 'a single High Class College', it placed 'its youth and young men of the middle class under a disadvantage . . . Scotland had provision for 4,000 of her sons . . . If Wales were equally favoured, its College students would number more than 1,000'.[110] A memorandum from MPs in support of the 'Memorial' claimed that 'the establishment of the proposed University College of Wales would be of signal advantage to young men of the middle class in the Principality'.[111] Similarly, in June 1871, at the general meeting subscribers at Westminster Palace Hotel, it was resolved that the establishment of a college was essential 'to the advancement of learning in the Principality, and the placing of young men on a footing of equality with those belonging to other portions of the United Kingdom'.[112]

However, girls were not completely excluded from the deliberations and developments relating to 'higher education' during the 1860s. Indeed, one of the most significant developments was the opening of the Howell schools at Denbigh and Llandaff. The pupil-teacher system and training colleges continued to provide post-elementary educational opportunities for many Welsh women, as also did the Sunday schools.[113] Female involvement in literary societies and Sunday schools was being seen in terms of a continuing education.[114] Welsh Sunday schools were not only for children: there were adult female classes taught by women. A limited, though valuable insight into the extent of female participation in Sunday schools, is provided by a survey conducted in 1850 by Sir Charles Reed, later chairman of the London School Board, on behalf of the Sunday School Union. Though his inquiry was focused primarily on south Wales, information was also acquired from parts of north-west Wales. He found that, comparatively, men played a more significant role.[115] Educational experiments for women in Huddersfield and Bradford which provided evening courses in general education and in domestic management were much praised and recommended for adoption elsewhere in England and Wales.[116]

Mechanics' institutes had also provided opportunities for further enlightenment in England and Wales since 1824. In Wales, the first was established at Swansea in 1826, and by 1840, there were seventeeen in south Wales.[117] However, they were overwhelmingly male institutions and the numbers of women who participated in their affairs were comparatively few.

One of the more successful was 'The Llanelly Mechanics Institute' which was formed at a meeting of 'forty gentlemen' at the Ship and Castle Inn in 1840. No woman was present at the gathering.[118] Though some lectures were held in the years 1840–46, the institute was not officially opened until 1847. The Athenaeum building, which became its famous home, was built in 1857 and opened in 1858. Membership trebled in the early 1860s, with 459 members in 1864. Most were from the upper-working-class strata of society. Though female membership was allowed — 'The Institution shall in all its departments be conducted on the basis of perfect equality for all parties and denominations'[119] — and some journals of female interest acquired for the library, the women associated with the enterprise in the 1860s, and indeed during the rest of the Victorian era, were comparatively few. The officers were invariably male. In 1864, the membership of 459 included seventeen 'lady' members, though there might also have been women amongst the forty-two shopkeepers, twenty shop assistants, thirty-five potters and five teachers. By 1891, twelve per cent of the members were female. Such a lecture as Bessie Inglis's 'Women Poets' in 1864 was the exception rather than the rule because there was no especial female dimension to the lectures, and women were conspicuous by their absence from the lists of lecturers, and non-involvement in debates.

Frances Hoggan: a Welsh woman's triumph in medicine and the quest for educational reform

At the time when 'the numerous educational gaps that now exist in the principality'[120] remained to be filled with elementary schools and when girls had hardly ventured into the few institutions of 'higher' education, far away in Zurich, a young Welsh woman who was shortly to exert a major influence on the cause of female education in her native land, had scored a notable scholastic victory for her sex.

Frances Elizabeth Hoggan was born Frances Elizabeth Morgan at Brecon in 1843 and died in Brighton in 1927. She was the eldest of five children of Richard and Georgina Morgan. Her father's family came from Pembrokeshire and her mother's from Carmarthenshire. Her father was a graduate of Jesus College, Oxford, and at the time of her birth, was curate at Brecon though he was soon to move to the living of Aberafan with Baglan where his daughter was brought up. He died in 1851 without seeing his daughter achieving considerable distinction as physician, educationist and philanthropist. Though almost completely ignored by Welsh historians, she was undoubtedly one of the leading feminist pioneers of Victorian Wales.[121]

The difficulties facing women wishing to enter the medical profession were a challenge which she triumphantly overcame. Prejudice and antipathy towards women enrolling for the study of medicine was particularly strong in mid-Victorian Britain.[122] Even in 1875, Rose Mary Crawshay referred to 'the tremendous opposition made to allowing women who have talent and taste, to become doctors'.[123] Following the Medical Act 1858, the Medical Register was instituted in Britain and to qualify for registration, one needed a degree in medicine from a British University. However, anyone holding a degree from a foreign university and who was practising medicine in Britain in 1858 could also be registered. Until 1845, Dr Elizabeth Blackwell, a native of Bristol, and a graduate of an American University, was the only women admitted to the register. When she came to London after qualifying in New York, she found that her American degree entitled her to professional recognition. However, it is unlikely that the conservative-minded Medical Council and medical schools had expected such a contingency. They acted quickly to frustrate the ambitions of other women wishing to enter the medical profession through revising the Charter, so that in future, the holders of foreign degrees could be excluded.

It was also possible to be admitted to the Medical Register through passing the examinations of the Society of Apothecaries. There was no rule that excluded women; it was never anticipated that there would be female applicants. In 1865, Elizabeth Garrett (later Elizabeth Garrett Anderson) had passed the society's examinations but was only admitted to the Medical Register with great reluctance, and only after legal action had been threatened. She thus became the second woman to be included on the register.[124] However, the medical establishment were determined that the restrictions on women could in no way be eased. In 1868 it was stipulated by the Apothecaries' Society that, in future, a period of study in a recognized medical school would be obligatory in order to qualify for their diploma, although it was known that no such school was available for women. For the next twelve years, the Medical Register contained the names of only two women — Elizabeth Blackwell and Elizabeth Garrett. But the fight for emancipation was under way, with Sophia Jex-Blake in the vanguard.[125]

Being fully aware of the difficulties facing her sex, Frances E. Morgan resolved in 1866 to study medicine and obtain a diploma from the Society of Apothecaries after being assured that there were no new prohibitory regulations in force. To satisfy its demands, she and two friends paid for an expensive course of lectures from registered lecturers at medical schools, and successfully passed a preliminary examination in January 1867. Immediately, however, the Council of the Apothecaries' Society, being afraid that the entry of many women into the medical profession was imminent, passed a resolution excluding women henceforth from any of its professional examinations.

Frances Morgan, who had already received some of her early education in Paris and Düsseldorf now again turned to the continent. In Switzerland, M. Nadjesda Suslova, a native of St Petersburg in Russia had become the first women to graduate in medicine at Zurich University in 1867.[126] A few weeks later, in the autumn of 1867, Frances Morgan entered the Faculty of Medicine and graduated in March 1870 at the age of twenty-seven years. From there, she proceeded to a postgraduate course at a leading Vienna clinic and thereafter to the University of Prague and finally to Paris. However, it was not until 1876, with the passing of an Enabling Bill permitting medical schools to examine women even if they were technically forbidden to do so by the terms of their charters, after many fierce battles (involving in particular Miss Sophia Jex-Blake and the University of Edinburgh) that her name was entered on the Medical Register. She had thus become the first Welsh, and second British woman to graduate in medicine. Several English women followed her almost immediately to Zurich and returned to practise in their own country. Fittingly, Frances Morgan was to spend the first few years of her career as a medical practitioner in association with Elizabeth Garrett Anderson at the New Hospital for Women in London, and also co-operated with Dr Elizabeth Blackwell to found the National Health Society in 1871 'to promote health amongst all classes of the population'.

Following her marriage to Dr George Hoggan in 1874, she continued to practise as a doctor and published numerous medical papers dealing in particular with women and children.[127] Her medical qualification, obtained so brilliantly, and after overcoming such great obstacles, paved the way to a highly successful career in medicine as well as helping to open the doors of medical education for women in Britain. In 1881 there were twenty-five women doctors in England and Wales.[128] Frances Hoggan had succeeded in fulfilling the objectives advanced by such pioneers as Miss Emily Davies and Miss Buss that education should enable middle-class women to earn a living in their own right and in the same professions as men. This was a significant departure from the prevailing Victorian ideal of femininity and its emphasis on seeking fulfilment in the home as wife and mother.[129]

But Frances Hoggan's impact on education in Wales was only beginning. In a study published in 1981, Brian Harrison showed that many of the pioneer women doctors in the 1870s and 1880s, including Elizabeth Garrett Anderson and Sophia Jex-Blake were 'decidedly feminist' in their outlook on contemporary political and social issues.[130]

At the end of the decade, the Meyrick Trust Funds at Oxford became a major educational issue in Wales. There were numerous meetings throughout the Principality and many articles and letters were published in the Welsh Nonconformist press. Principal Harper and the Fellows of Jesus College had proposed that the endowments of Jesus College, Oxford be thrown open to all male students irrespective of their place of birth. There were twenty Meyrick scholarships at Jesus College, hitherto limited to Welshmen. It was argued that the Jesus College endowments, which included the Meyrick Funds, were intended for the educational benefit of Wales.[131] Gee argued that from the time of its foundation, Jesus College and the Meyrick bequest were intended to serve Wales.[132] It was felt that £12,000 were in jeopardy if the proposed changes were implemented. It was feared that if the scholarships were thrown open, Jesus College would become an 'English College of ex-public schoolboys'. In 'Suggestions for Memorials to the Oxford University Commissioners', it was emphasized that the Meyrick Funds should be deployed more effectively for the benefit of Wales. Significantly, it was suggested that scholarships should be established for boys in the endowed grammar schools of Wales and at Aberystwyth. Edmund Meyrick had bequeathed moneys in his will to enable 'poor boys' from north Wales to receive education.

Concern about the deployment of the Meyrick Trust Fund was not confined to Nonconformists. Dean H.T. Edwards called for the proposed changes to be implemented judiciously. The Honourable Society of Cymmrodorion also expressed their disapproval: '. . . The Council desire to express their strong sympathy regarding opposition to the proposed alienation of Jesus College endowments, now tenable only by Welshmen from Wales'.[133]

The possibility of utilizing the Meyrick Funds to alleviate 'the educational poverty of Wales' was considered in terms of educational opportunities for boys. However, Dr Hoggan was determined that female education should be a key aspect of the debate. Towards the end of the 1870s — a decade that witnessed some attempt at a more equitable sharing of educational endowments — Dr Hoggan began expressing her concern about the lack of educational opportunities for girls in Wales. In 1878, she was incensed by Principal Harper's proposal and wrote at length to the *Western Mail* expressing her feelings and suggesting what should be done:

The endowments of Jesus College, being clearly designed by the founders as encouragement to learning in Wales, it may fairly be asked whether the time has not come to allow girls to participate in some of the advantages of the College, by throwing open some of the scholarships to Welsh persons of either sex, and by generously affording to Welsh female students co-education with their brothers. The educational wants of women are becoming daily more evident, and the subject has become of a national interest and importance, engaging the earnest attention of some of the most vigorous intellects of the age. The time has almost passed away for sneering at girls desiring the advantage of higher education; and I am sure all, who know Wales and the Welsh could point to more than one girl, no less promising than her clever brother, to whom the possibility of gaining a scholarship at Jesus College would mean just the difference between a life of monotonous drudgery in an uncongenial home, and a life of honourable and useful independence, in that circle in which her talents would entitle her to move.[134]

She maintained that if Jesus College had a larger income than it could dispose of in fulfilling the original intentions of the founders, there was a need for the affairs of the college to be reviewed by the Charity Comissioners. She noted that, elsewhere, they had recommended that girls should share in endowments which had been used for the exclusive benefit of boys:

Not until such scheme has been tried and has failed, does it seem fair to alienate from natives of Wales the special provision made for them at Jesus College by founders, chiefly of Welsh origin. First extend the provision to Welshwomen, and if they do not respond to the appeal within a reasonable time, then by all means let the resources of the college, which are said to have outgrown the needs of Welshmen, be utilised as generally and as widely as possible. But until Welshwomen have this chance afforded them, it seems premature to urge the claims of men, to whom all the ancient colleges of Oxford and Cambridge, and among them, one which owes its foundation to a woman, open wide their doors.[135]

Two years later, she returned to this theme whilst testifying to the Aberdare Commitee. By then, Dr Hoggan had also delivered a lecture *On the Physical Education of Girls* to the Annual Meeting of the Froebel Society on 9 December 1879. This was published the following year in a 28-page booklet.[136] It was a time when the female's quest for equality in higher education, employment, and the franchise was closely associated with much debate about her mental and physical condition.[137]

University College of Wales, Aberystwyth, 1872–1879: opportunities for women

At a meeting to celebrate the opening of University College of Wales, Aberystwyth in October 1872, speeches by such luminaries of the Welsh political and educational scene as Principal T. Charles Edwards, David Davies, Llandinam, George Osborne Morgan and Henry Richard were telling in their lack of reference to women. Attention focused on the intended unsectarianism of the college and on the need for financial support by the State. It was particularly emphasized that what was being requested for Wales, was already being provided for Scotland and Ireland.[138] In references to the newly established university college, the focus throughout was male-orientated.[139] There was no overt opposition to women students recorded — the possibility of opening the doors for their enrolment was simply not considered.

However, as early as 1873, the need for the college to admit women students was being acknowledged in *Baner ac Amserau Cymru* by John Griffith, 'Y Gohebydd'. He noted that five or more scholarships, worth between £15 and £50 were being offered by the Clifton Association for the Higher Education of Women, and tenable at University College, Bristol. The significance for Wales of Bristol's opening of the doors of its new college to women as well as men was underlined.[140] At Aberystwyth itself, there was also some support for opening the doors to women. At 'an entertainment' in the Examination Hall in December 1873, H.N. Grimley, Professor of Chemistry, said that he hoped that before long, women would be able to share the educational advantages provided by the University. The subject was immediately taken up by Gibson in the *Cambrian News* who heartily approved the suggestion and expressed the hope that '. . . women would speedily put to the test the willingness of the authorities to open the doors of the college to them as well as men'.[141] In his opinion, women would soon be asking for admission, and such appeal would be favourably met. The well-being of the Principality would be promoted if women were to enrol as students.[142] By early 1874, with sixty male students at the college, it was noted that more than once at public meetings, it had been intimated that the University College of Wales authorities would not be averse to admitting female students on the same terms as men. Professor Grimley was quoted as saying that all that was required was for women to 'knock at the doors of the College and demand admittance'. Significantly, it was recognized that separate classes would be formed if necessary. Gibson, stressing the economic and social advantages of female education, endeavoured to arouse support, recommending the establishment of scholarships and exhibitions for women at the college: '. . . Let women apply for admission, and we believe they will not only be received without hesitation, but will be gladly welcomed'.[143] He wanted the UCW authorities to be tested as to whether women would be admitted to the ordinary classes.

In these early days of the college's history, a distinction came to be made between the 'ordinary classes' in four different schools — modern languages and literature, classics and philosophy, mathematics, natural science — where students studied for London University degrees, and 'music classes' which did not provide a constitutent part of the Honours course.[144] Students of music studied for the qualification of 'Associate in Music of the University College of Wales' from 1876. A Department of Music had been established, with Joseph Parry, who returned from America as Professor in 1874 at a salary of £250 per annum.[145] Women as well as men attended his music classes, and were valuable members of the choir who gave concerts in the town and elsewhere in Wales. Joseph Parry had persuaded the college authorities to allow women students to be registered because he required female voices for the college choir.[146] A distinction was made between the ordinary students and those who attended the music classes. However, it appears that music students did attend some of the 'ordinary classes'.[147]

It is difficult to ascertain the precise number of female music students, because in the college reports for the 1870s, though a distinction is made between students of music and the others, male and female students of music are not differentiated. In October 1874, of the eighty-four students at the college, twenty-three attended the Musical Classes only'.[148] There were awards for women from 1874 as 'scholars and exhibitioners in music'. Two of the four exhibitioners in the Christmas term 1874 — who included David Jenkins, Trecastle, a future Welsh musician of distinction — were women. Lizzie Edwards, Cardiff held a singing exhibition tenable for one year, and Kate Rees, Aberystwyth held a pinaoforte exhibition tenable for one year.[149] The *Prospectus and Regulations* 1874-5 refers to 'one exhibition in music restricted to female candidates'. Four others were open to all without restriction. In an appendix, it stated '. . . The Department of Music open to women as well as men'.[150] By April 1875, thirty-nine of the 126 students enrolled, were students of music.[151] A photograph of music students, dated 1875-6, includes seven women and twelve men.[152] During the Christmas term 1875, three women were awarded music exhibitions and two others given 'honourable mention'. Likewise in 1876, two women gained awards in pianoforte and harmony and in singing and harmony. Of the first examinees in 1876 for the 'Associate in Music' examination, six of the sixteen candidates were women. In 1877, there were five female candidates, and three women held exhibitions each worth £10. In the Lent term 1878, one woman held an exhibition in singing.[153] During these years, male and female music students performed concerts both in the college building and in the town.

Though music students were registered at the college, they were tolerated rather than encouraged. In 1875, Hugh Owen advised Principal T.C. Edwards that it was 'not desirable' to have a 'second Professor or Assistant Professor of music' and '. . . the number of students in the Music Department should not be greater than Mr Parry could teach without help'.[154] He thought it most undesirable for women students to reside in the college building unless careful precautions were taken:

> It is not without hesitation that I express a doubt as to any proposal of yours, especially when it is backed by Mrs Edwards and Mr R.E. Roberts. I must however say that I should look with horror at the bringing of a lot of girls (I beg their pardon for thus referring to them) to lodge and board in the same building with a lot of youths — young men. You would of course have partitions, locks, bolts and all that sort of thing, and practically no mischief might arise from the arrangement. But the existence of the arrrangement would be certain to occasion surprise in the country, and subject the College to damaging criticism . . . I trust that you may find it possible to surround the girls with adequate protection.[155]

At the time, a committee had reported an arrangement for boarding and lodging students, rules of discipline and the utilization of the whole college building. It had recommended that '. . . accommodation be provided for the Musical Department in the Castle end of the building; and that alterations be made for the purpose of separating the Male from the Female Students in the rooms in the corridor over the Examination Hall'.[156]

However, the main issues of the day for the college were fund raising and allegations of Nonconformist intolerance.[157] In June 1875, the college council sent a memorial to the government requesting a grant in aid to the college. A deputation in support of the memorial was received by the Lord President of the Council. But there was no reference to the educational needs of women, only the emphasis on 'the absolute need of such an Institution in Wales, and the great advantages which it is calculated to confer on its youth and young men'.[158] They claimed that the establishment of the college had been welcomed as 'a national boon' by the middle and working classes, '. . . as shown by their spontaneously collecting funds among themselves to enable young men of talent . . . to enter the College'.[159] Similarly, at the prize day in June 1878, there was no reference to women students, the main issue being funds and the future of the college.[160] The principal's reports and the deliberations of the college council show that female education was not an issue in the 1870s.

However in 1878–9, by virtue of the Joseph Parry affair, the position of women students at Aberystwyth was adversely affected. At a meeting of the college council in London on 14 June 1878, the principal was requested to offer suggestions at the next meeting 'to lessen the relative cost of maintaining the College, say by reducing the staff or increasing the number of students'.[161] A report was discussed at the July meeting when consideration was given to the possibility of merging a number of chairs. The Music Department was also considered and it was resolved on 20 July 1878,

> That the Principal should confer with Professor Parry on his position at the University College, and propose to him a new arrangement based on his discontinuance of teaching Music to any but the ordinary male students of Arts at the college . . . Dr Parry should retain his Professorship on a salary to be agreed upon for such teaching as above-mentioned.[162]

He would also be allowed to provide private lessons outside the college. However, it should be 'clearly understood that during the Sessions of the College, Dr Parry should not give, nor professionally attend concerts in Aberystwyth or in its immediate neighbourhood'.[163] In June 1878, there were eighty-two students at the college, of whom twenty-two were music students.[164] By June 1879, there were seventy-seven students at the college including thirteen women studying music.[165] Faced with new conditions of service and a reduction in salary, Joseph Parry was unlikely to remain at Aberystwyth and tendered his resignation in 1880.[166]

Joseph Parry's brief tenure at Aberystwyth was highly controversial at the time, and has interested modern writers and film-makers.[167] In the *The Cambrian News*, John Gibson voiced strong opposition and questioned the constitutional propriety of a decision taken when all the members of the council were not present. He interpreted it as meaning the discontinuation of the music department and the virtual dismissal of Professor Parry: 'One of the most conspicuous features of the College is the music department. Professor Parry came from America to take charge of this department'.[168] Female students of music would henceforth be excluded as well as any male specialist students of music. On 1 August 1879, a public meeting was held at Aberystwyth, with the mayor presiding, to consider the action of UCW concerning Professor Parry. Much opposition was voiced.

Various factors accounted for the decision of 1878, which the Council claimed was in 'the interest of the College in its primary and essential objects'.[169] Financial problems (which also put the teaching of Welsh in jeopardy in May 1879), Joseph Parry's generous salary and frequent absences, all contributed to the events of 1878–9. But in addition, there was much criticism of the quality of the music students.

In the Principal's Report 1875, it was stated that music students would not be admitted unless they had passed an examination in that subject. Their disproportionate numbers may have caused envy, whilst their lack of discipline and supervision were regarded with disfavour and unbecoming for a new institution of higher education.[170] Nor was there any real enthusiasm for the admission of women students at the end of the decade. Sir J.E. Lloyd recalled that,

> ... the professor, wayward and impulsive like the true musician, was difficult to fit into the academic machine; the level of education among the students of his department was appallingly low, the presence of women — not yet admitted to ordinary classes — imported into the college a new and disturbing element.[171]

By the summer of 1879, the future of higher education in Wales was the subject of considerable public attention. On 1 July 1879 the subject was debated in the House of Commons, with Hussey Vivian, Lord Emlyn and Gladstone amongst the speakers. The main focus was the deficient state of education in the Principality, and the need for a state grant for the funding of the University College at Aberystwyth. In this climate, the debate on the educational needs of women was given scant hearing.[172]

5

Promotion of Educational Reform in the 1880s

(i) *The Aberdare Report and the quest for intermediate education for girls, 1880–1888*

> . . . a Committee to inquire into the present condition of Intermediate and Higher Education in Wales and to recommend the measures which they think advisable for improving and supplementing the provision that is now, or might be made available for such education in the Principality.[1]

The appointment of the Aberdare Committee was the culmination of many years of political pressure exerted by Liberal and Nonconformist Wales, previously on a Conservative, and now on a new Liberal Government. After much deliberation, which reflected prevailing religious and social divisions, the Departmental Committee was appointed by Gladstone's Government.[2] The members were Lord Aberdare (chairman), Viscount Emlyn MP, Reverend Prebendary H.G. Robinson, Henry Richard MP, Professor John Rhŷs and Lewis Morris. Significantly, the voice of Welsh Nonconformity was firmly represented.

The committee held meetings in fifteen different centres between 8 October 1880 and 10 February 1881, where evidence was given by more than 250 witnesses. As well as headteachers and teachers, college principals and professors, evidence was given by the four Welsh bishops, numerous clergymen and ministers of religion, several members of parliament, many laymen and a few women. The oral and written evidence was quickly assimilated, and a 72-page report, together with forty pages of appendices appeared in August 1881. The accompanying volume of evidence amounted to another 896 pages.

The appointment of the Aberdare Committee in 1880 was generally welcomed. Attention focused in particular on its 'religious' complexion, the need to remove Anglican control of endowments such as Howell's and to ensure a fair deal for Nonconformists. Though female education was not amongst the main issues discussed, it was given significant attention. The witnesses who testified before the committee included women as well as men. Undoubtedly, the most eminent feminist campaigner who gave evidence was Emily Davies. Though she was of Welsh extraction, she readily admitted that her knowledge of the Welsh scene was very limited, and she had nothing of major importance to say about Wales. However, she thought that there was a need 'to supply the want of girls' schools in Wales'. As was typical of the period, and in particular of the ethos that characterized the Aberdare inquiry and report, the extension of educational opportunity for girls was conceived in middle-class terms. She criticized the Howell schools for not encouraging girls to stay until eighteen years and aspire to the higher qualifications of the university local examination boards.[3] She also favoured the provision of degrees for women in a University of Wales and had no objection to co-education as long as 'proper discipline' was maintained.[4]

Mrs Verney of Rhianfa, Anglesey — who was later to become a leading campaigner for girls' education in Wales — was criticial of the quality of the education in private girls' schools, and claimed that there was 'a very great desire for better education in Anglesey among farmers' wives, and wives of small tradesmen'.[5]

From south-west Wales, Emily Higginson, widow of a Unitarian minister, stressed the need for 'middle class schools' in Swansea, teaching science as well as the arts. They should also cater for able working-class pupils from the board schools who had passed the sixth standard. She claimed that though there were numerous private schools in Swansea, none was able to provide tuition to meet the matriculation requirements of the University of London.[6]

At Aberystwyth, John Gibson, editor of *The Cambrian News* also thought that there was a great need for girls' schools in Wales. He welcomed the recently opened Dr Williams' School at Dolgellau. He even thought that the quality of the girls' schooling could be improved through 'the assistance of the professors at the Aberystwyth College'.

Inevitably, in Nonconformist Wales, the Anglican ethos of the Howell schools figured in the deliberations. Thomas Gee was highly critical of the exclusively Anglian control of the Denbigh school, where the eighty-five pupils were taught the Church catechism. He suggested that the control of the Drapers' Company, whom he claimed knew very little about Wales, should cease, and the charity's funds should be transferred into the hands of Welsh commissioners.[7] Similarly, the Llandaff school was subject to criticism for its denominational nature, and because its endowment could be used more advantageously.[8] Wales's most eminent pioneer of education in the Victorian age —

Hugh Owen — was also critical of the 'very defective' state of girls' education, and advocated the enlargement of the two Howell's schools and the Dr Williams' School at Dolgellau, and the utilization of the college buildings at Aberystwyth, if the University College were to move from the town.[9]

Another witness who gave particular attention to the education of girls was Eliza Peter of Rhianfa School, Towyn. She was the widow of the Reverend John Peter, a professor at the Bala Independent College. Educated in Liverpool and Chester, she had taken considerable interest in education in general, and girls' education in particular. In August 1880, at the Cymmrodorion Section of the Caernarfon National Eisteddfod, she read a paper on the higher education of girls. Until her death in 1889, she used her literary and organizational skills to promote the cause of women — 'dyrchafiad y rhyw fenywaidd'.[10]

In her evidence to the Aberdare Committee she criticized the Dr Williams' School for its high fees (£30 per annum for boarding and four guineas for tuition), and also the denominational element at the Howell schools at Denbigh and Llandaff which were 'practically Church of England schools'.[11] She had detected 'a considerable desire' among middle-class parents for higher education for girls, though there was also a need to convince some that education was as essential for their daughters as for their sons.[12] Regarding curricular provision, she emphasized that there should be no sexual differentiation other than the provision of domestic economy for girls. Wales required a network of intermediate schools with facilities for boarders as well as day pupils: whilst these facilities were likely to be at a lower level than those at Dr Williams' School, there was also need for scholarships to enable girls to attend such schools as the one at Dolgellau. Eliza Peter also emphasized the importance of opening up the educational opportunities of women as well as men by the establishment of a University of Wales.

On the matter of religious bias, the committee were informed that the Diocesan High School at Carmarthen had no appeal to the overwhelmingly Nonconformist community of the district who, nevertheless, required greater educational opportunities.[13] Similarly, the authorities at Ashford School remained unpersuaded by any arguments in favour of its conversion into an unsectarian school. Nor did they see any real disadvantage for Welsh girls on account of the school's location in London.[14]

The most well informed and persuasive witness on behalf of women's education was Dr Frances Hoggan, who was to continue to campaign for some years afterwards. At the outset, she stressed that she was no stranger to Wales, even though she had spent most of the previous decade in England, after graduating in medicine at Zurich in 1870.

On the basis of wide-ranging evidence both from within and outside Wales, she drew attention to the inadequate provision for the education of girls in the Principality.[15] She had prepared a 'Scheme for higher and secondary education of girls and women in Wales' which she submitted to the Committee, and elaborated upon, under questioning from Lord Aberdare, Revd. H.G. Robinson and Henry Richard.[16] Epitomizing the Victorian belief in self-help, she argued that it was not the function of the State to provide secondary schools, but rather to make it easier for girls (and boys too for that matter) to proceed from elementary schools, with the help of scholarships and exhibitions, to secondary schools raised by public subscriptions. Here, she acknowledged the influence of the Irish intermediate scheme. Such secondary schools might be provided on the model of those established under the auspices of, and with some assistance from, the Girls' Public Day Schools Company in England, or of the two Camden Schools: the North London Collegiate School for Girls and the Camden School. She admitted that there might well be cases where a building grant from public funds might be desirable, but in general, she was confident that there would be sufficient local interest 'to get the buildings'. Dr Hoggan would appear to have been unaware of the lack of appeal of the Girls' Public Day School Company in Wales, primarily because of its reputedly Anglican connections.[17]

As for the relative merits of co-educational and single-sex schools, Dr Hoggan was all in favour of the former, though she doubted whether they would be practicable until there was an adequate number of suitably qualified women teachers.[18] She thought she was 'the only Welsh woman who is able to speak from practical experience of co-education at a University'. Her own experience, and the views of one of the most eminent professors at Zurich, convinced her of the virtues of co-education:

> Women are benefited and in no way injured by this education, and . . . the young men also benefit; there is a certain softening influence which must always proceed from cultured and educated women.[19]

On being asked by H.G. Robinson whether or not a mixed teaching staff was a necessary prerequisite of a satisfactory co-education, she replied that '. . . we certainly require women to be largely represented in the education of girls, not only for their teaching, but for the moral influence they will exert'.[20]

In such schools as she envisaged — schools raised by public subscriptions, open to boys and girls from elementary schools who were bright enough to win an entrance scholarship or an exhibition — the needs of Welsh-speaking pupils should not be overlooked, as they had been to a great extent in the past:

> In all schools established in the Welsh-speaking parts of Wales, the wants of the Welsh-speaking children require to be specially considered, which they have not been so far, either in the case of boys or girls.[21]

The role of the Welsh language in education was only given peripheral attention by the committee, and unsurprisingly, Dr Hoggan was not pressed to elaborate. But in supplementary evidence submitted, she showed greater enlightenment than most. Nevertheless, her concern was less with the promotion of the language *per se* than with ways in which Welsh could be used in schools to further the pupils' understanding of the English tongue. Masters and mistresses ought to be able to understand Welsh so that 'they may be in sympathy with the people among whom they labour', but this was really in order 'to help their pupils intelligently to overcome the difficulties which necessarily arise in learning English when the home language is Welsh'.[22] But

> . . . the study of the English language ought to be made a special feature in secondary schools in Wales . . . In regard to the teaching of Welsh in secondary schools, it will, I believe, be generally found sufficient to place it on the same level as French, German and Latin, that is to say not making it compulsory but allowing it to be chosen as the modern language learnt.[23]

Though she herself was a clergyman's daughter, she stressed that the Aberdare Committee should give careful recognition to the strength of Nonconformity in Wales: '. . . the majority . . . are nonconformists. It ought to be kept prominently before the eyes of those who legislate, or make any arrangements for the education of Welsh people'.[24] Schools should be completely unsectarian, and the voice of Nonconformity should be heard on their governing bodies.[25] Women also should be members of governing bodies. They had already proved their suitability through participation in the affairs of chapels, churches and training colleges.[26]

She favoured the establishment of a degree-awarding university in Wales which would have obvious advantages for the poorer classes. Those families who could afford to do so, would probably continue to send their children to English universities. A university in Wales should be completely independent and not a college affiliated to a university in England. She naturally assumed that it would be open to men and women alike, and on perfectly equal terms. The dearth of highly qualified women teachers in Wales was an acute problem which degree examinations open to women would help to rectify: 'Nothing would tend more to raise both the status of women teachers and their general capability, than the power of obtaining the high-class teaching of a university and the sanction which only a degree would give'.[27] Rather than designating one of the colleges solely for women, she preferred their admittance to all the colleges that might be established: 'I have seen so much good result from the co-education of women, that I should be sorry that women should miss the advantage of co-education in Wales'.[28] If, however, mixed colleges would have to be ruled out, she suggested that at least two colleges for girls should be established — one for north Wales and another for south Wales. Women should also be adequately represented on the university's governing body. As for the suggestion that a degree course would impose too great a strain on women students, and that they should accordingly be admitted earlier and pursue a shorter course than men, she dismissed it out of hand. She recognized the danger of overstrain in examinations, which was true for boys as well as girls, but thought that if all students were given a wide choice of subjects from which they would be required to study only a few, and be examined in only a limited number in any given examination, the problem could be overcome. Furthermore, just as there should be scholarships and exhibitions to enable promising pupils from humble homes to proceed from the elementary school to the secondary, so too should there be similar arrangements to assist those who wished to continue their education in a university or technical institution. The success of the Irish intermediate examination scheme had influenced her views on scholarships and exhibitions.

Frances Hoggan believed strongly in the value of technical education for girls as well as for boys.[29] The need was there, probably more so for boys in the first instance, but the needs of girls should be provided for through nursing schools, dairy schools, and schools giving instruction in the various branches of domestic economy. Much of the existing educational machinery could be used to establish such schools in Wales — the Girls' Public Day Schools Company for example, and the newly established City and Guilds of London Institute, which catered for women as well as for men, and which had framed a most liberal course of study. Moreover, two of the largest charities were associated with Wales — the Drapers' and the Haberdashers' Companies — and if it proved impossible to recover the money which these two companies had wasted or misapplied over the years, and use it for the benefit of the children of Wales, surely some of it could be recovered indirectly by making provision for technical education. And much would be gained, she added, if an institution for higher technical education was established in a university town, as in Zurich, where the University and the Federal Polytechnic had been mutually helpful. There, 'many of the professors had classes common to both the University and the technical school and in that way all the students had a much larger range of instruction accessible to them'.[30]

Finally, there was the issue which ran like a thread throughout her evidence — the use, or rather the misuse, of educational charities in Wales. She thought it was urgent to institute 'a searching investigation' into the way in which charitable endowments for educational purposes were being administered or maladministered.[31] In particular, she pointed to how, on many occasions, girls had not benefited because the word 'children' in the original bequest had been interpreted to mean 'boys'. The actions of the administrators of the Howell charity distressed her because 'in the dispositions of the founder there is no question of restricting the application of the funds to the Church of England'.[32] Though the Court of Chancery had recently approved a new scheme for its administration, she maintained that it was heavily weighted against Nonconformists and even against girls from Wales in general.[33]

It was essential that all endowments be investigated and redistributed primarily in the interests of the girls of Wales; that endowed day-schools should be established at low fees in or near large centres of population (where local funds could be raised to supplement them); that any thoroughly efficient existing secondary schools should be endowed; that special technical schools for girls, such as nursing or dairy schools, should be established, and that exhibitions for entry into 'higher schools' should be founded which would be open to boys and girls of elementary schools. She reiterated her 1879 criticism of Jesus College, Oxford and doubted whether the college was really useful to Wales in its existing form. Its funds could be more effectively used to form the nucleus of the proposed Welsh university, but failing that, girls should be eligible to compete for Jesus College scholarships and exhibitions on a par with boys and live in halls of residence specifically provided for them, or in Lady Margaret Hall or Somerville Hall.

The Aberdare Committee concluded that the opportunities available for girls compared very unsatisfactorily with those for boys at the level of intermediate and higher education. The two Howell schools — at Denbigh and Llandaff — and Dr Williams' at Dolgellau had an enrolment of only 263 girls but were the only endowed schools offering a higher education for girls in Wales. Another 1,870 girls were attending a variety of seventy-three private schools.[34] These were comparatively small schools with an average of twenty-six pupils who paid fees of £6 per annum on average. It was concluded that the standards were very low. There were a number of schools offering education 'higher than elementary' who did not reply to the committee's quest for information. Thus the actual number of private schools was greater than seventy-three.[35] Schemes had been submitted to the Committee of Council for the utilization of part of the endowments of Beaumaris Grammar School and the Tasker's charity at Haverfordwest to establish schools for girls, whilst an endowment at Eglwysilan in Glamorgan, had been made available for the education of girls under a Charity Commission scheme.

Ironically, although Wales's most successful school at the time — Llandovery College — catered only for boys, its establishment in 1847 owed a great deal to the valiant efforts of Lady Llanover. Altogether, there were twenty-seven endowed grammar schools with an enrolment of 1,540 boys and an aggregate annual endowment income of approximately £12,788. Another seventy-nine private schools, catering for 2,287 boys, are listed in the Aberdare Report, though it is known that yet more private schools also existed.[36]

The committee thought it a matter of urgency to improve the educational opportunities available for middle-class girls: '. . . improved education for girls of the middle class may be described as urgent'.[37] The whole thrust of the report was directed towards a graded and differential conception of a middle-class secondary education. The system of intermediate schools was intended primarily to cater for the educational needs of middle-class families in Wales.[38]

The Welsh School at Ashford though retaining its 'nominal connexion with Wales', was doing 'little or nothing to promote the education of boys or girls who really belong to the Principality'. The report recommended its removal to Wales, and the channelling of its resources for the education of girls exclusively.

The utilization of public funds to provide additional schools for girls as well as boys was recommended. Women should be represented on the governing bodies of girls' schools. Changes were advocated in the constitution of the Howell Foundation to enable a much larger number of pupils to benefit. The Aberdare Committee found it difficult to reconcile the schools' claim of religious equality with the high proportion of Nonconformists in Wales, and the very small number of their daughters at the Llandaff and Denbigh schools. Likewise, the Anglican monopoly of their governing bodies was noted.

The Aberdare Report was to be one of the most significant events in the educational history of modern Wales. On the occasion of its centenary in 1981 its importance was acknowledged though it was assessed as less radical and enlightened than was previously considered.[39] Nevertheless, it was to exert considerable influence on the quest for greater and fairer educational provision for women. That quest for equality now came to be based on imitation — which meant academic education for girls as well as boys.

(ii)   *The quest for intermediate education for girls, 1882–1888*

During the long struggle in the 1880s for legislation to establish intermediate schools, the education of girls was given attention, though it was not the major priority. It was to receive considerable prominence because the few girls' schools in existence — Howell's and Ashford especially — were viewed by the Nonconformist–Liberal protagonists as bastions of Anglicanism and socio-economic privilege. Consequently, female education was propelled into the centre of the political, religious and educational arena in the 1880s. Though an increasing number focused on intermediate education for girls in its own right, the issue attracted greater attention as part of the wider educational debate, and the concomitant religious and political conflicts.

In April 1882, when it was announced that an Intermediate Education Bill had been drafted, and was to be introduced in the House of Commons, Thomas Gee stressed the need for the embodiment of all the recommendations of the Aberdare Report.[40] By June, however, criticism was being voiced at the delay in introducing legislation.[41]

On 15 June 1882, an 'influentially-attended meeting of Welsh members and others interested in Higher Education in Wales',[42] was convened by Lord Aberdare at the Westminster Palace Hotel to demand governmental implementation of the recommendations of the recent report. It became clear that the bill had not yet received the imprimatur of the Cabinet, though a measure had been promised in the Queen's Speech at the opening of the 1882 Parliament.[43] A draft had been prepared by the Education Department.[44] However, Lord Aberdare argued that various changes could be implemented without legislation. He spoke firstly about the education of girls, arguing that 'their wants were really the most pressing'. Though the two Howell schools were doing very satisfactory work they had been founded under a decree of the Court of Chancery before the 1869 Endowed Schools

Act was in force, and were established on principles which were unacceptable to the majority of the population. He reminded his audience that the committee desired that the number of pupils benefiting from the charity should be trebled or even quadrupled. He also thought that Betton's charity, worth £8,000 per annum, and Madam Bevan's charity, could be more effectively deployed for educational purposes in Wales. Having also discussed other aspects of intermediate and higher education, it was eventually decided that a deputation be sent to wait on Mr Mundella at the Education Department, though Henry Richard MP and others present warned of the dangers of fragmentary measures interfering with an ultimate and complete scheme of intermediate and higher education.

On 19 June 1882, an influential deputation of peers, MPs and representatives of the Council of the University College of Wales, met A.J. Mundella in Whitehall. They maintained that there were some recommendations of the Abderdare Committee that could be implemented without legislation, and without interfering with a more comprehensive scheme for intermediate and higher education that needed parliamentary approval. As well as providing financial assistance to the University College of Wales, advanced elementary schools could be established for boys and girls. Also, arrangements could be made for more effective application of such endowments as the £6,500 per annum Howell charity, Meyrick fund, Betton charity and Wells' charity. Mundella, however, was noncommittal on the question of endowments, but promised that a circular would be issued, dealing with advanced elementary schools.

On 10 August 1882, the 'Mundella Circular' was issued by the Education Department to the larger school boards of Wales.[45] Detailed instructions were provided as to the procedures for establishing advanced elementary schools, and an insight given into the operation of 'higher school boards' at Bradford. Though no especial attention was given to girls, it was clearly intended that both sexes should benefit from advanced elementary schools.

In February 1882, Dr Frances Hoggan had already argued the case for the establishment of higher board or advanced elementary schools in some of the densely populated districts such as Glamorgan. She believed that a maximum fee of 9*d.* a week would not place such schools beyond the reach of the lower-middle-class community. It would be essential that adequate curricular provision were made for the girls in such schools, with the establishment of a technical department giving particular attention to domestic economy.[46]

Already at Ffestiniog, the school board had considered the feasibility of establishing an advanced elementary school. In a report prepared for the board on 26 June 1882, Robert Roberts had stressed that the school should cater for girls as well as boys: 'The case of girls is a most important one'. Since such schools would be subject to state scrutiny, various subjects would be efficiently taught.[47] Shortly, Mundella's proposal was to lead to the establishment of advanced elementary schools at Blaenau Ffestiniog, Ystrad Rhondda, Cardiff, Merthyr Tudful, Swansea and Gelligaer.[48] At Gelligaer, the school was directly related to the decision of the Lewis's Schools governors to educate boys rather than girls. But the demand for secondary education still remained unanswered.

However in 1882 and 1883, it was higher education — the future of Aberystwyth College and the location of the North Wales College — rather than intermediate education that was the main focus of attention. A long struggle lay ahead for the advocates of intermediate education.

On 22 May 1885, Mundella moved the first reading of a Welsh Intermediate Education Bill. Inevitably, the bill was viewed from the standpoint of well established prejudices and, in general, it received a mixed reception.[49] The exclusion of the Howell and Ashford endowments from the terms of the bill figures prominently amongst the criticisms voiced. The measure reasserted the principle established by the Endowed Schools Acts of 1869 and 1873, that endowments given fifty years or more before 1869 could not be interfered with, except with the consent of the governing bodies of such schools.[50] However, before a second reading could take place in June, Gladstone's second ministry had fallen and the bill was lost. The lack of any special provision for the education of girls led directly to the formation of The Association for Promoting the Education of Girls in Wales.

However, the need for legislation was being reiterated in the Welsh press.[51] Thomas Gee and the Welsh MPs, including the Conservative G.T. Kenyon, were demanding action.[52] On 21 May 1886, a number of Welsh MPs including Osborne Morgan, W. Rathbone, Love Jones Parry, J. Bryn Roberts, G.T. Kenyon, Stuart Rendel and Cornwallis West saw Earl Spencer and Sir Lyon Playfair at the Education Department concerning a Welsh Intermediate Education Bill. Stuart Rendel MP emphasized that strong feelings had been aroused throughout Wales by the exclusion of important endowments from the bill. Spencer agreed to consider these representations and do what he could to introduce an amended or different bill before the end of the session.

Thomas Gee again took the occasion to call for the inclusion of all endowed schools in Wales (including Dr Williams' and Howell's) under the terms of the bill, otherwise it would be far from effective. He also responded to the proposal to establish an Association for Promoting the Education of Girls in Wales by expressing confidence that the educational needs of girls would not be overlooked in an Intermediate Education Bill.[53]

With the demand for parliamentary action continuing to be voiced,[54] G.T. Kenyon, Conservative MP for Denbigh, took the initiative on 24 April 1887 and introduced a private bill to establish intermediate education in Wales. Though there was some support for the measure, its failure to deal effectively with the management of existing schools was immediately highlighted.[55] There was no change proposed in the arrangements, whereby under the Endowed Schools Acts the agreement of the trustees or governors was needed prior to the introduction of any changes. Howell's was singled out as an example of an endowment unlikely to be affected, and it was particularly noted that there was no reference to Ashford School in the measure.[56] By May 1887, however, lack of parliamentary time and also opposition to the bill's financial proposals had ensured that the measure would make no further parliamentary progress.

By June 1887, following active deliberations in the Liberal ranks, another Intermediate Education Bill had been presented to Parliament by A.J. Mundella.[57] Significantly, and in contrast to earlier measures, the Ashford, Howell and Meyrick endowments were included within the powers of the bill. Mundella's bill did not receive a second reading, but the pressure for legislative action continued. The Cymmrodorion Society decided that its section meetings at the London National Eisteddfod in August should be assigned for educational problems. Consequently, the Cymmrodorion meetings held at the Central Technical Institute, Prince Gate took the form of an influential educational conference to discuss 'The Future Development of the Educational System', with women's education and the newly established Association for Promoting the Education of Girls in Wales being given considerable attention. A resolution proposed by Miss Dilys Davies (a leading member of the association) and seconded by Miss Armstrong (formerly of Dr Williams' School) was passed: '. . . that this meeting of the Cymmrodorion Section of the National Eisteddfod is strongly of the opinion that in any provision for Intermediate education in Wales, the interests of girls should be considered equally with those of boys'.[58] Miss Fewings, the new headmistress of Dr Williams', supported the claims of girls in Wales to cheap, unsectarian education. A resolution proposed by Owen Owen, Oswestry, and seconded by John Owen, Warden of Llandovery College, was also passed calling for an education conference of representatives of the colleges, and intermediate and elementary schools.[59]

This conference was summoned by the Cymmrodorion Society at Shrewsbury on 5 and 6 January 1888, to discuss 'The Future Development of the Welsh Educational System'. Between sixty and seventy representatives of various Welsh educational interests gathered in the Guildhall, with Professor Rhys as chairman. They included ladies prominently associated with female education in Wales — Miss E.P. Hughes, Miss Dilys Davies, Mrs Verney and Miss E.A. Fewings of Dr Williams' School, Dolgellau, the headteachers of private girls' schools at Aberystwyth, Welshpool, and Carmarthen as well as Miss Virgo of the Welsh Girls' School, Ashford. On the agenda were the establishment of a University of Wales, inspection of intermediate schools by the university, utilization of existing schools, establishment of a graduated system of scholarships to aid poor boys and girls to proceed from elementary schools to intermediate schools and the university colleges.

The first resolution passed called for the establishment 'of numerous and efficient Intermediate schools', whilst the second, proposed by Elizabeth Hughes and seconded by Dilys Davies, stated 'that this Conference is of the opinion that in any provision for Intermediate Education in Wales, the interests of girls should be considered equally with those of boys'.[60]

Unsurprisingly, the need for legislation for intermediate education figured very prominently in the deliberations. But the cause of female education was also given a most influential platform. It was discussed in the morning sitting on 5 January, when Elizabeth Hughes took up the cudgels in a lengthy, philosophical treatise on behalf of the daughters of her native land. Whilst alluding to the contemporary debate concerning the merits of differentiating between the education courses of boys and girls, she emphasized that 'at present, the only course open to us is to give boys and girls not only equal, but similar educational advantages'.[61] She did not subscribe to the view that a similar education for boys and girls would have an adverse effect on 'womanliness'. The study of Plato and the sciences did not make a female 'unwomanly'. Further, she demanded that every council and committee concerned with girls' education should include female representation.[62]

Dilys Davies pointed out that the principle was adopted in elementary and higher education, and only needed to be implemented in intermediate education. Schools modelled on the girls' public day-schools of England were needed in Wales. In rural areas, where circumstances would not permit the establishment of separate schools for girls, she pleaded for mixed schools, or the addition of a separate wing for girls. Professor Arnold of Bangor also spoke, emphasizing that the effect of passing this resolution would be that the conference endorsed a proposal to include a provision for the co-education of women and men in the Welsh University of the future.

It was also resolved to meet members of both Houses of Parliament to lay the conference resolutions before them. A meeting was duly arranged for 15 March 1888. Arrangements were made by the Cymmrodorion Society for those summoned to the Shrewsbury conference to meet at Westminster Palace Hotel prior to the meeting in Parliament, to name prolocutors.[63] The 'large and influential delegation'[64] including Elizabeth Hughes, Dilys Davies and Miss Armstrong as well as Professor Rhys, Beriah G. Evans, Viriamu Jones, T. Marchant Williams, Isambard Owen and H.R. Reichel was introduced by the Earl of Powis, President of the Cymmrodorion Society, who laid before the MPs the resolutions passed at the conference. Elizabeth Hughes was one of those who spoke at the meeting chaired by Henry Richard MP.[65] The Cymmrodorion Society believed that the Shrewsbury conference and the meeting in Parliament, which had given proper recognition to the claims of women, were significant events in advancing the cause of Welsh education. The action 'had powerfully urged forward the educational movement in Wales, and has caused it to take a very distinct step in advance'.[66] The impetus given by the Cymmrodorion Society made an important contribution towards the eventual legislation in 1889.[67]

By then, there were two intermediate education bills before the country. Early in the 1888 Parliamentary session, both the Kenyon bill, now proposing one board of education for the whole of Wales, and supported by all but one of the Welsh Conservative MPs, and Mundella's bill, approved by all the Welsh Liberal MPs, were again presented to Parliament but there was no further parliamentary progress in 1888.[68] Discussion continued over their respective merits and weaknesses.[69] The provision of intermediate education for girls was part of the debate: referring to the Mundella bill in May 1888, Revd Ellis Edwards expressed the hope that 'in this and similar Bills, the privileges extended to boys will be given to girls also'.[70] But the main issues were those of control, representation, finance and unsectarian education.

There were demands that the Government should introduce a

measure of its own. At the Wrexham National Eisteddfod in September 1888, Isambard Owen expressed the wish that the hand of the Association for Promoting the Education of Girls in Wales would be evident in the preparation of a Welsh Intermediate Education Bill, whenever it saw the light of day.[71] It was a time of much expectation and anticipation regarding intermediate education, but also, many felt that there was little chance of legislation in the immediate future. However, with the dawn of the year 1889, the long quest for legislation for intermediate education reached a successful climax.

By then, the Charity Commission had drawn up new schemes for the Tasker's charity at Haverfordwest and the William Jones charity at Monmouth which ensured that henceforth girls as well as boys would benefit from secondary education.

Furthermore, from their inception, the awards of the North Wales Scholarship Association were intended to be available for girls, as well as boys, of exceptional merit.[72] The involvement of Captain and Mrs Verney in the organization of the scheme was a virtual guarantee that the female interest would not be overlooked. The awards were intended to establish a passage from the elementary schools to grammar and high schools, and eventually the universities. By 1894, £2,453 had been paid out in scholarships and prizes in north Wales. The function of the association was then superseded by the provision for scholarships in the county schemes for intermediate education. Though the number of girls who benefited were comparatively few, for over a decade the association had played an important role at a crucial time in showing equal concern for the education of girls as well as boys. It had also focused attention on the meagre provision of efficient secondary schools for girls. It made a positive contribution towards ensuring that both girls and boys would be beneficiaries from the new scheme of intermediate education.[73]

The 1880s were years of continued success in the three girls' endowed schools in Wales. At Llandaff, Maria Kendall's appointment as headmistress in 1880 initiated significant organizational and curricular changes. The reputation of Dr Williams' School grew steadily with pupils being attracted from England and Ireland, as well as from Wales itself. From 1886 to 1893, Elizabeth A. Fewings was headmistress, and as a member of the Association for Promoting the Education of Girls in Wales, she was to be prominent in advancing the cause of secondary and higher education for women.

At Llandaff, Denbigh and Dolgellau in the 1880s, the girls' secondary schools had endeavoured to place a greater emphasis on academic standards and achievement, rather than accomplishments and trivial pursuits. They reflected a trend also evident in the new girls' high schools in England. Their objective was to redefine the prevailing conception of middle-class femininity in terms of the cultivated wife and mother and to prepare women for a limited, though growing number of acceptable job opportunities. For the modern feminist, they are open to criticism for their failure to challenge the sexual division of labour; to attempt to 'to subvert conventional concepts of femininity'; and to promote radical social change.

Evidence submitted to the Aberdare Committee and other testimonies during the 1880s, showed that secondary education of varying quality was available for girls in non-endowed private schools. In general, they were not regarded as meeting the real educational needs of middle-class girls, and criticisms of their condition strengthened the case for adequate attention to girls as well as boys in the intermediate education schemes of the 1890s. Some of the private schools had functioned for a number of years; others intermittently or for short periods, whilst some were newly established, such as Penrhos College.

By the eve of the Welsh Intermediate Education Act, Swansea was unique in Wales through being the location in 1888 of the only high school opened by the Girls' Public Day School Company in Wales. At the Diocesan High School Carmarthen, there was a modestly successful experiment in providing girls with a sound liberal education based on Christian principles.

Women's educational ideas 1882–1887: advocacy of secondary and higher education in Wales

Women's quest for intermediate and higher education in Wales in the 1880s generated a number of published speeches, addresses and letters. Many were associated with the Cymmrodorion Section of the National Eisteddfod, which ensured that the most influential protagonists in the Welsh political and educational debate were not oblivious to the educational needs of women. Nor could the politicians and educationists have been unimpressed with the considerable maturity of thought displayed.

In 1882, Dr Frances Hoggan was the author of a 59-page book — *Education for Girls in Wales* — published in London by the Women's Printing Society Limited. Much of the work consists of a verbatim account of the conclusions and recommendations of the Aberdare Committee, as well as her own evidence. The Aberdare Report met with her warm approval.[74] She argued that if the Aberdare Committee thought that sixteen boys in every thousand of the population should be receiving education higher than elementary, '. . . an equal number of girls ought also to be receiving it'.[75] Believing that there was an urgent need to extend the provision of girls' education in Wales, and that it was 'a time when the public mind was in a state peculiarly fitted to consider educational questions',[76] she had sent three letters to the *South Wales Daily News* in early 1882. These were not included in full in this volume.[77]

The first letter, dated 23 January 1882, dealt with university co-education.[78] Since the opening of a university college in south Wales was imminent, there should be an informed opinion in the Principality about the merits of co-education.[79] Frances Hoggan referred to co-education in the USA, Switzerland, Holland and France. She argued that many British qualms were not substantiated by the American experience. In the USA, co-education had enabled women to obtain enhanced career opportunities. In Switzerland, women had been admitted to university without any restriction for fifteen years, and had attended mixed classes.

Dr Hoggan favoured the establishment of a separate women's hall of residence in conjunction with a university college in south Wales, though she thought there were also advantages to be gained from some male involvement in the halls' administration.[80] She proposed that those who would be involved with the new Welsh college ought to be aware of the ways co-education was organized in foreign countries. It was essential to concentrate resources for higher education in Wales in co-educational institutions.[81] Later that year, she voiced similar sentiments at the Denbigh National Eisteddfod. Again, she used comparative educational data to support her arguments. She had been invited to read a paper on 'Co-Education at Different Ages' to the Cymmrodorion Section of the Eisteddfod.[82] An awareness of the experience of other countries could 'be helpful to Wales at the educational crisis through which it is now passing'.[83]

In any well structured scheme of education, it was essential that attention was also given to physical training. At this point, she referred to her Froebel lecture of 1879 — *On the Physical Education of Girls* — published in 1880.[84] There she had argued that with children generally, and with girls especially, the training of the physical powers should take precedence over the training of the intellectual powers.[85]

Dr Hoggan's second letter, dated 24 February 1882, focused on 'Intermediate Education for Girls'.[85] For her, it was a matter of urgency that intermediate schooling and higher education be made available for middle-class girls as well as boys. Like many others at the time, her conception of education reform only extended to the middle classes. She elaborated on her suggestion that the Girls Public Day School Company might extend its work into Wales. She had already ascertained that the company would be interested, provided its usual conditions of local co-operation and financial involvement were met.[87] If it was felt that 'the special circumstances of Wales' would not be given suitable attention by 'a managing board living out of Wales and bound to it by no ties of sympathy or kindred', a Welsh Public Day School Company might be established.[88] Though aware that many favoured State aid for the establishment and maintenance of intermediate schools for both boys and girls, she thought that since State aid for higher education in Wales was imminent, it would be wiser '. . . not to make exorbitant demands on the imperial exchequer, and to prove, by patriotic exertions and sacrifices, that a strong desire exists in Wales for sound intermediate education, and that parents are prepared to do what in them lies to obtain it for their sons and daughters'.[89]

A third letter, dealing with 'Endowments for Girls' Education in Wales', 29 April 1882, was returned unpublished, purportedly because of its length.[90] Again, she reiterated views already voiced to the Aberdare Committee. She claimed that the liberal intentions of so many of the Welsh educational endowments had been narrowed and circumscribed over the years by those administering them. In particular, many of them were intended to benefit both girls as well as boys. The Howell endowment was rightly utilized for the exclusive benefit of girls, but '. . . we must lament its wasteful application, its large unemployed surplus in the hands of the Drapers' Company, the practical exclusion of nonconformists from its benefits, and the exclusion of both nonconformists and women from its governing body'.[91] She called for a redistribution of the few endowments that could be utilized for the promotion of girls' intermediate education in Wales.

On matters outside Wales, she drew attention to the Ashford School, Middlesex, and was highly critical of the managers' attempts to forestall the proposals of the Charity Commission by creating a scheme which would retain the school's denominational or Anglican nature, the all-male board of management and the location at Ashford. She also reiterated her arguments in favour of allowing Welsh women to benefit from the £8,000 per annum accruing from the endowments of Jesus College Oxford. She called for '. . . substantial justice be done to girls who until now had been left out in the cold in all Welsh educational schemes'.[92]

Thereafter, Frances Hoggan proceeded to quote approvingly a passage from Lewis Morris: 'Higher Education in Wales' published in *The Contemporary Review* in April 1882, which advocated equal educational opportunities for girls as well as supporting the case for co-education. She concluded by emphasizing the importance of female education for national growth and prosperity.[93]

The following year, at the Cardiff National Eisteddfod 1883, she presided over a meeting of the Cymmrodorion Section of the National Eisteddfod where the main subject of discussion was education in Wales and particularly the education of girls. She also read a paper on *The Past and Future of the Education of Girls in Wales*. She contrasted the inadequate provision for girls' education in Wales with that of England.[94] Her concern was limited to the middle classes, assuming that whilst the labouring classes had already been provided for in 1870, there was '. . . no machinery for adequate schooling of the middle classes'.[95] Between 12,000 and 13,000 girls should be taught at a higher level than elementary education. 'What we have to do now is what we have not done in the past — to educate our middle-class girls'.[96] The education of middle-class girls was lamentably deficient, and for two years she had waited in vain for the formation of a 'Welsh Public Day School Company' or a 'Welsh Women's Education Union' similar to the body that had completed a decade of sterling work in England.[97] She stressed the need for women to be members of the governing bodies of schools and colleges, and was critical of the Council of University College Cardiff for not having a single female member.

As well as referring to the possibility of emulating the work of the Girls' Public Day School Company, she also recognized that since Wales could be regarded as 'educationally virgin soil', other schemes also merited consideration. The Swiss experience with cantonal and advanced schools, and the American methods of financing schools could be worthy of study.

Whilst recognizing that there was room for much divergence of opinion regarding the details of a scheme of intermediate and higher education for girls, there could be unanimity on the basic objective of providing equal educational opportunities for both sexes:

> Patriots, republicans, friends of the people and all who deeply care for the welfare of the Principality, all admit that it is only by making the foundations of education strong and deep — so strong and deep that it will reach not one sex only, but both — that the full measure of national prosperity, of national happiness and usefulness, and of national growth can be attained.[98]

For twenty-five years, this patriot had lived outside the land of her birth, but during a crucial period in the educational history of modern Wales, was to be in the vanguard of the quest for female education in the Principality. She espoused a most enlightened educational philosophy and was no less remarkable as an educational pioneer than as the first woman from Wales to graduate in medicine. She offered a valid diagnosis of the Welsh educational scene and pinpointed the importance of female education for the nation's well-being: '. . . Other nations have to re-model, we have to model and to make, other nations have to cast away from them the outgrown clothes of former systems of teaching; we have little but rags to throw away . . .'.[99] She had appeared suddenly on the Welsh educational scene and remained for only a short period. After the mid 1880s, educational and social reforms in India, the Near East and the USA became the foci of her interest. Following her letter of support in 1886 to the Association for Promoting the Education of Girls in Wales, she appears to have played no further role in the educational affairs of Wales. Though it is difficult to measure the extent of her influence, it is undeniable that she was Wales's leading feminist campaigner in the early 1880s. Thereafter, the cause of female education was championed by others — some of whom had appeared on the same platform as Frances E. Hoggan.

At the Cymmrodorion Section of the Denbigh National Eisteddfod in 1882 with Lewis Morris in the chair, Dilys Davies gave an address on 'A Model School for Girls'. She maintained that the only public schools of any real standing for girls in Wales were Dr Williams' School and the two Howell schools. She thought that Dolgellau could serve as a model for every Welsh county to establish new schools for upper and middle-class girls. Dolgellau had a scheme of management 'permeated by a broad liberal spirit and practical common sense'.[100] Whilst day-schools ought to be the rule, boarding schools might be justifiably established in certain districts as long as careful attention was given to their internal arrangements. In all the high schools that might be created, it was essential that women were represented on governing bodies.

Dilys Davies justified such developments by emphasizing the formative influence on character and intelligence exerted by an educated mother on a child, particularly during the years of infancy and early childhood.[101] For well-educated women who had to earn their own living, it was a time of increasing job opportunities. Unfortunately, when such contingencies as bereavement caused middle-class women to look for employment, their 'expensive but superficial education' proved disadvantageous.[102] They were compelled to work as nursery governesses, lady helps or household servants.

Careful attention should therefore be given to the curriculum of girls' high schools so as to ensure that 'a well-balanced training of all powers of mind and body' was offered and also provision for the cultivation of special gifts which might be particularly important in the job market. With the training of the body as well as the mind being important, it was essential that human physiology was taught, and adequate attention given to the need for ventilation in school buildings. In boarding schools, particularly as regards sleeping accommodation, both ventilation and privacy were important. Dilys Davies emphasized the importance of the playground in girls' schools and condemned the contemporary prejudice against gymnasia and exercise. The curriculum should include cookery and science, whilst religious instruction should be taught subject to a conscience clause.[103]

Four years later, she addressed the Cymmrodorion Society at the Caernarfon National Eisteddfod in 1886 on 'Higher Education of Girls in Wales'.[104] It was shortly after some considerable publicity had been given to an address by Dr Withers Moore, the President of the British Medical Association, at the annual meeting held at Brighton which had cast doubts on the suitability of women to undertake higher education.[105]

Dilys Davies regretted that 'higher education' was misunderstood by many, and equated with over-pressure, forced intellectual activity, and cerebral strain. She recognized that 'cramming', which occurred in some girls' schools, did have adverse physical and mental consequences. This often occurred when girls of fourteen to sixteen years endeavoured to assimilate a four or five-year course of studies in two years. This had generated unfortunate prejudice against the whole concept of higher education for women. However, there need be no danger as long as the education was well-rounded, balanced, and not one-sided.[106] She was particularly critical of overemphasis on the intellectual domain for the sake of examination success and to the detriment of physical education.

There was no place for mere concentration on the acquisition of accomplishments which characterized so many girls' schools: '. . . that smattering of a foreign language or two, and facility on piano or with pen and pencil as may appear necessary to make her a so-called accomplished member of society . . . instead of developing the powers which are innate, it lays on a thin superficial crust of artificiality'.[107] In these cases, powers of perception, observation, reasoning and sympathy were undeveloped.

Proceeding to examine the educational institutions in Wales, she noted that there was reasonable provision of elementary schools. However, she did not attempt to examine whether they required 'some modification to suit the Welsh characteristics'. She noted that the university colleges were open to both men and women, but she also pinpointed a major weakness in the system of education: 'There is still the fatal gap. We still want the means of bridging over the period between the Primary School standard and that of the University or University Colleges; the circle is incomplete. What have we to supply the means for the Intermediate Education of Girls in Wales?'[108] The existence of only three 'public schools' — at Dolgellau, Denbigh and Llandaff — was highlighted, as was the fact that the most valuable endowment for girls was located outside the Principality at Ashford and was 'of comparatively little value as an educational force in Wales'.[109] As regards the private schools, it was difficult to generalize about their standards, because their work was evaluated according to criteria which varied from school to school.

Though the supply of good schools for girls was clearly inadequate, the speaker felt that there had been no strong demand from parents for greater provision.[110] It was therefore necessary to arouse the enthusiasm of Welsh parents on behalf of their daughters' education, and also to foster a more perceptive appreciation of the nature and implications of a liberal education for girls.

Whilst recognizing that some might use the financial and demographic constraints in an argument against establishing a large number of new girls' intermediate and high schools, she believed that with regard to rural, thinly populated districts, the American experience should be taken into account. Referring in particular to a report on the public schools of St Louis, Missouri, she underlined the financial, pedagogical and social advantages of 'joint-schools'. But, wary of the reaction of her Nonconformist audience, she quoted the section that stated:

> Social intercourse in these joint-schools is not of course left to chance. Girls and boys need and get as careful attention at school as in their own homes. Usually they enter and leave the school building by different doors, and indeed, meet only when they are receiving instructions from the teachers, where they occupy separate forms on different sides of the room.[111]

It was also noted that schools in Scotland followed similar arrangements.

For Wales, the message of comparative education seemed clear: 'If we may not have joint-schools, where boys and girls are actually taught together, could we not institute dual schools, where there could be a girls' side and a boys' side?'[112] This was to be one of the key issues in the implementation of the Welsh Intermediate Education Act in the decade that followed. Whilst taking the opportunity of announcing the formation of an Association for Promoting the Education of Girls in Wales, Dilys Davies suggested specific objectives: the association ought 'to raise the standard or ideal of girls' education and arouse public opinion to a fuller appreciation of its value',[113] investigate the state of education in Wales, and consider the most appropriate methods of establishing new intermediate schools for girls. Significantly, Dilys Davies accepted the hypothesis that only a particular proportion of the population would avail themselves of these educational advantages.

In January 1887, she delivered an address — 'The Problem of Girls' Education in Wales' — to the Liverpool Welsh National Society. Again, she interpreted education as the harmonious development of all the powers of mind, body and spirit. In her view, the exclusion of religious teaching from some elementary schools under the terms of the 1870 Education Act had been misguided. Equally misguided were those who perceived womanhood as requiring no higher education. In fulfilling their duties effectively in the home, and in society at large, where there were growing job opportunities, women would be more effective following a liberal education. She proposed that, though a woman should be well acquainted with the domestic arts, her schooling should not be limited to these: she should also develop a cultivated intelligence.

Again, Dilys Davies reiterated the view that the machinery for the provision of such education for girls in Wales was seriously deficient in intermediate schools. The Anglican domination of the Howell schools and the location of the Ashford school outside the Principality were serious drawbacks. Many girls were sent to schools in England, often at considerable cost, for an unsatisfactory veneer of accomplishments. The lack of efficient intermediate schools contributed to the meagre stream of girls proceeding to the colleges. Legislation to establish intermediate schools for girls as well as boys was imperative. The network ought to include, in every large town, a girls' school similar to that of Dr Williams, or those schools opened by the Girls' Public Day School Company. In rural districts, the experience of America, Norway and Scotland suggested the feasibility of co-education. Here she quoted from Dr Hoggan's writings on co-education in the United States.[114] If co-education in mixed schools was too great an innovation, dual or joint schools might be more acceptable.

Dilys Davies also asked for a system of university local examinations which could improve the efficacy of the intermediate schools. She referred to the advantages of such examinations advocated by Dr Sophie Bryant in 1885,[115] and by Principal Reichel in his paper on *The Future of Welsh Education* published by the Association for Promoting the Education of Girls in Wales. Examination of the schools in this way by a future University of Wales would thwart any possible attempt at control by the Education Department in London. It would also link together in a harmonious whole, all the parts of a national educational system. Exhibitions tenable at institutions of higher education could be attached to the local examinations.

Being weary of the delay for an Intermediate Education Bill, she suggested that an Intermediate Education Board be established consisting of representatives of the three university colleges and other institutions of higher education. It might then formulate a scheme of local examinations and of school inspection which could provide a worthwhile yardstick for existing schools.

At the Cymmrodorion Section of the London National Eisteddfod in August 1887, she reiterated her plea for dual or joint schools in rural areas and the adoption of Dr Williams' School as a model for other girls' schools. Unsectarian religious teaching, and the facility of a conscience clause, were recommended for girls' intermediate schools.[116]

Dr Sophie Bryant was also to be closely identified with the movement to advance the education of girls in Wales. Born in Dublin, she had studied at Bedford College, London, served with Miss Beale at Cheltenham and in 1875 was appointed to the staff of the North London Collegiate School. In 1884 she became the first woman to be awarded the degree of Doctor of Science and succeeded Miss Buss as headmistress of the school until her retirement in 1918. In 1894, she was appointed one of the thirteen female members of the Bryce Commission.[117]

Though resident in England for many years, she retained a deep interest in the affairs of her native Ireland, and also in Scotland and Wales. In an article — 'The Sentiment of Nationality' — in March 1886, in the *Dublin University Review* where she discussed the claims of Ireland, Scotland and Wales to be independent nations, Welsh national 'feeling' was not seen as one demanding political separatism.[118]

In 1885, her name, together with that of Dr Frances Hoggan, appeared in the suffragists' letter to the House of Lords in the company of other leading feminists such as Millicent Garrett Fawcett, Frances Power Cobbe, Frances M. Buss, Elizabeth Blackwell, Josephine Butler, Sophia Jex-Blake and Emily Davies.[119]

Also in 1885 at the Cymmrodorion Section of the Aberdare National Eisteddfod, she participated in the discussion following Beriah Gwynfe Evans's paper on 'The Place of the Welsh Language in Education'. She found it difficult to understand why the Welsh Language was not given a central role in a national system of education. In her view, every attempt by the Government to destroy the Welsh language had failed.[120]

She also read a detailed, carefully argued paper to the Cymmrodorion Section on 'Welsh University Local Examinations in Wales' in 1885.[121] She maintained that the establishment of an efficient system of intermediate education was Wales's most pressing need. With an awareness of the relationship between educational systems and their cultural contexts, she called for intermediate education to be attuned to the needs and requirements of Wales and not be a mere transplant: 'The wisest and best of governments cannot give to a manufactured and still less to an improved system, the conscious life and elastic vigour of a native growth'.[122] In her view, 'the development of the national type' was of interest and concern for all nationalities.

She maintained that there were two pre-requisites of a sound system of intermediate education in Wales. Firstly, the means of establishing and maintaining a sufficient number of efficient schools charging moderate fees. Secondly, it was essential that the schools were not associated with any one political party but maintained a 'political equilibrium' to be free from party strife. She was confident that these two conditions, widely approved of in Wales, would be recognized in forthcoming legislation. The intermediate schools established in thinly populated rural areas would still be small. To ensure their efficiency and uniformity of standards, as well as providing mutual stimulus and guidance, it was essential that pupils' performances were determined with reference to the wider community of scholars. Some system of external assessment on the pattern of the Oxford and Cambridge local examinations was essential for boys and girls:

> All the scholars of the country, instead of those within one school are compared; each is judged, with the strict impartiality of personal non-acquaintance, as passing absolute standards of higher or lower degrees, and thus a comparison is instituted whether lists in order of merit are issued or not.[123]

In Dr Bryant's judgement, the university local examinations had played an important role in improving the condition of girls' education in England. In Wales also, the education of girls and boys, and the work of their teachers, would benefit from the stimulus of public examinations.

In theory, the organization of a system of examinations might be undertaken either by the State through the Education Department, or by the Welsh university colleges. Dr Bryant considered it highly undesirable that this role should be assumed by the State alone, because of the likelihood of some form of 'payment by results', inspection and control. The involvement of the university colleges was therefore crucial.

Though a university of Wales did not yet exist, a joint examining body could be established by the councils of the three university colleges to organize a system of local examinations. The colleges should act immediately and not wait for legislation for intermediate education. The machinery would then be established and would show the potential efficiency of the examination system. Unless the colleges took the initiative, Dr Bryant anticipated that state involvement could lead to control which was the inevitable corollary of state funding of intermediate education.

Dr Bryant recognized that there was one other alternative — examinations by the universities of Oxford and Cambridge. However, because of 'an instinct to preserve essential nationality under extraordinary difficulties',[124] control by an English university was unacceptable. Education in Wales should be subject to self-control by the Welsh themselves.[125]

In the discussion following the reading of Dr Bryant's paper, there were significant contributions from Principal Viriamu Jones, Principal H.R. Reichel and T. Marchant Williams. At University College Cardiff, the Senate had already established a committee to consider the feasibility of its future involvement in school examination and had already concluded that the task would be more than their overburdened staff could undertake. However, Principal Jones supported Dr Bryant's proposal for a central board comprising of representatives of all colleges, together with external assistant examiners. Her speech had underlined the need for a university of Wales to be established at the same time as intermediate schools. Principal Reichel also agreed with Dr Bryant's preference for university rather than state examination of intermediate schools. He was afraid of the consequences of centralization, and also wary that it would lead to the introduction of the system of payment by results already implemented in the elementary schools and in intermediate schools in Ireland: 'Under this system the pupil is not a mind to be trained, but a possible instrument by which fees may be wrung from an exacting and suspicious government'.[126] T. Marchant Williams was also fearful of a state-imposed mechanical system of 'payment of results', and in agreement with the sentiments voiced in favour of examinations and inspections being regulated by the university colleges: 'This is the only way to impose upon our system of education, the impress of our national character'.[127]

The following year, 1886, at Caernarfon, Dr Bryant participated in the lengthy discussion following Miss Dilys Davies's paper. She emphasized that women had been deprived of the opportunity of advancement, and were entitled to receive the same educational opportunites as men. In January 1887, at Cardiff, she addressed the first public meeting of the Association for Promoting the Education of Girls in Wales which was to receive her staunch support and to whose publications she made valuable contributions.

The name of Elizabeth P. Hughes became prominent in Wales for the first time in 1883. At that period, she was a student at Newnham College, Cambridge. Although absent from the 1883 National Eisteddfod at Cardiff, her paper on 'The Future of Welsh Education with special reference to the Education of Girls' was read out by T. Marchant Williams at the Cymmrodorion section meeting.[128] She believed that Wales stood at the dawn of a new era in her history. Her paper claimed that it was essential that before taking decisive steps regarding the country's edcuational future, careful consideration should be given to the needs and conditions of the Principality, rather than the mere adoption or transplantation of an English system. Furthermore, Wales could learn from the mistakes and weaknesses of her neighbour who had also been constrained and hindered by the weight of educational customs and ideas.[129] English education lacked a definitive aim, allowed too much importance for competitive examinations, overemphasized the learning of facts in such subjects as history, and was slow in introducing such subjects as the sciences.

In Elizabeth Hughes's view, any effective national scheme of education in Wales should recognize the difference in requirements and conditions between Wales and England. Music and poetry ought to be given prominence because 'the Welsh nation has shown an especial aptitude for music and poetry. The Eisteddfod is a noble monument of this fact'.[130] Whilst a non-religious education might be acceptable in England, she doubted whether this would even satisfy Wales, where the desire was for a religious but unsectarian education.

She gave particular attention to the education of girls and advocated the establishment of a Welsh Girls' Day-school Company. She felt it important that girls were taught hygiene and cookery. However, whilst recognizing the need for curricular differentiation between boys and girls, she considered it essential that for both sexes, education involved initiation into culture: 'I do not wish to depreciate the value of culture as culture in women's education'.[131]

At the Liverpool National Eisteddfod in 1884, with Lord Aberdare and Miss Gladstone adjudicating, Elizabeth Hughes won a £25 prize donated by John Roberts MP, for a substantial essay on 'The Higher Education of Girls in Wales with practical suggestions as to the best means of promoting it'.[132] The essay enunciated a detailed scheme of education, focusing, at the outset, on key parameters. Firstly, national character could not be overlooked in a scheme of education for Wales:

> Let us have a national education to preserve and develop our national type ... An ideal Welsh education must be national. It must differ from an ideal English education primarily because of the difference of race ... Differences of race, far from being a subject for regret, as far as possible should be deepened and perpetuated. The differences of race found within the bounds of the British Empire can become a source of strength and completeness.[133]

Like others of the same ilk in late-nineteenth-century Wales, Elizabeth Hughes appeared to find no conflict of interest in advancing national claims within an imperial framework. Wales needed its own system of education, so as to be able to play an effective role within the larger sphere of Empire.

Language was also part of the backdrop. With a million people speaking Welsh, she believed, somewhat optimistically, that if the language were recognized in the educational institutions, it could provide an inducement to a more prolonged period of study. In a scheme of Welsh higher education, the Welsh language should figure at least as an optional subject.[134] The religious division in the Principality made it essential that the educational system was unsectarian.[135]

It was also essential that there was a clear understanding throughout Wales that the primary purpose of higher education was the development of the individual though the acquisition of a liberal education.[136] The writer distinguished between a liberal education and a technical or professional education. Whilst recognizing that higher education could be valuable for the fulfilment of various occupational roles, that was not its primary objective. She acknowledged that the means of acquiring a liberal education was one of the most controversial issues of the day. Many regarded the study of the classics as the essence of a liberal education. However in the writer's judgement, it was the mode of teaching and study rather than the content that was crucial: 'Any subject if taught philosophically can be used as a means of a liberal education'.[137] The attributes of a liberal education were a philosophic habit of mind, a balanced judgement, and a perception of basic principles.

A professional and a technical education could, simultaneously, also be a liberal one. With detailed references to the history of European civilization, she maintained that there were solid reasons for regarding the study of German, and especially philosophy and art, as valuable as the classics in being effective instruments of higher education.[138] They provided the best material for the cultivation of mental culture.

The principle of curricular differentiation also needed consideration. Whilst acknowledging that girls and boys were likely to pursue dissimilar careers, Elizabeth Hughes believed that precise curricular differences would be difficult to determine. A scientific-based course in cookery, nursing and hygiene, and an artistic course in dressmaking and house decoration might well replace chemistry, physiology and painting, but the basic content of the education of both sexes should be the same. Educated women, themselves, might decide on further differentiation in the future.[139]

The pivot of the proposed scheme was the establishment of a 'Union for Promotion of Higher Education in Wales' with a committee representing a wide range of educational opinion specially responsible for the higher education of girls. It might consider launching a Welsh Girls' Public Day School Company with the object of opening a high school in any town where the inhabitants were willing to become shareholders. Since it was essential that there was a national ethos and dimension to education in Wales, it would be impractical to extend the activities of the existing Girls Public Day School Company into Wales. The schools would be unsectarian, and their fees, at no more than £8 per annum, would be relatively low. If such schools were ever to be economically viable, particularly in small towns, the greatest economy would be necessary. In particular, it was essential to follow American experience and adopt the principle of co-education, which would be advantageous in terms of buildings, resources and staffing. Initially, a 'twin school' was likely to be more acceptable than a fully-fledged mixed establishment.[140]

The possibility of enabling girls to share the endowments of existing grammar schools needed to be explored. If that were not feasible, communities might consider the possibility of starting, through public subscription, girls' high schools, which would be attached to existing boys' schools.

It was vital that teaching staff were well trained and more effectively deployed than in existing girls' schools. In particular, the best possible advantage should be taken of specialists in such subjects as science and geology, through using 'visiting teachers' to deliver a series of lectures to pupils from groups of schools.

Since the schools were to form a national system, they should be established with a certain uniformity of character, though there ought to be some degree of differentiation. The curriculum should not be a slavish emulation of English schools: 'It seems very undesirable that we should be fettered by the English course of study'.[141] It was suggested that girls' schools in England placed too much emphasis on written work at the expense of oral work. In girls' schools in Wales, it was essential that adequate attention was given to the spoken as well as the written word.[142] The danger of subjecting girls too soon to the over-pressure of external examinations, particularly when the medium of examination for a great many would be their second language, was also underlined.[143]

The essay recognized that the supply of private girls' schools in Wales had never been large. The writer estimated that approximately 1,300 girls attended establishments where the average enrolment was twenty-six pupils. These schools were obliged to charge low fees, with £6 per annum being the average. The quality of the teaching was poor, and many of the pupils were the daughters of farmers who only stayed for short periods of a term or one year. The better-off families sent their daughters to schools in England.[144]

It was suggested that if the three endowed grammar schools for girls were placed in the hands of a Welsh Girls' Day School Company, their funds could be utilized far more economically. It was essential that they be made unsectarian so as to meet the educational requirements of the Welsh community.

The establishment of a scholarship system was also advocated in order to link the elementary schools, high schools and provincial colleges. Until a university of Wales were established, scholarships tenable at English universities would be desirable.[145]

As well as discussing the provision of high schools, Elizabeth Hughes's scheme emphasized the need for suitable arrangements for women students in the three provincial Welsh colleges. It was essential that there were female hostels attached to the colleges at Aberystwyth, Cardiff and Bangor. As well as overcoming the moral evils of the alternative system of boarding-out, hostels could be eonomically viable residential units and provide necessary supplementary teaching to the main college course.

The provision of continuing education or aiding 'the self education' of girls who had left school was also advocated. An excellent model, worthy of emulation, already existed in the form of the Cambridge Extension Scheme, the Cambridge Correspondence Class and the Women's Lending Library. The writer was also aware of a correspondence class organized by women at Boston, USA. The proposed committee might consider establishing libraries, museums, loan exhibitions and associated lecturers in Wales. There was also scope for organizing evening classes in a variety of popular subjects. The Welsh people's love of music would be encouraged through lectures and singing classes.[146]

An efficient complement of trained teachers was essential for the implementation of this scheme: 'The best, and most rapid way to educate a nation, is to educate its teachers'.[147] One of the weaknesses of the system of education in England was the lack of adequate training for women teachers in secondary and high schools. Whilst recognizing that it was not financially possible at the time to open a training college in Wales for women teachers in high schools, the essay suggested that the committee could contribute towards improving their educational and pedagogical competence through organizing lectures on education, providing information about education on the continent and in the USA, administering a lending library of education books, and establishing scholarships for teachers tenable at English colleges, but conditional on taking up appointments for a specific period in Wales. The writer hoped that eventually the majority of teachers in Wales would be Welsh and that an association of male and female teachers of all grades would be formed in the Principality.[148] She also suggested that the committee might establish a Welsh technical college in which there would be a female department. The reform of the eisteddfodau was also advocated, with more attention given to educational issues. The National Eisteddfod, and particularly the educational section of the Cymmrodorion, could provide a suitable focus for the deliberations of the proposed 'Education Union' and Welsh teachers' union.

The implementation of these proposals would require large sums of money and the writer recognized this. She hoped that the Government would provide Aberystwyth with a grant equivalent to the provision being made for Bangor and Cardiff. Ireland had been given money for the building of the Queen's Colleges and also Scotland for the new university building at Glasgow. Though there was no precedent for government aid to intermediate education, circumstances were changing, and with the State already providing funds for elementary and higher education, there appeared to be no reason why intermediate education should not be supported. In Wales, where it was doubtful that fees would meet expenses, government grants for the purchase of sites and erection of buildings for high schools would be most welcome.

Though the establishment of a degree-awarding, university of Wales was a long-term rather than an immediate possibility, a national university was nevertheless viewed as essential: 'It is necessary that our education should be national, and for a perfect national education, a University is an essential requirement'.[149] The most feasible way of implementing plans for the university in Wales was seen as the formation of an examination board constituted from the staff of the three provincial colleges which would themselves be affiliated. The suggestion of the worthlessness of a Welsh University degree was rejected, and the writer believed that it would be at least equivalent to a Cambridge ordinary degree.

In January 1887, at the first public meeting of the newly formed Association for Promoting the Education of Girls in Wales, Elizabeth Hughes gave an address on 'The Education of Welsh Women' where she reiterated a number of key arguments.[150] Conscious of the differences between the Welsh and English, she favoured eventual Welsh control of their system of education:

> I think it is of vital importance that the Welsh should have a large amount of Home Rule in matters educational, so that in the future those who can alone rightly guide the plan of differentiation should have the power to effect the change.[151]

Whilst recognizing the eventual need for the educational system to differentiate adequately between the requirements of the two sexes, initially the provision for both boys and girls was likely to be similar. To ensure that teachers in girls' high schools were satisfactorily trained, she called for the establishment of a fund to be used to provide professional training for prospective female teachers at the three Welsh colleges.

The following summer she read a paper at an influential meeting of the Cymmrodorion Section of the London National Eisteddfod in August 1887.[152] Referring to the commercial rivalry of other countries, such as Germany, she underlined the economic value of education and the relationship between the provision of education and the strengthening and improvement of the Welsh race: 'Our greatest national need at present is an excellent national education . . . in that national education, a very important part is the Higher Education of Welsh women'.[153]

The girls' schools would have to be unsectarian, co-educational and primarily day schools. Women would be members of governing bodies.

Again, the national dimension was emphasized — schools in Wales would differ in some respects from those in England and should be administered from within the Principality: 'It is absolutely necessary we should keep our education in our own hands. It is Wales which can best decide what is good for itself'.[154] She rejected the arguments that higher education would damage a woman's health and render her 'unwomanly'. It was essential to realize that '. . . no nation can develop rapidly when half of it is being left behind'.[155]

Though a new concept of femininity was being advanced, and sympathy voiced in the columns of *Y Frythones* in 1887, it is also significant that the last word in the Cymmrodorion's discussion on the education of women — by Myddleton Evans — showed that the traditional Victorian ideal of womanhood was far from forgotten: '. . . If they thought they could make their way as doctors, or lawyers, or anything else, he would say let them have a chance. Only do not let them unwomanise themselves'.[156]

(iii)   *The Association for Promoting the Education of Girls in Wales (1886–1901) — its formation, objectives and leaders*

In 1886, the Association for Promoting the Education of Girls in Wales was formed, and during a decade of vital significance for education in Wales, it was to be active in the struggle for equal opportunities for girls in intermediate and higher education.

As with other important educational movements in Victorian Wales, it grew from small beginnings. A group of friends held a meeting in London, and voiced concern regarding the apathy and indifference shown to the education of girls in many parts of Wales. At the meeting held on 9 June 1886, Miss Dilys Davies assumed a high profile.[157] They decided to form an association with three main aims:

> . . . to diffuse knowledge as to what constitutes a good school and college of education for girls, and to point out the best means of securing it under the special conditions of life in Wales.

> . . . to collect information as to the present condition of education for girls in the various districts of the Principality.

> . . . to watch over the interests of girls in any future legislation affecting education, and in the re-arrangement of Welsh educational endowments.[158]

It was then decided to form a small provisional committee of twenty-two men and women, who had already expressed interest in the scheme. They included the principals of the three university colleges —

T. Charles Edwards, H.R. Reichel and J. Viriamu Jones — and other notable luminaries of late Victorian Wales, both male and female. Fifteen men and seven women were listed as members of this committee. They included T.E. Ellis MP, Professor Henry Jones, Dr Isambard Owen, A.C. Humphreys-Owen, T. Marchant Williams, W. Cadwaladr Davies, W.E. Davies, London and R.D. Roberts, Cambridge. Mrs Verney, Rhianfa, Bangor and Miss Dilys Davies, London, who were to be the leading figures of the association, were appointed honorary secretaries. Elizabeth Hughes, now Principal of Cambridge Training College, was also to be a leading supporter of the association from these early days. A prospectus was circulated, and this attracted more members to the association. Surprisingly, Frances Hoggan does not appear to have been a member, though she did send a letter of support to an important meeting held in Caernarfon in 1886. Also, Dilys Davies was informed in a letter from W. Cadwaladr Davies that '. . . Mrs Frances Hoggan feels strongly on the question and she gave evidence to the Aberdare Committee'.[159] Gee welcomed this initiative, noting that though the establishment of three university colleges had done a lot to extend educational opportunities to girls, there was a great need for intermediate schools.[160]

At the National Eisteddfod held in Caernarfon in September 1886, the Cymmrodorion Society placed one of its meetings at the disposal of the association. W.E. Davies had been a staunch supporter of such action.[161] The decision was welcomed because of the importance of the topic to be discussed.[162] A paper on 'Higher Education of Girls in Wales' was read by Miss Dilys Davies of London.[163] A resolution approving the formation of the association was passed unanimously on the motion of Isambard Owen, seconded by T.E. Ellis MP.

The Cymmrodorion Section of the National Eisteddfod was under the management of the Honourable Society of Cymmrodorion and had been established for the purpose of holding meetings in conjunction with the National Eisteddfod at which '. . . papers on science, literature and other subjects relating to the development of the national resources of the Principality and the intellectual advancement and general well-being of the inhabitants may be read and discussed'.[164] Its progenitor was Sir Hugh Owen.[165] In 1861, he founded the Social Science Section of the National Eisteddfod. It had lapsed but was re-established in 1879 as the Cymmrodorion Section of the Eisteddfod.[166] Already at the Denbigh National Eisteddfod in 1882, and at Cardiff in 1883, Frances Hoggan, Dilys Davies and Elizabeth Hughes had voiced the great need for female education in Wales. Henceforth, for more than a decade, the

Cymmrodorion Section of the National Eisteddfod was to be a vitally important platform for the newly founded feminist association.[167]

The foundations of the association were consolidated early in 1887 when meetings were held in Liverpool and Cardiff. On 11 January 1887, the Welsh National Society of Liverpool allocated one of its meetings to the association. Dilys Davies read a paper on 'The Problem of Girls' Education in Wales' and thirty new members were enrolled.[168] A week later, on 17 January 1887, the first annual meeting of members of the association was held in Cardiff with Principal Viriamu Jones presiding. Following a proposal by Dr R.D. Roberts, Clare College, Cambridge, seconded by Miss Fewings of Dr Williams' School, Dolgellau, the association was now formally constituted, its rules defined, and an annual subscription of 2*s*. 6*d*. agreed upon. The committee was to consist of twenty-four members, and it was resolved that those on the provisional committee, together with two other members, be elected as the committee for the year 1887. That evening, with the Mayor of Cardiff presiding, the first public meeting of the association was held, with addresses given by a number of prominent figures including Elizabeth Hughes, Dilys Davies, Principals Reichel and Viriamu Jones and Professor Thomas Powell of Cardiff and Professor John Rhys of Oxford.[169]

On 15 April 1887, a meeting of the association was held at the Queen's Hotel Assembly Rooms in Aberystwyth. The chairman, Principal T. Charles Edwards, underlined the great need for female education in Wales, and stressed the importance of careful thought and deliberation regarding the means of fulfilling their objectives:

> The object was clear, but the way to obtain that object seemed to be somewhat indefinite. They were groping in the dark, They had gone there with no cut and dried plan, but to assist one another with suggestions.[170]

Letters of support from a number of influential figures in late-Victorian Wales were read.[171] A resolution proposed by Elizabeth Hughes and seconded by William Williams HMI, was passed. It called for the education of girls to be an essential element in any intermediate education bill brought before Parliament. At the Cymmrodorion Section of the London National Eisteddfod in August 1887, prominence was given to the association and a resolution calling for equal provision for girls and boys in any legislation for intermediate education.

The association's formation was primarily due to the failure of the Mundella education bill of 1885 to make any special provision for the education of girls.[172] Unless they were specifically mentioned in such

legislation, girls tended to be passed over.[173] The association's formation also embodied a desire for equal opportunities for girls within
schools and for women on governing bodies. One of the association's
staunchest supporters was Principal J. Viriamu Jones, who regarded the
education of women as an essential concomitant of realizing 'the democratic ideal'. Equality of educational opportunity came to be interpreted in terms of curricular assimilation and uniformity. It was
deemed essential that women could show that they could reach the
same intellectual heights as men. At the first public meeting of the
association at Cardiff in January 1887, Elizabeth Hughes commented
that 'As men and women are essentially different, and have a different
work to do, I believe that eventually their education will differ; but at
present, our one chance as women of equal education is to receive a
similar one'.[174] Likewise, Dr R.D. Roberts called for a non-sexist
approach to women's education. They needed to be educated for every
position in life.

There was also a feeling that female education in Wales lagged
behind other parts of Great Britain. In 1887, Dr R.D. Roberts calculated that whilst there were about 4,000 boys in private adventure
and endowed schools, there were about 2,000 girls in private adventure
schools in Wales. It was assumed at the time of the Aberdare inquiry
that approximately ten out of every 1,000 boys in Wales ought to be
attending intermediate schools. There ought, therefore, to be 15,000
rather than 4,000 boys in intermediate schools. He saw no reason why
the estimate of girls attending intermediate schools should be any
lower. Not only was the provision of schooling for girls exceedingly
inadequate, but also the quality of the teaching in private adventure
schools was often very mediocre. Miss Fewings called for the more
equitable redistribution of existing endowments so as to provide unsectarian education for more pupils. In 1887 the association were advised
by William Williams HMI that because of their high fees, private
schools were beyond the reach of a large proportion of the lower middle
classes.[175]

It is also evident that some members of the association desired to
regard Wales as a national educational entity. In 1887, Dilys Davies
referred to '. . . the bounden duty of every patriotic Welshman to
further the 'national ideal'.[176] Such late-Victorian students of comparative education as Sir Michael Sadler would have concurred with Miss
Hughes's plea for a nation's system of education to be an organic
growth embodying that society's key traits and determinants rather
than an extraneous transplant. In Elizabeth Hughes's words:

> No system of education now prevalent would suit Wales . . . Every nation must make its own system, they could not transplant the Scotch nor the English, nor the German, nor the American to Wales, and make it practicable. They must make their own system in Wales.[177]

> I do not believe that there is any force strong enough to keep our nationality for us except the force of education . . . If we accept the education of England, in due time we shall become Anglicised. If we work at our own education we shall remain Welsh.[178]

In the 1890s, when Cymru Fydd was a force in the Principality, the issue of nationality was under much discussion. In an address to the Cymmrodorion Society on 28 March, 1895 Elizabeth Hughes claimed that '. . . if there is anything in nationality, then we must have a national education'.[179] She rejoiced in the fact that university and secondary education in Wales were 'at last in our own hands' and hoped that this would soon also be the position regarding elementary education. Indeed she called for the establishment of a Welsh education department. In an article — 'A National Education for Wales' — she stressed 'the need to keep the enormous force of education in our own hands. Our University education and our secondary education are practically so already. We must get our elementary education into our hands also'.[180] By 1901, in an address entitled 'The Renaissance in Education in Wales' to the Cymmrodorion Society of California, she was euphoric about the transformation in Wales since 1850. It was now 'a part of Britain where a national system of education was most perfectly organized'.[181]

Though, in general, Social Darwinism tended to consolidate traditional attitudes towards the role of women in the late nineteenth century, members of the Association were to employ such evolutionary concepts as 'the quality of the race' and 'the struggle between different races' to promote the cause of female education. At the Denbigh National Eisteddfod in 1882, where Miss Dilys Lloyd Davies addressed the Cymmrodorion Section on 'A Model School for Girls', she viewed the Dr Williams' School as a model upon which to found new schools, which '. . . alone can give our girls a fair chance of receiving such an education . . . as will enable them to leave a lasting impression for good upon the succeeding generations of our race'.[182]

The clearest exponent of Social Darwinism was Elizabeth Hughes. At the first public meeting of the association in Cardiff in January 1887, she said that '. . . the civilised world has yet to learn the power of women, and how to use it for the advancement of civilisation. No race can nowadays prosper greatly if half of it is uneducated or badly educated'.[183] For her, the well-being of the Welsh nation and the healthy progress of the race required an educated womanhood:[184]

> Men and women being so different, I believe that in the future, educated women will grasp some aspect of truth that has not yet been perceived, and that in their hands lies the key of some hidden mysteries and of some social problems, which the world will never understand until they open the door.[185]

She referred to an address — 'Race and Nationality' — given at the opening of the Cymmrodorion Section of the 1886 National Eisteddfod by Isambard Owen. It was later published as a pamphlet by the association. It delineated the history of the Welsh from the time of the Celtic invasions, focused on 'the Stock of the Welsh people', and attempted to define 'our racial position in the British Islands'. Owen's argument then turned to the necessity of intermediate education:

> Deprived of education, a Welshman is an organism incomplete, lacking its perfect development. His intellectual capacities are his fighting arm. What can avail him in the battle of life if his right arm be withered and stunted from childhood . . . The question is one of life and death for the country.[186]

Once again in 1887, this time at the Cymmrodorion Section of the National Eisteddfod at London, Elizabeth Hughes focused on the concepts of race and nationality, stating that 'education is a power of immense force — how immense the world has little conception. The Germans conquered the French in the Franco-Prussian War because of their better education, and the French sufficiently realized this to devote much energy to French education'.[187] She maintained that during an age of intense commercial rivalry, particularly from the Germans, 'a highly-educated man or woman is placed at an immense advantage in the world's battle . . in the struggle for existence which is going on now'.[188]

The association centred especial attention on the need for a Welsh Intermediate Education Act which provided equal opportunities for girls as well as boys. In a pamphlet — *The Problem of Girls' Education in Wales* (1887) — Miss Dilys Davies expressed weariness at waiting for the Welsh Intermediate Education Act and proposed the establishment of an intermediate education board consisting of representatives of the three university colleges and other institutions of higher education. The board would plan local examinations and school inspection, and thereby establish a standard by which existing schools could test their proficiency.

In 1888, when the Charity Commission was considering a sum of money accruing from the Monmouth School endowment, they were petitioned by the association for a portion to be allocated for the foundation of a high school for girls in Monmouth.[189] In June 1889, the association expressed satisfaction that the commissioners' draft scheme regarding the Monmouth endowment included provision for the education of girls. This was seen as 'a most liberal' proposal.[190]

In 1888, the association decided to establish an exhibition fund to provide financial awards for 'deserving and promising students'. It was thought that they might be used to supplement scholarships awarded to girls by the North Wales Scholarship Association or any other similar organization established in Wales, and also to assist female students in their studies in the University of Wales or in teacher training-colleges. Already, £50 had been donated by one of the association's members — Owen Owen of Liverpool.[191]

At Shrewsbury during January 1888, Dilys Davies and Elizabeth Hughes represented the association at a public conference on Welsh education and ensured that a resolution was carried stating that in any provision for intermediate education in Wales, 'the interests of girls would be considered equally with those of boys'.[192] Thereafter, they represented the association in a deputation which lobbied Welsh members of both Houses of Parliament on 15 March 1888, and Miss Hughes spoke in support of the claims of girls.[193]

In June 1889, with the Intermediate Education Bill in its final critical stage in the House of Commons, a meeting of the association was held at Blaenau Ffestiniog. T.E. Ellis MP, who was playing a crucial role in the Parliamentary deliberations, emphasized the need in an increasingly competitive age for girls to be given the same educational opportunities as boys.[194] At the same meeting, Professor J.E. Lloyd claimed that the cause of female education had not become prominent sooner because of male self-interest and the prevalence of the misguided idea that girls only needed a short period of education. Professor Henry Jones and the Reverend T.J. Wheldon called for the education measure to ensure that women would be adequately represented on every committee formulating schemes for intermediate education. The Ffestiniog School Board was congratulated for providing advanced elementary education for girls as well as boys. In this respect, it was one of the most innovative boards in Wales, and owed a great deal to the vision of Revd T.J. Wheldon, the father of a future Permanent Secretary in the Welsh Department of the Board of Education. He was a staunch supporter of intermediate education for girls as well as boys.[195]

By 1890, when joint education committees were being established throughout Wales to prepare schemes to implement the new legislation, the association decided to formulate a draft scheme embodying its views as to the kind of intermediate education needed to cater adequately for girls. Copies, dated January 1890, were sent to joint education committees and county councils throughout Wales. The document — 'Outline Scheme for Girls' Schools' — considered in detail the merits and disadvantages of the three possible variants that might be adopted according to the circumstances of the locality: separate girls' schools, dual schools and the conversion of private schools. Attention had been given to T.E. Ellis and Ellis Jones Griffiths's *Intermediate and Technical Education in Wales* which influenced the planners of intermediate education in numerous counties.

Although it was implicit in the legislation of 1889, and evident from the deliberations of the joint education committees during 1890 and 1891 that girls were to be given the same educational opportunities as boys, the association kept a watchful eye on the educational planners. Throughout the decade, the association sought to ensure that women throughout Wales acquainted themselves with the organization of the new intermediate schools and made certain that the interests of girls were safeguarded and promoted by the joint education committees and county governing bodies.[197]

In 1890, the association published pamphlets by A.H.D. Acland MP, on *Welsh Education* and Miss E.A. Carpenter's *Mixed Classes in Intermediate Schools* translated into Welsh by Revd Daniel Rowlands. At the fourth annual meeting at UCNW Bangor in September 1890, which was addressed by Professor Rhys, Mrs Verney, Mr J. Bryn Roberts and others, it was stressed that '. . . the distribution of literature of this kind is of considerable importance at the present crisis in Welsh education as it assists in forming a healthy public opinion on the subject of Girls' Education in the Principality'.[198]

At the eighth annual meeting of the association in Caernarfon in July 1894, an analysis of the various county schemes was given by Mrs Glynne Jones.[199] Attention was focused on the need for equal representation on governing bodies and equal status for headmistresses in dual schools. By the end of the decade, numerous issues pertaining to girls' education had been regularly highlighted. They included co-education, curriculum content and differentiation, the status and position of women headteachers in dual schools, and representation on governing bodies.

For over a decade, the association's leading protagonists were Lady Verney, Miss Dilys Davies (later Mrs Glynne Jones) and Miss E.P. Hughes. In 1935 it was stated that '. . . Lady Verney and Mrs Glynne

Jones, then Miss Dilys Davies, did for Wales what Mrs Emily Davies and her helpers were doing for England'.[200] Lady Verney, born Margaret Hay Williams at Bodelwyddan in 1884, married Captain Verney RN, and inherited 'Rhianfa', Anglesey, from her father, Sir John Hay Williams. This became her home in north Wales, though her main residence was the Verney family seat at Claydon, Buckinghamshire. There, where Florence Nightingale was a frequent visitor, Lady Verney collaborated with a relative on a two volume history of the Verneys of Claydon in the seventeenth century which was published in the 1890s. She had stressed the case for girls' education to the Aberdare Committee at Bangor in October 1880 and was to become Honorary Secretary and President of the Association for Promoting the Education of Girls in Wales. She was a member of the Council of UCNW from 1889. In 1916, the Privy Council chose her to be a member of the Council of the University of Wales, a post she held until her death in 1930. Her services to Welsh education were recognized in 1919 with the award of an Honorary Doctorate of Law by the University of Wales.[201] In an obituary in 1930, Principal D. Emrys Evans remarked that 'Lady Verney's name will be specially associated with the growth of higher education in Wales from its infancy . . . She was especially devoted to the cause of higher education for the women of the Principality'.[202]

Miss Dilys Davies, of 5 Gordon Square, London, in 1887, later Mrs Dilys Glynne Jones of Bangor, was one of the association's secretaries until 1898 when she was succeeded by Elizabeth Hughes. Thereafter, 'this moving spirit of the association for many years past' became Vice-President. She was the daughter of William Davies 'Mynorydd' an eminent London-Welsh sculptor and member of the Cymmrodorion Society, and sister of Miss Mary Davies a noted singer. In 1887 she taught at the North London Collegiate Schools for Girls where she came into contact with Dr Sophie Bryant who was also to be a staunch supporter of the association. Her interest in education extended to other spheres, and in 1912 she gave evidence on the work of the Central Welsh Board to the Consultative Committee of the Board of Education which eventually published its Report on the Examination of Secondary Schools.[203]

Elizabeth Phillips Hughes, born in 1851 in Carmarthen, was educated at Cheltenham Ladies' College, and taught for four years under the famous Miss Beale, before entering Newnham College, Cambridge where she gained a first in 1884 in moral sciences and was much influenced by Miss Emily Davies and Miss Clough.[204] In 1885, she was appointed the first Principal of the Cambridge Training College for

Women Teachers, established primarily through the efforts of Miss Frances Mary Buss. She held the post for fourteen years and the college was later renamed Hughes Hall after its first principal. During her long life, Elizabeth Hughes proved to be a '. . . tireless worker, and a gifted administrator with a profound interest in education both at home and abroad'.[205] In 1920, she was conferred with an honorary Doctorate of Law by the University of Wales for '. . . her services to Welsh education and social progress'. She was a governor both of University College Cardiff and of the University of Wales, and also an active member of Glamorgan County Council and Education Committee to within a few weeks of her death in 1925 at Barry where she had lived since 1899. She was a major influence in the establishment of the Training College for Women at Barry in 1914. Her death was marked with an obituary in *The Times*, whilst articles in the *South Wales News* and *Western Mail* referred to her as 'A leader among Welsh Women' and her death as 'A great loss to Welsh Education'. She was remembered in particular as 'one of the pioneers in the movement to provide facilities for the higher education of women'.[206]

The association adopted a variety of activities in its campaign, which included meetings, speeches, addresses and petitions, the publication of pamphlets as well as fund raising. The published pamphlets included the work of Dr Isambard Owen, Principal Reichel, Elizabeth Hughes, Dilys Davies, Dr Sophie Bryant, Miss E.A. Carpenter and A.H.D. Acland MP. These were the usual methods of a middle-class Victorian pressure group. By February 1889 the association had over 300 members. However, by 1897, the earlier momentum had been lost, and some members, claiming that the work had now been accomplished, favoured winding up the association.[207] Indeed, by then, little was heard of the movement except for the annual meeting usually held during National Eisteddfod week. However in 1896, the *South Wales Daily News* said that the annual meeting was regarded as one of the most important adjuncts of the Eisteddfod, and still attracted a large audience.[208] In 1897, it was decided that the association be continued, and though the thirteenth annual meeting at Cardiff Town Hall on 21 July 1899 was reported to be well attended, its heyday was past. Two years later the association disbanded. It is difficult to quantify the extent of its contribution to late Victorian educational reform, nevertheless, its basic objective had been accomplished by the dawn of the new century. There was now greater opportunity for girls and women in both secondary and higher education.

In a privately published volume *In Memory of Margaret Maria Lady*

Verney 1881–1930, Mrs Glynne Jones could justifiably claim that the association had successfully influenced the developing system of intermediate and higher education in late Victorian Wales:

> We wished to secure fair play to the claims of girls, and I think we may fairly take some credit for the fact that when the Intermediate Act 1889 came into operation, girls' education received equal attention with that of boys. Then, when the Colleges emerged, and later the Welsh University, the opportunities for women were equal with those for men, and all posts were open to them.[209]

Intermediate and Secondary Education for Girls, 1889–1914

(i)   *The Welsh Intermediate Education Act 1889 and the education of girls*

On 23 February 1889, an Intermediate Education Bill introduced by Stuart Rendel received its first reading in Parliament.[1] Basically, it was a revised version of the bill introduced by Mundella in 1887. County councils would submit plans for intermediate and technical education to the elected board of education for Wales.[2] In *The Cambrian News*, Gibson thought it a more satisfactory measure than the 1885 bill, and welcomed clause 17 in particular, which deemed the Ashford and Howell trusts, and Meyrick fund, to be applicable for the purpose of the bill '. . . with the consent of the governing body or otherwise'.[3]

There was widespread support for the bill's basic principles during the second reading on 15 May 1889.[4] The only dissentient was Stanley Leighton, MP for Shropshire, who objected to the inclusion of the Ashford endowment within the terms of the measure. T.E. Ellis MP, however, rejected the plea for its exclusion and reiterated the Aberdare Report's criticism of the school's geographical location. He drew attention to the meagre provision for girls' education in Wales. He was also critical of the Court of Chancery for changing the Howell trust, which 'had no denominational restrictions whatsoever', into an Anglican endowment which provided two girls' schools with an annual income of £6,500 but '. . . doing no good whatsoever to the great mass of girls in the Principality'.[5] Neither school had a single Nonconformist child nor governor. He proceeded to remind the Commons of the Aberdare Report's recommendation that charitable funds be shared more equitably through the establishment of more girls' schools in Wales. Unsurprisingly, the governors of Howell's School Llandaff unanimously objected to the inclusion of the school in the proposed legislation.[6]

On the understanding that amendments would be introduced by the Government in committee, Rendel's bill was given an unopposed second reading.[7] When the measure came to be discussed in committee, there were ten amendments, the majority of which had been called for during the second reading. The most significant was the establishment of joint education committees consisting of representation of the Privy Council and county councils, rather than the latter on their own, as the key administrative bodies for implementing the terms of the bill.[8] Most surprising was the exclusion of Monmouthshire from the terms of the bill. The Ashford endowment and Meyrick trust also were excluded.

Unsurprisingly, there was much criticism from Nonconformist Wales. It was seen that whilst county councils would have less power, there would now be greater power and influence for the Education Department, Charity Commission and Tory party in the formulation of schemes for intermediate education in the various counties. Three members of each joint education committee would represent the county council, and three would be nominated by the Privy Council.[9] The exclusion of Monmouthshire and the Ashford and Meyrick endowments were viewed as major omissions which would considerably weaken the measure's efficacy. Thomas Gee wanted the bill to be rejected, and intermediate education postponed until after disestablishment of the Church.[10]

When the bill's amendments were dealt with in committee in early July, attention focused primarily on the exclusion of Monmouthshire and on the composition of joint education committees. At a prior meeting, under the chairmanship of Lord Rendel, Welsh MPs had voiced determination to oppose these amendments. With the need for compromise essential if the bill was not to be lost,[11] the exclusion of the Ashford endowment was reluctantly accepted. The Government withdrew the amendment in respect of Monmouthshire and made concessions in respect of Privy Council representation of joint education committees. Two rather than three members, would now be nominated by the Privy Council.[12] With the Government conducting the bill through its final stages in the House of Commons and the Upper House, it received the royal assent on 12 August 1889, and was to be operative on 1 November.

In the process of legislating for intermediate education, the female cause as such had not been a major Parliamentary issue. However, the educational wants of girls had been given attention, particularly in conjunction with the criticism of the Anglican control of the Howell and Ashford schools. In the climate of late Victorian Wales, it was inevitable that Anglican domination of endowed schools should take precedence over any claims of the educational neglect of girls and women. It was also clear that their educational demands would not be divorced from the religious and political conflicts.[13]

By 1889, equal treatment of girls and boys was widely expected from an Intermediate Education Bill. In particular, the Association for Promoting the Education of Girls in Wales — a product of the quest for intermediate legislation — had, during its two-year existence, endeavoured to ensure that the parliamentary legislators for intermediate education would be under no illusions regarding the educational needs of girls. There can be no doubt, that by uniting so many influential people, organizing public meetings and petitions, publishing pamphlets and establishing exhibitions, the association did much to advance the cause of girls' education during the crucial period 1886–9.

Reservations were still being voiced about the legislation. As well as the powers of the Charity Commission, the lack of an elected education board for Wales, the composition and size of county committees, and the loss of the Ashford endowment for girls' education in Wales were also criticized. However, in general, the Welsh Intermediate Education Act was much welcomed.[15] The definition of intermediate education for both sexes in terms of instruction 'in Latin, Greek, Welsh and English Language and Literature, Modern Languages, Mathematics, Natural and Applied Science, or in some of such studies and generally in the higher branches of knowledge' was an opportunity for girls to receive the same intellectual education as boys. The advocates of equality for girls at this time realized the curricular importance of identity of standard — in dual or mixed schools. It was essential to show that the female was of the same intellectual calibre as her male counterpart. The Welsh Intermediate Education Act now provided the opportunity for the intellectual emancipation of the woman, that should, of necessity, be based on a theory of curricular imitation.

In a volume published in 1889 — *The Welsh Intermediate Education Act: How to Use it* edited by W. Cadwaladr Davies — there was an important contribution by Mrs Dilys Glynne Jones, the Honorary Secretary of the Association for Promoting the Education of Girls in Wales on 'The Education of Girls: Some Practical Suggestions'. Whilst recognizing that society in general still placed a higher premium on the education of its sons rather than its daughters, she maintained that '...there is at the same time, a rapidly-growing conviction in the country, that the educaiton of Welsh girls is a pressing necessity and must not be any longer neglected'.[16] In the intermediate schools which were required for girls throughout the Principality, it was essential that the fees be kept low and an accomplishments-oriented curriculum avoided. The course of studies which needed to be both thorough and 'useful' in nature, might be profitably modelled on the curriculum at Dr Williams' School, Dolgellau.

As far as possible, the schools should be self-supporting. But in Dilys Jones's judgement, the financial returns of the Girls' Public Day School Company, and other bodies, showed that this was only possible where schools were organized in rent-free buildings, and where there was healthy enrolment and income from comparatively high fees. An endowment was essential if fees were not to exceed £4 or £5 per annum. In her opinion, the Welsh Intermediate Education Act made this possible, through sanctioning a rate of one halfpenny in the pound.

Dilys Jones was opposed to the monies raised from the rates being deployed for the erection of school-buildings which ought to be provided by each local community: 'Let each locality which feels the need of such a school come forward to provide buildings free of rent'.[17] Schools were needed in the well-populated parts of Wales and especially in the large towns. She foresaw advantages in their location in, or near the university towns of Wales. Able young teachers would be attracted to places where there were opportunities for continuing education and support in their professional work from university lecturers.[18]

The author preferred day-schools to boarding-schools, though she recognized that there was a tradition of Welsh girls attending boarding-schools, because of the paucity of day-schools in the Principality. However, the establishment of boarding-houses in conjunction with day-schools was recommended as a means of providing intermediate education for girls living in outlying districts.

In rural areas, the economic feasibility of establishing dual schools also needed to be explored. She foresaw distinct advantages in terms of staffing and equipment. She even saw the possibility of mixed classes.[19] However, the writer was well aware of the novelty of her proposal and the prejudices of the age.[20] The position and authority of the head-teacher of a dual school needed careful attention. Dilys Jones was determined that women's positions would not be inferior: the quest for female emancipation and equal status demanded nothing less.[21]

The feasibility of adding 'girls' wings' to existing boys' schools in areas which would be unable to support separate girls' schools was also considered. Once again, matters of status and public recognition were not to be ignored. The writer emphasized that the head of the girls' side be well qualified and must enjoy absolute authority.

The editor of the volume, W. Cadwaladr Davies, also focused on dual and mixed schools, viewing them within the wider context of

Welsh educational development. He also foresaw mixed or dual-school arrangements as the only effective means of providing intermediate education for girls in somes areas. Whilst recognizing that there could be 'moral dangers' associated with such arrangements, he felt that the Welsh experience, particularly with Sunday schools, suggested that there was no need for real concern. The architects of intermediate education were soon to find that issues pertaining to co-education and mixed schooling, and others raised in 1889, were more complex than anticipated, as steps were taken to implement the long-sought-for legislation. A powerful lobby was determined that the claims of girls should not be overlooked.

(ii) *The establishment of a new system, 1889–1900*

Conferences of the joint education committees

In accordance with the terms of the Welsh Intermediate Education Act, a joint education committee was to be established in each county and county borough, consisting of three persons nominated by the county council and two persons 'well acquainted with the conditions of Wales and the wants of the people', who were to be nominated by the Lord President of the Council. Each joint education committee was to prepare a scheme or schemes for the intermediate and technical education of their area.

At the conferences of the joint education committees in the early 1890s, certain attention was given to the education of girls, though it was not a major issue. The principle of equal educational opportunities for both sexes had already been accepted by the legislators of 1889.[22] The main deliberations, therefore, concerned fees, the curriculum, and the functions of county governing bodies and local governing bodies. Considerations had also to be given to the respective advantages and disadvantages of mixed, dual and separate schools.

At the first meeting of the north Wales joint education committees in Chester on 12 April 1890, the third item on the agenda was 'the education of girls and the best manner of providing for it in Inter- mediate Schools'. Principal Reichel presented a paper on the subject and considered the merits of dual schools, which were seen as essential, if intermediate schooling was to be economically feasible for girls in some parts of the country. Their first advantage was that they would be much cheaper than the separate boys' and girls' schools. Moreover, he doubted whether the concept of mixed classes, common in the USA and Scandinavia, would meet with approval in north Wales, where he was aware there was strong opposition. Where there was already a good boys' school, such as Friars' School, Bangor, he thought it wiser to establish a separate school for girls. He also thought that in most instances, day-schools were preferable to boarding-schools for religious and social reasons. As well as being cheaper, there would be 'less danger of the religious difficulty appearing', and also 'greater chance of mixture of the different classes of society'. However, it would be desirable to have one or two boarding-schools, such as existed at Howell's Denbigh and Dr Williams', Dolgellau. Except for less provision of classics, there should be little curricular differentiation between girls' and boys' schools.[23]

The 'considerable demand' for girls' education in Montgomeryshire was voiced by A.C. Humphreys Owen as well as the prevalent 'decided opposition to any form of mixed education'. The provision of girls' education had also been considered in Denbighshire, and Thomas Gee said 'Decidedly they were in favour of it'. However, at some centres in Merioneth, the feeling was that the provision at Dolgellau was sufficient.[24]

Subsequent meetings of the joint education committees also gave some attention to various aspects of girls' education. At the third meeting of the north Wales joint education committees in Chester on 19 July 1890, the future role of Howell's School, Denbigh and also female representation on governing bodies were discussed.[25] In the first general conference of the joint education committees of Wales and Monmouthshire at Shrewsbury on 19 September 1890, the position of the Howell schools was raised, and the advantages and disadvantages of mixed and dual schools were considered.[26] At the fourth general conference on 29 May 1891, a report was submitted by Humphreys-Owen and Herbert Lewis on 'The Employment of Women as Teachers'. They referred to the position in Scotland and the USA and concluded that 'the suitability of women for teaching boys or mixed classes in Intermediate Schools may be taken as established as a general rule'.[27]

The prevalence of mixed elementary schools in rural parts of Wales, often under female teachers, was seen as likely to reduce the criticism in those areas of the employment of women as teachers and the establishment of mixed classes in the intermediate schools. In 1892 at Carmarthen, W.J. Evans, Principal of the Presbyterian College, maintained that evidence submitted to the fifth conference of joint education committees at Shrewsbury was overwhelmingly in favour of mixed schools. Problems relating to girls' education were to continue to involve the deliberations and policies of the county governing bodies in the 1890s.

Co-education

In 1898, in its review of the operation of the Welsh Intermediate Education Act, the Board of Education acknowledged that 'the idea of co-education of the sexes was a novel one, and public opinion was certainly unprepared for the general establishment of mixed schools'.[28] As yet, the English high schools had not been faced with this aspect of education. The Endowed Schools Commission and the Charity Commission had considered the feasibility of co-education in the 1870s, but found that there was no real support for the principle. Recent research has shown that neither the Education Department in the late nineteenth century, nor the Board of Education in the early twentieth century encouraged its implementation. In 1895 the Bryce Commission examined co-education in Canada and the United States, and in recommending its adoption in English secondary schools, saw no 'undesirable consequences' but rather 'some special advantages for the formation of character and general stimulus to intellectual activity'.[29] Until the 1890s, co-education was only adopted in the lower classes of elementary schools and a few higher-grade schools.[30]

In Wales, there had been support for the principle of co-education in the 1880s by the pioneers of female education. The implementation of the legislation of 1889 focused attention anew on the implications of different patterns of co-education. There was no unanimity in the 1890s in favour of the adoption of any one system of co-education. Some preferred mixed schools, others favoured dual schools with separate entrances, classrooms and playgrounds. There were also staunch opponents of co-education who opted for separate girls' and boys' intermediate schools.

There were significant contributions to the debate which included Charles T. Whitmell's paper, *A Plea for Mixed Schools*, presented in 1890 at Cardiff, and Miss E.A. Carpenter's *Mixed Classes in Intermediate Schools* presented in 1891. Both were later published as pamphlets by the Association for Promoting the Education of Girls in Wales.

By 1900, the ninety-three intermediate schools in Wales consisted of forty-three dual schools, twenty-two boys' schools, twenty-one girls' schools and seven mixed schools. Pupil numbers and costs, as well as attitudes to co-education, had been key determinants influencing the educationists and politicians who organized the new system of intermediate education.

The status and position of 'mistresses' in dual schools

Though dual schools were to become widespread in the 1890s, attention focused not only on the propriety of the arrangements for the education of the two sexes, but also on the position and status of the 'chief mistress' or headteacher of the girls' school. There was much debate and acrimony concerning the merits and disadvantages of dual schools.

In 'The Duty of Welshwomen in relation to the Welsh Intermediate Education Act', 1894, Dilys Glynne Jones noted that provision was made for the establishment of dual schools in most of the county schemes. She took the opportunity to voice a strong objection to the Charity Commission's interpretation of a clause in the Caernarfonshire scheme that 'the term headmaster includes headmistress'. This was seen as an unfortunate precedent for all other dual schools in Wales, because it gave the headmistress of the girls' department the status of an assistant mistress only, and allowed the headmaster to receive all the capitation fees in respect of girls. Dilys Glynne Jones, and others, pressed for equality of status for headmistresses of dual schools. In 1896, in an article entitled 'Progress of Women in Wales', Miss Anna Rowlands wrote about the injustice afflicted on women and the cause of girls' education through the appointment of a headmaster in every instance as head of a dual school.[31] At the end of the decade, John Gibson was still lamenting the injustice of 'the subordinate position imposed upon women teachers'.[32]

Adequate female representation on governing bodies

The Association for Promoting the Education of Girls in Wales also saw adequate female representation on governing bodies as crucial. In July 1893 it published an *Analysis of Schemes formulated under the Welsh Intermediate Education Act*. It was acknowledged that the education of girls had been recognized in all the schemes drawn up. But it was also noted that provision for female representation on governing bodies varied considerably. Only the Montgomeryshire intermediate education scheme included a clause stipulating that there must be women members on the county governing body. Of the total membership of twenty-one, there were to be four women including one co-opted member.

At the end of the decade in 1899, the association published another pamphlet dealing with this issue, entitled *The Position of Women on the Governing Bodies of Educational Institutions*.[33] Dr Sophie Bryant focused attention on the fact that for the whole of Wales, there were only thirty-five women members compared with 355 male members of county governing bodies. Twelve of these thirty-five women were in the county boroughs of Cardiff, Swansea and Newport, where there were separate schools for boys and girls. The 'deficiency of women governors' was most evident in those counties where most of the intermediate schools were of the mixed or dual type, and under the overall authority of headmasters. Dr Bryant claimed that in such schools, the women responsible for the girls 'had no independent access to the governing body'. In four of the Welsh counties, — Anglesey, Flintshire, Pembrokeshire, Monmouthshire — there was no female member of the county governing body, and in three of them, no girls' school nor headmistress to represent the rights of women. Furthermore, with only twenty-two women amongst the ninety-four head-teachers, there was insufficient power in the hands of women.

Other contributors to the pamphlet, including Miss E.A. Carpenter, demanded adequate female representation on governing bodies. She attributed the male domination of the governing bodies to the prevalence of the belief that men were better equipped to deal with the key issue of financing the schools. Miss Annie M. Dobell of Blaenau Ffestiniog County School also underlined the inadequate female representation on school boards. She strongly disagreed with the views of Mrs Humphreys-Owen, who believed that it would be misguided policy to increase female representation on county governing bodies at the expense of 'competent men'. In Mrs Humphreys-Owen's opinion, there was no reason to assume that the cause of female education in intermediate schools would be better served by women governors. However, she also believed it to be only a matter of time before women became headteachers of dual schools.

Curricular issues

During their first decade, the newly established intermediate schools of Wales were aware of the need to sell their educational wares and establish a worthy image. Unsurprisingly, they utilized the curricular tradition of the boys' grammar schools and girls' high schools for their purpose. Prevailing notions of a liberal education, and the associated academic curriculum and the praise of examination achievements, influenced the intermediate education of girls as well as boys. In 1890, the Association for Promoting the Education of Girls in Wales recommended the adoption of the curriculum of Dr Williams' School. Curricular deliberations involved a number of crucial issues which had important implications for the education of girls. They included the

validity of a general academic education, technical and scientific education, as well as curricular uniformity *vis-à-vis* differentiation.

The provision of a sound academic education had become a major
objective in English girls' high schools by the late nineteenth century.
In the Education Department's Special Reports, Volume 2, 1898, Dr
Sophie Bryant pinpointed the changes that had occurred: 'A scheme of
serious study' had replaced accomplishments, and girls' studies had
tended to assimilate those of boys.[34] Unsurprisingly, this tradition was
to be a prominent trend in girls' intermediate education in the 1890s.
The assimilation of the curriculum of girls' secondary schools to that of
boys was evident in both England and Wales in the late nineteenth
century. Since the 1860s, the quest for equal opportunities for girls had
led the pioneers of female education towards the existing model of a
liberal education for boys.[35] Such subjects as Latin, German and
mathematics were regarded as providing excellent means of sharpening
the intellectual faculties. Identity of curriculum and comparable examination successes were intended to show that girls possessed the same
intellectual calibre as boys. The intermediate schools were intended to
be agencies of a liberal and humane education.

In 1898, The Association for Promoting the Education of Girls in
Wales published a pamphlet entitled *The Teaching of Literature in our
schools*. Miss Kate Warren, lecturer in English Literature at Westfield
College, London and the North London Collegiate School, underlined
the value of literature in the education of girls. It trained the intellect,
the emotions and the imagination, and merited greater prominence in
secondary schools.

Though the merits of an academic-based, liberal education, were
widely recognized in girls' intermediate schools, attention also focused
on the implications of their obligation to provide technical education
which became equated with domestic economy, needlework and the
laws of health. Attitudes were influenced by developments elsewhere in
England and Wales which saw increasing importance given to the role
of domestic subjects in the education of working-class girls in elementary schools. Middle-class girls' secondary education was also influenced by the contemporary debate which saw differing views expressed
by headmistresses regarding the place of domestic subjects in a primarily academic curriculum. Sara Burstall, headmistress of Manchester
High School, was a leading supporter of the inclusion of domestic
subjects. Others, however, favoured the same academic and intellectual
education for girls as well as for boys.

This was a time when the Education Department, through changes in the Code, were endeavouring to ensure that girls in the elementary schools did receive some 'technical education', — needlework, cookery, dairy work and housekeeping. Recent research by Carol Dyhouse and June Purvis has focused on the attempts made in England in the late nineteenth and early twentieth centuries, to bias girls' education, especially in the elementary schools, towards domestic subjects and mothercraft.[36] In the 1890s, and in the first decade of the twentieth century, the Education Department and its successor, the Board of Education, were pressing the case for greater attention to domestic subjects in the education of girls in secondary, as well as in elementary schools. This trend led to opposition from the Girls' Public Day Schools Trust who favoured a traditional academic education.[37] The advocates of the inclusion of domestic and technical subjects in post-elementary education called for the utilization of funds raised under the Technical Instruction Act 1889 and Local Taxation Act 1890 to provide instruction in cookery, laundrywork, dressmaking, physiology and domestic economy. Significantly, curricular change was being justified in 1897 in terms of women achieving greater competence in the home.

In 1892, the Association for Promoting the Education of Girls in Wales expressed satisfaction that in all the schemes of intermediate education that had been drafted, there was provision for subjects which had a direct bearing on the home and domestic duties of women.[38] In 1894, the association published a pamphlet entitled *Manual Training for Girls in Wales*,[39] which emphasized the need for the intermediate schools' curriculum to include cookery, laundrywork, dressmaking and the elements of physiology, hygiene and domestic sanitation as well as a sound liberal education. The same year saw the publication of another association pamphlet — *Technical Education for Women* by Miss Hester Davies, Principal of South Wales and Monmouthshire Training School of Cookery. She argued that '. . . in the great expansion of education in Wales in the last decade, technical education of women had not revealed the share of attention its importance demands'.[40]

The quest for adequate attention to domestic subjects, which were equated with girls' technical instruction, also became associated with wider issues concerning the relationship of intermediate education to employment, and curricular uniformity *vis-à-vis* differentiation. In the various county intermediate schemes, the curricular structure was designed to provide a basis for a sound general education, and the local governing bodies were empowered to determine the relative importance and value to be given to the different groups of subjects. The responsibility for the nature and scope of the instruction given at each school rested entirely with the governors, subject to the provisions of their local schemes. It was in the power of every district to meet the needs of its own population. However by 1900, though the county intermediate schemes gave a degree of curricular freedom to the schools, it was curricular uniformity rather than diversity that characterized the emerging pattern of intermediate education in Wales. In general, domestic subjects were still on the periphery of the schools' curricula and, to avoid accusations of sexism, there had been little diversity in courses of study, other than in some counties such as Carmarthenshire where domestic economy including needlework and the laws of health could be provided for girls instead of natural science.

Traditional academic values ensured that this form of technical education for girls was a mere appendage to the intermediate schools' curriculum by 1900. Limited resources, costs, staffing difficulties and external examinations also ensured that in spite of the commitment of the legislation of 1889 to technical as well as intermediate education, languages, literature and mathematics were the core of Welsh girls' education.

(iii)   *Girls' intermediate education in the 1890s: years of achievement*

The 1890s saw a crucial contribution by politicians, administrators and educationists towards the provision of a fair deal for girls in the new intermediate schools.

In the Education Department's first comprehensive survey of 'The Welsh Intermediate Education Act 1889: Its Origin and Working' by W.N. Bruce in 1898, the arrangements for the provision of intermediate schooling for girls were regarded as satisfactory. The adoption of a dual system was regarded as justifiable for financial reasons, and because it was also thought to be attuned to the prevailing attitudes towards co-education. However it was foreseen that there could be further reorganization in the direction of both mixed and separate schools. It was conceded by W.N. Bruce that the current state of public opinion tended to give men an advantage over women for the posts of head-teachers of dual schools. It was also accepted that there was some justification for the criticism that 'the present system, which gives to a Head Master the control of the internal management of a school worked in two departments, is not desirable in the interests of either girls or Assistants'.[41]

By 1900, there were 3,513 girls and 3,877 boys in the ninety-three intermediate schools of Wales. Twenty-two of these were boys' schools, twenty-one were girls' schools, while forty-three were dual and seven were mixed schools. Evaluating 'The Welsh County School System: Its Merits and Defects' in August 1900, F.E. Hamer in the *Manchester Guardian* remarked that 'one of the most striking features is the increase in the number of girl pupils and the new level to which the system raises female education'.[42] By then, the intermediate schools of Wales were subject to regular inspection and examination by the Central Welsh Board. Whilst curricular issues and premature withdrawal of pupils were amongst the problems highlighted at the turn of the century, the education of girls appeared to be progressing satisfactorily, and was subject to no especial criticism by the Central Welsh Board. Although, by 1900, the Association for Promoting the Education of Girls in Wales was well satisfied with the operation of the legislation of 1889, it still called for vigilance to ensure that women were adequately represented on county governing bodies. The Association could also have criticized the staffing problems in schools, the blatant sexism embodied in the differing salary scales of male and female teachers, and insufficient curricular differentiation. Numerous difficulties had been overcome — sites, buildings, finance, resources and staffing. There was ample evidence to support W.N. Bruce's view in 1898 that though it had been intended to provide adequate schooling for girls, there was a tendency at first to favour boys when financial resources were scarce.[43] Lord Aberdare's plea to his son, Henry, in 1890 in relation to intermediate education at Neath — 'Don't forget due provision for girls' would also have been an apt instruction elsewhere in Wales.[44]

Other issues had been highlighted, but remained unresolved at the turn of the century. The limited educational background of elementary school pupils and their late entry to intermediate schools, remained a recurring problem in the early twentieth century, and caused numerous curricular and pedagogical problems. The premature withdrawal of pupils from the intermediate schools was equally annoying for head-teachers. In 1897, Miss Holme, headmistress of Carmarthen Girls' School deplored the fact that many girls stayed only one or two terms and '. . . some of these were the daughters of well-to-do parents who imagined that girls do not require education like boys'.[45]

In Cardiff, and also to a lesser extent at Swansea, the management of intermediate schools for girls had already generated problems of a socio-economic kind. At Cardiff in 1896, there were 196 pupils in the girls' school. It was noted by W.N. Bruce, during a Charity Commission inspection, that only twenty-four of the pupils had attended public elementary schools whilst another twenty-six had been pupils at higher grade schools. Tuition fees at the intermediate school were as high as

£7. 10s. per annum. The governors had 'deliberately suspended' the scholarship clauses of the scheme because of 'the fear of giving rise to some social difficulty if a large number of public elementary school children were admitted at the outset'.[46] The headmistress, Miss Collin, who was to be a powerful influence at the school until 1925, had previously been on the staff of the Girls' Public Day School Company's high schools at Notting Hill and Nottingham, was intent on establishing a socially exclusive girls' high school at Cardiff rather than a 'mere' intermediate school. She, and the governors, were critical of pupils from public elementary schools, who were insufficiently prepared, and stayed too short a time to benefit effectively from intermediate education.

W.N. Bruce had no sympathy with the school's policy, and informed the governors that the Treasury grant was 'gravely imperilled'. He was highly critical of this 'class' school, and recommended that there should be a reduction by one tenth in the maximum grant payable to the school. The scheme was originally intended to enable 'meritorious children of all classes' to benefit from intermediate education. The problem was not resolved, and later, O.M. Edwards was also involved in conflict with the school authorities. By 1900, conflicts of class and culture signalled the differing perceptions of the role of girls' intermediate schools in Wales.

(iv) *Secondary education for girls, 1901–1914*

Enrolment, fees, and free places

In the Edwardian age, there was a significant expansion in the provision of secondary education for boys and girls in Wales. As well as growth in numbers in the intermediate schools, there were twelve new municipal secondary schools established by local education authorities, with their powers under Part II of the 1902 Education Act, in the county boroughs of Cardiff, Swansea and Merthyr and the administrative county of Glamorgan. They were not subject to examination and inspection by the Central Welsh Board and charged lower fees. The dual system of secondary schools and educational administration thereby created, was to see much confrontation and conflict involving the Central Welsh Board and the Welsh Department, Board of Education.[17]

By July 1914, when the enrolment in the intermediate schools was the highest hitherto recorded, there were more girls and boys in the 100 intermediate schools — 7,396 girls and 6,796 boys. There were twenty-three girls' schools, twenty-two boys' schools, forty-six dual and nine mixed schools.[48] The numbers of both sexes had more than doubled since the beginning of the century. It had been noted by the Central Welsh Board in its report for 1913 that there was a significant preponderance of girls over boys in the industrial counties of Glamorgan — 1,894 girls to 1,534 boys — and Monmouth — 730 girls to 360 boys. This trend was also evident amongst older pupils and education authorities were advised to consider the implications:

> The excess of girls over boys . . . represents a very definite swing of the pendulum since the days not so long ago, when the number of girls receiving secondary education was considerably less than the number of boys and the fact may be commended to the very careful consideration of the responsible authorities.[49]

With a total of 363 assistant masters and 350 assistant mistresses, the proportion of male and female teachers was approximately equal. The qualifications of male and female teachers were comparable, there being ninety-six women and eighty-five men without degrees. A total of 163 assistant masters and 150 assistant mistresses were University of Wales graduates, whilst forty of the men and forty-two of the women held University of London degrees.

By 1914, the twelve municipal secondary schools consisted of four boys schools with an enrolment of 1,101; five girls schools with 1,227 and three boys and girls schools with 322 boys and 411 girls.[50] They had been established in large centres of population in south Wales, and reflected the increasing demand for secondary education. Whereas in 1901, 2.1 boys and 2.1 girls per 2,000 of the population of Wales were in secondary schools, by 1914 the proportion had increased to 3.6 boys and 3.9 girls.[51]

The pre-war years in England and Wales saw increasing criticism, by socialists and liberals in particular, of the elitism of secondary education. Though scholarships had been available in the intermediate schools since the 1890s, many able working-class children were denied access because of inability to pay the fees. The regulations of 1907, introduced by the reforming Liberal administration, were intended to increase the proportion of 'free places' in secondary schools to twenty-five per cent, and thereby in R.H. Tawney's famous words, strike a major blow at 'the walls of educational exclusiveness'. The municipal secondary schools in south-east Wales were to prove more generous than the intermediate schools in their allocation of 'free places'. For example, two-thirds of the pupils at the Dynevor Municipal Secondary School for Girls, Swansea in 1907 were exempt from payment of fees.[52]

At the Cyfarthfa Castle Municipal School for Girls, where forty-eight per cent of the parents of the 288 pupils were classified as artisans and ten per cent as labourers, no fees were charged in 1913.[53]

Consequently, by 1913, 47.82 per cent of girls and 46.23 per cent of boys in Welsh secondary schools were exempt from paying fees.[54] With the demand for secondary education still increasing, some educationists and politicians in Wales favoured the development of central schools, whilst others advocated secondary schools for all pupils over twelve years of age.

During this period of growth in secondary education in the years preceding the First World War, the education of girls as such was in no way a major issue. Girls were regarded as having the same educational opportunities as boys. Even to raise the issue of female education seemed anachronistic and a mere reminder of battles won long ago. Such was O.M. Edwards's impression at Rhuthun in 1913:

> I am going to begin my address by asking a question that will cause you considerable surprise — the question is — should women be educated? As soon as I have asked the question, I imagine that a spirit of amusement, not unmingled with some pity for me, has taken possession of you. And I also imagine that a question is forming itself in your mind and about me. It is — 'from what kind of geological formation does this ancient fossil emerge?'[55]

Sexist and socio-economic inequalities

Though the denial of the Parliamentary franchise to women remained the major bone of contention, the sexist inequalities in the growing system of secondary education also attracted some significant criticism. In most areas where women's work was equal to men's — in factories, schools and the post office — men were paid higher salaries.[56] Women were in a significant minority at headteacher level. In the intermediate schools, there were seventy-six headmasters but only twenty-four headmistresses in 1914. They were paid average salaries of £377 and £324 respectively. An assistant mistress's average salary of £125. 15s. 4d. was also significantly lower than her male colleague's £156. 2s. 9d. Moreover married women teachers were penalized in some areas such as Glamorgan in 1912 where marriage nullified service in the schools for all women teachers.[57] Likewise, at Swansea in 1913, there was some criticism of the restriction of the employment of women teachers to single women.[58] The payment of lower salaries to married women teachers than to single women in Carmarthenshire and Monmouthshire in 1913 was regarded as 'unfair treatment'.[59] In Caernarfonshire, there was an unsuccessful attempt to limit the service of married women to five years from the date of their marriage.[60]

The advocacy of greater working-class representation in secondary schools included only a few specific quests exclusively on behalf of girls. Where inspections revealed that less than twenty-five per cent of free places were awarded, the Board of Education brought the matter to the attention of the governing body. Some schools were reluctant to implement the new regulations. In 1908, the governors of Bangor County School for Girls agreed to provide twenty-five per cent of free places following a critical letter from the Board of Education.[61]

By 1913, when the intermediate schools of Caernarfonshire had an average of thirty-six per cent free places, at Bangor School only twenty-five per cent of the 156 pupils were admitted without charge. The school fees of £7.15s. per annum were the second highest in the county, and parents were complaining about their inability to pay. In 1910, the Board of Education had refused to approve a tuition fee of £8.[62] A report of the Special County Schools Committee in 1914 argued that 'the working class population desires an extension of the system'.[63]

At Cardiff, the local education authority proved reluctant to implement the 1907 regulations through increasing the proportion of free places in the boys' and girls' intermediate schools to thirty-five per cent. They preferred to channel the expansion of secondary education into the municipal schools, thereby preserving the social elitism of intermediate schools which they desired to designate 'High Schools'. Such class distinction, differentiating intermediate and municipal schools, proved unacceptable to O.M. Edwards and the Board of Education (Welsh Department).

The Cardiff Intermediate School for Girls figured prominently in the controversy involving the local education authority and the Board of Education (Welsh Department) in the years 1908–11. Reluctantly, the local education authority did eventually comply with Board of Education policy, though in 1910, only fourteen per cent of the places of the Boys' Intermediate School were free, and twenty-one per cent in the Girls' Intermediate School. By contrast, the proportion of free places in Howard Gardens Girls' School was twenty-six per cent, thirty-two per cent in Howard Gardens Boys' School, and thirty-three per cent in Canton Boys' School.[64]

However, the Board of Education also condemned the policy adopted at Howard Gardens Secondary School for Girls. In 1912 there was concern over the non-allocation of ten free places at Howard Gardens, and after scrutinizing the examination papers of the unsuccessful candidates for free places, the governors were advised that 'in future, care must be taken not to require of candidates for Free Places a higher standard than that expected for admission to the school'.[65]

Both at Howard Gardens, and at Canton Municipal Girls' School, the pre-war entrance examination was regarded as 'severely competitive'.[66] Miss Mary Collin, headmistress of Cardiff Intermediate School for Girls from 1895 to 1924 played an important part in the controversy. Deriving her inspiration from the public and high schools of England she endeavoured to establish an exclusively middle-class institution. Her dislike of the designation 'intermediate school' led her in the years 1906–11 to try and adopt the name 'high school'.[67] In 1905, she wrote to the Board of Education expressing concern regarding the reorganization of the higher grade school into a municipal secondary school. In her view, there was no need for two schools 'attempting to cover exactly the same ground'.[68] In 1908, the Board of Education drew the school's attention to the allocation of less than twenty-five per cent of free places.[69] Miss Collin's opposition to the 1907 regulations was particularly evident and, even in 1913, the Cardiff Local Education Authority and especially the Girls' Intermediate School, were criticized for not awarding the full number of free places.[70] In 1912, only 49.1 per cent of the 283 girls had attended public elementary schools and, at £7.10*s*. per annum, the fees were comparatively high.[71]

Though these instances of sexist and socio-economic inequalities inherent in the system of pre-war secondary education received attention in the communities concerned, they did not generate any significant debate in political and educational circles throughout the whole of Wales. Girls' secondary education was not a major national issue in Wales during the Edwardian and pre-war years.

Co-education

In Wales, with the establishment of dual and mixed intermediate schools following the debates of the early 1890s, a varying degree of co-education had developed. In England, however, the system of co-education was still subject to much discussion, experiment and criticism. It interested such leading educationists as Professor Michael Sadler and Professor Stanley Hall. It was an age of much interest in comparative education. The position in Wales was appreciated as being educationally significant. In the *Cyclopaedia of Education* edited by A.E. Fletcher in 1906, it was stated that '. . . in Wales, the new intermediate schools have, in several instances, adopted co-education rather than continue the system of dual schools originally founded'.[72]

There was particular interest in the well-established practice of co-education in the United States. In 1903, co-education in American Schools and colleges was examined by the Mosely Educational Commission whose members included Principal H.R. Reichel and Principal John Rhys, Jesus College Oxford. The commission, however, arrived at no consensus. Indeed, conflicting reports were submitted by members of the commission. Some praised co-education for its worthwhile moral and educational results; whilst others, including Professor Sadler and Principal Rhys, were distrustful because it had led to the growing influence of women in the teaching profession.

However, the quest for separate girls' schools in Glamorgan did lead to deliberations with the Board of Education (Welsh Department) in 1909–10. There were plans for new girls' schools at Barry, Porth and Pontypridd, and also a demand for a similar arrangement at Aberdare.[73] The education authority were of the opinion that the needs of the county would be best served by the establishment of separate-sex schools in the large and populous centres. By 1913, four new intermediate schools for girls had been opened at Barry, Porth, Pontypridd and Aberdare.

O.M. Edwards and the Board of Education were not enthusiastic about this trend, which they viewed as 'quite contrary' to developments elsewhere in Wales.[74] They considered it expensive, and instigated by women 'who wanted to retain headships open for themselves because no woman was yet head of a mixed school. The party now in power has taken up the policy of establishing girls' schools — a policy I believe, both uneducational and wasteful'.[75]

They grudgingly consented to the erection of new buildings, though the needs of Aberdare in 1918 were regarded more favourably.[76] The Glamorgan Education Authority were instructed to ensure that expenditure on buildings was as low as possible, and their attention also drawn to the advantages of having boys' and girls' schools in close proximity for the interchange of staff.[77]

Matters of health and welfare

The medical case opposing higher education for women, which had influenced attitudes in the late nineteenth century, had been given less credence by 1900. But overpressure, and physical and mental strain on girls in secondary schools attracted serious attention in the years before 1914. The danger was recognized both by the Board of Education and the Central Welsh Board who endeavoured to ensure that schools were aware of the problem. It was seen partly as an inherent physiological problem, but more as the inevitable consequence of short stay, an overloaded curriculum, and the control exerted by external examinations. Some educationists were influenced by the writings of G. Stanley Hall and his claims that an adolescent female's reproductive system might be harmed, if she were subject to undue intellectual rigour and mental strain. In a persuasive speech in 1908, the Board of Education's chief woman medical adviser has also highlighted the dangers involved.[78]

In 1907, in her presidential address to the Welsh County Schools Association at Shrewsbury, Miss Collin drew attention to the risk of overpressure in conjunction with the Honours Certificate.[79] She suggested that a woman inspector be appointed to the staff of the Central Welsh Board, because of the large number of girls being educated, and 'the many important questions bearing on their health, courses of work, and teaching of domestic subjects, etc'. In 1907, the Central Welsh Board voiced its fears that 'the great eagerness' of parents for their children to be entered for its 'higher' examination, was causing stress both for some pupils and teachers.[80]

In 1913, the Board of Education also recognized that overpressure seemed more acute in mixed schools, and recommended that 'girls may, with advantage, generally postpone such examinations to an age rather later than that which is usual for boys'.[81] In an address at Rhuthun Girls' School on 27 December 1913, O.M. Edwards raised the question of strain in girls' secondary education:

> The system of Welsh Education being what it is, can our daughters pass through it without undue strain? Can they stand the physical and the mental strain? If not, there is something wrong with the girls or there is something wrong with the system. Either the girls are incapable of being educated, or the system is incapable of educating.[82]

He discerned no physical or physiological reasons for the problem, but rather an unreasonable emphasis on cramming for examination results, an overemphasis on the academic side of a girl's education and the fact that,

> the parents and the governors demand unreasonable, immature, examination results. So their daughters must be hurried and crammed . . . And the tendency always is for the academic side, which is tested by examinations, to encroach on the domestic side. If there were a proper proportion, life in school would be happier and we would hear less about strain.[83]

By 1914, the relationship between education and social welfare had become more clearly understood. Legislation to establish the School Medical Service, and provide school meals in elementary schools were regarded as significant achievements of the pre-war Liberal administrations. In the Welsh intermediate schools also, hostel and lodging arrangements, travelling and midday meals were viewed as important aspects of educational policy. Their bearing on the education of girls often gave greater urgency to that policy.

The Welsh Department favoured the establishment of hostels in conjunction with intermediate schools, but it was recognized that many pupils were unwilling or unable to pay an economically viable fee. For both sexes, a hostel would have its advantages: '. . . clearly, unless in cases where the lodgings are especially good or the lodging-house keepers are of exceptional character, a hostel would be a great improvement both for the health and education of the children'.[84] However, for girls, hostels were also seen as providing support for consolidating and developing the 'domestic' element in their curriculum:

> Hostels would have an excellent influence, especially on girls . . . a hostel under a thoroughly competent matron might become a very useful democratic adjunct to the school as a house in which real practical cookery for the hostel, table, the buying of food, cleaning and decoration of the home et al. could be done with success.[85]

Curricular issues

The curriculum of intermediate and secondary schools attracted considerable attention during these years. Its alleged uniformity and rigidity led to the consideration of possible differentiation primarily between schools but also between the sexes. The Board of Education (Welsh Department) Report for 1909 was particularly critical, and soured relations with the Central Welsh Board for many years. It suggested that

> . . . the Central Welsh Board should now consider to what extent their rigid examination system may be the cause of the wooden and un-intelligent type of mind of which their examiners complain. Elasticity and adaptability of curriculum, and the development of differentiation among schools are difficult under such a highly centralised system of examinations.[86]

In a celebrated defence of the Central Welsh Board, Edgar Jones maintained that the Board of Education's own *Regulations for Secondary Schools* accounted for much of the curricular uniformity.[87] In a statement refuting the Board of Education's allegation of uniformity, the Central Welsh Board's exemplification of the diversity of the system of intermediate schools included reference to the curricular arrangements for girls:

> As a further instance of differentiation, it is a common-place to state that in some of the Welsh County Schools, boys and girls are taught together,

and that in others they are taught in separate departments or in separate schools . . . In one girls' school, a special technical department, the girls prepare and cook the midday meal and also learn dairywork.[88]

It was also stated that in a number of girls' schools, those who showed greater aptitude for domestic than for academic subjects received extra instruction in needlework, cookery, and health education. In some girls' schools, botany was taught instead of chemistry, but elsewhere, girls continued with their studies of chemistry and physics.[89] In the prefatory memorandum to the *Regulations for Secondary Schools in Wales*, 1908, it was stated that for girls over the age of fifteen years, science could be replaced by an approved course of instruction in domestic subjects. It was openly acknowledged that the intention was to underline the importance of training for domestic duties.[90]

Since the late nineteenth century, the quest for equality of educational opportunity for girls had involved the pursuit of equal identity with boys' schools and their overwhelmingly academic curriculum. Any significant differentiation of the curriculum between the sexes, based on domesticity, had been regarded as incompatible with the aims of higher education for girls, which were concerned with their equal intellectual status. In Wales, as in England, there was evidence that by 1914 in the curriculum of girls' intermediate and secondary schools was overwhelmingly academic. This trend had developed in spite of the advocacy of curricular differentiation by the Central Welsh Board and the Board of Education. There had been attempts in the 1890s to ensure that a 'technical' dimension was provided in the curriculum of the new intermediate schools, but with little success.

The academic bias of the curriculum of girls' schools was regularly criticized in the pre-war years. The Board of Education (Welsh Department) and the Central Welsh Board, advocated a policy of curricular bifurcation which involved a greater role for domestic subjects in girls' education. The late nineteenth century and early twentieth century saw growing concern about the alleged physical deterioration of the nation. The role of domestic subjects in girls' education was viewed within the context of wider issues relating to the role of the women in British society. Through general circulars, regulations in 1904, 1908 and 1909, annual reports, inspection of schools, and through a select committee in 1911 and a consultative committee in 1913, the Board of Education underlined its opinion of the importance of domestic subjects in girls' education.[91] Likewise, the Central Welsh Board was advocating a sexist approach to the curriculum.

Schools were regularly criticized by the two boards for giving insufficient attention to domestic subjects. Canton Secondary School for Girls was urged in 1912 to develop housecraft for those girls in their last year at school who had no aspirations of proceeding to a university.[92] Beaumaris County School was advised in 1911 that it would be 'desirable to strengthen the domestic course';[93] in 1912, Swansea Girls' Intermediate School was told that 'the subject of cookery greatly needs attention'.[94] Occasionally, schools were complimented on their attention to domestic subjects. Welshpool Girls' School was praised for its domestic course in 1912,[95] and likewise at Monmouth High School for Girls in 1913, the teaching of domestic subjects was 'highly praised'.[96] A more central role for domestic studies in such schemes came to be supported on the basis of utility, and the perceived role of women; their applied scientific nature was also used as justification for those subjects being taught as alternatives to pure physics and chemistry for older pupils who had already some understanding of basic scientific principles.

The attitude of the Central Welsh Board is clearly revealed in the reports of inspection of schools. In its report in 1910 on Hawarden Intermediate School, where the girls had been weak in chemistry at the senior stage, it was deemed desirable that 'some further differentiation should be made between the course for boys and that for girls. It is suggested that a course in household economics, with a sound scientific basis underlying it, should be established as an alternative to the more academic teaching'.[97]

By 1914, the sexist approach to the curriculum that was intended to cater for the needs of girls had grown. Physics and chemistry were being increasingly seen as 'boys subjects'. In 1910, the Central Welsh Board reported that for girls in the upper forms, botany had largely replaced chemistry. However, 'a further modification of the science course for girls seems desirable in order to bring about a closer association between the laboratory work and the schemes of instruction in domestic science'.[98] Though more girls were studying domestic subjects in most schools, they were still only on the fringe of a curriculum that remained overwhelmingly academic.[99]

In the years preceding 1914, the Central Welsh Board, the Board of Education and O.M. Edwards sought to ensure what they considered to be a balanced liberal curriculum, embodying a 'utilitarian' or 'technical' element as well as academic subjects for boys and girls: 'The problem of secondary education today is to make the pupils' education a preparation for the duties of life without ceasing to be a liberal education. The relations between the two aspects vary in different schools'.[100] Attention was drawn to the curricular needs of girls in agricultural districts, many of whom left secondary school after three years:

> For such pupils, a thoroughly good course in important subjects that appeal to them — Domestic Subjects, English Literature, Welsh Literature, and their allied subjects — is better than a wide course of subjects which they cannot appreciate or master. The aim of the Headmistress should be, not to bring such pupils up to a Junior Examination standard, but to give them such a course that they will be thoughtful and cultured housewives, able to do their work well and enjoy the best literature of their county.[101]

Occasional articles in *Y Gymraes*, espoused the same curricular standpoint. With many girls staying for only a short period of one to three years in intermediate schools, the study of Latin, French, Algebra and Chemistry rather than cookery, needlework or domestic economy was regarded as misplaced.[102] Average school life was still very short at this time (in 1910 the average was 2.11 years for girls and 2.7 years for boys), and the proportion remaining beyond 16 years was low (average leaving age being 16 years for girls and 15.8 for boys).[103] Of the pupils staying on at school, 23.5 per cent of the boys and girls were aged fifteen years and 9.4 per cent aged sixteen years.[104]

The provision of short courses in domestic studies at UCW Aberystwyth in conjunction with local education authorities dated from the 1890s. They were welcomed in *Y Gymraes* in 1911, which again criticized the academic orientation and irrelevance of much of the teaching in secondary schools for thousands of Welsh girls who left school at fourteen years.[105] The greater attention given to technical instruction in overseas countries, and the accompanying economic benefits in terms of job opportunites were highlighted. But the main thrust of the article was its emphasis on the need for educators to note the implications of the woman's role in society. Household duties and competence in the home were still being advanced as essential requirements.[106]

(v)   *The endowed and private secondary schools, 1890–1914*

The late Victorian era proved of utmost importance for the future management of Wales's leading girls' endowed schools. Their development became immersed with contemporary political and religious conflicts, and they were affected to a varying extent by the establishment of county schemes for intermediate education. Under the terms of the 1889 Education Act, each scheme for intermediate and technical education which was to be submitted to the Charity Commission from each county, was to specify the educational endowments within the county, which in the opinion of the framers ought to be used for the purpose of the county scheme. However, endowments given since the passing of the Endowed Schools Act 1869, could only be utilized with the consent of the founder or of the governing body. The assumption underlying the 1889 Act was that intermediate education was to be, in the main, provided by endowed schools, and out of funds which could be derived in a large proportion from endowments.

However, among the special problems which each county had to decide for itself, none presented greater difficulties than the treatment of the existing grammar schools. By 1898, seventeen endowed grammar schools in Wales had been adopted as intermediate schools. But some of the most well-known boys' schools — Llandovery College, Christ College Brecon, Cowbridge and Rhuthun — remained outside the new system of intermediate education, whilst the Pontypool, Monmouth and Abergavenny boys' schools were also outside the Monmouthshire county scheme, though not entirely unrelated to it. Numerous complex factors accounted for this state of affairs, including religion, the attitude of trustees and the fear of losing status.

Problems were also encountered in the 1890s with the endowed girls' schools already established in Wales, and with one located outside the Principality. At Monmouth and Haverfordwest, the girls' schools opened in 1891 and 1892 respectively, worked in close relationship with the Pembrokeshire and Monmouthshire schemes of intermediate education but continued to enjoy the financial benefits and higher status accruing from the Tasker and William Jones endowments. At Swansea, the only girls' public day high school to be opened in Wales became the Girls' Intermediate School in 1895.

The older endowed girls' schools at Dolgellau and Llandaff were also subject to a new element of administrative control by the State, by virtue of the local arrangements for intermediate education. In Merioneth, the less than generous financial arrangements associating the Dr Williams' School with the county's scheme for intermediate education caused much acrimony, which was not quelled for over a decade. The dispute between Dr Williams' School and the county governing body assumed wider significance when it was taken up by John Gibson to champion female education in Wales. In 1899 he claimed that, 'this starvation process is part of the traditional scheme for benefiting boys at the expense of girls, an old but pernicious policy of which surely in these days there should be an end'.

The benefits of the Howell charity were to be divisible between the county of Denbigh and the Diocese of Llandaff. Though reluctantly, the governors of Howell's School, Llandaff entered into arrangement with the Glamorgan, Cardiff, Newport and Monmouthshire schemes for intermediate education. Representative governors were now appointed, and income from the Howell's charity was to maintain thirty Howell scholarships providing exemption from boarding and tuition fees at the 'Howell's Glamorgan County School'.

In Denbighshire, the outcome was to be very different, and exceedingly acrimonious. In August 1892, after consultation with the Howell's School Committee of the north Wales counties, the Joint Education Committee submitted proposals for a scheme dealing with Howell's School to the Charity Commission.[107] Following some slight amendments regarding details of representation ensuing from deliberations between the Charity Commission and the Joint Education Committee, a draft scheme was published on 17 July 1894. There was to be a governing body of twenty-two, consisting of nineteen representatives and three co-opted governors. The North Wales County Governing Body would be in a majority whilst the Drapers' Company were given one representative. The university colleges at Bangor and Aberystwyth were also represented. At least four of the governors were to be women and the school was to be both a day and boarding-school. With preference being given to girls who were orphans or had one parent deceased, forty boarding scholarships of the total value of £1,000–£1,500 were to be competed for annually by girls resident in the north Wales counties, with the exception of Merioneth, whose county governing body was to receive an annual payment of £120 towards the maintenance of the Dr Williams' School at Dolgellau. Twenty day-scholarships, which gave exemption from tuition fees, were to be available for those girls resident in the Denbigh school district and educated for at least three years in a public elementary school. Another thirty day-scholarships were to be available for girls from other parts of north Wales. No religious catechism that was distinctive of any particular denomination was to be taught to a day scholar, nor indeed in any of the school's boarding-houses, though the Charity Commission had not given final approval to the proposal by the Joint Education Committee.

It had been evident even before the draft scheme was published, that there would be opposition from the Anglican Church in the Diocese of St Asaph. The Warden of Rhuthun School — Revd Bulkeley O. Jones — and Captain Griffith Boscawen protested against the proposal to give 'an overwhelmingly preponderance' to representatives of the county governing bodies on the school's governing body.[108]

In the meantime, the Joint Education Committee's general scheme for intermediate education in Denbighshire, approved by the Education Department in April 1894, and which incorporated Rhuthun grammar school, had been opposed in the House of Lords on 19 June 1894. By a majority of fifty-eight, a motion was passed, requesting the withholding of royal assent to the inclusion of Rhuthun grammar school in the county scheme. Significantly, the Bishop of St Asaph played a key role, claiming that the original foundation of 1595 at Rhuthun was an Anglican school, and that since its character was unchanged in 1869, it was outside the jurisdiction of the 1889 Act. Having tasted victory at Rhuthun, the Bishop and his friends were unlikely to acquiesce in the changes proposed for Howell's School Denbigh. In October 1895, the local governors, whose chairman was the Bishop, informed the Education Department that they desired to submit certain suggestions for amending the scheme.

At the Education Department, Sir George Kekwich was surprised, particularly since the scheme for Llandaff had met with no objection, and also because in the Denbigh scheme a certain amount of concession had been made to denominational instruction through the boarding-house conscience clause. Girls resident in a school hostel or boarding-house could attend whatever place of worship and also received whatever religious instruction that their parents wanted for them. He realized that the hand of the Bishop lay behind these machinations, and was determined that 'before granting an interview, I most certainly insist on having the objections before us in writing'.[109] When these were received, the main emphasis was on changing the constitution of the governing body. It was proposed that the Bishop of St Asaph should be chairman ex officio, and that there should only be six representatives from north Wales county councils. The universities of Oxford, Cambridge and Wales should each have one representative, whilst the Drapers' Company and the Lord President of the Council should have six representatives each. There was also objection to the allocation of an annual sum of £120 to Dr Williams' School. However, the Education Department was not sympathetic to these proposals, which would have given only one representative for Denbighshire and similarly only one for each of the other north Wales counties, and thought it desirable that the school be brought into the system of intermediate education since the locality needed a girls' school to cater for day pupils. A perceptive departmental memo noted: 'Of course the Bishop of St Asaph is the real objector .. but whether the Bishop would go so far as to move the rejection of the scheme in the House of Lords I cannot say. I think he would however'.[110]

On 16 July 1897, in the House of Lords, Dr Temple, the Archbishop of Canterbury, rose to speak in a debate that led to a motion being passed by a majority of seventy-two to thirty-three requesting the Queen to withhold her assent to the scheme to administer the Denbigh share of the Howell's charity.[111] Inevitably, the rejection of the scheme aroused widespread anger in Nonconformist circles, and was criticized widely in the press. Thomas Gee reacted sharply in the columns of *Baner ac Amserau Cymru*. He saw the Bishop of St Asaph, who had already succeeded in having Rhuthun Grammar School excluded from the county scheme, as the architect of another unjust Anglican victory — 'gwraidd y drwg'.[112] T.E. Ellis MP wrote in the *Manchester Guardian* attributing the instigation of the whole affair to Bishop A.G. Edwards, and claiming the action to be part of the Bishop's determination to thwart the advance of Nonconformists in educational institutions. He claimed that the Church had gained control over the endowment in the 1850s through 'theological piracy'.

For denominational reasons, the Bishop of St Asaph had succeeded in thwarting the plans of the Joint Education Committee, and Howell's School Denbigh as well as Rhuthun Grammar School remained outside the county's intermediate education scheme. A decade later, in response to criticism of the lack of a girls' intermediate school in the Denbigh school district, the Denbighshire Joint Education Committee in 1909 prepared a new scheme dealing with Howell's School. Again, they were to be thwarted by Bishop A.G. Edwards and the House of Lords.

On 26 April 1910, in the House of Lords, the Bishop of St Asaph moved that an address be presented to His Majesty requesting the withholding of royal assent to the scheme proposed for Howell's School, Denbigh. He maintained that the school was intended to serve the whole of north Wales and there was no justification for its conversion into a degraded Denbighshire county school. It was claimed that the Welsh Intermediate Education Act had led to the disastrous appropriation of educational endowments by county authorities. Only such fine schools as Llandovery and Brecon, which had preserved their independence, could be ranked with the superior public schools of England.[113]

Bishop A.G. Edwards defended his action on the basis of freedom, independence and diversity of type in schools: 'If the present status is sacrificed to a craving for rigidity of system and uniformity of control, secondary education in North Wales will receive a heavy blow'.[114] He was dishonest in claiming that he had acted purely from an educational motive, and that sectarianism or party bias had never entered into his calculations.[115]

The school had retained its splendid isolation and, by 1913, an extensive new building scheme was contemplated. Whilst the head-mistress claimed that 'the danger is now past', and looked foward to 'serving the truest interests of education in Wales',[116] it was destined to be a girls' school in, rather than of Wales.

Likewise, the Welsh Girls' School, Ashford was determined to retain its independent status. Legislation for intermediate education in Wales was viewed with unease by the authorities of the Welsh School, Ashford. Mundella's Intermediate Education Bill 1887, which did not receive a second reading in the House of Commons, had included the Ashford, Howell and Meyrick endowments within its terms of refer-ence.[117] During the second reading of Rendel's Intermediate Education Bill on 15 May 1889, Stanley Leighton, Tory MP for Shropshire, and a member of the school's governing body, voiced 'the only real opposi-tion' to the measure. As well as objecting to the provisions that would place control of education in Wales in the hands of county councils, which he regarded as political bodies, he also objected to the inclusion of the Ashford endowment within the terms of the proposed legislation. He called for the bill to be referred to a select committee. However, T.E. Ellis MP had no sympathy for Leighton's plea: 'What a grotesque position this institution holds for a school designed for the good of the boys and girls of Wales. Before they can obtain the slightest advantage, the must leave their hillsides and valleys and cross to the further-most corner of England'.[118]

During the debate, William Hart-Dyke, Vice-President of the Council, suggested that the bill be re-drafted by the Education Depart-ment for consideration by a House of Commons committee.[119] On 28 May, on the proposal of Lord Powis, the trustees of Ashford School decided to petition the House of Commons, and if necessary the House of Lords, that they be allowed to voice their opposition to section 17 of the Welsh Intermediate Education Bill by which the whole property of the Ashford School was handed over to the proposed Board of Education for Wales together with the Howell and Meyrick endow-ments. They voiced various objections to this forcible annexation. They claimed that the funds at the disposal of the school could not really be classified as 'endowments' but rather 'the accumulated results of the liberality of living benefactors, or the families they represent'. Further-more, 'the charity had always been a London Charity, not for Wales but for the Welsh'. They argued that at one time, it had been exclusively restricted to Welsh children born in or near London, whilst under the terms of an Act of Parliament in 1847, the beneficiaries were to be the children of parents born in Wales or in the parishes of Oswestry, Selattyn and Llanymynech in Shropshire. The school, which had always been located near the metropolis, had an enrolment of 127 pupils from Wales, and another thirty-six from England who were of Welsh parentage. It was claimed that 'the Society at present educates more Welsh children than any other similar educational establishment', and since October 1882, 508 pupils had been admitted. No scheme could be devised whereby the charity's funds could be used for the education of a larger member of Welsh children. This was extremely dubious in view of the society's declared investments of £49,500 as well as a school building and land valued at £19,826.19s.11d.[120] The latter figure was a very conservative one, for in 1882, a figure of £30,000 was suggested.[121] The school's academic achievements in external examinations were underlined, as well as 'the efficiency and tone' of the school. Significantly, it was claimed that the applications for admission, which exceeded the number of places available, attested to their confidence in the institution: 'The parents of many Welsh girls, realising the fact that their children have to make their way in the world, not merely in the Principality, prefer sending their children out of Wales for their education'. Copies of this memorial were sent to all MPs, asking them to oppose clause 17 so far as it related to Ashford School, and to the Education Department and also to every parent. In addition, the trustees sought legal advice in June.[122]

The revised bill was considered by a House of Commons committee in June, and in its amended form, approved. The powers originally proposed for the county councils were now given to joint education committees, whilst the clause establishing a Board of Education for Wales was struck out. So also was the wording of clause 17 which had placed the Ashford and Howell trusts and Meyrick fund within the scope of the bill. There was criticism of these amendments from Thomas Gee and other Welsh Liberals, but the main bone of contention was the decision — later revoked — to exclude Monmouthshire from the scope of the legislation.[123] The action of the Ashford trustees had triumphed, and a valuable endowment was made unavailable for the purpose of intermediate education in Wales. It was seen as success for the 'Church Party' and a blow to the quest for equal opportunities for Nonconformists.[124] In *Y Goleuad* the exclusion of the Ashford charity and Meyrick fund were equated with removing 'the soul' of the Intermediate Education Bill. The significance of the decision of 1889 concerning Ashford, was seen primarily as part of the Anglican–Nonconformist conflict over educational endowments. Its significance for female education was perceived only within that context. During the deliberations of the Joint Education Committee in Wales in 1891 and 1892, it was felt by many that Ashford School should still be brought under the 1889 Act.

The school continued in splendid isolation. Ironically, at the end of one of the most progressive decades in the history of education in Wales, Ashford School's official handbook stated that 'the school is available for all Welsh parents who desire to obtain Intermediate Education for their daughters and provides a First-Class Education ... The religious instruction ... shall be in accordance with the Principles of the Church of England'.[125] Here, were the real paradoxes which explained why the attitude of the Ashford trustees and the objectives of the architects of Welsh intermediate education had proved irreconcilable.

At Ashford, the Welsh Girls' School celebrated its thirtieth anniversary as an exclusively female establishment in 1912. Miss A.H. Jones had been headmistress for twenty-one years and was to remain till 1930. Dean John Brownrigg was still a powerful influence on the school's governing body. Inevitably at a time of celebration, attention focused on change and development. In contrast to 1882 when there were only an enrolment of forty-eight, a staff of three, no public examinations, a timetable that was 'a very simple affair', no tennis court or hockey, there were by 1914 a staff of eighteen, 169 pupils — 151 boarders and eighteen day pupils; in 1915, a wide curriculum, preparation for Cambridge local examinations and pupils regularly attending concerts and recitals.[126] A magazine — *Welsh Girls' School Gazette* — was begun in January 1912, attesting to the existence of a successful, confident school. In the pre-war years, applications for admission were 'far in excess' of the accommodation available.[127] It was stated that every district in Wales was represented at the school. However, the school's tenuous links with the Principality could not be disguised by the claim that 'the School maintains Welsh national, as distinguished from a Welsh local, character'.[128] It was not until 1920 that a detailed insight into the school's curriculum and organization was provided by a Board of Education inspection.[129]

During the Edwardian and pre-war years, Dr Williams', Ashford and Howell's were synonymous with the most prestigious secondary schools for girls. They were perceived as being superior to the intermediate schools. Whilst the girls' schools at Ashford and Denbigh were to remain in isolation, the schools at Dolgellau and Llandaff were influenced by the administrative and financial relationships with the local education authorities emanating from the local arrangements for intermediate education in the 1890s.

Various trade directories and newspaper advertisements showed that there were numerous private schools of varying quality at the turn of the century. Many were adversely affected by the opening of intermediate schools.

The Carmarthen High School for Girls continued to function under the management of the Diocesan Council. By 1900, there was an enrolment of sixty pupils consisting of twenty-one boarders, and thirty-nine day pupils. Ever since its opening, the school had been dependent on voluntary subscriptions and pupils' fees. There was constant concern about the school's financial viability in the 1890s and early 1900s. On the north Wales coast, there were important developments at Penrhos College. In 1895, a magnificent building, hitherto used as a 'Hydropathic Establishment', was bought and became the nucleus of the school in the twentieth century. By 1900, a school-house, gymnasium, classrooms and dormitories had been erected. Pupil numbers showed a steady growth from thirty-five in 1895 to 152 by 1914. Though increasingly on the periphery of girls' secondary education in Wales by the beginning of the twentieth century, the private non-endowed girls' schools were a reminder of an important source of female education in Victorian Wales long before the establishment of intermediate schools.

Teacher Training for Women in Wales, 1880–1914

(i) *The quest for expansion and links with the university colleges*

Throughout the 1880s, the only training-college for women in Wales was at Swansea. It was a time of growing demand for teachers with the Education Department referring regularly to 'the great and increasing proportion of female teachers now employed in elementary schools'.[1] In 1880, fifty-eight per cent of certificated teachers, sixty-six per cent of assistant teachers, and sixty-nine per cent of pupil-teachers in England and Wales were women. By 1889, the respective proportions were sixty per cent, seventy-five per cent and seventy-four per cent. There was substance to the editorial in *The Cambrian* in 1890 which stated that 'every year, the demand for well qualified mistresses was becoming more urgent . . . Good work at Aberystwyth, Cardiff and Bangor must not be allowed to shadow the claims of the Swansea Training College — the only College of its kind in Wales'.[2] Indeed, its uniqueness had not passed unnoticed during a period that saw investigation of the facilities for teacher training. At a meeting of the Association for Promoting the Education of Girls in Wales at Blaenau Ffestiniog in June 1889, T.E. Ellis MP expressed regret at the lack of teacher training-colleges for women in north Wales, which would have enabled hundreds of Welsh women to become teachers not only in the Principality, but also in England. In October 1886, in evidence to the Cross Commission, he had emphasized the need for training-colleges for schoolmistresses to be conveniently situated for north and mid-Wales. He maintained that there was no difficulty in placing Swansea students in teaching posts. With so many small rural schools, he foresaw a growing demand for schoolmistresses.[3] Principal David Williams of Swansea told the Cross Commission that undenominational colleges were required. Many young people were debarred from Anglican training-colleges.[4]

At a conference of educationists convened in Cardiff in March 1887 by C. Whitmell HMI, to discuss the training of teachers, Lewis Williams, chairman of the Cardiff School Board contrasted Scotland's facilities for training 545 schoolmistresses with the seventy places available in Wales. On the basis of a population of 3.7 million in Scotland and 1.6 million in Wales, he maintained that there ought to be provision in the Principality for training 230 women teachers. There was an increased demand for female teachers consequent upon the organization both of girls' departments in mixed schools and also infants' departments. He noted that in the years 1869–86, there had been an increase of twenty-five per cent in the number of male pupil-teachers, but the increase in female pupil-teachers had been 158 per cent. Wales, he maintained, was not providing its fair share of the supply of teachers. To be on the same footing as Scotland, Wales could justly claim facilities to train another 160 mistresses every year.

At Aberystwyth in April 1887, at one of the first all-Wales meetings of the Association for Promoting the Education of Girls in Wales, Principal J. Viriamu Jones focused attention on the need for more Welsh women to be trained as teachers: 'The most prominent numerical deficiency in connection with Welsh elementary education is the deficiency of Welsh schoolmistresses, so that the schools have to be provided with mistresses from England and Scotland'.[6] He also contrasted the provision for training in Wales with that in Scotland. It was essential that Welsh girls were encouraged to regard schoolteaching as providing excellent opportunities for the well qualified. But it was also essential to increase the training facilities in the Principality.

In the 1880s, J. Viriamu Jones was advocating the establishment of links between training-colleges and the universities, and enabling elementary school teachers to have the benefits of a university education. At Sheffield, through the medium of evening classes in Firth College, he had enabled some elementary school teachers to savour higher education.[7] At Cardiff, he wanted the Government to establish a number of Queen's Scholarships, tenable at the University College, which would enable prospective elementary school teachers to study various subjects in common with the University students, and also be instructed in the principles and practice of pedagogy. In 1885, the idea, mooted in addresses to elementary teachers of Cardiff and Merthyr district, was supported by Lord Aberdare:

> I like your plan of having the College accepted by the Government in substitution of the Training College, and see much in it that would be acceptable at least to a Liberal Government, who are sometimes sore pressed by objections as to the denominational character of the majority of the training colleges.[8]

Such an idea, however, was not entirely novel in Welsh educational circles. In 1880, in her evidence to the Aberdare Committee, Dr Frances Hoggan had emphasized the need for more women teachers. Their training by the University of Wales and 'the sanction which only a degree could give' would raise both the status and general capability of women teachers.[9] There was also support from Lewis Williams, chairman of the Cardiff School Board. In April 1886, the board decided to ask the Education Department to found a number of Queen's Scholarships for the training of elementary school teachers. In March 1887, with the concurrence of the University College Council, Lewis Williams voiced support in evidence to the Cross Commission. He advocated the establishment of university day training-colleges.[10] At the first annual meeting of Aberdare Hall in January 1887, support was expressed for the action of the Cardiff School Board. It was anticipated that in the future, some prospective elementary school teachers would reside in Aberdare Hall. Lady Aberdare maintained that the 'superiority of Scotch over Welsh teachers' could be attributed to a more liberal university training. Charles Whitmell HMI, said he had been constantly stressing the importance of teachers acquiring the benefits that could accrue from residence in a university college hall. Such a scheme would alleviate difficulties caused by the denominational nature of many training-colleges and their lack of accommodation for enrolling more students. Lewis Williams foresaw Aberdare Hall and the University College enabling Welsh women teachers to acquire that 'wider culture' which was already a significant attribute of Scottish teachers. In 1887, J. Viriamu Jones reiterated his plea for the Government to establish Queen's Scholarships tenable at the university colleges so that elementary school teachers could be trained within a university environment.

Elizabeth Hughes was also in favour of a role for the university colleges in providing Wales with an adequate complement of women teachers. At Cardiff in January 1887, she anticipated the implications of legislation for intermediate education: 'In a short time a large number of girls' schools will be opened in Wales, and we teachers cannot help asking the question: Who are going to teach in them? We have not at present in Wales a supply of efficient teachers to meet the new demand'.[11] Wales should avoid being 'flooded with second-rate and third-rate English teachers'. It would be much better for Wales to train her own women teachers at the three university colleges: 'As a rule it is far better that the teacher should be of the same race as his pupils . . . They understand and sympathise with one another far better because they have much more in common'.[12] She claimed that the need for competent Welsh teachers was particularly important at this time, because trends in the USA indicated that schoolteaching was becoming increasingly a female profession: 'Let Wales be a pioneer in using a new social force, that of women invigorated by receiving equal educational advantages with men'.[13] Elizabeth Hughes favoured the establishment of an 'Exhibition Fund' to help deserving and promising students to complete their education. Financial assistance was provided from 1888 by the Association for Promoting the Education of Girls in Wales. In October 1888, the first exhibition of £10 was granted to Miss Emily Payn, a student at University College Cardiff.

At the Association's sixth public meeting which took place at Blaenau Ffestiniog on 14 June 1889, an appeal was made for funds and attention was given to the importance of granting exhibitions in order 'to enable a girl to complete a University degree or obtain that special training, without which a teacher is but an unskilled labourer at the work'.[14] The association regarded the provision of financial assistance to poor students as one of its most valuable activities because without this help many were 'unable to carry on their education beyond 16 years. They are often compelled to seek a livelihood at an age when they are not qualified in any one direction'.[15] The importance of the provision of funds was particularly recognized because the growth of intermediate education for girls would necessitate more women teachers. However, the association did find it difficult to raise sufficient funds, and although the records of the association are incomplete, making it impossible to determine the exact amount of funds allocated, it would not appear to have been very large.

During 1887, other prominent figures also focused attention on the lack of training facilities for women teachers in Wales. Miss Dilys Davies blamed this situation for the influx of English schoolmistresses into Welsh schools. T.E. Ellis MP urged the Association for Promoting the Education of Girls in Wales to exert its influence to connect elementary with university teaching through emphasizing 'the immense advantage' of having women teachers educated at the university colleges. Both the elementary and also the intermediate schools of Wales would thereby gain teachers who had acquired 'a broad education'.[16] A large number of women teachers, in the elementary schools of Wales were uncertificated. In 1887, William Edwards HMI told the Cymmrodorion Section at the National Eisteddford in London that only fifty-three per cent of the female teachers had passed through a training-college whilst the proportion of male teachers was not much higher.

That year, the Cymmrodorion Section had discussed whether or not university colleges should establish teacher-training departments. In his lengthy address advocating the establishment of day training-colleges in connection with the university colleges, Principal Viriamu Jones referred to the dilberations that had already involved the University College and the Cardiff School Board. If such a scheme were established, the community at large would benefit because 'the University becomes a familiar thought to the elementary teacher and therefore also to boys and girls in the elementary school'.[17]

It was a time when the future pattern of teacher training in England and Wales was one of the key issues being considered by the Cross Commission of 1886–8. Attention was given to various proposals for extending the facilities for teacher training, such as the establishment of university day training-colleges advocated by Lewis Williams, Chairman of the Cardiff School Board in his evidence in March 1887. In its Final Report, the Cross Commission recommended a limited system of day training-colleges though it did not specifically advocate the establishment of new day training-colleges attached to universities. The Minority Report was much more enthusiastic in its support for 'A large extension of facilities for training in day training colleges in connection with places of higher education existing, or to be established . . .'.[18] It was a time when teacher training was regarded by many as being a course of study for the working classes that should be confined to residential training-colleges. Naturally, the training-colleges were suspicious of any proposals that would impinge upon their monopoly, whilst on the other hand, the establishment of day training-colleges was seen by some university personnel as an opportunity to increase student numbers. The early 1890s saw the beginning of day training-colleges for women as well as men in the three university colleges in Wales. This was a most significant development for women's higher education in Wales. By 1897, there were 131 female and 126 male students enrolled. Also, in 1891, in conjunction with University College, Cardiff, a 'Training School of Cookery and Domestic Arts' was opened, whilst at Bangor, the St Mary's Training College was converted into an exclusively women's institution, and at Swansea, the training-college continued to function successfully.

Unsurprisingly, the provision of greater training facilities for women teachers in Wales was welcomed by the Association for Promoting the Education of Girls in Wales. In particular, the implications for the training of women teachers of the establishment of girls' intermediate schools were highlighted: a supply of trained and qualified women teachers was essential.[19] In 1890, Miss E.P. Hughes had argued that the elementary schools had already benefited from the growing number of trained teachers, and as befitted the Principal of the Cambridge Training College established to provide suitable training for women in secondary schools, she stressed the need for the new intermediate schools of Wales to be staffed with trained teachers. In 1890, and in 1892, the influential Welsh journal *Y Traethodydd*, published articles — 'Arbrawf mewn Hydfforddi Athrawesau: Ymarfer Addysgawl'[20] and 'Nodweddion Gwers Iawn'[21] — which provide a succinct synopsis of her pedagogical philosophy emphasizing the need for a careful blend of theory and practice. Effective lessons required a careful definition of objectives, a carefully structured scheme of work, suitable attention to pupils' interest and experience, and utilization of knowledge in a purposeful and active manner. Her ideas epitomized the careful attention to pedagogy that is evident from the teacher-training manuals and the HMI reports of the late Victorian era. There was sound precept, the relevance of which is in no way outdated a century later.

By 1894, the Association for Promoting the Education of Girls in Wales was well aware of the need for teachers in intermediate as well as elementary schools to be trained. At its request, Elizabeth Hughes wrote a pamphlet — *The Educational Future of Wales* — which claimed that for the first time in history, educationists in England were turning towards Wales.[22] The Principality should show the educational world its commitment to three key principles, the first two being 'the democratic principle that education is for all' and 'the Christian principle' which meant that neither sex or creed ought to be a reason for disqualification from enrolment or appointment at an educational institution; the third principle was 'the practical principle' which involved a commitment to the professional training of teachers.

> Wales was the educational experimenting-ground of Great Britain, and could do another stroke of good work for advanced educational reformers by insisting on professional preparation.[23]

In 1894, at the eighth annual meeting at Caernarfon, the association expressed satisfaction that women could now qualify as elementary or secondary school teachers and take the professional part of their training in the University of Wales. Later — in 1898 — Miss Hughes was to maintain that one of the mistakes involved in the introduction of intermediate education in Wales was the appointment of too many former elementary school teachers, who were out of touch with secondary education.[24]

Pupil-teacher centres became increasingly important in the 1890s. They were usually located in a particular elementary school or higher grade school or in a separate building often in close proximity to, or in conjunction with, an elementary or higher grade school. There was a high proportion of girls attending such centres because of the appeal of the teaching profession to women. In the 1890s, centres opened in such areas as Llanelli, Swansea, Cardiff and the Rhondda played an important role in extending educational opportunities for girls through their preparation for pupil-teacherships and eventually for the teaching profession. Occasionally, in some localities, such as the Rhondda, the pupil-teacher centre enjoyed greater prestige than the local higher grade school. By the end of the decade, the trend was developing towards locating the training of pupil-teachers in intermediate schools. A period in an intermediate school was approved by the Central Welsh Board since it 'postponed to a time nearer to maturity the beginning of their professional training'. Though the various schemes differed in detail, their main intention was that a period of two or three years as ordinary pupils in an intermediate school and studying for the Central Welsh Board's Junior Certificate, would be followed by approximately the age of sixteen by an apprenticeship — usually in the pupil's former elementary school.

In the teacher training-colleges in Wales, the female presence was consolidated by 1914 with the development of colleges controlled by local education authorities as well as the Church of England. Under clause 23 of the 1902 Education Act, the power given local education authorities to supply or aid the supply of education other than elementary education, included the power to train teachers. When introducing the bill, Balfour commented strongly on the deficiency in the means of teacher training in England and Wales. In July 1903, the Board of Education issued regulations for the training of teachers. Local education authorities were invited to help increase the number of training-college places by providing subsidies to existing colleges, or by establishing new colleges. However, local education authorities did not respond enthusiastically because they were not afforded financial help to meet the capital expenditure. In 1905, the Government offered voluntary societies and public authorities a grant of £25 per student towards the cost of enlarging or erecting colleges. However in 1906, the position changed when the Liberal Government offered a much higher grant of up to seventy-five per cent for the capital expenditure incurred by local education authorities in providing sites and buildings for training-colleges.[25] Nothing, however, was offered for maintenance.

Even more significant, the new grant was restricted to local education authorities' colleges and the previous building grant offered to voluntary societies was withdrawn.

Swansea Training College was immediately affected by this State initiative. Also, by 1906, the idea of establishing another training-college for women in Glamorgan was being mooted. In north Wales, women students were being admitted for the first time to Bangor Normal College.

Significant questions were also being raised concerning the future pattern of teacher training in Wales. As well as the perennial problem of matching supply and demand, attention was also given, in the deliberations concerning Swansea and Barry, to the relationship between teacher training-colleges and the university colleges and also the whole ethos of teacher education. Control of teacher training by Whitehall or by a Welsh National Council was also an accompanying issue. Also, significant changes were occurring in the pupil-teacher system which was becoming intermediate rather than elementary-school based.

(ii)   *Swansea Training College*

At the Swansea Training College, the 1880s were years of steady progress. Enrolment was satisfactory, but constrained by limited space. Demand greatly exceeded the number of places available throughout the decade. An enrolment of fifty-six had increased to seventy by 1883, at which figure it was to remain. There was no shortage of candidates for admission, though, of course, not all were from Wales. Admission was not restricted to pupil-teachers; it was by selection from candidates who were successful in the entrance examination for Queen's Scholarships in accordance with Article 41 of the Code.

Every year many of the women failed to reach the standard deemed necessary for a pass in an examination encompassing English, geography, history, domestic economy, music, needlework and school management. Marks could also be gained for proficiency in Latin, Greek, French, German, drawing and the sciences.[26] Of the 118 candidates in 1880, only sixty-nine were successful and twenty-seven of them were admitted into the college.[27] Likewise, at the end of the decade in 1889, seventy-eight of the 187 candidates failed the examination. The best thirty-four examinees were selected for admission.

The students' work was examined by college staff, Her Majesty's Inspectors and the Science and Art Department. In general, results compared favourably with other training-colleges. In 1880, there was much satisfaction that 'on the general certificate list just issued, the College occupied a higher place than three-quarters of English Colleges, and in the last published report of the Education Department, only two of the aforesaid Colleges stood better in the important subject of "Teaching" than Swansea'.[28]

As well as its good work, its unsectarian nature, strictly adhered to throughout the decade, was viewed as a particular virtue: 'The fact that so many students of various denominations lived and studied together in love and harmony, is a pleasing feature of the Institution and a conclusive proof of the soundness of the principles on which it is founded'.[29] There were members of various churches on the college management committee and likewise amongst the staff. Though government grants and students' fees were the college's major sources of finance, the need for voluntary subscriptions was reiterated throughout the 1880s. It was felt that the supporters of education in Wales could have been much more generous in their support.[30] There was much expense involved in purchasing 12 Nelson Terrace in 1883, in improving the sanitary condition of the buildings, and in erecting a new kitchen and out-offices.[31] The college was run on a tight budget with income and expenditure in the region of £2,000 to £3,000. In some years, there were shortfalls.

The curriculum showed little difference from the 1870s and included Bible study, school management, penmanship, reading, English language and literature, arithmetic, geography, history, drawing, vocal music, domestic economy, needlework and cutting out. Animal physiology was introduced in 1889.

Teachers trained at Swansea Training College in the 1880s, were, as ever, subject to the dictates of the regulations and policies of the Education Department and HMI and their concept of womanhood and the role of elementary education.[32] The importance of needlework and domestic economy in girls' elementary education, and *ipso facto* in training-college courses was reiterated with even greater force in the 1880s.[33] Cookery now attracted particular attention in elementary schools. International exhibitions at South Kensington in the 1870s, lectures by J.C. Buckmaster of the Science and Art Department, the establishment of training-schools for cookery in 1874–5, the second Report of the Royal Commission on Technical Instruction 1884, as well as the HMI and the Education Department reports in the 1880s — all underlined the need for a more systematic, practical approach to cookery in schools.[34]

Though the 1882 Code included cookery as a subject for girls, the report of William Williams HMI for the Welsh Division in 1886–7 suggested that its 'teaching was not spreading so fast as its importance deserves'.[35] The lack of suitable equipment was a problem that needed to be overcome. In its report for 1889, the Education Department emphasized the importance of cookery: 'After the three elementary subjects and sewing, no subject is of such importance for the class of girls who attend public elementary schools'.[36] In the 1880s, the training-colleges were associated with the elementary schools to fulfil well-established educational and social roles. In his evidence to the Cross Commission in 1886, T.E. Ellis MP referred to the interrelationship of educational and social reform. In advocating the provision of more places for the training of schoolmistresses in Wales, he was conscious of recent evidence which had highlighted the misery of many homes caused by 'ignorance of domestic economy and lack of habits of thrift'. Schoolmistresses could exert a formative influence on girls, and sharpen an awareness of 'feminine qualities'.[37] By 1897 in England and Wales, sixty-one per cent of certificated teachers, eighty-five per cent of assistant teachers and seventy-nine per cent of pupil-teachers were women.

The demand for well-qualified women teachers remained high throughout the 1890s and was much greater than for men. At Swansea, there was a healthy enrolment throughout the decade. Regularly, there were far more candidates for admission than could be accepted. For example, in the summer in 1890, 225 sat the admission examination. Of the 126 who passed, thirty-six were selected for admission.[38] At the end of the decade, the average of forty students enrolled every year represented only a quarter of those who applied.[39] For an analysis of the students' geographical origins, data is limited. In 1895, twenty-two were from Glamorgan, eleven from Monmouthshire, eleven from other Welsh counties, ten from Gloucestershire and twenty-six from eleven other English counties.[40]

In the Code of 1890, not only was provision made for the establishment of day training-colleges attached to universities but also for the admission of a few day-students to existing residential training-colleges.[41] At Swansea in 1894–5, seven day-students were enrolled for the first time with the other seventy students in residence. By 1897, their number had increased to fourteen.[42]

The moderate increase in student numbers was governed by the limited accommodation available on the premises. Better buildings were called for on numerous occasions. The lack of a well-equipped model school was also a significant disadvantage, though it was alleviated to some extent through recourse to three local elementary schools for purposes of teaching practice. The feasibility of acquiring a new site was actually discussed in 1895. However, costs of approximately £15,000 were anticipated, and in view of the college's meagre finances, it is not surprising that a few minor alterations were the most that could be contemplated.

In the 1890s, inadequate financial support from the public was regularly highlighted in meetings of the management and in *The Cambrian* where there were appeals for more subscriptions.[43] In 1893, B.J. Binns HMI argued that in spite of the college's successes, unsectarian nature, and unique position as the only residential training-college for females in Wales, the public were apathetic concerning its welfare and, but for government grants and students' fees, it would have collapsed long ago. This was a fair judgement. In 1895, subscriptions barely reached £50.[44]

In spite of the mediocre facilities, the quality of the teaching and the students' examination performance remained high throughout the 1890s. Indeed, the growing number of students awarded a first-class grade in their final examination attested to the college's efficiency.

The prospective schoolmistresses' course of studies was orientated towards efficacy in the elementary education sector where cookery and domestic subjects remained important for the fulfilment of a well-established social role. However, in the 1890s, Her Majesty's Inspectors welcomed attempts to provide a broader liberal education:

> It is not merely as a seminary in which the students are to be prepared to pass certain examinations and to learn certain technical rules of school keeping, but as a place for the formation of character and tastes, for broadening and liberalising the mind and for encouraging generous aspirations, that the training college has its chief value.[45]

It was believed that the establishment of day training-colleges 'stimulated the older colleges'.[46] J.G. Fitch HMI was advocating courses in the history and philosophy of education so that students would be versed in the principles underlying methods of teaching.

It was customary for deputations from various school boards in England and Wales to visit the college to select prospective teachers. In 1897, it was said that the difficulty was not in finding schools for the newly qualified students, but in finding teachers for all the managers who applied.[47] Students were appointed to schools in various parts of England and Wales. In 1894, for example, twelve went to Glamorgan, seven to other parts of Wales, and nineteen to six different English counties.[48]

In 1891, Principal David Williams, a native of Haverfordwest, and a staunch Independent, retired after fifteen years loyal service in the post. He had been a pioneer in advancing the cause of teacher training for women. In his successor, David Salmon, the college acquired another worthy leader who was to remain at the helm for over a quarter of a century, becoming one of the Principality's most well known education-ists.

In 1901–2, when forty-two students were admitted, proposals were being considered to erect a new building on a site at Town Hill, and at a luncheon on 13 March 1902 a fund-raising campaign was initiated. Within a short time, over £4,250 was promised. However, the introduc-tion of Balfour's Education Bill checked the flow of subscriptions and, by 1906, following the introduction of new regulations regarding building grants, the proposed scheme for a new and enlarged building had been abandoned.[49]

However, this was a time when the Swansea Education Committee saw the need for more teacher-training places for local women. It proposed an increase in the number of day students from sixteen to forty and to reserve the additional places for candidates from Swansea. This provision could not be implemented without an additional class-room. Since building grants were now to be available to local education authorities' colleges rather than voluntary institutions, it was not sur-prising that the Education Committee invited the College Council to a Conference on 21 January 1907, whereupon the latter agreed to recom-mend to the British and Foreign School Society that the Swansea Training College be handed over to the Swansea Local Education Authority on condition that a new college be erected. A scheme for transfer was prepared by the Board of Education under the Charitable Trusts Act.[50]

At the time, the work of the college was highly complimented. O.M. Edwards reported that the teaching of the college was excellent. He praised the library, and also the increase in the numbers studying Welsh.[51] The numbers seeking admission — 220 in 1909 — far exceeded the fifty-six vacancies (thirty-three resident and twenty-three day students) available annually.[52] The college magazine — *The Swan* — portrayed a very active and full student life. There were numerous societies, and excellent articles were contributed on various educational and topical issues such as the suffragette struggle.[53]

The proposed erection of a new building at Swansea was strongly condemned in the *Western Mail* as 'A reckless Swansea Proposal'.[54] It was viewed as a needlessly expensive venture amounting to 'careless extravagance'. At a time when the possibility of training-colleges at

Barry and Caerleon was also being considered, it was argued that vast sums of money were being spent on training-colleges in England and Wales, although the supply of trained teachers was far in excess of demand. Not only was it claimed that an unnecessary financial burden would be imposed on the ratepayers through the training of more teachers than the area could possibly absorb, but it was also noted that many newly trained teachers were unable to secure posts. Of the 1,920 women who left five residential colleges in England and Wales in July 1908, 418 had been unable to secure teaching posts. Likewise, 352 of the 1,064 men and women who left day training-colleges were without jobs.

Similar sentiments were voiced at a meeting of the Swansea Education Authority on 20 January 1909. During the following weeks, much hostility to the scheme was still being voiced locally and especially in the *Western Mail.*[55] In particular, the critics argued that it was impossible to justify the expansion of teacher training at a time of unemployment among teachers. It was also maintained that training-colleges should be located in close proximity to university institutions.[56]

By 1911, however, the foundation stone was laid for the new training-college to accommodate 120 residential and eighty day students. The Government provided seventy-five per cent of the estimated cost of £40,000.[57] The building was opened on 2 October 1913.[58] Whilst C.P. Trevelyan, Parliamentary Secretary to th Board of Education, viewed the new college as epitomizing the achievements made towards equal provision of educational opportunities for both sexes, the *Western Mail* continued to question the wisdom of the venture. The paper thought it unreasonable that the inhabitants of Swansea should be expected to support a training-college for students primarily from outside the borough: central government rather than local education authorities should be responsible for colleges which were primarily national in their purpose.[59]

(iii)   *St Mary's Training College, Bangor*

A teacher training-college for male students — The North Wales Training College — was opened by the National Society at Caernarfon in 1856. In 1891, part of the building was destroyed in a fire. It was then decided to erect a new college providing accommodation for sixty students. However, in 1892, the local management committee noted that there were significant changes occurring in teacher training. It was anticipated that a considerable number of student teachers leaving training-colleges in the near future would be graduates. The establishment of a degree-conferring University of Wales was also regarded as very likely. It was regarded as 'an absolute necessity that Church teachers should not fall behind other teachers in secular learning'.[60] Consequently, it was decided to locate the new college in or near Bangor, and by October 1892, land had been leased from Lord Penrhyn and a building committee appointed.[61] By 1895, building work had begun on a site overlooking the town. In 1896, the new college buildings were much praised.[62]

It had been intended that the new college would be a training establishment for men, and initially it assumed this role. However, in May 1895, H.E. Oakeley HMI drew the attention of the management committee to 'a serious falling off' in the numbers of male pupil-teachers in the country and advised that the conversion of the college into a women's training-college merited consideration. It appeared that there was 'an abundant supply of female pupil teachers'.[63] In January 1896, at the annual committee meeting at the Bishop's Palace, St Asaph, the Principal placed before the committee a plan for changing the college into an establishment for women. However, it was not accepted and, instead, it was decided to send a circular to the managers of Church schools drawing their attention to the scarcity of male candidates for the college and advising them of the advantages of the new institution at Bangor.

Later that month, at a management committee meeting, Oakeley again referred to the recruiting difficulties caused by the decline in the number of male pupil-teachers. In contrast to 100 applications for entrance to the college in 1886, there were now only nineteen. Vacancies in English training-colleges had aggravated the difficulty at Bangor because 'the College depended largely on English students who could not gain entrance into the English colleges'.[64] One poor year for recruitment would ruin the college financially. Consequently, Oakeley again suggested the desirability of converting the college into one for women. The Principal then pressed 'the critical position' of the college and it was decided to convert The North Wales Training College for Men into a women's training-college.

The Education Department consented to a request for a one-year transition (1896–7) into a female institution. During that year, the second-year students would be men, whilst women would be the first-year students.[65] Canon Fairchild remained as Principal, and was assisted by four mistresses as well as visiting mistresses for needlework, music and drawing. By 1899, there were sixty-four women — thirty-three in their first year and thirty-one in their second year — in residence at 'The North Wales Training College for Church Schoolmistresses, Bangor'. The HMI report in 1899 was satisfactory and Principal Fairchild believed that 'the Institution now was one that could challenge the confidence of the country'.[66]

At St Mary's College Bangor there was much concern regarding the implications of the 1902 Education Act. Initially there was anxiety that the local education authorities would undersell denominational colleges through establishing their own colleges and providing scholarships for student teachers. The college authorities were in no doubt that the country was on the eve of a very considerable increase in training-college accommodation. However, the governing body's natural concern for self-preservation was expressed in a resolution that it was 'earnestly to be hoped that the intention of the Bill will be borne in mind that new colleges are to supplement and not supersede existing Colleges, and should not put them at a disadvantage'.[67]

There was also concern that St Mary's might be adversely affected, if new arrangements for teacher training were to lead to the localizing of existing colleges, or any new colleges that might be founded. At the time, the enrolment pattern showed little change:

1900: 77 students	1904: 84 students
1901: 75 students	1905: 86 students
1903: 84 students	1906: 85 students[68]

During these years, there was no shortage of candidates for admission. For example in 1906, there were 120 candidates, of whom 100 were from England and twenty from Wales. The college was held in high regard by His Majesty's Inspectorate and received very satisfactory reports.[69]

In 1909, the Principal, the Reverend Canon John Fairchild MA, completed twenty-five years at the college. By 1911, extensive additions were made to the buildings, with the erection of a handsome new wing costing over £4,000. This expenditure was incurred in order to enable the college to compete with modern establishments being erected by local education authorities. There was now accommodation for 107 students, and, by 1914, the debt had been reduced to £1,500.[70] In his report of inspection in 1911, O.M. Edwards was highly complimentary: 'The college was very progressive, its tone quite excellent; it was one of progress in education'.[71] Significantly, however, a more thorough course in the teaching of domestic subjects was deemed as necessary. Teacher training could not be divorced from prevailing notions of the role of women and the requirements of girls' elementary education. Equally significant was the observation of the Inspector of Church Colleges that St Mary's was 'one of the most attractive in England'![72]

However, by this time, St Mary's, like other Anglican colleges, began to experience a fall off in the number of applications for entry from 225 to 1909 to 187 in 1910 and 106 in 1911. This decline was attributed to the increase in the number of training-colleges administered by local education authorities, of which there were twenty by 1914, and also to the difficulties in obtaining employment.[73] 'The future of the Church Training Colleges is now in serious question. Excessive building of Training Colleges by LEA's with unlimited funds, and a dearth of candidates for the profession on the women's side making it difficult for the voluntary colleges to fill'.[74]

Enrolment was also adversely affected by the replacement of the pupil-teacher system which was elementary-school based, by the student-teacher and bursar systems which were secondary-school based. The latter became the key elements in the Board of Education's teacher-training strategy as revealed in the 1903 and 1907 Regulations.[75] The introduction of the bursar system in 1907 encouraged prospective teachers to complete a course of secondary education.

A local education authority could recommend for approval as bursars, pupils who intended becoming elementary school teachers and who were attending full-time at a secondary school but required financial assistance in order to remain at school. Bursars were prepared for the CWB Senior examination or the matriculation examination of the University of Wales or the University of London. Girls were usually obliged to include needlework as part of their course of studies. At seventeen years of age, bursars were engaged as 'student-teachers', spending part of their time teaching in an elementary school and also continuing their studies in the intermediate school. At the end of the year's training, a student-teacher would, as a general rule, be recommended by the Board of Education as an uncertificated assistant or as a training-college student.

As the number of pupil-teachers in England and Wales declined, the total number of entrants from the secondary schools was less than anticipated by 1909.[76] For voluntary colleges in general, the immediate pre-war years were a period of anxiety concerning recruitment. In 1914, Principal Fairchild was referring to 'a crisis in Church Training Colleges'.[77] At St Mary's, there were 103 residential students and twenty-three day students in 1913. The college council decided in 1914 to send a letter to all the clergy of Wales requesting them to inform prospective female teachers of the advantages of training at St Mary's. The quality of the training at St Mary's on the eve of the First World War was deemed to be most satisfactory. Following a visit in May 1914, O.M. Edwards wrote:

The training is resourceful and very successful. The teaching is of a kind to arouse thoughtfulness and originality. Much attention is paid to the place of Handwork in teaching and the development of Domestic Subjects teaching is receiving the careful attention of the College.[78]

(iv)   *Bangor Normal College*

At Bangor Normal College, the fiftieth anniversay of its establishment as a training-college for male teachers saw the admission of the first women students in 1908. No especial significance appears to have been attached to this innovation. Nationally, attention focused on the Nonconformist–Anglican hostility and controversy generated by the Education Bill's proposal to establish a National Education Council.[79] Locally, the college's transfer to local education authority control was a far more significant event.

In 1905, D.R. Harris was appointed Principal of the exclusively male college of seventy students and within a very short period showed that he was very much aware of the changing world of teacher training. It was realized that the Glamorgan and Monmouthshire local education authorities were considering establishing their own training-colleges for men and women. If prospective teachers from south-east Wales were to continue to be attracted to Bangor, the new Principal's objective of increasing the total enrolment was to be achieved, better student accommodation and teaching facilities were essential.[80]

With the anticipation of a large financial outlay on buildings of approximately £18,000, it was decided that it would be opportune to transfer control of the property to local education authorities in order to qualify for the newly available government grants. There was a feeling that 'the era of voluntary effort in elementary education, and the training of the state teacher is drawing to a close'.[81] In 1906, at a time when the establishment of a Welsh national council for education was being mooted, the management committee at Bangor were also much aware of the 'national role' that had always been fulfilled by the Normal College.[82] There was a desire for the new controlling authority to be representative of the whole Principality, or at least the whole of north Wales.[83] However, it was soon evident that this was not feasible, and following consultation with the British Society and the Board of Education, an approach was made to Caernarfonshire County Council to take over control of the college, providing that building extensions were undertaken immediately. Anglesey Education Committee also showed interest and, on 23 May 1907, a conference was held with the Caernarfonshire and Anglesey local education authorities when it was decided that the transfer of the college, whose buildings and equipment were estimated to be worth £25,000, should be effected at an early date. On 14 April 1908, with the scheme for the constitution of the Caernarfon and Anglesey Training College Committee having been approved by the Board of Education, the property was transferred to a Joint Committee comprising representatives of both county councils, together with three co-opted members representing UCNW and elementary secondary school teachers in the two counties.[84] Representation of UCNW epitomized the attempts at closer co-operation between the two institutions in the years 1905–10.[85] By August 1909, Flintshire and Denbighshire county councils were also participating in the scheme of management of the North Wales Training College and its accompanying financial commitment. Merioneth was to join in 1919 and Montgomeryshire in 1935.[86]

In June 1908, deliberations were begun with the Board of Education concerning approval and financial support for the provision of further accommodation in new halls of residence and the conversion of the existing buildings for use as a teaching block. On 6 June 1908, a deputation from the College Committee stated that 'the Committee were strongly in favour of the College being mixed' with an anticipated enrolment of 120 men and eighty women. As yet, however, the College Committee had not come to a final decision regarding the admission of women.[87]

It was anticipated that there would be opposition from Principal Fairchild who feared that a second training-college at Bangor would have an injurious effect on St Mary's. However, the Board of Education were told by the Bangor Normal College deputation that St Mary's drew a large proportion of its students from Liverpool and Birkenhead. Furthermore, it also had 'the Church atmosphere' which made it unattractive to a large number of prospective women teachers in north Wales. Denbighshire Education Committee had also intimated a desire to be associated with Bangor Normal College if it were a mixed institution. Otherwise, there was a possibility that there would be a request for a training-college for women to be opened at Wrexham. The Bangor deputation viewed the Normal College as an institution providing undenominational residential training on a national rather than a local basis. At that time there were no facilities for undenominational teacher training for women in north Wales. The Board of Education officials, including O.M. Edwards, were 'strongly in favour of some provision being made for women here'.[88] It was not thought that St Mary's would be adversely affected: 'Being the only Church College for women in

Wales, it is not really a local College in any way; also it draws a large number of students from Liverpool'.[89]

On 12 June 1908, the Board of Education asked the Bangor Normal authorities to make a final decision concerning the admission of women. It was a time when various other proposals for the provision of training-college accommodation in Wales were also under consideration.[90] On 17 June the Board of Education were informed that the Training College Committee were in favour of Bangor Normal College providing accommodation for eighty women and 120 men.[91] The Board of Education welcomed the proposal, and viewed the provision for women as no more than sufficient to meet the needs of the four north Wales counties, particularly if the college continued to enrol a quarter of its students from England.[92] In November 1908, Board of Education approval was given to the college enlargement scheme and, by February 1909, the building contract for £32,374 had been awarded.

Not everyone was enthusiastic for the proposed expansion. There was concern that large numbers who left training-colleges in 1908 were still without jobs and cries of 'the market overcrowded' and 'national scandal' were voiced. Others, however, were content to believe that the Board of Education would be unlikely to sanction the proposed enlargement if extra provision was not necessary. It was also argued that it was the duty of the Caernarfonshire Education Committee to encourage the large number of unqualified, ex pupil-teachers to become certificated teachers. Furthermore, it was argued that in Wales there were only 296 student teachers in residential training-colleges though the numbers of pupils on the school rolls increased annually by 3,000.[93]

In June 1910, the post of Warden of Women Students was advertised at a salary of £150 per annum and Miss Hawtrey appointed. Shortly afterwards, three other women members of staff were appointed. However, the women's hostels were not ready by September, and consequently the first women students enrolled at Bangor Normal were accommodated in approved lodgings. The following session, eighty-four women students became the first residents to occupy two well-built hostels adjacent to the college buildings.[94] There were a total of 198 students, who by 1914 had increased to 203 male and female students. However, men and women were taught in separate classes and, even half a century later, the principle of co-education was not fully implemented at Bangor Normal. By 1914, with a large proportion of the students from north Wales, Welsh was taught, and the bilingual problem studied. Significantly, domestic and rural science was being considered.[95] Within a comparatively short period, Bangor Normal

College had undergone one of the most important changes in its history. But for the college in general, and the female presence in particular, even greater change was to be ushered in following the outbreak of the First World War.

O.M. Edwards testified to the 'high efficiency and the leading character' now attained by the college among educational institutions.[96] He praised the attention given to domestic and rural science which 'would ensure for Welsh elementary schools a position of influence and power in the national economy'.[97]

(v)   *Barry Training College*

The implications of the Education Act 1902 for teacher training, and a speech by Principal Salmon of Swansea at the Shrewsbury Conference on the Training of Teachers 1904, where he drew attention to the inadequate provision for the training of women teachers in Wales, were to generate interest in the possibility of establishing a new training-college for women in the county of Glamorgan.[98] Two years later, in a letter to the Board of Education, the idea of establishing a training-college for women, in conjunction with the pupil-teacher centre at Pontypridd, was mooted by the Glamorgan County Council. The idea was not unconnected with the announcement of building grants of seventy-five per cent. However, the Board of Education showed no enthusiasm for the proposal.[99]

In May 1908, the Board of Education were informed that the Glamorgan County Council were desirous to establish a training-college for women teachers accommodating 100 resident and twenty-five day-students,and had arranged to purchase four acres at Barry.[100] On 19 May 1908, following the consideration of a sub-committee's report, the Glamorgan Education Committee decided that a training-college be erected at Barry.[101] It was soon evident to the Board of Education that Aberdare Borough Council also wanted a college for women teachers and claimed to have a suitable site and premises available at Abernant House. There had been negotiations between the Aberdare Education Authority and Lord Bute regarding the purchase of Abernant House and four acres of land as a site for a training-college, at an estimated cost of £7,500.[102]

Responding to a request from the Board of Education for details, the County Council estimated that approximately 100 new teachers would need to be trained annually to meet the requirements of the area. It was also said that there were adequate facilities in the area for school practice. In the meantime, the Board of Education received an application from Monmouthshire for a training-college for sixty women and forty men. It was decided to consider the Glamorgan and Monmouthshire requests together. The possibility of providing teacher training for women only in one college serving the needs of both counties, and providing for men only in another college, appeared to be the most feasible arrangement.

However, a potentially significant dimension to the Board of Education's deliberations was provided in a memo from O.M. Edwards who favoured the close association of teacher training with the university colleges.

> My hope is that each of the three University College centres, there should be a Training College on the lines of the arrangement we have sanctioned at Bangor, so that the students, while thinking first and chiefly of the professional training will get some of the advantages of university life.[103]

He wanted the conference arranged by the Monmouthshire, Glamorgan and Cardiff education authorities to consider the possibility of suitable teacher-training students being enabled to transfer to the University to conclude their studies.

At the conference on 23 November 1908, it was claimed that Glamorgan and Monmouthshire were experiencing great difficulty in appointing suitable women teachers. A resolution was carried, requesting the Board of Education to sanction the establishment of a training-college for women at Barry, and for men at Caerleon. At a later meeting, on 1 December 1908, where especial attention was given to possible numbers, it was decided that Glamorgan would seek a training-college for 150 women, and Monmouthshire a similar institution for 100 men. A nine-and-a-half acre site near the Barry intermediate school was already earmarked as a suitable location.[104]

The Board of Education noted that nothing more had been heard from Aberdare, and that the Glamorgan County Council were not advocating the location of a training-college there. Likewise, proposals to open a training-college at Merthyr had not been pursued. Barry was preferred by the Board of Education because of the high quality of its elementary schools and its proximity to Cardiff from where occasional assistance by university lecturers might be obtained.[105] A decision regarding a training-college for men at Caerleon appeared much less complex than the proposed women's college at Barry. The Board of Education wanted to ensure that the market would not be oversupplied with women teachers, and a final decision regarding Barry could not be divorced from the deliberations concerning the enlargement of Swansea Training College. However, it was not thought that these developments would lead to an excess of teachers because the population was increasing.[106]

The Board of Education were also aware that there were objections in south Wales to the proposed location of training-colleges at Barry and Caerleon. In the *Western Mail*, doubts were voiced about the wisdom of increasing the supply of teacher training at a time of teacher unemployment.[107] But equally significant was the criticism of the location of training colleges 'in places far removed from centres of life and learning and activity'.[108] Students trained at Barry and Caerleon would not receive degrees and would be 'outside the stream of University culture' through being side-tracked away from the university colleges.[109] Moreover the colleges would be controlled from Whitehall and not by a Welsh National Council which it was hoped to establish. As well as vigorous editorials, the *Western Mail* carried numerous articles to support its thesis that there was 'A Crisis in Welsh Education'.[110] William Jones MP argued that all teachers should receive university education.[111] The National Union of Teachers also disapproved of the location of a training-college at Barry — 'a place remote and far removed from the centre of learning'.[112] It was argued by the *Western Mail* that generous building grants would be wasted if deployed to establish 'limited and extremely localised institutions' which would not attract good staff and only train teachers with a limited outlook on education.[113] The plan was condemned as 'a policy of drift' which would cripple the future development of elementary education in south Wales, through its inefficiency and waste.[114] The *Western Mail* argued that teacher training should be carried on in conjunction with the university colleges, and the paper welcomed the trend towards strengthening the relationship between Bangor Normal College and the University College.[115]

Unsurprisingly, the Barry Chamber of Trade rejected these criticisms, claiming that the National Union of Teachers did not want to increase the supply of teachers for reasons of self-interest.[116] It was also argued that a college at Barry would enable working-class girls to enter the teaching profession.[117] In the *South Wales Gazette*, Elizabeth Hughes, one of the pioneers of women's education in Wales and now a resident at Barry, wrote an article on 'The Training of Teachers: A Grave National Problem'.[118] She argued that the proper supply of the right kind of teacher is the most important educational problem for every nation. In her view the establishment of training-colleges at Barry and Caerleon was the most satisfactory solution to the educational needs of populous south-east Wales. She also upheld the training of teachers in a residential college rather than in a university normal department. More time could be allocated to professional work, and overpressure, which was 'of grave importance' in women's education, could be more easily prevented in a residential non-degree college. The colleges at Barry and Caerleon would not have an adverse effect on teacher training at the university colleges at Bangor and Cardiff. In 1910, Elizabeth Hughes was given an interview at the Board of Education where, significantly, she emphasized the need for adequate attention to domestic subjects at Barry.[119]

By June 1909, Board of Education approval was given for the erection of a women's training-college at Barry providing accommodation for 120 Glamorgan students with further provision for thirty Monmouthshire students. Male students from both counties were likewise to be trained at Caerleon.[120] The Board of Education were somewhat uneasy that their decision, together with their earlier approval of enlargement at Swansea, might cause an oversupply of teachers.

In 1910, the Glamorgan Education Committee authorized plans for the erection of a residential college for 130 women students at an estimated cost of £41,000. In October 1914, with Miss Hilda M. Raw — a former teacher at Gelligaer Intermediate School — as Principal, and a staff of four lecturers, the new Glamorgan Training College at Barry was officially opened with seventy-five students in residence.[121]

It was not a propitious moment. Britain was at war, and there was a shortage of students in many colleges. The payment of low teachers' salaries by the Glamorgan Education Committee was not regarded as conducive to recruitment.[122] At Barry itself, the distance from places of worship, and the drafting of soldiers to the area, immediately concentrated the minds of the college authorities on questions of morality as well as education.[123]

Women in the University Colleges of Wales, 1880–1914

(i) *General orientation*

> It must not be forgotten that the higher education of women was a plant of very modern growth.[1]

The 1880s were of major importance for the future pattern of higher education in Wales. Decisions were taken concerning the location of the university colleges and their finance, and arrangements made for their administration and public accountability. Though the education of women was neither a premier nor really controversial issue of that time, the various deliberations were influenced by the quest for higher education for women in terms of access and growth in numbers, the provision of halls of residence and constitutional safeguards for their involvement and participation in college affairs.

In contrast to the anti-feminist attitudes of Oxford, Cambridge and Edinburgh universities for much of the Victorian era, the university colleges in Wales were quite enlightened in their attitude to women's education. Women students had been admitted to the three Welsh colleges by 1884, but female representation on governing bodies was still to be formalized.

Lewis Morris remained a staunch supporter of the female cause and called for constitutional safeguards for women on college governing bodies. He wanted provisions for admitting women to governing bodies included in any charter granted to a Welsh college. In October 1884, when the charter of University College Aberystwyth was being considered by the governors, he sent a memorial to Lord Carlingford, Lord President of the Council, concerning the Welsh colleges. It emphasized the need for the presence of women on the councils and governing bodies.[2] His attention had been drawn to the fact that, in statutes of the Cardiff and Bangor colleges, women were ineligible to sit on the various governing bodies, including the Court of Governors and the Council. He had been involved in revising the constitution at Aberystwyth and a clause to alter this state of affairs was to be submitted for deliberation at the next Council meeting.[3] He recognized that at the three colleges, all the benefits and emoluments were available for both sexes. At the recent examination at Aberystwyth, one scholarship and two exhibitions were awarded to women, and likewise at Bangor, one scholarship and three exhibitions were awarded to women. Since the colleges were thus open to women as well as men, it was essential that there was female presence on the college's councils and governing bodies.[4] Thomas Gee supported Lewis Morris's plea for female participation on the governing bodies of colleges, and suggested that the vacancy on the Council of Bangor College be filled through a female appointment. Gee believed that women should be involved in the college's affairs, both as governors and teachers.[5] Lewis Morris's action was supported elsewhere in the Welsh press.[6]

The Bangor College Charter included no specific provision for the inclusion of women as members of the Court of Governors or Council. Indeed, women were conspicuous by their total absence from the lists of members of the Court and Council.[7] However, there were no legal impediments to their representation, nor a desire to exclude women from participation in college affairs. By 1887–8, Mrs Verney was a governor by virtue of having paid a subscription, and in 1891–2 was the only female member of the Council.

At Aberystwyth, where Lewis Morris had been pressing for a charter since 1884, the college constitution was revised by the Court of Governors in January 1885 and endorsed by the Education Department. It was not stipulated that women were eligible to be members of the Governing Body, Council and Senate.[8] Aberystwyth eventually followed Bangor and Cardiff and received its charter in February/March 1889, which stipulated that 'Female students should be admissible to all the benefits and emoluments of the college, and women should be eligible to sit on the Governing Body, on the Council and on the Senate'.[9]

The previous year, at Cardiff, the Executive Council of Aberdare Hall requested the election of a woman as a member of the Council of the University College. It was pointed out that the councils of Bangor and Aberystwyth colleges already included female members.

Although by the end of a most significant decade in Wales's educational history, decision-making in the three university colleges remained overwhelmingly under male control, women had taken significant steps towards participation in a system of higher education that was beginning to acquire a more representative character. From Cambridge, a Welsh observer noted in 1888:

> The Welsh Colleges seem to have settled at their birth the vexed question of the Educational Rights of Women. But the cautious authorities of the Universities of great traditions and jealously-guarded privileges, are very difficult to move.[10]

During the 1890s, the female presence in the three university colleges was consolidated. The erection of new halls of residence, developments in teacher training and the establishment of the South Wales Training School of Cookery were significant events in the development of higher education for women. Moreover, through schemes of agricultural education, many girls were given the opportunity to develop an interest in worthwhile post-elementary education. The charter awarded to the University of Wales in 1893 gave further legal sanction and safeguard to women's rights in higher education. Principal J. Viriamu Jones regarded the position assigned to women in 1893 as unique, and interpreted it as indicating 'the desires and aspirations of the Welsh people who are signally interested in the education of women'.[11]

In the University of Wales Charter 1893, which marked the apogee of the Principality's educational achievements, provision was made for placing women in complete equality with men.

> Women shall be eligible equally with men for admittance to any degree which the University is, by this our Charter, authorised to confer. Every office hereby created in the University, and the membership of every authority hereby constituted, shall be open to women equally with men.[12]

In the lengthy deliberations during 1892–3 concerning the Charter, female representation was not an issue: equal treatment of women was taken for granted. The first degree awarded by the University of Wales was conferred on a woman student from Cardiff — Maria Dawson.

Such recognition of the educational claims of women led to a view of the University of Wales as 'the most liberal'[13] of all British universities and as being 'in the van of progress'.[14] In particular, the position was contrasted with Cambridge which still excluded women from degrees.[15] In 1896, the Association for Promoting the Education of Girls in Wales voiced its criticism of the attitude of Oxford and Cambridge universities to degrees for women. In 1895, in a lecture — 'The Future of Welsh Education' — Elizabeth Hughes rejoiced that 'in our Welsh University, unlike our English University, it is no disqualification or drawback to be a woman'.[16] Dilys Glynne Jones expressed satisfaction 'with the justice extended to women in the Charter of the University of Wales'. Though there had been no major problem to overcome, the association had kept a watchful eye to ensure that women were fairly and adequately represented on the colleges' governing bodies, and this principle had been embodied in the charters which provided for women members of the council and court of governors of the three university colleges.

However, equal opportunity for women in higher education could not be taken for granted, and the Association for Promoting the Education of Girls in Wales realized the importance of orchestrating public opinion in support of equal opportunities and rights for women as students, and as members of governing bodies of training-colleges and of the University of Wales. The possibilities opened to women by the University of Wales Charter were far-reaching. *De jure*, they had gained educational equality, but *de facto*, the University of Wales remained a male-dominated institution.

Elizabeth Hughes was the only female member of the committee that drafted the University of Wales Charter. At the first meeting of the Court of Governors on 6 April 1894, there were only six women but seventy-six men. Lady Verney and Elizabeth Hughes were Crown nominees, whilst the Guild of Graduates, the University College of South Wales and Monmouthshire, intermediate schools and elementary schools were represented respectively by Miss Foxall, Lady Aberdare, Miss Fewings and Miss Rule.[17]

Progress was still hampered by controversy and prejudice. In 1895, Principal T.F. Roberts maintained 'there is still a great deal of prejudice against higher education of women, but the prejudice is breaking down and it is for the women of Aberystwyth and Wales generally to strike another blow at it by providing, if possible, the money required to complete and furnish the Hostel'.[18] There was fear in some quarters associated with Aberystwyth College that if once women outnumbered male students, it would have a detrimental effect on the college's status and prestige.[19] At Bangor, an insignificant dispute at the women's hall of residence developed into one of the most remarkable legal *causes célèbres* in Welsh educational history.

Though the university colleges and the University of Wales adopted a liberal policy towards female education, the numbers of women students were still comparatively few at the turn of the century. But it was undeniable that the doors of these institutions of higher education in Wales were open for women. This was a tribute to the enlightened principals and it also attested to the democratic and liberal ideas being voiced in a society where the status and expectations of women, particularly of middle-class background, were undergoing a slow but significant change.

With women having been given due recognition in the Charter of the University of Wales, it was not surprising that in the deliberations of the University Court and University Senate in the early twentieth century no especial attention was given to women students as such. The decisions and pronouncements of the University applied equally to both sexes. The University of Wales administrators and representatives on Court and Senate were not faced with any significant and exclusively female issues. Yet women representatives were still in a small minority in an overwhelmingly male-controlled institution, even though such representatives as Lady Verney and Miss E.P. Hughes participated fully in the democratic decision-making.[20]

In 1909, the Raleigh Committee on 'The University of Wales and the Welsh University Colleges' published its report. Female education was conspicuous by its absence from the numerous deliberations and recommendations. It was noted by J.H. Davies, Registrar of the University College of Wales, that women students were now in a majority at Aberystwyth. The increase in the number of women students from Wales was attributed to the establishment of the network of intermediate schools.[21]

(ii)   *Aberystwyth*

The quest for survival at Aberystwyth, 1882–1884: an educational establishment for women?

In the aftermath of the publication of the Aberdare Report, the future role of the college at Aberystwyth seemed uncertain. The report had recommended the establishment of a college in Glamorgan to cater for the higher-education needs of south Wales; and the retention of the college at Aberystwyth, or its removal to Caernarfon or Bangor to provide for north Wales. In May 1882, the Government decided to allocate an annual grant of £4,000 to the north Wales college 'at Aberystwyth or elsewhere' and likewise to the college for south Wales provided they were established within two years.[22]

The survival of the Aberystwyth College, and the provision of government grants were key educational issues in Wales in the years 1882–4, and the provision of higher education for women became an important aspect in the ensuing deliberations.

Following a conference of representatives of educational opinion in north Wales held in Chester on 23 January 1883, it became clear that Aberystwyth was unacceptable as the location of the college for north Wales. Thomas Gee was prominent at the time in advancing the claims of Denbigh, whilst various other towns were also seeking the north Wales college.[23] With the closure of Aberystwyth College seemingly unavoidable a few saw the possibility of its conversion into an educational establishment for girls or women.

On 18 May 1883, a letter from Captain Edmund H. Verney of Rhianfa, Anglesey was published in *The Cambrian News*. Verney argued from a sexist premiss — 'Wales urgently needs that building, that museum, that library — if not for her sons, yet for the mothers of her sons to be'.[24] He maintained that Dr Williams' School was the only girls' high school open to the public in north Wales. Unless they were amongst the privileged few who were admitted to Howell's or Ashford, girls had to travel to such places as Chester, Liverpool or Manchester for their education.

Given these circumstances, he appealed to his fellow members on the council of Aberystwyth College to consider whether the cause of higher education would be advanced through 'transforming our college into a high school and college for girls, on the same strictly unsectarian principles as must rule in the college for men'.[25] He raised the possibility of financing the establishment as a self-supporting unit on the lines of the Girls' Public Day School Company. Financial assistance might also be obtained from either Howell's charity or the 'Society of Ancient Britons'. He foresaw the establishment of scholarships and exhibitions, and a request being made to the Government for financial assistance for the only college for girls in Wales. As long as the fees were reasonable, he anticipated an immediate enrolment of between 200 and 300 girls.

The proposed conversion led John Foulkes Roberts, a future Lord Mayor of Manchester, and a close confidant of T. Charles Edwards to write to the Principal describing Verney's ideas as 'absurd and insulting'.[26] The proposals also met with hostility from John Gibson, both a staunch supporter of the female cause and, at the time, an even more vigorous defender of Aberystwyth College. In 1883, he wanted Aberystwyth to remain open, in addition to new colleges in north and south Wales. He believed that a number of the leading figures in public life in Wales — including Lord Aberdare and Lewis Morris — were, at best, lukewarm in their support for the college. He maintained that even before the Departmental Committee concluded its inquiry, one of its members, Lewis Morris — who was also Secretary to the College Council — had favoured its conversion into a school for girls and there is evidence to suggest that Morris had contemplated this possibility. Gibson maintained that if Aberystwyth were regarded as a convenient location for a girls' school, the same principle applied as regards the continuation of its collegiate role. There was no justification for destroying 'a successful college' at Aberystwyth in order to establish a girls' school. A school for girls could co-exist at a convenient location in north Wales.

During summer 1883, public meetings in support of the continuation of the Aberystwyth College were held in various parts of Wales. A new role as an educational establishment for girls was not an issue. Nevertheless, a few influential figures still saw such a solution as a convenient answer to the problem of Aberystwyth. In July 1883, Thomas Gee, whilst presupposing that there was little chance of Aberystwyth being recognized as the north Wales college, welcomed the strong possibility of the relocation of the Ashford School in the college building. However, by September 1883, Gee, whose stance in opposing Aberystwyth as a north Wales college had been criticized, was supporting Aberystwyth as a third college to provide higher education for up to one third of the Welsh population in south-west and mid-Wales. He also saw Aberystwyth as an effective counterpoise to the cathedral city of Bangor, chosen in August 1883 as the location of the north Wales college.

In summer and autumn 1883, Lewis Morris was still advocating the conversion of Aberystwyth into an establishment for females. In his inaugural address at the Cymmrodorion Section of the Cardiff National Eisteddfod in 1883, the idea was mooted.[27] Also, in correspondence with A.J. Mundella, he contemplated a role for the college in female education. Initially, a high school for girls was considered a more realistic proposition than a women's college. In September 1883, with two colleges being seen as the formula for Wales's higher education needs, Mundella wrote to Morris:

> You agree with me as to the best method of utilizing Aberystwyth. You say I look forward with you, as I have done from the first to the utilization of Aberystwyth for the Higher Education of Girls, but I do not think that public opinion in Wales is ripe to the experiment of a Women's College. I agree as to the prematureship of a 'Women's College', but before a women's College can succeed, girls must first obtain better education. Why not then begin with girls? Why not apply for the transfer of Ashford and make it one of the best schools for girls in Britain? I will promise you vigorous help.[28]

An unsigned article in Volume v of *Y Cymmrodor*, 1882 — 'Higher Education in Wales and the Proposed University Colleges' — also indicates that Aberystwyth's conversion into an education institution for girls was one role being advanced in 1883 in the aftermath of the Chester Conference. Captain Verney was also continuing to support the location of a female establishment at Aberystwyth. This was evident at a conference convened in the town in October 1883 to consider what steps might be taken concerning the retention of the college. A letter from Verney was read out. However, Verney's proposals were not taken up at the conference, nor at a stormy meeting of the College Council on 16 October, when there were demands for the resignation of Lord Aberdare as the college president. The struggle for the survival of Aberystwyth College was entering its most critical phase. The conditional offer of a government grant to two colleges expired in March 1884. Cardiff College had opened in October 1883 and Bangor was already chosen as another location.

When the Council of Aberystwyth College met in London on 3 December under the chairmanship of Captain Verney, Lewis Morris proposed that the college be as open to women as men. Whilst this was given a favourable reception, his further proposal that boarding in the college building should be exclusively for women caused more controversy.[29] The matter was referred to a sub-committee which was to report to the council. Gibson thought that it would have been disastrous if the motion had been accepted at such a crucial moment in the college's history.[30] Male students would have had to find other accommodation, and this would have weakened the college's case for survival:

> The first step would have been taken towards converting the college into a girls' school, an object which everybody knows lies very near the heart of Mr Lewis Morris. It is pitiful to observe the attempts being made to prevent the college from having even a chance for existence.[31]

Gibson condemned Lewis Morris's 'absurd resolution' and called for his resignation.[32] When the College Council met again on 8 January 1884, to consider sending a deputation to impress on Gladstone the case for the college's retention and for provision of government aid, A.C. Humphreys-Owen suggested that firstly the Council itself ought to be unanimous in its views regarding the future of the college. Humphreys-Owen had circulated a letter impressing on Council members the need to decide what role Aberystwyth College could best perform in the future for education in Wales. Some wanted its role to be the same as Bangor and Cardiff and be the College for mid-Wales. Some wanted it to be used partly, if not wholly, for the education of women, whilst others favoured its conversion into an agricultural college or intermediate school. These issues were discussed at the meeting.[33] The retention of the college at Aberystwyth was the key issue when the proposals concerning its role as an institution for women were raised. Lewis Morris's proposal for allocating the boarding accommodation in the building for women students was seen as inopportune, and further discussion was postponed.

On 12 March 1884, under the chairmanship of A.C. Humphreys-Owen, the College Council discussed the seventeen-point memorial to be submitted to the Government, calling for the retention of the college and provision of annual financial aid. The sixteenth point dealt with 'the peculiar advantages offered by the buildings of Aberystwyth for the reception of young women' — an advantage which the colleges at Bangor and Cardiff did not have. The memorial was presented, and following a resolution moved by Rendel calling for state support for the college, the position of Aberystwyth College was debated in Parliament on 14 March 1884. Questions of finance dominated the parliamentary proceedings. Rendel called for Aberystwyth to be given the same financial support as the Bangor and Cardiff colleges. If this were done, he hoped some suitable arrangements would be made concerning the education of girls which had been much neglected. There was no other reference to female education as such in this crucial parliamentary debate, but the need for adequate provision for women in higher education was evident.[34]

A grant of £2,000 per annum offered on that day was raised to £2,500 in July 1884 following intense lobbying in Parliament and the holding of meetings throughout Wales. Though other serious problems lay ahead, by 1884 it was resolved that Aberystwyth College was to remain open as one of the Welsh university colleges. It was to cater for both sexes and not to be converted into an educational establishment for women. At a meeting in support for the college in April 1884, John Gibson referred disparagingly to Lewis Morris's attempt to convert the college into a girls' school.[35]

The admission of women students

The announcement in May 1884 that the Oxford University Convocation intended allowing women to take examinations and gain honours was welcomed in the Welsh press. It provided Thomas Gee with the opportunity to make comparisons with the position of women in the Welsh university colleges and advocate equal treatment for the two sexes.

In fact, the two new colleges at Cardiff and Bangor, and now also Aberystwyth, were to admit women on the same terms as male students. At Aberystwyth, though there had been female students in the 1870s, the first woman student enrolled for a full degree course was Miss Louise Davies from Carmarthenshire in the Lent Term 1884. She had been awarded an entrance exhibition, and for some months was the only woman student there. Within six months, however, there were half a dozen more women students and this had increased to ten by the end of the session. By October 1885, a total of nineteen women were enrolled. By 1888, there were forty women students at UCW Aberystwyth and forty-two in October 1889. Many years later, Aberystwyth's first woman student wrote that 'We could have met with kinder and more chivalrous reception from Professors and men students alike'.[36] When A.J. Mundella addressed students at Aberystwyth in October 1884, he showed his support for the higher education of women: 'Without educated women, we can never be an educated nation. It is to the intelligent wives and mothers we must look for well-trained and well-educated youth'.[37] By 1888, women constituted forty of the 165 students at Aberystwyth, forty-one of the 120 at Cardiff, and thirty-nine of the 101 at Bangor.[38]

The establishment of a hall of residence

An important consequence of the admission of women to all three colleges was the realization of the need for halls of residence. Their establishment in the 1880s heralded a significant step forward in the development of higher education for women. Aberystwyth and Bangor were praised in 1886 in *Baner ac Amserau Cymru* for following the example of Cardiff not only in admitting women, but also for providing hostel accommodation.[39]

Reviewing the position at Aberystwyth at the beginning of 1885, John Gibson suggested that the two items requiring the immediate attention of the college authorities were obtaining a full grant of £4,000 from the Government and opening a hostel for women which was the *sine qua non* for the growth of female education at the college.[40] During the 1884–5 session, women students had to find lodgings in the town. During the year, University College of Wales was to be given the same annual grant of £4,000 as Cardiff and Bangor, and a hostel for women students was opened in October 1885 under the supervision of the Lady Superintendent, Mrs Powell, widow of the late Reverend Ebenezer Powell, Holt Academy. It was located in Abergeldie House, on the Victoria Marine Terrace, which was rented for the session for £90.[41] The College Council hoped that its establishment would be accompanied by a steady increase in the number of women students.[42] The terms were £35 for the session, payable in advance.

Thomas Gee viewed the hostel as a major landmark in the advancement of higher education for women in Wales which was much appreciated by parents. Gee had regularly warned his Nonconformist audience of the moral dangers facing young women away from home in large towns and cities. Henceforth, in Aberystwyth at least, Welsh parents could rest assured that their daughters' pursuit of higher education would be bereft of any moral danger. There were twenty-four women students at Aberystwyth in the 1885–6 session, and twenty-eight in October 1886, out of a total of 146 students.

When, in May 1886, the College Council reviewed the position of the hall of residence, it was felt that in the light of the considerable financial loss caused by lack of support from women students, it should be closed at the end of the session. Henceforth, female students would reside in 'houses approved by the Senate' or with their relatives or guardians, though the Council hoped that the hostel would be reopened at a future date.[43] In fact, women students already had the option since the 1885–6 session of residing either in one of the registered houses in the town or in the hall of residence.[44] Principal T.C. Edwards thought that the 'interesting experiment' would probably have been successful if it had been continued for a longer period. However, the college's acute financial position did not permit such development.[45]

Gibson, however, called for a more businesslike approach from the college authorities in its handling of the hall of residence.[46] However, after an intermission of only one year (1886–7), which had seen an increase in the number of women students, a hall of residence for women students was opened again in October 1887 when Abergeldie House was rented once again. In June 1887, the Senate had considered the question of the discipline and lodging of the female students, and passed a resolution stating that it was 'very important that a hostel for women students should be re-established under a lady superintendent capable of exercising a salutary influence, and entrusted with general disciplinary authority over women students'.[47] Significantly, in order to ensure the success of the hostel, it was also recommended that residence be compulsory for all women students unless resident with their parents or guardians. On 15 June 1887, on the proposition of Lewis Morris, a staunch champion of the female cause, the College Council decided that it was desirable to re-establish a women's hostel and that 'a Lady Superintendent be appointed and entrusted with a general disciplinary authority over Female students, whether resident in the Hostel or not'.[48]

Out of eighty-three applicants for the post, Miss E.A. Carpenter was appointed at an annual salary of £80. A long, distinguished period of service for the college thereby began in 1887 and continued until 1905. By the opening of the new session in October 1887 with thirteen students in the hall, a set of regulations to govern students' conduct at the hall had been drawn up. Reflecting the prevailing Victorian social and moral attitudes which exerted considerable influence on women in Aberystwyth halls of residence for many years, they stipulated that all women students should be in their rooms by 10.00 p.m., permission was needed to be out ater 6.00 p.m. in winter, and 8.30 p.m. on Sundays in the summer. They were not allowed to enter the rooms of male students and were expected to attend a place of worship regularly. They were obliged to allocate at least one hour a day to walking or some other physical exercise. A former student at the hall in 1887 recalled:

> In those days, wherever we went after hours except to church or to chapel, the Lady Principal diligently accompanied us; the wall of her poky little back sitting-room . . . was adorned with a careful synopsis of our classes, so that at any moment she could tell where we were or rather ought to be; on return from evening classes every student reported herself to the dragon in her den; and undeviating punctuality at all meals was obligatory.[49]

The Principal recognized that the compulsory rule concerning residence might have had an adverse effect on the recruitment of students for the 1887–8 session, but he emphasized the educational and social value of residence: 'the influence of our Lady Principal will be of more value to her students than even the Professors' lectures'.[50] He was convinced that once parents appreciated the merits of residence in such a hall, there would be a steady growth in the enrolment of women students.[51]

At a time when there were criticisms voiced concerning the deficient nature of the education of many male and female students who entered the university colleges, and when the quest for intermediate schools was entering a crucial phase, the Lady Principal at Aberystwyth in 1888 welcomed the more thorough preliminary education that most of the women students had received.[52] In particular, she referred to the college's links with such recognized establishments as Cheltenham College; North London Collegiate School; Wyggeston School, Leicestershire; Orme's School, Newcastle under Lyme; Aske's School, Hatcham and High Schools at Blackburn, Bury, Dulwich and Southport.[53] Although there was a growth in the number of Welsh girls attending the college, the total was still comparatively low — eleven in the 1887–8 session of whom six were new students, whilst in the previous session, there were only two.[54]

For the following session, 9 Marine Terrace became the women's hall of residence, and because the number of female students was larger than expected, accommodation was also acquired for eight students in 10 Marine Terrace.[55] In October 1888, there were forty female students out of a total of 177 at the college. In December 1888, Miss Carpenter referred to the growing popularity of the hall, and expressed the hope that it would be self-supporting.[56] A financial loss of over £200 had been incurred in establishing the hall.[57] By the end of the session in 1889, the crowded conditions in the hall of residence were drawn to the attention of the College Council who regretted the lack of funds to provide a more suitable residence.[58]

Though the college authorities at Aberystwyth in the 1880s had not shown the same initiative and enthusiasm that had characterized the founders of Aberdare Hall in Cardiff, there had been a growing appreciation of the importance of the female presence, and the need for a suitable hall of residence: 'The Council look forward with great interest to the continued development of this branch of the College and they will hail with pleasure a further increase in the number of students connected by birth or residence with Wales'.[59]

At Aberystwyth the presence of women was consolidated in the 1890s, especially with the opening of a purpose-built hall of residence. From the beginning of the decade, with an increasing number of women students seeking admission, the Lady Principal — Miss Carpenter — had been emphasizing the need for more accommodation. The numbers of women enrolled at the college increased steadily:

1890–91:	33
1891–92:	45
1892–93:	84
1893–94:	102[60]

In 1891, whilst submitting a very favourable report on the academic work and successes of the women students in arts and science courses, she noted that most of them entered the college two or three years after leaving school, often after a period of schoolteaching. They wanted the privacy of a single room and she hoped 'the time has now come when the College authorities will see that buying a site and furnishing a Hall for our women students is an urgent necessity'.[61] With considerable foresight, she also suggested that in July and August, there was a rich vein to be tapped through accommodating visitors at the hall.

Primarily for financial reasons, the College Council was very slow in responding to a long-felt need, and consequently 'the Hall of Residence, oscillated, session after session between the North and South ends of the Terrace'.[62] Until the erection of Alexandra Hall in 1896, women resided in the Queen's Hotel rented from 1892 to 1893, and in 'overflow halls' such as 'Balmoral' and 'Brighton House'. The decision to establish a day training department for up to fifteen men and fifteen women contributed directly to the decision to take the Queen's Hotel.[63]

The strict surveillance introduced by Miss Carpenter remained much in evidence throughout the 1890s. Though the college authorities claimed that 'mixed' classes indicated the equality enjoyed by women students, the various rules and regulations operating inside, and even outside, halls of residence, were designed to keep male and female students separate as much as possible. Indeed, John Gibson, a staunch advocate of perfect equality between the sexes, was led by a celebrated disciplinary incident in 1898 to condemn the application of strict rules to one sex only — the women.[64] He even questioned the practice of making it obligatory for women, but not for men, to reside in hall. Women students should be allowed to lodge in town under the same rules and conditions as men: 'Even able women like Miss Carpenter may be afraid of freedom and may think that restrictions are good for women which she would not think were good or necessary for men.[65] However enlightened Miss Carpenter might have been as a pioneer of female education, she meted out harsh penalites for minor breaches of discipline. In the 1892–3 prospectus, all women students were obliged to be in their rooms by 10.30 p.m. with lights out by 11.00 p.m. Permission was needed to be out after 6.30 p.m. on weekdays in winter or after 8.30 p.m. on Sundays and in summer.[66] The college's failure to establish a purpose-built hall had been regularly criticized by Gibson in *The Cambrian News*. On the occasion of Principal T. Charles Edwards's departure in 1891, reference was made to 'the hostel confusion . . . the project still a mere project'.[67] The failure fuelled Gibson's demand for reform of the college management.

Principal T. Charles Edwards had been a cautious leader of the college. Financial constraints, rather than lack of enthusiasm for the higher education of women, explained the lack of a purpose-built hall of residence. He was undoubtedly aware that some members of the College Council were not in favour of women students outnumbering the men.[68] In accepting the principalship of Bala Theological College in 1891, he made it clear in his terms of acceptance that its doors should be open to women as well as men.[69] The new Principal at Aberystwyth, T. Francis Roberts, was left in no doubt as to the urgency of the hostel problem.[70] The women students' academic achievements, careful supervision and 'true collegiate life' under Miss Carpenter, were used to pressurize the college authorities to erect a hall larger than Queen's Hotel, that would allow for further development of women's education at Aberystwyth.[71]

An appeals committee was set up by the College Council in late 1891 to raise funds for the erection of a hall. Though the venture was supported by such well-known names as Miss Buss, Dr Sophia Jex-Blake, Miss E.P. Hughes, Miss Fewings, Miss Winter and Lady Rendel, donations and promises amounted to only £300 to meet a target figure of £6,000–£7,000.[72] The relatively poor response, as well as the debt on the college building itself, caused the women's hostel scheme to be left in abeyance until 1893, when circumstances were more encouraging.

Primarily through the influence of Lewis Morris, a sum of £2,000 was received from the Pfeiffer trust, and by early 1894, Aberystwyth Corporation provided a site on the seafront for a new hostel.[73] However, not all of the College Council were enthusiastic: John Gibson argued that 'the movement to build a hostel was being opposed, and obstacles were being thrown in the way of a project that ought to command the earnest support of every friend of Wales, and of Aberystwyth and of women'.[74] Nevertheless, architects were commissioned, and in March 1895, the foundation stone of a new five-storey hall of residence (initially for 100 women students and eventually for 200), was laid on the seafront at the northern end of Victoria Terrace. The adjoining Balmoral House, with room for twenty-five students, was bought in 1894, and the whole venture, including furnishings, was estimated to cost over £16,500.[75]

It was an exciting financial undertaking for the college. Except for the Pfeiffer bequest, and donations received following the 1891 appeal, no other reserves were available for the enterprise, and the scheme would not have gone ahead without the £12,000 borrowed from Edward Davies, Llandinam. A successful appeal for funds was now essential.

At the ceremony of laying the foundation stone, for which Lewis Morris had composed on ode, Principal T. Francis Roberts viewed the new hall as further embodiment of the advance of women's education at Aberystwyth. Miss Carpenter drew attention to the ever increasing numbers clamouring for admission. Enthusiastic support for the venture was expressed by Gibson in *The Cambrian News*, which regularly listed donations to the appeal fund.[76] He was critical of what he saw as the over-cautious attitude of the College Council in deciding to postpone the erection of one wing.[77]

On 26 June 1896, during the royal visit by the Prince and Princess of Wales, and in the presence of Gladstone, Alexandra Hall of Residence was officially opened. With the completion of the north wing in 1898, the new hall could accommodate 200 women students. By then, the cost of the hall, including furnishings, was put at £29,000.[78] The fund-raising appeal emphasized the successful development of women's education at the college which was reflected in a distinguished roll of academic honours, and growth in the enrolment of women students:

1893–94:	102
1894–95:	132
1895–96:	151
1896–97:	169
1897–98:	175

Of the factors contributing to Aberystwyth's success as a centre for higher education of women, especial attention was focused on the close relationship between hall and college, reasonable fees averaging £50 per annum, healthy environment, thorough implementation of the 'mixed' system of teaching, and the recognition of the equal educational claims of women in the college Charter of 1889 and the University of Wales Charter of 1893. Reference was also made to the opening of a secondary training department which provided further opportunities for women. A day training college for elementary teachers was opened at Aberystwyth in October 1892, when twenty of the thirty students admitted were women. In June 1898, sixty of the 200 students in Alexandra Hall were prospective elementary school teachers.

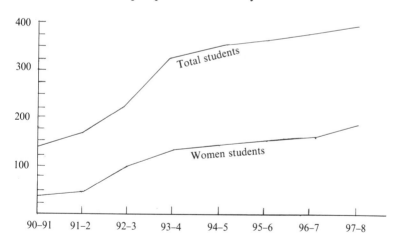

Figure 8.1
University College of Wales, Aberystwyth: Growth in Numbers from 1890 to 1897
(Upper line shows total growth; lower line growth in number of women students)
Source: University College of Wales Archives.

Women students, 1900–1914

The minutes of the College Council and reports to the Court, including the Principal's annual reports from the late 1890s to 1914, reveal no especial attention to women students except as regards the cost of hostel accommodation.

Following the opening of Alexandra Hall in 1896, there was a steady growth in the number of women students. By 1908–9, there were 218 women and 212 men enrolled at the college. However, by the outbreak of war, numbers had declined, there being 171 women and 223 male students in 1914–15.

Miss Carpenter remained as Lady Principal until 1905 when she reached her seventieth year. At the time, there were 215 women students at the college. After eighteen years of loyal service to the college, this pioneer of women's higher education now retired. In the *University College of Wales Magazine*, it was correctly recorded that since 1887:

> she has been an essential figure in the lives of all the women students of Aberystwyth . . . The students could not fail to feel how earnestly she had set at heart the cause of the higher education of women.[79]

Reference was made to her competent management of the hall, the establishment of the hall library, the fostering of intellectual activity, and her marvellous energy. Such praise was well merited, but more debatable is the view that she had been 'broad and liberal in her way of looking at social life'.

The rules and regulations in the Alexandra Hall prospectuses, with their focus on discipline and moral propriety, had changed little since her arrival in 1887. By the early twentieth century, they were often the cause of student irritation. Lady Stamp (née Olive Marsh), a student at Alexandra Hall between 1898 and 1900, recorded not only the rich social life of the college with its concerts, operas, literary and debating societies and swimming, but she also noted in a letter that 'Miss Carpenter is away. There is such an air of freedom about the place'.[80] In 1904, there was much dissatisfaction and there were rumours of a 'revolt' following a directive from Miss Carpenter that women students were to have 'as little intercourse as possible with any men outside the College buildings'.[81] Such restrictions were being increasingly seen by the students as betraying a lack of confidence of the authorities, and a slight on students' 'worthiness and true womanliness'.[82]

John Gibson published a worthy tribute in *The Cambrian News* where he referred to the conspicuous success of a remarkable woman who fought against the reactionaries represented on the governing bodies of the College who were against steadily increasing the number of women students.[83]

Miss Carpenter had to deal with people holding the misguided belief that, with the growth in the number of women students, the prestige of the college would thereby be adversely affected. However, the support accorded her by Lord Rendel and Principal T. Francis Roberts was also acknowledged.

Miss Carpenter's influence on women's education at Aberystwyth had been considerable. In 1955, H.J. Fleure, one of the college's most distinguished students, suggested that in Miss Carpenter, the college appointed 'a genius as Lady Warden', who was regarded as 'a very mighty atom' by the student body.[84] Though she might not have been beloved by her students, there is abundant evidence to support the judgement of the college's official historian in 1972 that 'she won and retained the respect of men and women students. She had an unmistakable air of authority'.[85]

Her successor, who came to be regarded as Warden of Alexandra Hall rather than Lady Principal, was Miss H.M. Stephen, whose academic excellence had impressed the staffing committee. Her appointment was seen by Rendel as the opportunity to strengthen the academic side of hall life, and infuse the women students with the wide intellectual and cultural values of the best Oxbridge tradition.

> We need not be provincial because we are Welsh . . . We must, if we can, touch the level of the older universities. This is a great opportunity of raising the whole tone and level and standing of the women's side of the College.[86]

But she was also aloof and was to hold the post for only three years, marked by conflict between students and staff, which reached a climax in the so-called Alexandra Hall 'revolt' of 1907. An outdated code of discipline, and petty regulations, were regarded with increasing irritation in an age of growing female militancy.[87]

In 1908, Miss Stephen was succeeded as Warden of Alexandra Hall by Miss E.A. Fewings, a former headmistress of Dr Williams' School, Dolgellau, and a leading advocate of female education. Within a year, there was an even more serious revolt against college discipline, which led to the suspension of proceedings by Sir Isambard Owen at a meeting of the University of Wales Court on 22 November 1909.[88] Though primarily orchestrated by male students, and not directly associated with life in Alexandra Hall, the women were in no way innocent bystanders. Whilst the UCW senate met on 25 and 26 November to impose penalties on the student body, it was reported in the press that women students had demanded that if there was to be any punishment, men and women should be treated alike.[89]

Women students participated in debates which reflected a keen awareness of contemporary issues. As well as demands for the extension of a parliamentary suffrage to women, which was debated in November 1903, attention was also given to enabling women to be admitted to all occupations on an equal basis with men.[90] The issues raised, focused on the principle of justice, the advantage to the economy of the definition of the woman's natural sphere, the question of intellectual capacity. Unsurprisingly, attention was also given to the principle of co-education in universities.[91] In 1906, it was maintained that co-education exerted a mutual influence on character and discipline and was a success in universities in Britain and the USA. Separation of the sexes was said to be contrary to natural laws and the numerous 'petty restrictions on social intercourse' at the college were condemned.[92] Co-education was also viewed as a more economical system, and it was maintained that the presence of women tended to raise the moral tone.[93]

In Edwardian and pre-war Aberystwyth, there was much dissatisfaction among the students concerning rules and regulations which aimed to erect a barrier between the sexes. Conscious of the demands for political, economic and social emancipation, they found it increasingly difficult to obey a senate rule in force in 1913–14 which forbade conversation between male and female students outside the college except at 'public meetings, at athletic matches, and at such social functions as are sanctioned by the Warden of Alexandra Hall'.[94]

Little evidence is available about the socio-economic origins of the women students in Edwardian and pre-war Aberystwyth. However, in the University College of Wales archives, there are seventy-four hall entrance forms for 1905–6, and forty-eight for 1913–14, which provide a useful, though limited insight. They show that the daughters of fathers engaged in business, trade and the professions, were well represented.[95]

Father's Profession/Trade

Grocer	2	Metal manufacturer	1
Butcher	1	Coal proprietor	1
Outfitter/shopkeeper/draper	4	Engineer	2
Provision dealer	2	Carpenter	1

Leather merchant/manufacturer	2	Wheelwright	1
General merchant/iron monger	2	Monumental mason	1
Farmer	7	Workhouse master	1
Minister/clergyman	5	Commercial traveller	1
Solicitor/barrister	2	House furnisher	1
Schoolmaster	6	Iron/steelworks manager	1
Inspector of schools	1	Lodging-house keeper	1
Insurance/Inland Revenue/customs	6	Railway goods foreman	1
Shipbroker	1	Quarryman	2
Medicine	1	Collier	1
Builder & contractor	2	Traffic manager	1
Registrar	1	Not given	10
Woollen/cotton manufacturer	2		

In 1911, women pursuing teacher training at Aberystwyth, as elsewhere, were affected by new regulations introduced by the Board of Education. Henceforth, grants were offered to universities that provided four-year courses — a consecutive three, plus one arrangement — for graduate certification. At Aberystwyth, from 1910 to 1911, prospective secondary school teachers were to pursue a one-year professional course leading to certification by the University of Wales instead of the University of Cambridge.

On the eve of the First World War, the college magazine — *The Dragon* — recorded the interests and activities of a student body highly conscious of significant trends in society at large. Outdated rules and regulations which impinged upon the development of a healthy co-education were particularly resented. Both male and female students felt the need for 'representative government and not senate government'. Not all would have agreed with O.M. Edwards's inspection report that women students at Alexandra Hall were under 'sympathetic and tactful rule'.[96]

(iii)   *Cardiff*

The admission of women students

Cardiff was the first Welsh college to admit women on the same terms as men. In his inaugural address at the opening of University College Cardiff on 24 October 1883, Lord Aberdare emphasized that the higher education of women would not be overlooked, and undeniably, a most enlightened approach was being shown: 'In all our arrangements we have borne in mind that our college must provide for the education of women as well as of men; our classes and laboratories, our scholarships and exhibitions, are open on equal terms to men and women'.[97] He referred to the scholarships and exhibitions won by women in the recent examination and foresaw that 'the intellectual superiority' assumed by men would soon be refuted.

From the outset in 1882, when the Cardiff College Scheme Committee prepared a draft scheme, it was intended that women students be admitted on equal terms with men. In the petition to Parliament in December 1883 requesting the grant of a charter for the college, clause 9(b) had stipulated 'that female students shall be admited to attend any of the courses of instruction established in the College'.[98] This was included in the college Charter.[99] Fourteen women and 103 men were admitted in the first session in October 1883 and a female student was awarded the chief entrance award. In the 1885–6 session, there were seventeen women and 107 men enrolled, and by the end of the decade, in 1888–9, sixty-three women and 102 men.[100]

The educational significance of the policy adopted at University College Cardiff was pinpointed at the time. It was noted that at the opening of the college 'all the advantages of Higher Education were thrown open for the first time in Wales to women students and men students alike'.[101] At a meeting of the Court of Governors in October 1886 when there were 107 men and seventeen women in the college, Lord Aberdare expressed satisfaction that in the distribution of prizes, female students had held their own.[102] Principal Viriamu Jones and his wife were staunch supporters of equality of educational opportunity for both men and women.

Establishment of Aberdare Hall

The opening in 1885 of the 'Aberdare Hall of Residence for Female Students' was a considerable achievement. It was to be the second-oldest university hostel for women students in Britain — the first being College Hall, London, founded in 1882.[103] Its establishment attested to the foresight, initiative, and vigour of a small group of devoted women who enjoyed the enthusiastic support of the Principal J. Viriamu Jones and the President, Lord Aberdare.

Its foundation must also be viewed within the context of late-Victorian perceptions of femininity. Criticisms had already been voiced concerning the mixed college at Cardiff, and the Principal — an enlightened supporter of female education — wanted to ensure that the admission of both sexes would generate neither misunderstanding nor opposition from the public.[104] In his report on the College's first session of 1883–4 he referred to:

> The experiment, if experiment it can be called, of classes composed of students of both sexes, has been most successful. I desire to point out to

the Council the necessity of opening a Hall for women students. I cannot too strongly recommend the Council to give this point their most careful consideration.[105]

In addition, he was aware of the disadvantages of residence in lodgings when lack of physical exercise and inadequate diet often had an adverse effect on women's intellectual study.[106] Mrs Viriamu Jones and Lady Aberdare wanted to ensure that young women were 'properly sheltered from the hazards of life in a mixed company away from home'.[107]

Early in the 1884–5 session, a General Ladies Committee was formed under the chairmanship of Lady Aberdare and with Mrs Viriamu Jones as secretary. It was decided to raise subscriptions in order to secure suitable premises for a hall of residence. In November 1884, following a report from Mrs Viriamu Jones and the Honourable Isabel Bruce, a daughter of Lord Aberdare, it was decided to adopt Keswick House in Richmond Road as a hostel for twenty students. Subscriptions of £600 were soon raised and further donations promised. Rules and a constitution for a ladies hall were drawn up. Significantly, the hall was to be undenominational, and was to be managed by an executive committee of twelve.[108] Though the establishment of the hall was an independent venture, and its affairs managed by a committee independent of the college, the College Council were to be the trustees of any property that the executive committee might acquire. But the hall did not receive any financial help from the University College.[109]

The hall was viewed as an essential means for increasing the numbers of women in higher education, and generating greater equality of educational opportunity.[110] Corporate life in a hall of residence was seen as a vital means of widening the experience of young women destined for the professions. Writing in *Women's Suffrage Journal* in April 1885, Mrs Viriamu Jones pinpointed the significance of the event as 'a new and important departure in higher education' in Wales. It was seen as a 'necessary adjunct to the success' of the women students who merited 'equal residential privileges' with male students in the various colleges in the country. The benefits of residential education for male students had been proven at Oxford and Cambridge. Thomas Gee saw the arrangements being made in Cardiff as superior to the alternative of lonely lodgings.[111]

The committee endeavoured to raise funds to establish awards for women and to acquire books. By 1886, the generosity of private donors enabled a scholarship of £20 and two prizes of £12.10*s.* each, awarded on the result of the entrance examination, to be made tenable at the hall. Dr Frances Hoggan donated thirty volumes to establish a library.

With the hall proving a success, its management was formalized in autumn 1886 through being placed in the hands of a body of governors instead of the general committee.[112]

The hall's register of students for the 1880s shows that whilst some students had attended private schools in such places as Ammanford and Mumbles, others had been pupils at Ashford School, North London Collegiate School, and various other high schools in England. In 1889, sixteen of the thirty students at the hall were Welsh.

Miss Bruce resigned as Honorary Principal in January 1887. It was undoubtedly accurately recorded in the college Calendar that 'the Hall had progressed under her'.[113] In May 1887, Miss Isabel Don was appointed the first salaried Principal of Aberdare Hall. As befitted a tutor in English at Oxford, she was 'a cultured personality' with experience of the supervision of women students at Somerville Hall, Oxford.[114] During her brief stay at Cardiff, there were eighteen women in residence at the hall in the session 1887–8. The fees of £35 for a 31-week session were deliberately fixed at a very low rate, in order to attract students. At the first annual meeting of the newly constituted governing body in January 1887, the philosophy underlying the hall's foundation had been reiterated. Lady Aberdare had emphasized that proper supervision was essential for students not living with their parents and that this was only possible in a hall of residence. More perceptive on this occasion was the Archdeacon of Llandaff's view of the merits of residence:

> Aberdare Hall is not merely an appendage of the South Wales College, but an absolute necessity . . . Only a small part of the required higher education can be obtained by a mere attendance at lectures . . . but Aberdare Hall which brought mind into contact with mind supplied exactly that education which was required.[115]

Though much enlightenment characterized the hall's management in these early years, its decisions were unlikely to be entirely divorced from prevailing social attitudes and sexual mores. It is thus not surprising that in 1885 the executive committee of Aberdare Hall showed concern for effective chaperoning of women students, and deemed picnics unsuitable.

> . . . all entertainments in which both men and women students take part are attended with certain risks, but that these dangers become much greater when the amusement takes the form of a picnic as the unrestrained intercourse during a long walk makes it difficult for those ladies who act as chaperones to exercise sufficient vigilance.[116]

No theatrical rehearsal should take place without the presence of a responsible chaperone.

In 1888, Miss Frances Hutchins became the third Principal of Aberdare Hall at a salary of £80 per annum, and held the post until 1892. Scholarships and library funds were established, as it was realized that many potential students would be unable to enter the hall without financial assistance. Amongst the scholarships tenable at the hall, there was now one from the Association for Promoting the Higher Education of Girls in Wales.[117]

With Aberdare Hall seen to be making 'steady and satisfactory progress' and its 'establishment and success . . . a most interesting chapter in the history of Higher Education in Wales', the acquisition of new premises was being contemplated before the end of the decade.[118] On the eve of the implementation of the Welsh Intermediate Education Act, the Hall's governing body passed a resolution calling for the interests of girls to be given equal consideration with those of boys.[119] Aberdare Hall itself was obviously likely to benefit from such a policy. Its governing body remained steadfast in its high estimation of the educational and cultural value of a hall of residence:

> It is not enough to have given women in our University College the means of intellectual culture, no one who has thought seriously on the subject will question the great importance of providing them those moral and refining influences which can only be ensured for students from a distance in such a residence as Aberdare Hall.[120]

At Cardiff, a new Aberdare Hall was opened for women students in October 1895, and was a most significant testimony to the continued progress of women's higher education. It was the first hall of residence for female students to be located in purpose-built premises.[121] By 1890, the number of female students was increasing and, with the opening of a day training department, it was clear that more accommodation would be required.[122] It was decided to erect a new building and, in August 1891, the support of the College Council was given to the venture and the appeal for funds.[123] The enterprise now became the joint initiative of the Aberdare Hall Executive Committee and the College Council. Eventually, in 1893, an acre of land in Corbett Road was acquired on a 99-year lease from Lord Bute for a ground rental of £100 per annum.[124] A hall to accommodate forty-three students, and costing £5,870, was to be erected. A decision was taken to finance payment through subscriptions and a mortgage.

At a most opportune moment, money was acquired from the Pfeiffer trust under the will of Mrs Emily Jane Pfeiffer (née Davies) who died in 1890. Born in 1827 of Montgomeryshire stock, she had married a wealthy German merchant, resident in London. A cultured lady, she had written poetry and also articles reflecting on the social position of women. Under the terms of her will, £70,000 was left in trust for the advancement of women's higher education. A sum of £2,000 from this fund was now allocated by the trustees towards the cost of erecting and furnishing the new hall in Cardiff.[125] By June 1894, together with the Pfeiffer donation, over £4,000 had been donated to the building fund.[126] A letter in the Aberdare Hall archives, dated 30 July 1892, shows that Lady Aberdare wrote to the Pfeiffer trustees emphasizing the feeling throughout Wales in favour of 'forwarding' the higher education of women. In her view, 'no more effectual aid' could be rendered to women's higher education in Wales than the provision of financial assistance towards establishing the new hall.[127]

From January 1895, the Richmond Road premises were vacated and students were accommodated at the new hall. At the opening ceremony, Mrs E.M. Sidgwick, Principal of Newnham College, addressed a large gathering. In a wide-ranging speech, she recognized the overall significance of the event: 'In Wales they were far ahead of Cambridge both in the provision for women and in the admission of these even to the teaching staff'.[128] The opportunity was taken to comment on the debate that had exerted such a major influence on attitudes to female education in the Victorian era and to refute a major misconception: 'A retrospect over 25 years showed clearly that the education of women was a good thing, and instead of injuring their health, had made them all better sisters, wives and mothers, housekeepers and educators of children'.[129] Likewise, the *Western Mail* rejected the view that education had an adverse impact on 'womanly feelings': 'Whatever mental culture she may possess, her heart never goes wrong by reason of it'.[130] Furthermore, such great strides in higher education being witnessed in Wales had sound economic justification. Through education, 'a thousand avenues of usefulness were opened for women'.[131]

From 1892 to 1898, Miss Ethel Hurlbatt was Principal of Aberdare Hall, which was described in the Minutes of the Committee of Council as 'a handsome well-planned building'.[132] She possessed strong personality, was endowed with a wide vision and was a staunch supporter of greater educational advantages for women. Ethel Hurlbatt played a crucial role in establishing the hall and raising subscriptions. With furnishings it was eventually to cost nearly £9,000.[133]

By October 1896, 106 students had passed through Aberdare Hall since 1885.[134] Whilst fifty-two had home addresses in Wales, the other fifty-four came from outside Wales. Such well-known schools as the North London Collegiate, Roon School, Greenwich, and Redland

High School, Bristol, were well represented in the hall. By October 1897, thirteen past students were headmistresses in Wales, and twenty-eight were assistant mistresses. But the hall was also home to girls educated in far less fashionable private establishments such as Golden Grove School and St Catherine's, Cardiff.

In 1893, with the approval of Elizabeth Hughes in particular, a decision was taken for the new hall to admit female students of the Normal Department who were training to become elementary teachers.[135] Hitherto, they were accommodated in a rented house elsewhere in the city. By the end of the century, students resident in Aberdare Hall were taking various courses. Following the establishment of medical studies at the University College in 1893, Aberdare Hall's appeal for funds stated that the number of women students would increase. In 1898, they included twelve arts and three science undergraduates, seventeen Normal Department students, one student in the Secondary Training Department, one medical student and three students studying for the Diploma of the School of Cookery. By 1899, the possibility of extending the hall was being mooted.[136]

At a time of considerable activity in the sphere of intermediate education throughout Wales, the Aberdare Hall Committee kept a watchful eye on county intermediate schemes. In 1890, resolutions were passed calling for girls and boys to be given equal consideration; the establishment of dual schools where there were insufficient resources for separate schools, and for the representation of women on governing bodies.[137]

Following Miss Hurlbatt's resignation in February 1898, on her appointment as Principal of Bedford College, London, her sister, Kate, was chosen as Principal of Aberdare Hall — a post she held until 1934. Within two years of assuming office at a very well established and successful hall, the need for more accommodation was being considered. The number of women students enrolled at the college had steadily increased throughout the decade and consequently only an increasingly smaller proportion were accommodated at Aberdare Hall:

1889–90:	86 men and 64 women
1892–93:	196 men and 137 women
1893–94:	210 men and 138 women
1894–95:	256 men and 139 women
1895–96:	229 men and 162 women
1896–97:	268 men and 163 women
1897–98:	301 men and 169 women
1898–99:	333 men and 178 women[138]

Not only were women enrolling for undergraduate courses in the arts and sciences, but the establishment of the Day Training Department and the South Wales Training School of Cookery had significant implications for the presence of women at University College Cardiff.

Opening of the Day Training College

The involvement of the University College in the training of teachers had been advocated since 1885 by Principal Viriamu Jones. In 1890, a day training college was established at Cardiff. An important new principle in the training of teachers in England and Wales was introduced in the Code, through revised Regulations of the Education Department in 1890, enabling day training colleges or normal departments attached to universities and colleges of university rank to be established. Together with Birmingham, Nottingham and Bristol, Cardiff had been amongst the first to request recognition to open such a department. In that year, nineteen males and thirteen females were admitted.[139] The minimum educational standard required for admission was a first or second-class result in the Queen's Scholarship examination.[140]

In the first report to the Education Department in 1891, William Williams HMI stated that:

> It is with the liveliest satisfaction that I can now report that a Day Training College department is in full operation in connexion with the Cardiff University College . . . A normal master has been, and a normal mistress will shortly be, appointed to give instruction in method, and to exercise a general supervision. . . . The more promising students will, it is hoped, remain for 3 years and obtain a London degree. By doing this, and by mingling with the general body of students, a more widely cultured and higher type of teacher will be formed.[141]

Such sentiments concerning teacher training had already been voiced by Principal Viriamu Jones.

The HMI with special responsibility for the training of schoolmistresses, J.G. Fitch, also visited the new department in its first year and wrote a complimentary and optimistic report.[142] Teacher training in university colleges, just as in residential training-colleges, was perceived within well-established Victorian social conventions. The Education Department recognized that students in day training departments would enjoy greater freedom than in residential colleges and consequently careful attention would be required in matters of discipline. There was 'need for governing bodies to exercise the most watchful supervision in regard to the conduct and associations, especially of the female students, during the period of their training'.[143]

In mixed colleges, it was vital that prospective female teachers were under the careful supervision of a mistress who would ensure that attention was given to such essential Victorian values as punctuality and regular study. Domestic economy and needlework were to be compulsory elements in their course of studies. The experiment was viewed as a most significant educational development, as 'a new fact in our educational history and one fraught with important consequences not only to popular education, but even to the provincial colleges themselves'.[144] Its particular attractions were the intellectual advantages — the broadening and liberalizing of the mind — which were expected to accrue for elementary school teachers from training in a stimulating university environment. The 'influence and public usefulness' of the university would also be strengthened.

At Cardiff, in 1891, with thirteen women in the Normal Department, arrangements were made for Miss Duncanson, headmistress of the Cardiff Higher Board School, to deliver lectures on domestic economy to the women students, whilst Miss Moxey superintended the needle-work. Professional training and school management for both male and female students was conducted by 'a normal master', Mr. T. Raymont BA. Arrangements had also been made with the Cardiff School Board for their regular attendance for observation and teaching practice at the Higher Grade School and Stacey Road School. At the University College itself, arrangements were under way for the provision of a suitable educational, library and special accommodation for the Normal Department.

In November 1891, following a proposal by Elizabeth Hughes, seconded by Principal Viriamu Jones, the governors of Aberdare Hall, who had enthusiastically welcomed the admission of women to the Normal Department, passed a resolution 'that in the interests of inter-mediate education in South Wales and Monmouthshire, a Training Department for Intermediate Teachers should be established at the University College'.[145] It was a most opportune moment. In his report for 1891 on the training of schoolmistresses, J.G. Fitch HMI expressed much approval of the training of secondary school teachers at the Cambridge Training College under its 'accomplished' principal, Miss E.P. Hughes. By 1892, an extension in the role of the day training-colleges was being contemplated: 'The need for some form of profes-sional preparation for the teachers in secondary schools is likely to be more and more strongly felt each year'.[146] In the press and on public platform, Elizabeth Hughes was advocating the involvement of the university colleges of Wales in the training of teachers for the new intermediate schools.

In 1892, a 'Department for the Training of Women Teachers in Intermediate or Secondary Schools' was opened 'to meet the need that will arise from the establishment of intermediate schools'.[147] Students, who were expected to be graduates or to have gained the London Matriculation or Cambridge Higher Certificate, were trained to meet the requirements of the Teachers' Diploma of the University of London and Cambridge. The course of study included psychology, history of education, school management, hygiene, elocution and school practice. However, primarily because of the unavailability of grant-aid for secondary training departments, the number of students remained small — there being only seven in 1894–5, fourteen in 1898–9 and only seventeen even in 1910–11. By contrast, the enrolment of students for elementary school training continued to increase:

> 1894–1895:   61 women and 44 men
> 1896–1897:   54 women and 44 men
> 1897–1898:   52 women and 40 men[148]

The best board schools in the city were used for regular teaching practice.

Though the separate teaching arrangements for male and female students were criticized as a waste of resources, the work of the department attracted favourable comment during the regular annual inspections:

> There is much vigour and high promise in this new college and in its Normal Department. The professors speak most favourably of the students, who mingle freely with the rest, and share to the full, not only the lectures, but the social life, the library, the debating society, and the athletics of the college.[149]

In a letter to Lady Aberdare in 1893, J.G. Fitch considered the merits of university day-training departments *vis-à-vis* residential training-colleges. Referring to the department at Cardiff, he foresaw it as providing 'training of another type — broader and more liberal in its aims'.

The establishment of the South Wales and Monmouthshire Training School of Cookery and Domestic Arts

In 1891, under the aegis of the Council of University College, Cardiff, and the city's School Board, a 'Training School of Cookery and Domestic

Arts' was established. Concern had already been voiced concerning the lack of training facilities for women teachers in Wales by the Cardiff School Board, whilst C.T. Whitmell, the local HMI, had been a staunch supporter of the inclusion of needlework, cookery and domestic economy in the elementary-school curriculum. As well as being conscious of the need to improve the quality of life in working-class homes, there was also an awareness of the demand for competent domestic servants in middle-class homes. Furthermore, the Education Department were endeavouring to ensure that girls in elementary schools received some 'technical' education. Cookery had been an optional grant-earning subject since 1883 and, in the 1890 Code, a model syllabus was included. In the 1890s, it was to be joined by dairy work, housewifery and domestic economy. In the curricular schemes for the new intermediate schools in Wales, adequate 'technical education' for girls was an issue of considerable importance at that time. Also, in both England and Wales, the implications of the Technical Instruction Act 1889 focused attention on the need to cater adequately for both sexes. Miss Hester Davies had underlined its educational and social importance:

> The necessity for providing instruction for women in all matters appertaining to the home is becoming more pressing year by year. In all classes, the conditions of modern life have tended to cause the loss of that domestic lore which in previous generations was handed down from mother to daughter, with the result that now women are almost universally dependent on external sources for knowledge.[150]

However, until 1890, no steps had been taken in Wales to provide specific instruction in technical work for women. Facilities for training cookery teachers were available in training-schools in London, Liverpool, Leeds, Edinburgh and Glasgow in the 1870s. They held their own examinations and awarded their own certificates independently of the Education Department. Now, however, in the early 1890s, a second wave of training-schools for cookery were opened at Bristol, Sheffield and Aberdeen in 1891, Newcastle 1893, and also at Cardiff.[151]

In 1890, a movement was initiated in Cardiff for the establishment of a school to train teachers of cookery. It is unclear whether the actual initiative came from the School Board or from the University College. Both parties were supportive of the idea and, from its inception, the training school was a joint venture.[152] It made concrete the desire of a number of Welsh educationists, keenly aware of the educational and social importance of cookery, to have training facilities within the Principality. In November 1890, a meeting of the Cookery School

Committee of the University College was held. Present were Principal Viriamu Jones, C.T. Whitmell HMI, Dr Treharne representing the School Board and Miss Hester Davies of the Cardiff Higher Grade School. The committee had assembled to meet Miss Harrison, Chief Inspector of Cookery at the Education Department. It was felt that a training-school of cookery should provide the opportunity for students to gain practical teaching experience in local elementary schools. It was thought desirable to have an entrance examination similar to the Queen's Scholarship examination. Fees of fifteen guineas were proposed for a full diploma course taught through lectures and demonstrations, and subject to inspection by the Education Department.[153] In December 1890, it was made clear that though the Education Department would recognize the teachers' diploma, grants to students would not be available. Miss Davies was appointed 'Mistress of the School of Cookery' at an annual salary of £100, payable in equal halves by the University College and the School Board. The kitchens of the Higher Grade School were made available to the committee now appointed by the Council of the University College to oversee the work. The members included Mrs Viriamu Jones, Mr and Mrs Lewis Williams, who had long associations with the School Board, and C.T. Whitmell HMI.[154]

On 7 April 1891, in the Higher Grade School in Howard Gardens, the South Wales and Monmouthshire Training School of Cookery was opened with Miss Davies, now styled Superintendent. Within a short time, it was carrying out a wide range of work. Its main role was to train teachers of cookery and be responsible for cookery instruction in the Cardiff Board's elementary schools. By 1893, there was a 'travelling teacher' conducting classes elsewhere in south Wales. By 1894, thirty cookery teachers had been trained, and awarded their diplomas, and hundreds of classes and lectures had been organized throughout south Wales. In day and evening classes, instruction was given in 'artisan, household and high-class cookery' as well as instruction and the award of certificates of competence to professional cooks. By then, the staff included six teachers as well as the superintendent. As well as aiding school boards, arrangements were being made to provide cookery instruction to a large number of voluntary schools. In the women's department of the Technical School of the County Borough of Cardiff, classes were held in cookery, dressmaking and domestic economy. As the numbers attending these classes grew steadily, the pressing need for larger premises was considered. This led to the training-school being moved, firstly to Stacey Road Hall in 1894, and subsequently to 6 St

Andrew's Place, near the University College, in 1897.[155] By then, instruction was also given in housekeeping, laundrywork, domestic economy and dressmaking, and in 1895 the title of 'The South Wales and Monmouthshire Training School of Cookery and Domestic Arts' was adopted.[156] In 1897, forty-two students were training as teachers for the diploma in cookery, two were training for high-class cookery, six studying for the laundry certificate and eight in domestic economy.[157]

From 1891, free studentships were maintained at the training-school by the Cardiff Technical Instruction Committee and later by Glamorgan, Pembrokeshire and Monmouthshire county councils. Until 1899, the training-school conducted its own examinations and awarded the diplomas in cookery to students.[158] Arrangements were changed in 1899 when the Board of Education introduced its own examinations and diploma in the training-schools of cookery.[159] Some of the diploma students resided with other undergraduates in Aberdare Hall. As well as securing teaching posts in elementary schools, some of them also proceeded to teach in the new intermediate schools in Wales and high schools in England.[160]

By the end of the century, the training-school was firmly established and was unique in being the only one of its type organized in conjunction with a university or university college. This arrangement was viewed by Miss Hester Davies as placing it on 'a higher level than any other school of the kind in the kingdom'.[161]

Women at the University College of South Wales and Monmouthshire, Cardiff in early twentieth century

At University College, Cardiff, there were 407 men and 169 women students by 1913–14, with another 123 at the Training School of Cookery and Domestic Arts. In 1902, with the new Aberdare Hall full and an 'overflow house' — 37 Corbett Road — leased, an appeal was made for funds to erect a new wing.[162]

Part of the mortgage on the 1893 building, which had cost £9,000 and accommodated forty-two students, was still outstanding. The cost of the proposed extension was estimated at £4,000 and was intended to accommodate about thirty-five students. Within a month, over £2,000 was subscribed by donors, who included Lord Tredegar, Lady Aberdare, Sir Isambard Owen and Sir Alfred Thomas MP, and by 1904 the extra accommodation was provided.[163]

Miss Kate Hurlbatt, Principal at Aberdare Hall 1898–1934, gave careful attention to corporate life and, through invitations to guest speakers, ensured that the women students were well versed in such key issues of the day as the suffragette movement.[164] In 1908, Miss Caroline Williams, President of Aberdare Hall, bequeathed £800 for the establishment of the Catherine Buckton Scholarship.[165] Following an inspection in 1910, O.M. Edwards found that Aberdare Hall remained 'in a most satisfactory state of efficiency'.[166]

The Aberdare Hall Appeal had referred specifically to the hall's important influence on 'the efficiency of those who will in future be teachers in Secondary and Elementary Schools'.[167] Careers in teaching attracted a fair proportion of the women students at University College, Cardiff. By 1913–14, seventy-nine women were registered in the Elementary Training Department and twenty-one in the Secondary Training Department.[168]

Ever since their establishment in 1890 and 1892 respectively, the Women's Day Training Department and the Secondary Training Department for Women had been organized as separate entities though they had the same staff and were under the same head, Professor H. Millicent Mackenzie (née Hughes) who was Professor of Education from 1904 to 1915. Although it was regarded elsewhere in Wales as a reactionary step, prospective male teachers were trained in a separate, parallel department with Professor T. Raymont as Profesor of Education from the 1904–5 session onwards.[169] There were separate departments at Cardiff until 1932 when they were amalgamated under the headship of Professor Oliver Wheeler. In her student days at Aberystwyth, she had been a staunch advocate of female emancipation.[170] In the Women's Secondary Training Department, the annual enrolment of students was comparatively low — with no more than twenty-three in any year before 1914.[171]

As well as utilizing various local schools for teaching practice, a well-equipped demonstration school, known as College School, was established at 34 Cathedral Road, under the direction of Professor Mackenzie. A private venture, located in property donated to the Women's Secondary Training Department, it included a kindergarten and preparatory school for boys and girls up to ten years of age. It was opened in 1901–2; a high school for girls only, up to eighteen or nineteen years of age, followed in January 1909. The admission of pupils of secondary-school age was intended to constitute a demonstration school in connection with the University College that would qualify for grants under the Secondary Training Regulations. However, this objective was not realized, because the Board of Education ruled that the company established in 1909 to take over the preparatory school was not a charitable trust.[172] Nevertheless, students attended demonstration lessons given by the school staff and undertook periods of teaching practice there until 1924. In 1912, the Board of Education judged that the school made 'a most important addition to the practical side of the equipment of the Secondary Training Department. The students are expected to share in the life of the school as well as that of the College'.[173]

For the South Wales and Monmouthshire Training School of Cookery and Domestic Arts at St Andrew's Place, Cardiff, which remained under the management of a committee appointed by the Council of the University College of South Wales and Monmouthshire, the early twentieth century saw a healthy enrolment of students. By 1905, there were 113 studying for diplomas. Since its foundation in April 1891, it had widened its curriculum to include laundrywork, dressmaking and housewifery as well as cookery. It continued with its pioneering work in organizing and examining domestic science classes in elementary, intermediate and technical schools, and supplying well-qualified teachers throughout Wales. There was much justification for the self-appraisal in 1902 that 'from small beginnings with 14 students, it had grown to be regarded as one of the biggest and most successful of Domestic Schools in the Kingdom'.[174]

For admission to the training-school, students had to be at least eighteen years of age, and unless they had passed the matriculation examination of the University of Wales, or other equivalent examination, they had to pass an entrance examination.[175] A number of free studentships were offered by Cardiff, Glamorgan, Monmouthshire and Pembrokeshire education authorities.

Until 1899, the school had conducted its own examinations and awarded Diplomas in Cookery. Thereafter, students were prepared for the new Board of Education teachers' diplomas in cookery, laundrywork and housewifery. In 1900–1, seventy-seven were registered as day-students in training for diplomas, and as many as 502 were pursuing courses in the women's departments of the Technical School of the County Borough of Cardiff.

By 1906, larger premises were desperately needed. Board of Education inspectors urged the management committee to make the necessary extensions and, at considerable expense, three adjoining houses were modified and added to the premises at St Andrew's Place. This new property belonged to University College. By October 1907, the departments of cookery, housewifery and dressmaking commenced work in large well-equipped premises, which were formally opened by Lady Llangattock on 11 November 1908. The management committee was proud that 'this is the only School of its kind in the Principality, and the only one in the United Kingdom that is a department of a University College'.[176]

By 1909, however, the training-school's future was in jeopardy. Aspects of its work, which could partly be attributed to understaffing, were criticized in a Board of Education report.[177] There were also acute financial problems, with a deficit of £600 in 1909 accruing from interest payments on the mortgage of the building.[178] University College Cardiff announced its intention to break its ties with the training-school from 1910.[179] Miss Hester Davies took the initiative to defend the institution and, in a letter to the University College Council in October 1909, emphasized its importance in Wales where there was an increasing demand for teachers of domestic subjects in secondary schools. Its closure would be 'a calamity' for the country. To avoid its closure, she proposed a scheme that would transform the school into a department of the University College, and extend the Secondary Training Department for Women to include technical training for secondary-school students, which could only be provided by the Training School of Cookery and Domestic Arts. Anticipating objections on the basis of the educational qualifications of students admitted to the Training School, she emphasized that an increasing number had gained their matriculation.[180]

By 1909, almost 600 students had followed the various training courses, and teachers' diplomas in one or more of the domestic subjects had been awarded to 411 students. There were eighty-one students enrolled in 1909, but in addition, large numbers were also attending classes in the various domestic subjects.[181] In contrast to domestic arts training-colleges in England, it had not received financial grants from public bodies. The building alterations and extensions had been implemented in response to Board of Education demands, and by 1909 the entire school building had cost £10,000.[182]

Faced by the University's unwillingness to continue the existing arrangement on account of the annual deficit of £600 accruing because of its association with the training-school, support was sought from the local education authorities.[183] It was emphasized that similar schools in England were supported financially by local education authorities. It was essential that this 'excellent school' should be enabled to continue, particularly at a time when 'a thorough training in the domestic arts is being recognised more and more'.[184] It was a time when speeches at the Women's Congress, and an address by the headmaster of Eton, had focused attention on 'the Profession of Housewife'. There were fears that the quality and efficiency of home life was weakening. The need for a more balanced education in schools that included domestic subjects was being advocated.[185]

With the exception of Carmarthenshire, who declined the invitation, representatives of local education authorities in south Wales — Glamorgan, Monmouth, Cardiff, Merthyr, Swansea — attended conferences at Cardiff in January and February 1911, when they decided to establish a joint management committee, including two representatives of the University College, and assume financial responsibility for the School of Cookery and Domestic Arts.[186]

In May 1912, on the occasion of the training-school's twenty-first anniversary celebration when 109 students were enrolled, Principal E.H. Griffith referred to it as 'the daughter of the University College' which had now been handed over to stronger financial hands.[187] Correspondence in the *Western Mail* stressed the need for women of intellect, as well as others, to study domestic subjects. It was essential that a university standard should be established in the teaching of these subjects. The training-school at Cardiff, with its long record of achievement, could play a vital role in ensuring that the kitchens of Britain were no longer 'unscientific laboratories'.[188] At the first public meeting of the South Wales and Monmouthshire Association of Teachers of Domestic Subjects at University College Cardiff in January 1912, Elizabeth Hughes, one of the members of the new management committee, delivered an address on 'The relation of general education and domestic subjects', where she emphasized the need for much greater correlation.[189]

In 1912, the new joint committee decided that the institution's official title was to be 'The Training School of Domestic Arts for South Wales and Monmouthshire'. In conjunction with other colleges in England, pressure was exerted in 1913 on the Board of Education for increased grants. By 1914, there were 124 students enrolled, and the standard of the entrance examination had been raised.[190]

There were to be further changes in management. In 1929, under a new scheme, the University College was to take control once more. Following the Second World War, there was to be greater administrative participation for the local authorities in south Wales. However, the University College's involvement continued, leading eventually to the development of degrees in home economics.[191]

(iv)   *Bangor*

Admission of women students

At Bangor, there was no antipathy shown to the admission of female students. Of the fifty-eight students enrolled in the 1884–5 session, twenty-nine were women students.[192] The college Charter stipulated that '. . . female students shall be admitted to attend any of the courses of instruction established by the College'. Indeed, the first name on the Students' Register at UCNW is that of Mary Elen Williams of Bangor.[193] In his address at the opening of the college in October 1884, Principal Reichel stated that no distinction would be made between female and male students: 'The ladies would have the same advantage and in no way would discouragement be shown to them'.[194] He noted that women already constituted twenty-five per cent of the students enrolled, and that amongst the thirty-three scholarship holders and exhibitioners, there were three female exhibitioners and one female scholar. He was applauded when he stated that female education was 'one of the first principles upon which the new college was founded'.[195] By 1889–90, forty-two of the ninety-seven students were women.[196] In an address at Bangor in June 1889, Principal Reichel, G. Osborne Morgan and others expressed disappointment that the college's proportion of women students from Wales was low. However, the middle-class and Anglicized background of a large number of women students at Bangor in the 1880s was not unwelcome to the college authorities.[197] Professor Morley complimented the college for implementing the principle that men and women 'were alike in mind and soul' and had an equal claim to higher education.[198] Many years later, in 1934, a former student recalled that Principal Reichel was particularly supportive of women students and was 'a pioneer in the movement for co-education in the modern university'.[199]

Establishment of a hall of residence

At Bangor, a hall of residence for women students opened on 1 October 1886, with Miss Frances E. Hughes as Lady Principal. In 1885 the Council of UCNW sought the advice of Principal T. Charles Edwards, Aberystwyth: 'We at Bangor, are thinking of following your example and that of Cardiff by establishing a ladies' hostel'.[200] Information and guidance was requested regarding the lady principal's stipend, rent and size of hostel, estimate of expected expenditure and scale of fees.

During the session 1885–6 at Bangor, the College Council had 'warmly approved' a proposal to establish such an institution though it was made clear that the college should not incur any additional financial burden as a consequence.[201]

At the college's opening ceremony in October 1884, Lord Aberdare had emphasized the necessity for the university colleges to open halls or hostels if they were to cater effectively for women. Likewise, Principal Reichel said that the admission of women students made it essential to have a hostel 'to protect students from one of the most pernicious forms of adulteration, unhealthy and impure lodgings'.[202] But also, a healthy enrolment of women students was dependent on the availability of such an institution:

> Unless a hostel is established, it is vain to hope that the college can even draw a steady supply of female students except from the immediate neighbourhood of the town. Let me, then, urge upon the patronesses of higher education for women the pressing claims of a Girls' hostel.[203]

The key event leading to the decision to establish a hostel, occurred in May 1886, when a meeting of the College Council was attended by such staunch supporters of the female cause in higher education in Wales as Mrs Verney, Mrs Dilys Glynne Jones, Dr Bryant and Principal Reichel. The latter explained that the meeting had been summoned at short notice following receipt of a communication from the North London Collegiate School which stated that a regular supply of students would enrol at UCNW as long as a women's hostel was established in the town. He was attracted by the possibility of 'lady students of rather a high class' attending the college. He referred to Dr Bryant (a member of the London school's staff) and her links with north Wales, which appear to have been the reason for North London Collegiate's interest. He wanted 'special attention' given to any 'lady students' that Miss Buss might send.[204] A middle-class, Anglicized element amongst the student body was not unattractive to the college authorities in those early days:

> About half are ladies, some of them ladies of position i.e. the daughters of Lord Penrhyn, the Wests, Mrs Verney etc. whose very presence gives tone to the classes.[205]

There was already a feeling amongst a number associated with the college that a women's hostel was essential if the education of women was to be successfully developed at Bangor. It had already been ascertained that parents had strong objections to their daughters staying in ordinary lodgings in a strange town.

In the deliberations that followed, reference was made to hostels already established at Cardiff and Aberystwyth. It was noted in particular that Aberdare Hall had not experienced any religious difficulty, and provided a valuable precedent. Though there was enthusiasm for a similar establishment at Bangor, it was made clear that the college had no financial resources available for such a project. Furthermore, since the college charter did not allow students to reside in the college itself, the college authorities were precluded from directly establishing such an institution. It would have to be the province of friends of the college, responsible to an independent management body. Consequently, a committee including Lord Penrhyn, the Honourable Misses Eleanor and Louisa Pennant, Mrs Verney, Mr and Mrs W.A. Darbishire and Mrs Richard Davies, together with the Principal H.R. Reichel and Professor Henry Jones, was appointed to consider the best means of establishing a hostel at Bangor.[206]

In its report, following the inspection of a number of houses, it recommended the adoption of Aberdare Hall as a model for a three-year experiment beginning in October 1886. In particular, no religious or theological teaching should be provided by the institution's staff. The students would be expected to attend a place of worship chosen voluntarily. Under the supervision of a lady principal, the hall should be permeated by a family rather than a lodging-house ethos.[207] Whilst eventually the hall might be self-supporting, it was anticipated that initially there would be a financial shortfall of £120 per annum, which would have to be met by voluntary subscriptions. The subscribers would become governors of the hall.

When the hall opened in October 1886 in rented premises, the committee included such luminaries as Miss Buss, Dr Bryant, Miss Elizabeth Hughes, Miss Dilys Davies, Mrs Verney, Mrs Rathbone and Miss Armstrong as well as the headmistresses of girls' schools in Bangor and Penmaenmawr. The fee for board and accommodation would be in the region of £30 to £35, and would depend on the precise accommodation provided.[208]

The venture was a success, and the decision taken to formalize arrangements. On 13 August 1887, with a capital of £2,210, 'The University College Hall for Women at Bangor Ltd.' became a registered company. The articles of association stipulated that there were to be between fifteen and thirty-six directors. Significantly, no religious test was to be provided as a condition of admission to or of residence in the hall.[209] By the autumn, arrangements were under way to acquire a new building, providing accommodation for twenty-eight students. The new hall was opened in October 1888 by Lady Penrhyn.[210] It was intended to be self-supporting and not incorporated in any way with the University College. It was, therefore, not under the control of the college authorities.

The hall was under the supervision of Frances E. Hughes who was appointed 'Lady Principal'. It is possible that her appointment was not uninfluenced by her family connection. In 1886, W. Cadwaladr Davies wrote that 'it is something in her favour that she should be the sister of Miss Hughes of Cambridge'.[211] However, within a short time there was considerable acrimony concerning her style of management of the hall. By 1887, she was told by W. Cadwaladr Davies that Miss Buss, Dr Bryant and Miss Dilys Davies were 'losing all interest in the Hall because of circumstances towards which she contributed'.[212] The Registrar would have been pleased if her dismissal could have been possible.[213] Within five years, Miss Hughes was embroiled in a far more serious conflict.

Principal Reichel expressed the hope that the establishment of the hall would contribute towards improving the status of female education in Wales which he deemed to be much lower than in England. He expressed disappointment concerning the small proportion of Welsh women at the college. Likewise, contrasting the position with England, A.H.D. Acland MP called for the establishment of middle-class girls' schools in Wales so that the college could be adequately supplied with students.

Women at the University College of North Wales in the 1890s and 'The Bangor College Scandal'

At Bangor, student numbers showed a steady increase during the 1890s although the growth in the numbers of female students was much less prominent:

1890:	42 women and	55 men
1898:	91 women and	176 men
1899:	93 women and	222 men[214]

The opening of a Day Training Department in October 1894 and the admission of fifteen men and fifteen women students marked the beginning of an important development for the college. By 1897–8, thirty-two men and forty women were enrolled in the normal department, which provided students with practical teaching experience: 'A novel and very interesting experiment is made in the annual migration of this department with its teachers to Blaenau Ffestiniog where some of the best schools in Wales are put at its disposal'.[215]

The Association for Promoting the Education of Girls in Wales was offering loans to Welsh women to train as teachers and this helped the department at Bangor. During the 1896–7 session, provision was also made for the training of graduates as secondary-school teachers.[216]

As at Aberystwyth, the establishment of a scheme of agricultural education was of importance to the University College of North Wales. Young women attended dairy classes at Bangor, Denbigh and Welshpool, and a college certificate in buttermaking and cheesemaking was awarded.[217]

'The Bangor Women's Hostel Co. Ltd.', at a cost of approximately £7,600, erected a hall of residence for fifty women students in Upper Bangor. The company was formed in August 1893 with a nominal share capital of £3,000 to provide for the erection of the building and temporary accommodation for female students during its construction. Funds were also raised on mortgage from University College North Wales. Until 1920, the company, which was administered as an educational trust, was responsible for all matters affecting hostel accommodation and administration.

The new hall was opened on 9 October 1897 by Miss Helen Gladstone. The opportunity was taken to underline its significance for UCNW and for Welsh education in general. William Rathbone, the college President, saw the event as 'a very important step in the completion of the UCNW in all its branches, which was one of the first to admit ladies to its studies'.[218] Others, such as A.H. Acland MP, and J.W. Mackail a civil servant in the Education Department, viewed the hall as reflecting the University of Wales's enlightened attitude to women students:

> The opening of the Hall was a new sign of the life and growth of the Welsh educational system. It had been the fate of the older Universities to have to face in one form or another, the sex problem. It was the distinguished glory of the University of Wales that from the first she determined that men and women should be alike, human, within her borders.[219]

Unsurprisingly at a time of rejoicing, there was no reference to the events surrounding the women's hall of residence earlier in the decade — the Bangor controversy of 1892–4 which Principal Reichel later recalled had 'threatened to wreck the women's side in UCNW altogether'.[220]

Since 1886, a licence had been granted by the college council to Miss Frances E. Hughes, to admit women students to a hall of residence which was administered by a limited company. It was not obligatory that all women students should reside in the hall, and those staying in private lodgings were often referred to as 'out-students'. In 1890, there had been disagreement amongst the hall's directors concerning the relationship between these two categories of students and the implementation of a rule forbidding any visiting between them. It was therefore agreed by the hall's directors that 'out-students' could visit the hall by invitation and with the approval of the lady principal. However, in-students were not to visit their fellow students in lodgings.[221] In October 1892, a graduate out-student aged around twenty-five years — Miss Violet Osborn — who had previously been a resident, was prohibited from visiting the hall. It would appear that she was disliked by the lady principal who regarded her as an undesirable companion for younger students such as the apparently very innocent 18-year-old daughter of John Rhys of Jesus College Oxford. The girl's mother — Elspeth Rhys — was informed 'in confidence' that the two students were associating. Miss Osborn was alleged to be 'untruthful', to possess 'a corrupt and impure mind', to have shown 'an indecorous behaviour towards men' including one of the Bangor professors — Keri Evans — and to be 'a woman of the world'. She came to hear of these allegations and complained to the College Senate. She was supported by two prominent local citizens — Dr Griffith Evans and Mr (later Sir) Henry Lewis — and a number of well-known educationists such as Dr Sophie Bryant and Miss Frances Buss who, although not personally acquainted with her, believed 'the proper conduct of her case essential to the interests of the Women's Educational Movement in North Wales'.[222]

A thorough Senate inquiry was held between 14 and 26 November. There were ten meetings in all, and eighty-nine pages of statements and evidence relating to the incident considered. Although fifteen persons gave evidence, Miss Frances Hughes refused to attend. In the unanimous verdict on 29 November 1892, the senate found that 'the charges were utterly without foundation . . . Miss Osborn's conduct and character had been those of a refined and honourable woman'.[223]

On 21 December, the minutes of the inquiry were laid before the College Council who expressed satisfaction that Miss Osborn had been exonerated. However, Miss Hughes still refused to withdraw the allegations, and likewise in 1893, when the Council formally accepted the verdict of Senate by a 13:9 majority.

By March 1893, the hall directors were informed that the licence would be withdrawn on 29 June. The view was taken that unless Miss Hughes withdrew the allegations, the effective safeguard of students would only be possible under a new hall administration. The dispute was now given considerable publicity in the national press. As well as such eye-catching headlines as 'Extraordinary Proceedings at Bangor

College', 'Principal versus Lady Principal' and 'Academic Stupidity' in the *North Wales Chronicle*, there was vigorous correspondence in *The Times* from the Reverend H.P. Hughes, a prominent Wesleyan minister and brother of Miss Frances Hughes, and a lengthy article by Principal Reichel in *Education Review*.[224] Following an article in the *Weekly Dispatch* that included such epithets as 'base' and 'dishonourable', Miss Hughes brought a libel action against the newspaper's proprietors. During a four-day trial at Chester Assizes in July 1893, where evidence was given by the leading figures associated with UCNW, details of 'the Bangor College Scandal' were given wide publicity and, at the end, Miss Hughes was awarded £350 compensation. Prior to the hearing, six members of the College Council, including the chairman, Col. W.E. Sackville-West, Vice-Chairman W.A. Darbishire and Richard Davies, Treborth, resigned in protest at the treatment of Miss Hughes. The senate inquiry, and particularly the role of Principal Reichel and Professor Arnold, were criticized.[225]

On 15 August, Stanley Leighton MP raised the matter in Parliament and, unsuccessfully, called for an impartial inquiry before the UCNW was given its annual grant of £4,000. On 29 August 1893, the Bishop of St Asaph raised the matter in the House of Lords. He asked the Lord President to take action to remedy the injury afflicted not only on the Lady Principal and shareholders of a successful Hall of Residence, but also on the cause of women's education in Wales. The Lord President, the Earl of Kimberley, reiterated Acland's reply in the House of Commons that the Government had no jurisdiction over the college's internal affairs.

However, by the time the Court of Governors assembled on 25 October 1893, Miss Mary Maude had been appointed Lady Superintendent of a new hall for women students. A proposition moved by John Roberts MP and seconded by Lloyd George MP, approving the conduct of Senate and Council throughout the dispute, was carried by a majority of thirty-one to four.[226] Numerous issues had been highlighted by the whole complex affair. It was construed by Miss Hughes and her supporters, including the hall's directors, as an example of the sectarian and political prejudice of the Senate and a majority of the Council against an Anglican. In Victorian Wales, where educational disputes were too easily prone to assume political and religious dimensions, such an interpretation was inevitable. Nevertheless, the evidence tends to corroborate the considered judgement of Dr Thomas Richards, in *Atgofion Cardi*, that a sectarian or political explanation is an oversimplification and unproven.[227]

Much of the evidence supports the view of the *North Wales Chronicle* that 'the whole dispute is the outcome of merest tittle-tattle and ought never to have arisen'.[228] It was well known that Miss Hughes had taken a strong dislike to Violet Osborn: 'I am sure that girl has a history, she is coming back [to College] to catch a professor'.[229] An alleged 'incident' involving one of the college professors and another man at Bickley during the vacation, which Miss Hughes had heard about, had some bearing on this perception. In the dispute, there were references to the 'Professor incident' and 'familiarity' and 'reputation'. The name of Professor Keri Evans, Professor of Philosophy, became associated with the charges against Miss Osborn:

> . . . the charge was that he had on one occasion tapped the cheek of a young lady with examination papers, and that on another occasion he held the hand of the young lady perhaps longer than was necessary in bidding her good-bye.

He withdrew from the Senate inquiry, and in a statement on 21 November 1892 said:

> I had dismissed the class and Miss Osborn remained behind I think to make some excuse about her work. As she was about to leave, some papers which I had in my hand came into contact with her face, brushed her face . . . it struck me a moment after Miss Osborn had left, that she looked embarrassed and hurt.[230]

Inevitably, this aspect was highlighted in the press. A letter in *The Times* on 5 May 1893 from Principal Reichel denied that there was any substance to the charge of 'familiarity'. Keri Evans himself accused the *North Wales Chronicle* of libel and received an apology and £50 damages. However, in February 1894, the College Council passed a resolution critical of his conduct, claiming that he 'did not act with that due discretion and reserve which ought to characterise the Professor's duty in relation to the lady student'.[231] Eventually, in 1895, he felt obliged to resign. Miss Osborn was later married to Professor E. Arnold — one of her most valiant supporters during those years.

However, the issues of real importance for the whole college, as well as the development of women's education, were those of management, authority and discipline, and particularly the relationship between a hall of residence and the college Senate and Council. Although licensed by the Council, the Lady Principal was not an official of the college, but a paid servant of the directors of a limited company and not contractually obliged to appear before the Senate. There were, undoubtedly, clashes of personality and imprudence and obstinacy on all sides. From the comparative calm of Aberystwyth, the Bangor dispute was not inaccurately viewed as having been caused by the hall of residence's virtual autonomous management — *imperium in imperio*. Arrangements similar to Aberystwyth, where the college Senate and Council had authority over the women students and where the Principal of the women's hostel was a college official directly responsible to Senate and Council, were regarded as essential.[232]

At the time, the scandal was seen as a threat to the very existence of UCNW and a danger to the development of higher education of women in Wales: 'the squabble which has done so much to endanger the higher education of women in the Principality'.[233] It is difficult to quantify the precise impact of the dispute on the fortunes of women's education in Wales. The number of women students continued to increase, albeit slowly; it led eventually to a clearer definition of the connection between the college and the women's hall. The Lady Superintendent's control over women students was subject to the general disciplinary authority of the Senate over all students. New rules and regulations concerning women students at the college were approved in October 1893. Following the revelations of 1892–3, their strict paternalistic nature was not unexpected.[234] As elsewhere in late Victorian educational institutions, moral attitudes dictated that male and female students were to be kept apart as much as possible:

> No rule as to the places to be occupied by men and women attending the same class, but the invariable practice is that the women students sit together upon front benches. In the Library and Refreshment Room, fixed places were reserved for the use of women students.[235]

Women students had to observe strict rules when attending evening meetings, they were forbidden to use the tennis court on the same afternoon as the men, or to row in the same boat as men. Likewise, mixed parties to visit places of antiquarian interest were not approved. Not surprisingly, the scene was set for 'the student strike' of 1901.

University College of North Wales, Bangor: 1900–1914

By 1899, with the turbulent events of that decade being gradually forgotten, there were 222 male and ninety-three female students enrolled, and a new women's hall of residence, opened in 1897, was now functioning. Mary Maude was Warden of Women Students 1893–1901 and built up the women's side of the college anew.[236]

However, the college's disciplinary code, especially the strict regulations enforced at University Hall primarily to keep the sexes apart, caused much friction. Indeed, they sparked off a student strike in February 1901 following the disciplining and suspension of both male and female students for breach of rules.[237] In an era when such themes as 'The New Woman' and the extension of parliamentary suffrage to women were debated in the students' Literary and Debating Society, such conflict was not surprising.[238]

On the occasion of the college's twenty-first anniversary in 1905, Principal Reichel reviewed the work and growth of the college. Yet, although Bangor was an institution committed to working towards equality between the sexes, Reichel made no particular reference to women students.[239] In the Edwardian and pre-war years, the attention of the college authorities focused primarily on the erection of new buildings which were opened by King George v in July 1911. During the first years of the twentieth century, the fight for more places for women at the college was no longer a major issue. Nevertheless, representation of women on the College Council remained token: three out of the thirty-six Council members were women. In 1911, the Board of Education noted the large number of women students enrolled compared to the handful of women on the Council; the Board then recommended the appointment of Helen Gladstone to fill a vacancy on the Council and become its fourth woman member.[240]

In 1914, the women students at Bangor, who would shortly participate in responsible war work, were subject to strict college rules which included the need to secure the sanction of the Warden of Women Students

> ... before any arrangements are entered upon for a picnic or excursion in which both men and women students are concerned. No such picnic or excursion may take place unless the Warden is able to accompany the party, or to arrange for another lady to take her place.[241]

At Bangor, as elsewhere in the University of Wales, there was to be little fundamental change in the authorities' strict, outdated code of discipline until well after the major social changes ushered in by the First World War.

9

Conclusion

By 1914, the foundations of the educational system of modern Wales had been firmly laid. The schools and colleges providing secondary and higher education had come of age. For boys, and particularly for girls, the educational vacuum that existed in Wales in 1847 had been filled. The final decades of the Victorian age, in particular, had witnessed a transformation in the provision of secondary and higher education for Welsh women. The termination in 1901 of the activities of the Association for Promoting the Education of Girls in Wales may seem precipitate today to feminists conscious of sexism and inequalities in the educational sytem of contemporary Wales. But in many ways it was an approriate moment, marking the successful fulfilment of the objectives of a highly influential organization in Victorian Wales. The educational gains made in the sphere of girls' secondary and higher education had been consolidated further by 1914. After decades of educational neglect, limited opportunities and male supremacy, women appeared to be receiving far more equitable treatment in secondary and higher education by the outbreak of the First World War.

It was primarily the middle class who gained from the establishment of, and access to, secondary schools and university colleges in Victorian and early twentieth-century Wales. But by 1914, during the formative years of the Welfare State, the Liberal administration were gradually extending these educational opportunities to working-class girls.[1] Initially, in the Victorian era, middle-class girls benefited from significant private educational ventures which have been given only peripheral attention in studies of the development of education in nineteenth-century Wales. As well as such prestigious establishments as the Howell schools at Llandaff and Denbigh (founded in 1860), and Dr Williams' School, Dolgellau (founded in 1878), numerous lesser known schools of varying quality made important contributions in educating generations of girls in Wales before the establishment of a network of intermediate schools in the 1890s (see pp. 55–62; 76–9). At Carmarthen, a Diocesan

High School functioned successfully from 1880, whilst in north Wales, Penrhos College had been opened by the Wesleyan Methodists, and Bangor was home to St Winifred's — one of the Woodard schools. At Swansea, in 1888, the Girls' Public Day School Trust opened its only high school in Wales. Elsewhere in the Principality, primarily in urban centres and on the coastal belt, there was a variety of non-endowed girls' schools.

Some of them, undoubtedly, merited criticism for their overemphasis on social accomplishments and also for poor academic standards. The accomplishment-orientated curriculum — usually including the study of music, art and modern languages, as well as the grammar, literature, composition and elocution, which constituted an 'English education' — reflected the prevalent middle-class notions of culture and womanhood. The economic changes of the late eighteenth and early nineteenth centuries had divorced the home from the workplace. In a patriarchal society, conscious of complementary sex differences and presuming different educational abilities, the home was deemed the proper sphere of the middle-class lady.

During the 1870s and 1880s, the growing demand in Wales for a greater provision of secondary education for girls was accompanied by an attempt to reject the assumed intellectual inferiority of girls. There was some response by schools, through modification of their curricula, to accommodate more academically challenging subjects and preparation for recognized examinations. By the end of the Victorian era, the two Howell schools and the Dr Williams' School at Dolgellau were recognized as the premier girls' schools in Wales and on a par with the best English high schools. In the quest for status, their curricula had become increasingly academic and examination orientated.

The State assumed a higher educational profile in the 1870s and 1880s, not only through the establishment of a network of elementary schools but also through the reform of educational endowments. The reforms of the Endowed Schools Commission and Charity Commission played an unimportant part in securing secondary education for girls in the endowed schools of Wales (see pp. 72–6). However, it was the Welsh Intermediate and Technical Education Act 1889, the product of a long campaign for greater educational opportunities for both sexes, that proved to be the most decisive event in the provision of greater educational opportunities in Wales in the years before 1914. In 1889, A.H.D. Acland MP wrote that:

> The Welsh Intermediate Education Act gives an opportunity to Wales,

such as no part of the United Kingdom has yet obtained. If this opportunity is well used, the benefit to Wales will be great, and the example set by the Welsh piorneers of organised Scondary Education to the rest of the country may be undeniable.[2]

The legislation has been viewed ever since, as one of the most significant achievements of Victorian Wales.[3] The foundations of the modern system of Welsh secondary education were firmly laid in the 1890s through the implementation of the terms of the Act. In 1939, on the occasion of the jubilee celebration of the 1889 Act, Mr Edgar Jones, an eminent headmaster of Barry County School and President of the Welsh Secondary Schools Association, maintained that:

> Fifty years ago, the men of vision who laboured to found our schools looked to them to bring forth in Wales wise and enlightened leaders and an educated people whose eyes had been opened to enjoy the treasures of literature and behold 'the gains of science and gifts of arts'. As we look backwards at the first fifty years that have gone by, I believe the schools of Wales can justly claim that they have not been unfaithful to the trust bequeathed to them.[4]

A century later, the benefits that accrued to Wales are still recognized as considerable, though there is now a greater awareness of the shortcomings of the legislation and of the system of intermediate and technical education established in the 1890s. A Board of Education for Wales was not included amongst the provisions of the 1889 Act nor was the Ashford endowment brought within the ambit of the Act to be used for the purpose of intermediate education for girls. Recent studies have highlighted the limited access and enrolment, the rigidity of the examination system, the curricular uniformity and the neglect of the Welsh language and technical education.[5] Hitherto, however, the educational gains for girls have been given little attention.

By 1889, equal treatment of girls and boys was widely expected from a Welsh Intermediate Education Act. In particular, the Association for Promoting the Education of Girls in Wales had endeavoured to ensure that MPs would be well aware of the educational needs of girls. The principle of equal educational opportunities for both sexes was accepted by the legislators of 1889. The network of intermediate schools to be established throughout Wales was intended to make adequate provision for girls as well as boys. By 1900, 3,513 girls and 3,877 boys were enrolled in the ninety-three intermediate schools. Unsurprisingly, the architects of intermediate education in Wales in the 1890s were influenced not only by the prevailing perceptions of the role of women in a society where gender stereotyping was well established, but also by the curricular tradition of the boys' grammar schools and their emulators in the girls' high schools. By 1914, the female presence in the developing system of intermediate and secondary education had influenced curricular, organizational and management issues (pp. 153–76).

With the establishment of state education, the heyday of the private girls' school in Wales appeared to be over. The private sector was to remain, comparatively small but influential. It survived primarily for reasons of snobbery and social class. Though some endowed schools were adopted as intermediate schools under the terms of the 1889 Act, others were determined to preserve their independent status (pp. 176–84). The inclusion of the Dr Williams' School in the Merioneth scheme of intermediate education caused much acrimony which was not quelled for over a decade. The governing body of Ashford School succeeded in excluding the endowment from the terms of the 1889 Act. Howell's School at Llandaff became associated with the Glamorgan scheme of intermediate education, but the school at Denbigh was excluded from the county scheme following celebrated debates in the House of Lords in 1897 and again in 1910, which were instigated by Bishop A.G. Edwards in order to safeguard Anglican influence and control at the school. In general, the growth in provision of state secondary education increased the non-local character of some of Wales's most famous schools.

By the outbreak of the First World War, women were also established in the three university colleges. Here, also, a significant transformation had been witnessed. During the 1860s and early 1870s, women were conspicuous by their absence from the deliberations of the protagonists of university education in Wales. During its first decade, the University College of Wales, Aberystwyth did little to advance the cause of women. But during the 1880s and 1890s, a far more enlightened attitude characterized the policies of the three university colleges. Though women students were still subjected to petty restrictions and occasional prejudice, policy making in the three colleges and the formulation of the University of Wales Charter in 1893 ensured that women would be given the opportunity to enjoy the fullest educational opportunities (pp. 96–100).

There had been encouraging developments in teacher training for women in Wales by 1914. Swansea and Bangor Normal colleges were now under the control of local education authorities, as was the newly opened Barry Training College. St Mary's College at Bangor ensured the continuation of the Anglican Church's involvement in the training of women teachers in Wales. Teacher training had provided a limited form of higher education for Welsh women for many decades. The domestic ideology fed to working-class girls in elementary schools was a notable feature of the training of women teachers in Victorian and Edwardian Wales. By the early twentieth century, not only was there a greater awareness of the dangers of gender stereotyping, but there was also concern over such issues as government control of teacher training and the relationship between teacher training-colleges and the University of Wales — issues which are not irrelevant to the current debate on teacher education (pp. 185–92).

The educational gains for girls and women had been caused by a wide range of factors: the contributions of strong-willed individuals, influential groups and societies as well as religious, social and economic determinants. In particular, there had been the triumph of reason and enlightenment over the forces of tradition, conservatism and prejudice from many quarters including churches and chapels, and the legal and medical professions. Tradition, buttressed by the prevailing feminine-domestic ideology, was the most formidable obstacle to the provision of wider educational opportunities in Victorian Wales. On the eve of the Welsh Intermediate Education Act, gender stereotyping was already evident in the elementary schools equipped to educate future wives and mothers. Until well into the twentieth century, this domestic orientation was to have a most restrictive and detrimental effect on attitudes to girls' education; schooling was regarded as less important for the girl than for the boy.

In 1918, in *Rhamant y Rhos* and in 1927 in *Cwrs y Lli*, the Welsh writer 'Moelona', steeped in the tradition of Cranogwen, criticized those farmers in rural Wales who still regarded education as of less importance for girls than boys.[6] In his novel *Flesh and Blood* (1974), set in the 1920s, Emyr Humphreys indicated the attitude of Welsh society towards the 'social' role of university education:

> '. . . A university education is something of the first importance. You know that don't you? . . . Socially I mean. It's the only safe ladder to move up from one class into anotehr . . . What degree do you want to take?'
> . . . The Rector frowned not altogether pleased.
> 'That's B.Sc.', he said, 'B.A. you know would be better for a woman. More becoming. It sounds more cultivated somehow.'[7]

The changes in the educational position of women did not occur in a social and political vacuum. they were the product of the wider movement for female emancipation that influenced both England and Wales over the previous half century. John Gibson's *The Emancipation of Women* (1891), which influenced the educational deliberations in

Wales, was one of the most vigorous expositions of the case for female enfranchisement since J.S. Mill's *On the Subjection of Women* (1869), whose message had also been highlighted inthe Welsh press. The quest for female emancipation in England exerted a profound influence on events in Wales. Welsh exiles in London, well informed about developments in England, were in the vanguard of the campaign to provide adequate educational opportunities for girls and women in their homeland. But they were also motivated by the Liberal–Nonconformist struggle for equality within the Principality (pp. 35–41). This proved decisive because equal access for girls to undenominational, intermediate schools and university colleges was an essential element in that campaign. It generated the Aberdare Inquiry and Report, the reform of endowments, and eventually the legislation of 1889. The involvement of the Association for Promoting the Education of Girls in Wales, the Honourable Society of Cymmrodorion and the National Eisteddfod ensured that the intermediate and higher educational needs of girls and women were not overlooked the crucial deliberations of the 1880s and 1890s.

In 1882, at the beginning of a crucial decade for the development of secondary and higher education in modern Wales, Dr Frances Hoggan had exhorted the Welsh people for the hard task that lay ahead:

> Other nations have to re-model, we have to model and to make; other nations have to cast away from them the outgrown clothes of former systems of teaching; we have little but rags to throw away, but we have, let us hope, amongst us all the fervour, all the vigour, and all the deeply-rooted persistence of individuals who have long been kept out of their natural birth-right of education to aid in laying deep and strong the foundations of higher education in Wales.[8]

A quarter of a century later, the gap between the educational opportunities of boys and girls was closing. However, it is unlikely that Dr Hoggan and the pioneers of the women's educational cuase would have been completely satisfied with the structure that had been established in pre-war Wales. The annual reports of the Central Welsh Board and Board of Education (Welsh Department) in the pre-war years highlighted insufficient attention to curricular differentiation and technical instruction, as well as the brief duration of the schooling of many girls (see pp. 166–76). The CWB encouraged the teaching of domestic subjects, particularly in the upper forms of Welsh intermediate Schools, where the curriculum was too academic and modelled too closely on that for boys. Also, the peripheral attention given to the language, literature and history of Wales, and the over-assimilation of Welsh secondary schools to the pattern of their English neighbours were evident to perceptive educationists by 1914.

Echoes of the Victorian concept of 'the weaker sex' still lingered on. In 1913 O.M. Edwards spoke of the fears of physical strain and over-pressure:

> The system of Welsh Education being what it is, can our daughters pass through it without undue strain? Can they stand the physical and the mental strain? If not, there is something wrong with the girls or there is something wrong with the system. Either the girls are incapable of being educated, or the system is incapable of educating.[9]

He believed that the conscientious pursuit of studies could involve physical and mental strain, but that girls could cope as long as there was no undue emphasis on examination results and academic education. His opinion was that 'The academic side of a girl's education is made too prominent at the cost of . . . the domestic side'. A worthy education should look 'back to her home or on towards University. She must think of both'.[10] This view was also evident later in 1923 in the Consultative Committee's Report on *The Differentiation of the Curriculum for Boys and Girls Respectively in Secondary Schools*[11] The training of girls 'to be makers of homes' characterized official government policy towards elementary and secondary education for many years.

A unified system of girls' secondary schooling had not been created. Elizabeth Hughes and other pioneers of the women's educational movement in the 1880s had advocated the deployment of the endowments of all of Wales's girls' secondary schools, including Ashford, for the benefit of the whole nation. But by 1914, the endowed girls' schools at Ashford and Denbigh as well as other private non-endowed schools tended to be merely on the periphery of the Welsh system of secondary education. There was a feeling that those girls' and boys' secondary schools such as Howell's, Ashford, Llandovery College and Christ College which had not been incorporated in shcemes drawn up under the Welsh Intermediate Education Act, and had become increasingly 'non-local schools', should play a more significant role in a co-ordinated national system of education. In 1920, the Bruce Report on Secondary Education was to recommend the establishment of a National Council of Education for Wales with jurisdiction over 'non-local schools'.[12]

By 1914, the training of women teachers was no longer a major issue. As well as free-standinig colleges at Swansea, Bangor and Barry, women were well established in the education departments of the three university colleges. The training-colleges' relationship with the University of Wales had been raised in particular by Principal J. Viriamu Jones and Elizabeth Hughes (see pp. 185–92). But by the outbreak of war, little had been done to establish a more effective relationship and promote the training-colleges as schools of the University for the professional training of teachers. Within the teaching profession in Wales, opposition was being shown on the one hand towards the employment of married women teachers, and on the other towards the payment of lower salaries to married than to unmarried women teachers. The ideology which equated the woman's place with the home and housewifery still remained a potent force in 1914. In the University of Wales, women were perceived to be on an equal footing with men as regards admission, eligibility for degrees and appointment to official positions. But the female presence on the teaching staff of the university colleges was minimal in 1914. Miss E.P. Hughes, Miss M.F. Rathbone a leading pioneer of extension lectures in north Wales, and Miss Mary Collin, headmistress of Cardiff High School for Girls, were conscious of the need to increase the number of female tutors and lecturers in all three constituent colleges.[13] Women students were still subject to out-dated regulations governing student discipline, particularly regarding social events and drinking in public houses. Shortly, these were to be challenged by students such as Idwal Jones who were veterans of a world war.[14]

The War generated a growth in the demand for secondary education in England and Wales, and by 1920 enrolment in intermediate and secondary schools had increased considerably. In the 119 intermediate and municipal secondary schools in Wales eligible for grants in 1919–20, there were 25,754 pupils — 12,026 boys and 13,728 girls. This revealed a marked contrast with the position in 1914–15 when 18,377 pupils — 9,057 boys and 9,320 girls — were enrolled.

Ever since the establishement of the university colleges and the implementation of the terms of the Welsh Intermediate Education Act, the democratic character of the system of education had been highlighted. However, in 1914 only a small proportion of girls from elementary schools benefited from secondary and higher education.[16] The education of the daughters of most working-class families remained limited.

Gradually in the inter-war years, with growing criticisms of the limited educational opportunities for working-class boys and girls, the proportion of free places was increased, until eventually, with the implementation of the Education Act 1944, oportunities for free secondary education and greater access to higher education were made available for both sexes. Whilst attempts were thus made to adjust the socio-economic bias of the educational system, it was not until the growth of modern feminism in the 1960s and 1970s that there was to be any significant attention to the educational implications of gender, sexism and sex-role stereotyping.

From the vantage position of the last decade of the twentieth century, one hundred years after the implementation of the most significant of the educational developments of the Victorian Age, an examination of the Welsh experience during the years 1847 to 1914 focuses attention on issues of significance both for educationists and historians. The inter-relationship of educational change and the political, social and economic context have been clearly demonstrated. Major agents of educational change and development and impediments to change, were located within a complex cultural and social backdrop as well as within educational institutions themselves. In particular, the promotion of female secondary and higher education in Wales was an integral part of the wider quest for emancipation motivated by developments else-where in Britain and overseas. At an opportune moment, a small group of middle-class, professional people, succeeded in promoting an educa-tional movement that led successfully to the establishment of, and access to, institutions of secondary and higher education. Not until the campaign to establish bilingual secondary schools in the 1960s and 1970s was Wales to see such a vigorous and equally successful educa-tional movement promoted by the professional classes. In the nine-teenth and early twentieth century, however, only peripheral attention was given to the native language and literature. The trend in education was to assimilate existing English patterns.

The triumph of female education in Victorian Wales was gained through the establishment of a state system. The whole campaign had gained credibility from evidence of the inadequacy and inequity in the private and endowed sector. In general, those schools that retained their independent status — and other to be established in twentieth century Wales — were, primarily by virtue of their fee-paying tariffs, to be on the periphery of the evolving system of secondary education. Occasionally, the opportunity was taken to utilize the freedom and opportunity provided by a wealth of resources for educational experi-ment.

The Welsh experience displayed trends in curriculum development that were to characterize the emerging pattern of girls' education elsewhere in Britain and overseas.[17] An overemphasis on so-called 'feminine' accomplishments was to be undermined by the quest for sexual equality. Identical curriculum and examinations for both sexes came to be regarded as the *sine qua non* of academic respectability. The girls' secondary schools imitated the academic-orientated curriculum of the well-established English grammar schools. However, by 1914, there was a demand for a balanced liberal education that could include a degree of differentiation which was reminiscent of the gender stereotyping of the late Victorian elementary school. A more central role for domestic studies as a valid alternative to foreign languages, mathematics and science in the secondary education of girls was regularly advocated by 1914 on the basis of utility, perceptions of femininity and gender stereotyping. Seventy-five years later, sex-role stereotyping and sexism in the curriculum are of considerable interest to educationists in Britain and overseas.

Study of the educational history of girls and women in Wales highlights significant issues pertaining to the methodology of women's history. It requires adequate attention to the fortunes of both sexes; the struggle for the education of girls and women in Victorian Wales was not divorced from the quest for better opportunities for boys and men. It is essential to ensure that over-enthusiasm for a separate feminist past does not distort the historical record anew. The history of female education and emancipation in Wales from 1847 to 1914 involves attention to the experience of a whole society.

Appendix A

Extracts from Thomas Howell's Will

Howell's Will was written in the Castillian tongue, and the material clause of it as translated (Hare's Reports on Charities under the Management of the Drapers Company, PRO, Ed. 27/6390) reads as follows:

> Item, I comaunde myne executers that I leve in Syvell, that incontynent, after my deathe, they doo send to the citie of London 12,000 duckats of gold, by billes of cambio, for to delyver to the House called Draper's Hall — to delyver theyme to the Wardeynes thereof; and the said Wardeynes, so sone as they have receyved the same 12,000 duckats to buy therewith 400 duckats of rent yearly for evermore — in possession for evermore. And it is my will, that the said 400 duckets be disposed of unto four maydens, being orphanes — next of my kynne and of bludde — to theire marriage — if they can be founde — every one of them to have 100 duckats — and if they cannot be founde of my lynnage, then to be geven to other foure maydens, though they be not of my lynnage, so that they be orphanes honnest of good fame, and every of them 100 duckats — and so, every yere, for to marry four maydens for ever. And if the said 12,000 duckats will bye more lande then the said 12,000 duckats to be spente to the marriage of maydens, being orphanes, increasing the foure maydens aforesaide as shall seme by the discretion aforesaide of the Master and Wardeynes of the saide House of Draper's Hall; and that this memoria to remain in writing in the Booke of Memoryes in the said House in suche mannere as it shall at no time be undone for ever.

Appendix B

Hall of Residence for Women Students, University College of Wales, Aberystwyth: women enrolled 1887–1890

Lady Principal: Miss E. A. CARPENTER.

(¶ Prize gained.   † Exhibitioner.   §Scholar.   *Non-resident Student in previous Session.   ‡Has been to Training College.)

Entered	Left	Students	Previous Preparation	Examinations passed	Subsequent Appointments
Oct. 1887	June 1890	*Elizabeth Victoria Cornell†	Univ. Coll., Cardiff	Matriculation, 1886; Intermediate in Arts, 1887	Visiting Mistress
Oct. 1887	June 1890	*Mary Elizabeth Fluck†	Private study.	Matriculation, 1885; Inter. in Arts, 1887 (Honours in French); BA, 1890.	Head Mistress of the Hastings High School for Girls
Oct. 1887	June 1889	*Mary Margeret Price Howard James¶	Univ. Coll., Cardiff.	Matriculation, 1887; Inter. in Arts, 1888 (Honours in English); BA, 1891 (Hons. in Mental Sc).	
Oct. 1887	Mar. 1888	*Annie Gwen Jones	Univ. Coll., Cardiff.	Matriculation, 1888.	Private Governess in Russia.
Oct. 1887	June 1891	*Ellinor Morgan†¶§	Wintersdorf, Southport.	Matriculation, 1889; Inter. in Arts, 1890; BA, 1891	
Oct. 1887	June 1891	Emma Aston Barrs...	Wesleyan School, Clapham Park.	Matriculation, 1889; Inter. in Arts, 1890.	
Oct. 1887	June 1889	Margaret Davies†§	Private study.	Matriculation, 1888.	Assistant Mistress in the Clergy Endowed School, St. Mary's Hall, Brighton.

Entered	Left	Students	Previous Preparation	Examinations passed	Subsequent Appointments
April 1891		(Entered again)...		Intermediate in Science, 1891.	
Sept. 1887	Dec. 1887	Lizzie Mercy Finch	Lady Hollis's High School, Hackney		
Sept. 1887	June 1888	*Mary Elizabeth Robinson	North London Collegiate School.		
Sept. 1887	June 1891	Sarah Jane Robinson	St. Martin's Middle-class School, London, W.C.		
Sept. 1887	June 1889	Phoebe Sheavyn§	Private study.	Matric, 1887; Inter. in Arts, 1888 (Hons. in English); BA, 1889 (Hons. in Eng.)	Assist. Mist. in the Aske's School for Girls, Hatcham.
Sept. 1887	Dec. 1889	Sarah Ann Walker†	Private study.	Matriculation, 1888; Intermediate in Arts, 1889; BA, 1891.	Assist. Mist. in the Clifton High School, St. Helens.
Sept. 1887	Dec. 1888	*Helen Jane Wilks	Cheltenham High School.	Matriculation, 1889	Private governess.
Sept. 1888	June 1889	Frances Mary Eastwood†	Wyggeston High School, Leicester.	Matriculation; Inter. in Arts, 1888; BA, 1889.	Assist. Mist. in Central High. Grade School, Leeds.
Sept. 1888	June 1891	Ada Emily Emmerson†	Aske's School, Hatcham, and Private study.	Matriculation, 1887; Inter. in Arts, 1889.	
Sept. 1888	June 1890	Helen Mary Freeman*	North London Collegiate School.	Matriculation; Inter. in Arts, 1888; BA, 1890 (Hons. in English).	Assist. Mist. in North London Collegiate School.
Sept. 1888	Nov. 1890	Lucy Helen May Freeman¶	North London Collegiate School.	Matriculation, 1888; Inter. in Science, 1889.	Assist. Mist. in Clergy Orphan School, St. John's Wood, Lond.

Sept. 1888	June 1889	Blanche Gardiner	…	Wyggeston High School, Leicester.	Matriculation; Inter. in Arts, 1888; BA, 1889.	Visiting Mistress.
Sept. 1888	June 1889	Annie Beatrice Hewart†	…	Bury High School.	Matriculation, 1889; Inter. in Science, 1891.	
Sept. 1888	June 1889	Susan Anne Hughes	…	Univ. Coll., Nottingham.	Matriculation, 1888; Prelim. Scientific (Chem. and Physics) 1888; (Biology) 1889.	
Sept. 1888	June 1891	Maud Mary Jeffrey¶	…	Aske's School, Hatcham.	Matriculation, 1888.	
Sept. 1888	April 1889	Mary Matilda Jones	…	Caerleon House, Aberystwyth.		
Sept. 1888	June 1889	Margaret Elizabeth Monk¶	…	Ladies' Coll., Cheltenham.	Matriculation, 1885.	
Sept. 1889	June 1889	Frances Mordue	…	Aske's School, Hatcham.	Matriculation, 1888.	
Sept. 1889	Mar. 1890	Alice Paffard¶	…	Blackburn High School.	Matriculation, June, 1889.	Private Governess
Sept. 1889	Mar. 1890	Ida Amelia Perman†§	…	Private study.	Matriculation, 1888; Inter. in Arts, 1889 (Hons in English); BA, 1891 (Hons in Classics).	
Sept. 1889	Dec. 1889	Laura Mabel Powell	…	Private study.	Matriculation, 1888; Inter. in Science, 1891 (Hons in Zoology).	
Sept. 1889	Nov. 1891	Winnifred Mary Ross	…	High School, Southport.		
Sept. 1889	Dec. 1888	Alice Shannon†	…	Bedford College.	Matriculation; Inter. in Arts, 1888; BA, 1890.	Assist. Mist. in Manchester High School.
Sept. 1889	June 1889	Helena Storey	…	Ladies' College, Hereford.		
Sept. 1889	Dec. 1889	Mary Bartle Thomas	…	Univ. College, Cardiff.	Matriculation, 1889	
Sept. 1889	Nov. 1888	Harriet Eliza Viggars†	…	Orme's School, Newcastle under Lyme.		

(¶ Prize gained   †Exhibitioner.   §Scholar.   *Non-resident Student in previous Session.   ‡Has been to Training College.)

Entered	Left	Students	Previous Preparation	Examinations passed	Subsequent Appointments
Sept. 1888	June 1889	Lucy Lipson Ward	Wyggeston High School, Leicester.	Matriculation; Inter. in Arts, 1888; BA, 1889.	Assist. Mist. at the Aske's School, Hatcham.
Sept. 1888	June 1890	Ethel Julia Windley†	North London Collegiate School.	Matriculation; Inter. in Arts, 1888; BA, 1890.	
Sept. 1888	June 1890	Emma Harling Wood	Birkbeck Institute.	Matriculation; Inter. in Arts, 1888; BA, 1890.	Assist. Mist. in the Burton High School.
Jan. 1889	June 1891	Winifred Anna Ellis	Dr. Williams' School, Dolgelley.	Matriculation, 1891.	
Jan. 1889	June 1891	Lilian Mary Martha Macdermott	Private study.	Matriculation, 1883;	
Jan. 1889	June 1889	Ada Alice Ridewood‡	Queen's College, Harley Street, London.	Inter. in Arts, 1889.	
May 1889	June 1889	Charlotte Reid Bingham	Sandholm School, Waterloo.		
Sept. 1889	June 1889	Margaret Findlay Anderson† ...	Tottenham High School.	Matriculation, 1889; Inter. in Science, 1890.	
Sept. 1889	Dec. 1890	Mary Steele Bickley	Orme's School, Newcastle under Lyme.	Matriculation, 1889; Inter. in Arts, 1891.	Assist. Mist. in the Orme's School, Newcastle under Lyme.
Sept. 1889	Dec. 1890	Ruth Ellen Brooks†	Blackburn and Middlesborough High Schools.	Matriculation, 1890; Inter. in Arts, 1891.	
Sept. 1889	June 1891	Emily Croft†	The Salt Schools, and The Yorkshire Coll., Leeds.	Matriculation, 1888; Inter. in Arts, 1890; B.A. 1891.	
Sept. 1889	June 1891	Marian Firth†	The Salt Schools.	Matriculation, 1889; Inter. in Arts, 1890.	
Sept. 1889	June 1890	Alice Lucas Marshall	Belmont House School, Leicester.		

Entered	Left	Name		School	Examinations passed	Present position
Sept. 1889	June 1890	Edith Mary Monk†	...	Ladies' Coll., Cheltenham.	Matriculation.	Assist. Mist. in Rotherham High School.
Sept. 1889	June 1890	Jane Bella Partridge§	...	Bedford College, London.	Matriculation, 1888; Inter. in Arts, 1889, (Hons. in French (Prize) and in English).	
Sept. 1889	June 1891	Emma Palmer Pratt†	...	Royal Holloway College.	Matriculation, 1886; Inter. in Arts, 1890; BA. 1891.	Matriculation; Inter. in Arts, 1889; BA, 1891.
Sept. 1889	June 1890	Laura Caroline Trevor†	...	Private study.	Matriculation, 1890.	
Sept. 1890	June 1891	Edith Mary Bartholomew†	...	North London Collegiate school.		
Sept. 1890	June 1891	Ethel Catharine Biggs§	...	Private study.	Matriculation, 1888; Inter. in Arts, 1890.	
Sept. 1890	Dec. 1890	Lucy Davenport†	...	Private study.	Matriculation. Inter. in Arts, 1890.	
Sept. 1890	Dec. 1890	Rosa Davey§	...	Private study.		
Sept. 1890	Dec. 1890	Edith Gadsby†	...	De Montfort House School, Leicester.	Matriculation, 1889; Inter. in Arts, 1891.	
Sept. 1890	Dec. 1890	Alice Mabel Hewart†	...	Bury High School.	Matriculation, 1891.	

Notes

CHAPTER 1

1. 'What is Women's History?' *The Times Educational Supplement*, 19 April 1985.
2. Foreword, M. Bryant, *The Unexpected Revolution*, 1979.
3. Deirdre Beddoe, 'The Lost Sex', *Arcade* No. 3, November 1980.
4. 'Towards a Welsh Women's History', *Llafur*, Vol. 3, No. 2, 1981.
5. Theodore Zeldin in Review of E.O. Hellerstein (and others) *Victorian Women, Observer*, 24 May 1981.
6. Angela John, 'A Miner Struggle? Women's Protests in Welsh Mining History', *Llafur*, Vol. 4, No. 1, 1982, p. 72.
7. L.J. Williams and Dot Jones, 'Women at Work in Nineteenth Century Wales', *Llafur*, Vol. 3, No. 3, 1982, p. 20.
8. Held at Polytechnic of Wales, April 1983. Lectures and workshops focused on topics which included: 'Welsh Working Class Women, Past and Present'; 'Women in Employment'; 'Women in Welsh Coalmining Communities'; 'Women: Self Help and Philanthropy in the Nineteenth Century'; 'Images of Women in Nineteenth Century Welsh Women's Magazines'.
9. *Y Traethodydd*, Rhifyn Arbennig: Merched a Llenyddiaeth, Vol. CXLI, No. 598.
10. See Sian Rhiannon Williams, 'Nid Siôl a Het Uchel', *Y Faner*, 9 January 1981. Idem, *Y Faner*, 29 April 1983; Beddoe, op. cit.
11. Iorwen Myfanwy Jones, *Merched Llên Cymru o 1850 i 1914*, unpublished MA Wales, 1935. R. Tudur Jones, *Coroni'r Fam Frenhines*, 1976. Idem, 'Daearu'r Angylion. Sylwadau ar Ferched mewn llenyddiaeth 1860–1900', *Ysgrifau Beirniadol*, XI, 1979.
12. D. Jenkins and M. Owen, *The Welsh Law of Women*, 1980.
13. *The Times Higher Education Supplement*, 1 February 1985.
14. Malcolm I. Thomas and Jennifer Grimmett, *Women in Protest 1800–1850*; D.J.V. Jones, 'Chartism', *History*, Vol. 68, No. 222, February 1983, pp. 1–21.
15. See Barbara Taylor, *Eve and the New Jerusalem*, 1985.
16. *The Times Educational Supplement*, 19 April 1981.
17. Martha Vicinus (ed.), *Suffer and Be Still: Women in the Victorian Age*, (1977), p. vii.
18. P. Branca, *Silent Sisterhood: Middle Class Women in the Victorian Home* (1975).

19. M. Bryant, *The Unexpected Revolution: A Study in the History of Education of Women and Girls in the Nineteenth Century*, 1979.

20. S. Fletcher, *Feminists and Bureaucrats: A Study in the Development of Girls' Education in the Nineteenth Century*, 1980.

21. See also: C. Dyhouse, 'Social Darwinistic ideas and the development of women's education in England, 1880–1920', *History of Education*, Vol. 5, No. 1, 1976, pp. 44–58. Idem, 'Good wives and little mothers: social anxieties and the schoolgirls' curriculum', *Oxford Review of Education*, Vol. 3, No. 1, 1977, pp. 21–35.

22. J. Purvis, 'Separate Spheres and Inequality in the Education of Working Class Women 1854–1900', *History of Education*, 1981, Vol. 10, No. 4, pp. 227–43. Idem, 'Women and Teaching in the Nineteenth Century', in *Education and the State*, Vol. 2, ed. R. Dale, G. Esland, R. Fergusson and M. MacDonald, 1981, pp. 359–73. Idem, 'Domestic Subjects since 1870' in J. Goodson (ed.), *Social Histories of the Secondary Curriculum*, 1981, pp. 148–156.

23. G.E. Jones, 'Education in Wales: The Need for a Historical Perspective', *Education for Development*, Vol. 10, No. 1, 1985, pp. 2–12.

24. Frances Hoggan, 'The Past and Future in the Education of Girls in Wales', *Report of National Eisteddfod Association*, 1883, p. 50.

25. *The Cambrian News*, 28 July 1899. Speech by Dr R.D. Roberts on the occasion of the twenty-first anniversary of Dr Williams' School.

26. R.D. Roberts, Clare College, Cambridge, in ibid., 7 March 1884.

CHAPTER 2

1. See Dyhouse, C. 'Social Darwinistic ideas and the development of women's education in England 1880–1920' in *History of Education*, Vol. v, No. 1, 1976, pp. 44–58. Purvis, J., 'Separate Spheres and Inequality in the Education of Working Class Women 1854–1900', ibid., Vol. x, No. 4, 1981, pp. 227–43.

2. Branca, P., *Silent Sisterhood*, 1975, p. 152.

3. Bridenthal and Koong (editors), *Becominig Visible: Women in European History* (1977), pp. 5–8.

4. J.R., 'Addysg y Fam Gartref', *Y Cronicl*, 1849, p. 335.

5. R. Hughes in *Y Dysgedydd*, October 1850, p. 307.

6. Letter: 'Dyledswyddau Gwŷr a Gwragedd', *Baner ac Amserau Cymru*, 14 October 1857.

7. *Baner ac Amserau Cymru*, 28 December 1859.

8. Quoted in R.T. Jones, 'Daearu'r Angylion', *Ysgrifau Beirniadol* XI, pp. 212–3.

9. M.A. Williams, 'Merched Cymru' *Cymru* 1893, p. 60.

10. See: W.E. Houghton, *The Victorian Frame of Mind 1830–70* (1957), pp. 350–2; Mrs Ellis, *Daughters of England and The Wives of England: their Relative Duties, Domestic Influence and Social Obligations* (1843).

11. R.T. Jones, op. cit., p. 16.

12. Cf. 'Awdurdod Mamaidd', Chapter 2, p. 9.

13. *Yr Eisteddfod*, April 1864, p. 158.

14. Ibid., p. 220.
15. 'Dylanwad Mam yn Ffurfiad Cymeriad yr Oes', *Y Gymraes*, 1898, pp. 84–5.
16. R.T. Jones, op. cit.; A.H. Williams, *Cymru Oes Fictoria*, 1973, p. 21; Olive Banks, *Faces of Feminism*, 1985.
17. G.M. Young, *Portrait of an Age*, 1977, p. 24. M. Bryant, *The Unexpected Revolution*, p. 69.
18. *Yr Eisteddfod*, 1864, p. 144. Essay at Caernarfon National Eisteddfod 1862 by Mrs Richards, Garth, Bangor.
19. Hannah Hughes, *Y Gein-Flwch, neu Neilltuolion Gwraig Dda*, 1871, p. 15.
20. 'Gwerth y Rhyw Benywaidd': written originally in an 1845 review in *Y Traethodydd*. Quoted in *Y Drysorfa* 1885, pp. 61–2. See also E. Davies and A.D. Rees (eds.), *Welsh Rural Communities*, 1966.
21. R.T. Jones, *'Coroni'r Fam Frenhines*, 1977. See: Roger Edwards, *Cartref* (1st edition 1855, 2nd edition, 1870), pp. 76–7; O.M. Edwards, *Cartrefi Cymru*, 1896; Houghton, op. cit., p. 372, Vicinus, op. cit., p. 372.
22. Williams, op. cit.; Angela John, *By the Sweat of their Brow: Women Workers at Victorian Coalmines*, 1980.
23. Wanda F. Neff, *Victorian Working Women*, 1929, p. 37.
24. R.H. Williams, *Y Dysgedydd*, 1874.
25. L.J. Williams and Dot Jones, Women at Work in the Nineteenth Century, *Llafur*, Vol. 3, No. 3, 1982, p. 23. See also Table p. 30.
26. 'Addysgiaeth a Disgyblaeth Plant', *Baner ac Amserau Cymru*, 21 December 1859.
27. 'Y gwersi angenrheidiol i Ferched Ieuainc', *Y Drysorfa*, 1863, pp. 136–7.
28. *The Cambrian News*, 22 April 1887: J. Gibson's Editorial.
29. 'Trefniadaeth Deuluaidd', *Yr Adolygydd*, 1853.
30. R.J. Derfel, 'Cymdeithasau Llenyddol', *Y Traethodydd*, 1854, pp. 345–6.
31. *The Cambrian News*, 22 September, 1876. See also M.A. Williams in *Y Traethodydd*, 1894, p. 188; *Baner ac Amserau Cymru*, 19 June, 1889; *Caernarvon and Denbigh Herald*, 5 October 1888.
32. R.J. Derfel, op. cit., pp. 373–4; Ieuan Gwynedd, *Y Gymraes*, 1850, p. 5; Newcastle Report, Vol. IV, p. 449; Evan Jones (Tredegar), 'Dirwest a'r Rhyw Fenywaidd', *Y Drysorfa*, 1854, pp. 335–6; Editorial: 'Troseddau ac Addysg', *Baner ac Amserau Cymru*, 20 March 1857; ibid. 'Addysg a Moesau', 3 October 1860; 'Y Gwersi Angenrheidiol i Ferched Ieuainc', *Y Drysorfa*, 1863, pp. 136–7; *Y Drysorfa*, 1865, pp. 254–5.
33. Ibid., 7 December 1881; PRO Ed. 119/71.
34. *The Cambrian*, 29 June 1900.
35. W. Boyd, *The History of Western Education*, 1957.
36. P. Branca, *Women in Europe since 1750*, p. 63.
37. Bryant, op. cit., p. 56.
38. 'Merch y Llafurwr: Pa fodd y dylid ei dysgu?', *Cyfansoddiadau Eisteddfod Genedlaethol Conwy 1861*, p. 335.
39. 'Gallu a Dylanwad Merched', *Y Beirniad*, July 1871, p. 5.
40. 'Byddai yn anfenywaidd gweled A.C. (h.y. B.A.) yn dilyn ei henw', ibid., 1864, p. 159.
41. *Y Traethodydd*, 1854, p. 372.
42. 'Introduction', *Yr Athrawes o Ddifrif*, 1859, p. xv. Lewis Edwards, *Traethodau Llenyddol*, 1867.

43. Mrs Manuel, traethawd ar 'Addysg Merched', *Cyfansoddiadau Buddugol Eisteddfod Dinbych 1860*, p. 96.
44. Ibid., p. 101–103.
45. Revd William Williams, 'Addysgiad Benywod', *Yr Eisteddfod*, 1865, p. 255.
46. *The Cambrian News*, 22 April 1887.
47. *Caernarvon and Denbigh Herald*, 5 October 1888.
48. 'Hawliau ein Merched', *Baner ac Amserau Cymru*, 21 December 1870.
49. 'Dyfodol ein Merched', *Baner ac Amserau Cymru*, 7 May 1873.
50. Ibid.
51. Ibid.
52. Y Gohebydd, *Baner ac Amserau Cymru*, 14 June 1873.
53. Ibid., 7 May 1873.
54. Y Gohebydd, 'Dyfodol ein Merched', *Baner ac Amserau Cymru*, 14 June 1873.
55. Margaret Ellis, Ruabon, 'Addysg Merched', *Baner ac Amserau Cymru*, 17 October 1883.
56. Revd J.M. Morgan, 'Menywod Cymru ac Addysg a Llwyddiant eu Gwlad', *Y Traethodydd*, 1893.
57. Eisteddfod Genedlaethol 1891. National Library of Wales MSS BXl.
58. 'A Plea for Girls', *The Cambrian News*, 29 June 1894.
59. *The Cambrian News*, 14 February 1888.
60. *The Cambrian News*, 26 October 1888.
61. Dilys Glynne Jones Papers, UCNW, letter dated 17 April 1887.
62. *The Cambrian News*, 8 July 1898.
63. Miss Edmunds Bangor, 'Merched Blaenllaw yn Nheyrnasiad Victoria', *Y Gymraes*, 1899, p. 22: '. . . mae traddodiadau oesoedd wedi bod yn dal, ac i ryw fesur yn haeru eto mai unig safle merch mewn bywyd ydyw — y teuluaidd.'
64. R.J. Derfel, *Y Traethodydd*, 1854, p. 371.
65. Ibid., p. 372.
66. Mrs Edmunds Bangor, op. cit., pp. 55–6.
67. Mrs Manuel, traethawd ar 'Addysg Merched', *Cyfansoddiadau Buddugol Eisteddfod Dinbych 1860*, p. 96.
68. Mrs Richards, 'Cyfansoddiadau Buddygol Eisteddfod Caernarfon, 1862'; *Yr Eisteddfod* 1864 Vol I pp. 140–61.
69. 'Gallu A Dylanwad Merched', *Y Beirniad*, July, pp. 5–15.
70. Ibid., p. 6.
71. Y Gohebydd, 'Dyfodol ein Merched', *Baner ac Amserau Cymru*, 14 June 1873.
72. Ibid., quoting Dr Neil Arnot, *Observations on National Education*.
73. Lord Aberdare, *Lectures and Addresses*, p. 349. See also Thomas Gee, 'Ymenyddiau Merched', *Baner ac Amserau Cymru*, 24 April 1888.
74. *Minutes of Committee of Council on Education*, 1852–3: Report on British and Wesleyan and other Denominational Schools in the Midland District of England and Wales, p. 109.
75. *Minutes Committee of Council*, 1874–5; ibid., 1877–8, 16 January 1878; ibid., Tingling Report, p. 638.
76. *National Eisteddfod Association Report*, 1886.
77. *Western Mail*, 18 January 1887.

78. *Oswestry Advertiser*, 11 January 1888. See also *Caernarvon and Denbigh Herald*, 5 October 1888.
79. 'The Education of Girls in Wales', NLW MSS BXl.
80. Ibid.,
81. *Caernarvon and Denbigh Herald*, 9 October 1897. See also Principal T. Francis Roberts in *Y Gymraes*, August 1898, p. 114.
82. Brian Harrison, op. cit., p. 25; C. Dyhouse, *Girls growing up in late Victorian and Edwardian England*, p. 121.
83. Viz. Dr Henry Maudsley, 'Sex in Mind and Education', *Fortnightly Review*, Vol. xv, 1874, pp. 466–83.
84. Cf. J. Thorburn, *Female Education from a Physiological Point of view*, 1884.
85. Mrs H. Sidgwick, *Health Statistics of Women Students of Cambridge and Oxford and of their Sisters 1890;* Emily Pfeiffer, *Women and Work: An Essay*, 1888, *National Eisteddfod Association, Report, 1886; The Lancet*, 1886, p. 315; *Proceedings of British Medical Association*, 1886, pp. 338–9.
86. Jo Manton, *Elizabeth Garrett*, p. 66; Emily Davies (daughter of Revd John Davies and Sister of John Llewelyn Davies, also a champion of female education — see *Dictionary of Welsh Biography*, p. 135), *Questions Relating to Women, 1860–1908*, p. 40; Philip Guedalla, *The Queen and Mr Gladstone*, Vol. 1, 1933, pp. 227–9.
87. *Carmarthen Journal*, 28 March 1879, quoting *The Lancet*.
88. Dyhouse, op. cit., 1981, p. 91.
89. Burstyn, op. cit., pp. 75–9; Bryant, op. cit., pp. 114–15.
90. Jill Conway, *Stereotypes of Femininity in a Theory of Sexual Evolution*, pp. 140–54.
91. See: National Eisteddfod Association Report, 1886–7.
92. Dyhouse, op. cit., 1976; idem, 1981.
93. Note especially *The Cambrian News* and the publications of the National Eisteddfod Association.
94. John Gibson in *The Cambrian News*, 2 October 1885.
95. Ibid., 25 July 1890.
96. See Vicinus, *Suffer and Be Still*, 1977.
97. B. Harrison, 'Women's Health and the Women's Movement' in *Biology, Medicine and Society* 1840–1940, ed. Charles Webster, 1981, p. 51.
98. *The Cambrian News*, 29 November 1893.
99. Y Gohebydd, 'Dyfodol ein Merched', *Baner ac Amserau Cymru*, 14 June 1873.
100. *The Cambrian News*, 14 May 1873.
101. Thomas Gee, 'Yr Etholfraint i Ferched', *Baner ac Amserau Cymru*, Editorial, 11 May 1870.
102. Golygyddol, 'Meddiannau Merched Priod', *Baner ac Amserau Cymru*, 25 May 1870. See also ibid., 17 March 1869; 7 August 1869.
103. 'Hawliau ein Merched', *Baner ac Amserau Cymru*, 21 December 1876.
104. Ibid. 'Yr Etholfraint i Ferched', *Baner ac Amserau Cymru*, 10 May 1871. See also: 8 May 1872; 7 May 1873; 14 June 1873; 'Hawliau Merched', *Y Cronicl*, 1872, pp. 166–7.
105. Ibid., 14 June 1873.
106. *Baner ac Amserau Cymru*, 2 June 1886.
107. Editorial, 'The Education of Girls', *The Cambrian News*, 22 April 1887.

108. Ibid. See also: Dilys Glynne Jones Papers, UCNW, letter dated 17 April 1887.
109. *Y Dysgedydd*, 1848.
110. Letter, ibid., 11 July 1866.
111. *The Cambrian News*, 21 November 1879.
112. Revd H.M. Thomas (Huwco Meirion), *Mêl Myfyrdod: Pregethau, Traethodau, Barddoniaeth* (Pittsburg), 1882, pp. 224–5.
113. J. Gibson, *The Emancipation of Women*, 1891, p. 58. See also *The Cambrian News*, 12 October 1885.
114. Ibid., 26 October 1888.
115. Gibson, op. cit., p. 16. See also: *The Cambrian News*, 26 October 1888.
116. Bryant, op. cit., p. 60.
117. Bridenthal and Koong (eds), op. cit., p. 4.
118. Bryant, op. cit., p. 23.
119. R. Deem, *Women and Schooling*, 1978, p. 12.
120. Newcastle Report, Vol. IV, p. 443. Williams, op. cit., p. 37. *Re* difficulties of defining middle class, see Branca, op. cit., pp. 38–40.
121. Cf. Aberdare Report 1881.
122. *Cyfansoddiadau Buddugol, Eisteddfod Genedlaethol Conwy, 1861*, p. 338.
123. Deem, op. cit.
124. E.R. Phillips, ' The history of the teaching of domestic subjects 1870–1944', unpublished M. Ed. thesis, 1979, pp. xi–xii.
125. Deem, op. cit., p. 11.
126. D. Crow, *The Victorian Woman*, 1971, p. 51; Census Returns 1851–91.
127. *Committee of Council Minutes*, 1860–1, p. 163; see also, ibid., 1877–8, Revd Burns' Report on Glamorgan.
128. Winter, op. cit., NLW MSS.
129. Letters of Right Honourable Lord Aberdare, Vol. II, letter dated 29 June 1875.
130. *The Cambrian News*, 2 January 1880.
131. Ibid., 10 June 1898.
132. Bryant, op. cit.
133. J. and O. Banks, *Feminism and Family Planning* (1964). Bryant, op. cit., p. 35.
134. Ibid.
135. Ibid., pp. 35–40; Deem, op. cit., p. 110.
136. *Baner ac Amserau Cymru*, 7 April 1875.
137. Crawshay, op. cit., p. 28.
138. Ibid.
139. *The Cambrian News*, 7 March 1884.
140. Ibid. See also H.J. Fleure, UCW, Aberystwyth: 'An Old Student looks at the College, *Trans. Cymmrodorion Society*, 1955, p. 58.
141. See also: Banks, op. cit., p. 37; Gordon, op. cit., p. 165; Taunton Report, Vol. 1, p. 570: *Re* 'new openings for women in branches of employment . . . not much can be said with confidence. Even in America it cannot be said to have made such progress; and in this country it is spoken of as still uncertain; tentative and prospective'.
142. Bryant, op. cit., p. 23, p. 58.
143. Ibid.
144. Dyhouse, op. cit.

145. *The Cambrian News*, 15 April 1887.
146. Ibid., 22 April 1887.
147. See Tables 1 and 2: *Llafur*, No. 3, 1982.
148. Williams and Jones, op. cit., p. 21.
149. Ibid., pp. 23–8.
150. Ibid., p. 28.
151. Y Gohebydd, 'Dyfodol ein Merched', *Baner ac Amserau Cymru*, 14 June 1873.
152. Idem., 2 December 1874. See also Revd D. Evans MA in *The Cambrian News*.
153. *Baner ac Amserau Cymru*, 27 November 1874; *The Cambrian News*, 23 October 1874 and 22 September 1876.
154. Holland in *The Cambrian News*, 22 September 1876.
155. Y Gohebydd, *Baner ac Amserau Cymru*, 20 January 1875.
156. 'Women and the U.C.W.', *The Cambrian News*, 13 February 1874.
157. Y Gohebydd, *Baner ac Amserau Cymru*, 11 October 1876.
158. 'Dyrchafiad Merched', *Y Frythones*, 1886, pp. 235–6.
159. Ibid., 15 April 1887; *South Wales Daily News*, 6 January 1888.
160. *Baner ac Amserau Cymru*, 19 June 1889.
161. *The Cambrian News*, 22 March 1895.
162. Gordon, op. cit., p. 102.
163. J. Kamm, *Hope Deferred*, 1965, p. 184.
164. Frances Cobbe Papers NLW.
165. E.P. Hughes, 'The Higher Education of Girls in Wales', *Transactions of the Liverpool National Eisteddfod*, 1884, p. 41.
166. Y Gohebydd, 'Dyfodol ein Merched', *Baner ac Amserau Cymru*, 14 June 1873.
167. *Baner ac Amserau Cymru*, 20 October 1874.
168. Ibid.
169. Ibid.
170. Y Gohebydd, *Baner ac Amserau Cymru*, 2 December 1874. See also 11 October 1876.
171. Ibid., 7 April 1875.
172. 18 July 1890.
173. Letter from 'Cymro', *Caernarvon and Denbigh Herald*, 12 September 1863.
174. Ll.M. Rees, 'A Critical Examination of Teacher Training in Wales 1846–98', unpublished Ph.D. 1968, pp. 16–17; J.R. Webster, 'The Place of Secondary Education in Welsh Society 1800–1918', unpublished Ph.D. 1959, p. 155.
175. See H.M. Jones, 'History of the Cymmrodorion Society', unpublished MA, 1939, pp. 230–4.
176. See Chapter 3.
177. See H.M. Jones, op. cit.; H. Ramage and R.T. Jenkins, *History of the Honourable Society of Cymmrodorion*, Y Cymmrodorion, 1951.
178. *Baner ac Amserau Cymru*, 21 November 1883.
179. *Baner ac Amserau Cymru*, 22 February 1888.
180. 11 September 1890.
181. Webster, op. cit., p. 2.
182. E.P. Hughes, op. cit., 1884, pp. 53–4.

183. *Y Frythones*, July 1887, p. 200, commenting on Miss E.P. Hughes' address in Cardiff at first meeting of the Association for Promoting the Education of Girls in Wales.
184. Report of Nonconformist Conference at Aberystwyth. *The Cambrian News*, 24 September 1880.
185. See *Cymru Fydd*, 1888–91.
186. *Y Dysgedydd*, July 1889, p. 266.
187. Cf. Howell Schools. There were Anglican members of the Honourable Society of Cymmrodorion.
188. Aberdare Report, Vol. 1, p. XLVIII. See also E.P. Hughes, op. cit., pp. 3–4; Williams, op. cit., p. 36; Webster, op. cit., p. 136.
189. *Y Beirniad*, 1876, p. 320.
190. J. Myfennydd Morgan, *Y Traethodydd*, 1893, p. 370.
191. Ibid., p. 378.
192. See Chapter 3 (below).
193. *The Cambrian News*, 15 March 1895.
194. 'Merched: Eu Safle mewn Cymdeithas', *Y Gymraes*, 1913, pp. 106–7.
195. 'Y Gymraes yn yr Ysgol', *Y Gymraes*, 1898, pp. 24–6.
196. *The Cambrian News*, 28 March 1890.
197. Ibid., 13 May 1898.
198. Ibid., 11 June 1897; 16 July 1897.
199. John Gibson, *The Emancipation of Women*, (second edition) 1894, pp. 9–11.
200. *Y Gymraes*, 1896, p. 2; Ibid., 1905, pp. 3–5; Ibid., 1910, pp. 2–4; Ibid., 1913, pp. 106–7.
201. Miss Edmunds, Bangor, 'Merched Blaenllaw yn Nheyrnasiad Victoria', *Y Gymraes*, 1899, pp. 21–2.
202. M.A. Williams, 'Merched Cymru', *Cymru*, 1893, pp. 55–64; *Y Tyst*, 10 August 1894.
203. *The Cambrian News*, 27 April 1900.
204. Ibid., 7 February 1902.

CHAPTER 3

1. Editorial: *Yr Amserau*, 24 September 1846 — 'Addysg Gyffredinol yw pwnc mawr y dydd'.
2. William Williams MP, quoted in D. Salmon, 'The Welsh Education Commission 1846–7', *Y Cymmrodorion*, 1913, p. 193.
3. Minutes of Committee of Council on Education, 1839–40, p. 28.
4. Ibid., p. 182.
5. Ibid., p. 191; 192.
6. *Children's Employment Commission, Second Report*, 1843, pp. 145, 159, 193.
7. Mair Elvet Thomas, *Afiaith yng Ngwent*, p. 145.
8. D. Salmon, The Welsh Education Commission 1846–7, *Y Cymmrodor, Vol.* XXIV, 1913, pp. 193–222; F. Price Jones, 'Effaith Brâd y Llyfrau Gleision', *Y Traethodydd*, 1963, pp. 49–59.

9. *Reports of the Commissioners of Inquiry into the State of Education in Wales* (1848 edition), p. 32.

10. Ibid., p. 36.

11. Ibid., p. 227.

12. Ibid., p. 484.

13. Ibid., p. 535.

14. Ibid., p. 299.

15. Ibid.

16. Ibid., p. 35.

17. See *Yr Amserau*, 1848–50. Correspondence and press cuttings relating to Ieuan Gwynedd in Edward Griffiths MSS NLW.

18. Evan Jones, *Facts, Figures and Statements in illustration of the Dissent and Morality of Wales*, 1849, p. 31.

19. C. Tawelfryn Thomas, *Cofiant Ieuan Gwynedd*, p. 90.

20. Ibid., pp. 37–8.

21. *Y Dysgedydd*, January 1849.

22. See Sian Rhiannon Williams, op. cit., p. 446.

23. See W.E. Houghton, *The Victorian Frame of Mind*, pp. 341–53.

24. *Y Gymraes*, 1850, No. 2, p. 53.

25. R.J. Derfel, 'Cymdeithasau Llenyddol', p. 9, (Winner of essay competition at Bethesda Eisteddfod 1854) in *'Traethodau ac Areithiau*, 1864.

26. *Y Traethodydd*, July 1854, pp. 370–9.

27. H.E. Thomas, *Y Llenor, sef Traethawd ar Gymru a'r Cymdeithasau Llenyddol*, 1854, p. 17.

28. Dyhouse, op. cit.

29. See *Y Traethodydd*, 1850, pp. 108–11; ibid., 1856, p. 117; *Yr Amserau*, 23 January 1850; ibid., 18 May 1853; *Y Diwygiwr* 1851.

30. Minutes of Committee of Council on Education, 1850, p. 578.

31. Minutes of Committee of Council on Education 1864–5, p. XLVI, Revised Code; and 1866–7, p. LXVI.

32. Ibid., 1860–1; 1869–70.

33. *Report of Pakington Committee on Education 1865–6*, p. XVI.

34. Leslie Wynne Evans, *Education in Industrial Wales 1700–1900*, pp. 95–110.

35. Earl of Ressborough (ed.), *Lady Charlotte Schreiber. Extracts from her Journal*, 1853–1891.

36. *Report of the Committee on the Employment of Children, Young Persons and Women in Agriculture*, Vol. XIII, 1870.

37. Ibid., pp. 6–7.

38. Ibid., p. 18.

39. Ibid., p. 13.

40. Ibid., p. 19.

41. Ibid., p. 57.

42. Thomas Rees, *Miscellaneous Papers on Subjects relating to Wales*, 1867, pp. 29–33.

43. Published in 1866 at Merthyr Tudful.

44. Newcastle Commission, Jenkins' report on *The State of Popular Education in the Welsh Specimen Districts*, Vol. 4, p. 443.

45. Evans, op. cit., p. 2; Rowland Williams, 'The Church & Education in Wales', *Quarterly Review*, Vol. 87, 1850, p. 231; H. Barber & H. Lewis,

The History of Friars' School Bangor; W.H. HOuse, *School and Bell: Four Hundred Years of a Welsh Grammar School Llanrwst Grammar School 1610–1960*; K.M. Thompson, *Ruthin School: The First Seven Centuries*; D.G. Osborne-Jones, *Edward Richard of Ystradmeurig*; Iolo Davies, *A Certaine Schoole — A History of Cowbridge Grammar School.*

46. *Yr Haul*, Vol. XIV, 166, April 1849, pp. 127–9. W. Davies, Athrofa Ffrwdfâl: 'Addysgiaeth'.

47. *Pigot's Directory of Wales and Monmouthshire*, 1835 and 1844; *Robson's Commercial Directory*, 1841; *Slater's Directory of North Wales*, 1844 and 1850; *Hunt's and Company's Directory*, 1849.

48. Other well-established schools in north and mid-wales in the 1840s and 1850s included Misses Babington and Leigh's Ladies Boarding School, Bangor; Misses Pring's Boarding and Day School, Bangor; Mary Ann and Mary Bucks' Boarding School, Struet, Brecon; Mrs Hugh Jones School for the Education of Young Ladies, Red-Hill Mansion Beaumaris; The Misses Stenhouse Boarding and Day School, Denbigh; Green Lodge Ladies' Boarding School Llangollen; Ladies Boarding and Day School, Uxbridge Square, Caernarfon; Miss Maria Leslie's Boarding and Day School, Mold; Miss Hollis Boarding School, Newtown; Miss Charlotte Ann Williams Boarding and Day School, Pwllheli; The Misses Withy Boarding School Welshpool; Miss Mary Astle's Ladies Boarding School, Holywell; Mary Ann Ellis' Boarding and Day School, Rhuthun; Miss Mary Davies (Ladies Boarding), Holt; Miss Harriet Owen Ladies Boarding School, Wrexham; Miss Jane Rogers' Ladies Boarding School, Wrexham; Miss Charlotte Hughes' Boarding and Day School, Wrexham.

49. At Cardiff, the most well-known establishments were Miss Mary Allum's in Charles Street, Miss Maria Brown's in St Mary Street, and Miss Martha Vaughan's in Crockherbtown. Others in the region included The Misses King's Ladies Boarding School, Newport; Miss Howell's Boarding School, Abergavenny; Miss Alic Dixon's Boarding School, Usk; The Misses Huggin Boarding and Day School, Swansea; Miss Amelia D'Austein Boarding and Day School, Swansea; Miss Eliza Hunnam's Boarding and Day School, Swansea; The Misses Ballard's Establishment for the Education of young Ladies, Cowbridge; The Misses Hill's Boarding School, Haverfordwest; The Misses Barfield Boarding and Day school, Carmarthen; The Misses Waldegrave Boarding School, Milford Haven; Miss Sarah Howells' Boarding School, Llandovery; Miss Catherine Jenkins' Boarding School, Aberystwyth; Miss Mary Augusta Jones' Boarding School, Aberaeron; Miss Mary Ann Saunders Boarding School, Pembroke; Miss Ann Langford's Boarding School, Kington.

50. 1851 Census.

51. *The Welshman*, 26 January 1855.

52. *Caernarvon & Denbigh Herald*, 3 January 1852. See also ibid., 22 January 1859, 10 July 1852, 10 July 1852; *North Wales Chronicle*, 7 July 1855; S. Harrison, *Short Notes on Private Adventure Schools in Wrexham & District*, Wrexham Public Library.

53. *Cardiff and Merthyr Guardian*, 1 January 1859.

54. L. Edwards, Rhagarweiniad, *Yr Athrawes o Ddifrif*, 1859.

55. *Baner ac Amserau Cymru*, December 1859; See also Lewis Edwards, Rhagarweiniad, *Yr Athrawes o Ddifrif*, p. xv, 1859.

56. *Cardiff and Merthyr Guardian*, 10 January 1868.
57. They included Miss Sadler's School for Young Ladies, Wrexham; Misses Ingram, Establishment for Young Ladies Upper Bangor; Mrs Mercier, Bulkeley Square, Llangefni; Misses Ann and Sarah Groom, Welshpool; Misses Hughes, Welshpool; Mrs Marian Armstrong, Ladies Boarding, Holt Hall; Mrs Trubshaw, Aberystwyth; Misses Buck, Boughrood House, Brecon; Catherine Pierce, Brecon; The Misses' Jenkens, Newcastle Hill School, Bridgend; Miss Allum's Establishment for Young Ladies, Cardiff; The Misses Ayling, Cardigan; Miss Sarah Davies, Quay Street, Carmarthen; Miss Catherine Harris, Cowbridge; Miss Hill, Goat Street, Haverfordwest, and Misses Habakkuk, Swansea. Provision was made for both day pupils and boarders. There were also a number of schools which appeared only briefly.
58. Newspaper advertisements in the 1860s.
59. Taunton Report, Vol. VIII, pp. 45–6.
60. Ibid., pp. 40–1.
61. Ibid.
62. Ibid., pp. 41–2.
63. Ibid., p. 42.
64. Ibid., p. 43.
65. Ibid.
66. Ibid.
67. Ibid., p. 44.
68. Ibid., p. 47–8.
69. Ibid., pp. 49–50.
70. Ibid., p. 50.
71. Ibid., p. 51.
72. Ibid., p. 7. See also Bompas's views on Welsh language at Llandovery College: W.G. Evans, *A History of Llandovery College* (1981).
73. Taunton Report, Vol. VIII, pp. 53–4.
74. Ibid., p. 53.
75. Ibid., p. 54.
76. See Appendix A: copy of relevant parts of Thomas Howell's will.
77. I am grateful to the archivist of The Drapers' Company, Drapers' Hall, London for allowing me to consult the sources on which this section is based.
78. Jean McCann, *Thomas Howell and the School at Llandaff*, p. 31.
79. Ibid., p. 34.
80. Ibid., p. 37.
81. Scheme, 1853.
82. McCann, op. cit., p. 37.
83. 1853 *Scheme*, section 44.
84. Ibid., section 46.
85. Purvis, op. cit., Dyhouse, op. cit., Joyce Sanders Pedersen, 'The reform of women's secondary and higher education: institutional change and social values in mid and late Victorian England', *History of Education Quarterly*, No. 19, 1979, pp. 61–91.
86. See below: Judge Falconer's critique.
87. McCann, op. cit., pp. 39–41.
88. Pamphlet dated 1923. See also *Building News*, 1859.

89. Thomas Falconer, *The Mystery of Improvidence*, p. 17.
90. Falconer, op. cit., p. 20.
91. Ibid.
92. Ibid., p. 21, p. 4, p. 5.
93. Ibid., pp. 17–19.
94. *Merthyr Telegraph*, quoted in Falconer, *op. cit.*, p. 17. See also *Caernarvon and Denbigh Herald*, 3 December 1859.
95. Falconer, op. cit., p. 19.
96. Ibid.
97. Ibid.
98. *Caernarvon and Denbigh Herald*, 12 May 1860.
99. *Y Beirniad*, 1861, pp. 64–74. See also *Baner ac Amserau Cymru*, 13 October 1869.
100. E.T. Davies, *Monmouthshire Schools and Education to 1870*, pp. 33–4.
101. *Baner ac Amserau Cymru*, 7 December 1864.
102. Schools' Inquiry Commission (or Taunton Commission), *Terms of Reference*, December 1864.
103. Taunton Report, Vol. I, p. 546–9, 564, 553; Vol. V, p. 256, p. 241, p. 135; Vol. IX, p. 792; Dyhouse, p. 441.
104. *Baner ac Amserau Cymru*, 11 November 1863.
105. *Hansard*, 3rd Series, Vol. 196, pp. 1752–5.
106. Alice Zimmern, *The Renaissance of Girls' Education*, 1898, p. 83.
107. Taunton Report, Vol. xx Preface, Part IV.
108. Ibid., p. 152.
109. Ibid.
110. *1865 Scheme*, Clause 39.
111. Taunton Report, Vol. VIII, p. 70.
112. Ibid., pp. 72–3. See also Vol. xx, p. 152.
113. Ibid., Vol. xx, p. 152.
114. Ibid., p. 264.
115. Ibid., p. 153.
116. Ibid., Vol. VIII, p. 71. See also Vol. xx, p. 152.
117. Ibid., Vol. VIII, p. 71.
118. Governors' Minute Book, 4 July 1861. See also Miss Baldwin's Report, 23 June 1863 in Llandaff School Archives. Governors' Minute Book, 4 July 1861; McCann, op. cit., p. 104. See also pp. 132–3; Register of Day Scholars, Llandaff School Archives.
119. Taunton Report, Vol. xx, p. 153.
120. Ibid., p. 153.
121. See Examiners' Report Book, Llandaff School Archives.
122. *Taunton Report*, Vol. xx, p. 265.
123. Public Record Office (PRO) Ed. 27/6388, letter of 12 March 1863 and other correspondence in 1863.
124. *Caernarvon and Denbigh Herald*, 3 June 1865.
125. PRO Ed. 27/6390, Hare Report, 12 June 1865.
126. Ibid., letter 17 July 1865; Mrs Booth ready to resign.
127. PRO Ed. 27/6390.
128. *Baner ac Amserau Cymru*, 13 October 1869.
129. Ibid.

130. Thomas Gee's editorial, *Baner ac Amserau Cymru*, 27 March 1872; See also ibid., 2 February 1870, 9 February 1870.
131. Gee's editorial, ibid., 19 January 1870.
132. Ibid., 26 January 1870 — 'Dangosid gwrthwynebiad cyffredinol i addysg enwadol', See also Aberdare Report, pp. 31–32.
133. D.L. Lloyd, *The Mising Link in Education in Wales* (1876), pp. 1–5.
134. Ibid., pp. 9–10.
135. H.M. Jones, 'The History of the Cymmrodorion Society', unpublished MA thesis, 1939, p. 236.
136. T. Marchant Williams, *The Educational Wants of Wales*, 1877, pp. 31–32.
137. Ibid., p. 32.
138. Ibid.
137. *North Wales Chronicle*, 25 October 1879; 29 November 1879.
140. Ibid., 25 October 1879; North Wales Scholarship Association Reports 1–6.
141. 'Scholarships for Public Elementary Schools', NLW MSS XLB 2848, p.5.
142. Ibid., p. 6. See *North Wales Chronicle*, 25 October 1879.
143. *Y Frythones*, Vol. 1, No. 1, 1879, p. 5.
144. Sian Rhiannon Williams, op. cit., pp. 48–9.
145. Williams, op. cit., p. 48.
146. Peter Gordon, *Selection for Secondary Education*, 1980.
147. *Caernarvon and Denbigh Herald*, 16 April 1870.
148. J.R. Webster, op. cit., p. 289.
149. Webster, op. cit., p. 277; R.G. Jones, ' The development of secondary education in Dolgellau 1889–1946', unpublished M. Ed. 1972.
150. PRO Ed. 25/6578, letter dated 21 July 1874.
151. Samuel Holland's obituary, *The Cambrian News*, 30 December 1892. See also ibid., 23 October 1874; 21 August 1874.
152. *The Cambrian News*, 30 December 1892; ibid., 22 March 1878; ibid., 3 January 1879.
153. *Baner ac Amserau Cymru*, 2 December 1874.
154. *The Cambrian News*, 8 February 1878.
155. See Dyhouse, op. cit.
156. D. Pretty, *Two Centuries of Anglesey Schools*, p. 229.
157. *North Wales Chronicle*, 16 January 1875.
158. Ibid., 11 January 1879.
159. Pretty, op. cit., pp. 227–8. Mrs Verney's Evidence to Aberdare Committee, para. 2854–2870.
160. *Worrall's Directory of North Wales 1874; Worrall's Directory of South Wales 1887; Cassey's Directory of North Wales 1876.*
161. Anita M. Thomas, 'The Implementation of the Welsh Intermediate Education Act 1889 in the Wrexham Area to 1918', M. Ed., pp. 16–19.
162. *The Wrexham Advertiser*, 19 May 1877; Ibid., 6 January 1878.
163. *North Wales Chronicle*, 22 July 1876; ibid., 23 June 1877; ibid., 4 December 1875, 11 January 1879, 9 August 1879.
164. Ibid., 22 July 1876; 5 January 1878.
165. See Newspaper advertisements. See also *Caernarvon and Denbigh Herald*, 30 July 1874; *Worrall's Directory of North Wales 1874.*
166. *Brecon County Times*, 26 January 1878, *The Aberystwyth Observer*, 15 January 1878.

167. *The Cambrian News*, 4 January 1878.
168. *The Cambrian*, 6 January 1878.
169. Ibid.
170. *Cardiff Times*, 9 January 1875.
171. McCann, op. cit., p. 144.
172. *Brecon County Times*, 26 January 1878.
173. Ibid., 30 December 1876.
174. Carmarthen High School Minutes; *Carmarthen Journal*, 29 July 1887.
175. Carmarthen High School Minutes, 26 September 1879.
176. Ibid., 17 October 1879.
177. Aberdare Report, Vol. II, Evidence, 12,139–12,345.

CHAPTER 4

1. Ll.M. Rees. 'A critical examination of teacher training in Wales 1846–98', Ph.D., 1968, p. 101.
2. F. Widdowson, *Girls growing up into the Next Class: Women and Elementary Teacher Training 1840–1914*.
3. Minutes of Committee of Council on Education, 1856–7, F.C. Cook's Report.
4. Ibid., 1854–5.
5. Minutes of Committee of Council on Education, 1852–3; Matthew Arnold's Report 1852. See also Newcastle Report, Vol. 1, 1861, p. 104.
6. Minutes of Committee of Council on Education, 1850–51, letter, 22 January 1851.
7. Ibid., Circular, 18 February 1851.
8. Minutes of Committee of Council on Education, 1867–8, pp. vii–viii.
9. Ibid., 1864–5.
10. Rees, op. cit., p. 189; Minutes of Committee of Council on Education, 1863–8.
11. Ibid., 1867–8, pp. vii–viii.
12. Ibid., 1866–7, Bowstead's Report on south Wales.
13. Ibid., 1865–6: Revised Code 1866, Clause 89, pp. xxvi–xxvii.
14. J. Purvis, 'Domestic Subjects since 1870' in Goodson (ed.). *Social Histories of the Secondary Curriculum*, p. 183.
15. B.L. Davies, 'An Assessment of the Contribution of Sir Hugh Owen to Education in Wales', Ph.D., 1971.
16. Minutes of Committee of Council on Education, 1848–50, p. 220.
17. R. Meredith, 'Early History of the North Wales Training College', *Trans. Caern. Hist. Soc.*, 1946, pp. 4–19.
18. PRO Ed. 88/16.
19. Newcastle Report, Vol. 1, 1861, p. 643.
20. *The Educational Record*, Vol. 3, includes the name of Mary Phillips, Pembroke Dock amongst the twenty-four women who obtained Queen's Scholarships and were admitted into the Borough Road College in 1854. Four women with home addresses in south Wales were admitted. Most of the relevant documentation relating to students at Borough Road in the 1840s and 1850s does not specify home addresses. But some letters of

application and testimonials for applicants concern women with home addresses in Wales (MSS in The British and Foreign School Society Archives Centre). See also John Phillips, MSS NLW 5479E.

At Cheltenham Training College, three of the forty-two women students in 1851 and three of the seventy women students in 1852 had home addresses in south Wales. (Archives, The College of St Paul and St Mary Cheltenham).

See also: K. McGarry, 'Joseph Lancaster and the British and Foreign School Society', Ph.D. 1986, p. 336.

21. Annual Reports, Church of England Training Schools, Cheltenham.
22. Minutes of Committee of Council on Education, 1850-1, Revd F.C. Cook's Report, p. 217.
23. Minutes of Committee of Council on Education, Revd F. Walkin's Report 1848, p. 80; ibid., pp. 83–125; ibid., 1856-7, F.C. Cook's Report, p. 725; ibid., 1851, pp. 249–50; ibid., 1852-3, p. 339; ibid., 1854-5, p. 70.
24. Ibid., 1847-8, pp. 515-6; 1850-1, pp. 83–125.
25. Ibid., 1866-7, pp. 247-8.
26. Rees, op. cit., p. 276.
27. Stockwell College was opened in 1861 and women students were moved from Borough Road. Precise numbers from Wales cannot be ascertained but it is evident that a few enrolled virtually every year:

1861:	6 from Wales	1866:	3 from Wales
1863:	2 from Wales	1867:	15 from Wales
1864:	3 from Wales	1868:	3 from Wales
1865:	7 from Wales	1869:	4 from Wales

(Documents in The British & Foreign School Society Archives Centre).
28. See Annual Reports, op. cit.
29. Newcastle Report 1861, Vol. 1, p. 123.
30. Ibid., p. 141.
31. *Y Gymraes*, pp. 113–116, August 1911.
32. Lewis Edwards, Rhagarweiniad, *Yr Athrawes o Ddifrif*, 1859, pp. xiv–xv.
33. Minutes of the Committee of Council on Education, 1855-6, pp. 547.
34. Ibid., 1854, p. 320.
35. Newcastle Report, John Jenkins's Report on 'The State of Popular Education in the Welsh Specimen Districts', 1859.
36. Ibid., p. 612.
37. Minutes of the Committee of Council on Education, 1850-51, p. 655-6.
38. Ibid., 1866-7, pp. 247-8.
39. Ibid., 1867-8, p. xx.
40. Ibid., 1868-70, pp. 142-3.
41. Ibid., Revd B.J. Binns' Report on Breconshire, Glamorgan, Gloucestershire and Monmouthshire, 1869-70, p. 85.
42. Ibid., 1868-9, p. 176.
43. Ibid., p. 176.
44. Purvis, op. cit., p. 364; Dyhouse, op. cit.
45. Editorial, *The Cambrian*, 5 April 1872.
46. Correspondence and Agenda Minutes, British and Foreign Schools Society, 8 May 1871, quoted in Davies, op. cit., p. 321.
47. Minutes of the Committee of Council on Education, 1872-3, p. 244.
48. *The Cambrian*, 16 April 1875.

49. Ibid., 5 April 1872; *Baner ac Amserau Cymru*, 20 April 1872; Davies, op. cit., p. 323; Rees, op. cit., p. 72.
50. Davies, op. cit., p. 324; Tribute, *The Educational Record*, 1882, p. 54.
51. Swansea Training College Report, 1872, p. 7.
52. University for Wales, Minutes and Memoranda, UCW, Archives, folio 49: letter, 17 August 1871.
53. Ibid., letters, 31 July 1871, 14 September 1871.
54. Ibid., letter, 14 September 1871.
55. Swansea Training College: Booklet, 1913.
56. *The Cambrian*, 17 November 1871.
57. *Baner ac Amserau Cymru*, 27 December 1871.
58. *The Cambrian*, 5 April 1872.
59. *Baner ac Amserau Cymru*, 20 April 1872.
60. *The Cambrian*, 5 April 1872.
61. Ibid., 21 November 1873.
62. Ibid., Editorial, 20 November 1874. See also *Baner ac Amserau Cymru*, 25 November 1874.
63. *The Cambrian*, 20 November 1874.
64. Editorial, *The Cambrian*, 20 November 1874.
65. See *Baner ac Amserau Cymru*, 1874 for details of support for Swansea Training College from J.H. Griffith — 'Y Gohebydd'.
66. *The Cambrian*, 20 November 1874.
67. Editorial, *Baner ac Amserau Cymru*, 25 November 1874.
68. 'Y Gohebydd', ibid., 20 January 1875.
69. Ibid.
70. *The Cambrian*, 16 April 1875.
71. *The Cambrian*, 21 April 1876; Swansea Training College Report 1875, p. 5.
72. *Baner ac Amserau Cymru*, 31 March 1875.
73. Swansea Training College Report, 1875 and 1876.
74. Swansea Training College Report, 1877, p. 6.
75. Ibid., 1879.
76. *The Cambrian*, 21 April 1876.
77. Swansea Training College Report, 1879.
78. *Y Dydd*, 22 September 1876; *Baner ac Amserau Cymru*, 2 May 1877.
79. Swansea Training College Report, 1878, p. 6.
80. Ibid., 1873, p. 6. See also Minutes of Committee of Council on Education 1875-6, p. 469.
81. Ibid., 1872-3, p. 244. At Cheltenham College, three of the fifty-eight women students in 1871 were from Wales, and four of the eighty in 1872. (Archives, The College of St Paul and St Mary).
    At Stockwell, seven of the sixty-nine students in 1870 were from Wales. (The British and Foreign Society Archives Centre).
82. Ibid., 1873-4, p. 263; 1876-7, p. 712.
83. Ibid., 1872-3, p. 321.
84. Ibid., 1874-5, p. 263.
85. Ibid., 1873-4, p. 264.
86. Committee of Council on Education, 1872-3, 1873-4; 1876-7, p. 651.
87. Swansea Training College Report, 1875.
88. Minutes of Committee of Council on Education.

89. Ibid., 1873–4, 1874–5, 1975–6.
90. Ibid., 1872–3, pp. 111–112. See also 1873–4, pp. 186–7; 1874–5, p. 210; 1875–6, p. 175; 1876–7, p. 555.
91. *The Principles of Collegiate Education Discussed and Elucidated in a Description of Gnoll College — A National Institution Adapted to the Wants of the Age* (1859).
92. Ibid., p. 14.
93. Ibid., pp. 6–7.
94. George Eaton, A Girls' Grammar School at the Gnoll? *Neath Antiquarian Society Transactions*, 1982–3, pp. 78–9.
95. Details in *The Cambria Daily Leader*, 19 September 1863.
96. Ibid.
97. Ibid.
98. Ibid.
99. Ibid.
100. Ibid.
101. Ibid.
102. Ibid.
103. *Baner ac Amserau Cymru*, 11 November 1863.
104. Provisional committee's letter, *Baner ac Amserau Cymru*, 2 December 1863.
105. Gee quoting provisional committee, ibid., 2 March 1864.
106. *Baner ac Amserau Cymru*, 31 August 1864.
107. Ibid., 3 April 1867, Gee's editorial. See also 30 December 1868.
108. Ibid., 26 August 1868. See also 19 July 1869.
109. 'Outline of Plan', *Slater's Directory 1868*.
110. Document dated 24 March 1871, UCW Archives.
111. UCW Archives.
112. UCW Archives.
113. *Y Beirniad*, 1869, pp. 20–1.
114. Taunton Report, Volume VIII, 1868, p. 7. See also *Yr Amserau*, 24 May 1854.
115. Sunday School Union Magazine 1850, pp. 271–5, quoted in Revd D. Evans, *The Sunday School of Wales*, 1883.
116. Editorial, *Baner ac Amserau Cymnru*, 30 November 1864.
117. H.M. Davies, 'The Place of the Royal Institution of South Wales in the history of Scientific and General Eduction in the Nineteenth Century', MA, 1940.
118. Prospectus, Llanelli Mechanics' Institution, 1840.
119. Forty-fifth Annual Report, 1891.
120. *The Cambrian News*, 12 October 1870.
121. Onfel Thomas, 'Frances Elizabeth Hoggan, 1843–1927'. 1970. I am also deeply indebted to Mrs Onfel Thomas for allowing access to her late husband's manuscripts, the product of many years of meticulous and painstaking research.
122. J.G. Manton. *Elizabeth Garrett Anderson* (London, 1963).
123. Rose Mary Crawshay, *Domestic Service for Gentlewomen* at a meeting of the British Association, Bristol, 26 August 1875.
124. Manton, op cit., p. 78.
125. Onfel Thomas MSS.

126. Ibid.
127. Ibid., Y Gohebydd, *Baner ac Amserau Cymru*, 14 June 1873.
128. B. Harrison, op. cit., p. 51.
129. Joan M. Burstyn, *Victorian Education and the Ideal of Womanhood*, p. 58.
130. C. Webster (ed.), *Biology, Medicine and Society* 1840–1940, p. 51.
131. *Baner ac Amserau Cymru*, 16 July 1879.
132. Ibid., and also 21 June 1879.
133. Cymmrodorion Society Report, 9 November 1878.
134. *Western Mail*, 20 August 1878.
135. Ibid.
136. F.E. Hoggan, *On the Physical Education of Girls*, 1880.
137. Webster (ed.), op. cit., and S. Delamont and L. Duffin (eds.), *The Nineteenth Century Woman: Her Cultural and Physical World.*
138. *Baner ac Amserau Cymru*, 15 October 1872; 23 October 1872.
139. Ibid., 5 February 1873.
140. Ibid., 11 October 1876.
141. Editorial, *The Cambrian News*, 26 December 1873.
142. Ibid.
143. Editorial, ibid., 13 February 1874.
144. UCW *Calendar* 1877–8.
145. College Reports, 1870s.
146. E.L. Ellis, *The University College of Wales Aberystwyth 1872–1972*, p. 55. See also: O.T. Edwards, *Joseph Parry, 1841–1903*, pp. 29–41.
147. College Reports, 1870s. College Council Minutes, 22 June 1875. See also Principal's Report 1875.
148. College Council Minutes, 21 November 1874.
149. UCW *Calendar.*
150. *Prospectus and Regulations* 1874–5: Appendix p. 38, p. 54. Ibid., 1875–6, p. 51.
151. College Council Minutes, 13 April 1875.
152. UCW Archives.
153. UCW *Calendar.*
154. T.I. Ellis (ed.), 'T. Charles Edwards' Letters', National Library of Wales Journal, vol. III, 1952–3: Letter No. 162, Hugh Owen to T.C. Edwards.
155. Ibid., Letter No. 163, Hugh Owen to T.C. Edwards, 24 November 1875.
156. College Council Minutes, 22 June 1875.
157. *The Cambrian News*, 1876.
158. College Council Minutes, 6 June 1875, p. 33.
159. Ibid.
160. *The Cambrian News*, 21 June 1878.
161. College Council Minutes, 20 July 1878, p. 152.
162. Ibid.
163. Ibid.
164. College Council Minutes, June 1878.
165. College Council Minutes, June 1879; *The North Wales Chronicle*, 12 July 1879.
166. See O.T. Edwards, *Joseph Parry* 1841–1903, pp. 35–9.
167. Viz. Edwards, op. cit. Jack Jones's novel *Off to Philadelphia in the Morning* and subsequent TV film of the same name.
168. Editorial, *The Cambrian News*, 2 August 1878.

169. UCW Report to Court of Governors 1878–9, pp. 12–13, UCW Archives.
170. Edwards, op. cit., pp. 33–5.
171. 'A Retrospect 1877–81' in Iwan Morgan (ed.), *The College by the Sea* (1928), p. 72. See also Ellis, op. cit., p. 55; Edwards, op. cit., pp. 33–9.
172. *The Cambrian News*, 4 July 1879.

CHAPTER 5

1. Aberdare Report, 1881, Vol. 1, pp. i–ii.
2. Sir Ben Bowen Thomas, 'The Establishment of the 'Aberdare' Departmental Committee, 1880. Some Letters and Notes', *Bulletin of the Board of Celtic Studies*, XIX, pt. IV (May, 1962).
3. Aberdare Report, Vol. 2, Evidence, pp. 318–321.
4. Ibid.
5. Ibid., p.. 131–5.
6. Ibid., p. 573.
7. Ibid., p. 183.
8. Ibid., p. 746. Evidence of Lewis Williams, Vice-Chairman of Cardiff School Board.
9. Ibid., p. 18. See also Vol. 1, XL–XLIII.
10. Ibid., Evidence, 260–4; See *Y Gymraes* 1896, pp. 21–3; *Y Dysgedydd* 1889, pp. 268–71.
11. Aberdare Report, Vol. 2, Evidence, p. 261.
12. Ibid.
13. Ibid., p. 512.
14. Ibid., pp. 381–3.
15. Ibid., p. 344.
16. Aberdare Report, Vol. 1, pp. XIX–XXX; Evidence, pp. 345–9.
17. Aberdare Report, Evidence, p. 570.
18. Aberdare Report, Evidence, p. 349.
19. Ibid., p. 348.
20. Ibid.
21. Ibid., pp. 348–9.
22. See Frances Hoggan, *Education for Girls in Wales, 1882*, pp. 51–2.
23. Ibid.
24. Aberdare Report, Evidence, pp. 345–6.
25. Ibid., p. 344; Report, p. xxx.
26. Ibid., p. 346.
27. Ibid.
28. Ibid.
29. Ibid., p. 349.
30. Ibid.
31. Ibid., p. 348.
32. Ibid.
33. Ibid., p. 349.
34. Ibid., p. L–LXV.
35. See Anita M. Thomas, op. cit.
36. Aberdare Report, Vol. 1, p. L–LXV.

37. Aberdare Report, Vol. 1, p. LXL.
38. W.G. Evans, 'The Aberdare Report and Education in Wales', *The Welsh History Review*, Vol. Xl, December 1982, No. 2, pp. 150–173.
39. Ibid.
40. *Baner ac Amserau Cymru*, 29 April 1882.
41. Ibid., 28 June 1882.
42. *The Cambrian News*, 23 June 1882.
43. J.R. Webster, 'The Welsh Intermediate Education Act of 1889', *The Welsh History Review*, Vol. IV, No. 3, 1969, pp. 278–91.
44. Ibid., p. 278.
45. 'Mundella Circular' — *Circular No. 213*, 1882.
46. Letter, 'Intermediate Education for Girls', *Western Mail*, 24 February 1882.
47. *The Cambrian News*, 30 June 1882.
48. Webster, op. cit., p. 279.
49. Thomas Gee, *Baner ac Amserau Cymru*, 27 May 1885.
50. John Gibson, *The Cambrian News*, 5 June 1885.
51. Editorial, *The Cambrian News*, 14 May 1886; See also, 14 January 1887.
52. *Baner ac Amserau Cymru*, 27 March 1886; 14 April 1886.
53. Ibid., 11 August 1886.
54. Webster, op. cit., pp. 282–3.
55. *The Cambrian News*, 6 May 1887; *Baner ac Amserau Cymru*, 11 May 1887.
56. Ibid.
57. Webster, op. cit., p. 283.
58. Minutes of Honourable Society of Cymmrodorion 1887. See also *Seventh Annual Report, National Eisteddfod Association*, 1888.
59. *Y Frythones*, 1887, p. 200.
60. *South Wales Daily News*, 6 January 1888.
61. Ibid.
62. *Oswestry Advertiser and Border County Herald*, 11 January 1888.
63. Ibid.
64. *The Times*, 16 March 1888.
65. Minutes of Honourable Society of Cymmrodorion. See also 'Y Ddirprwyaeth ar Addysg Ganolradd', *Cymru Fydd*, April 1888, pp. 207–13.
66. *Y Cymmrodor*, Vol. X, 1889, pp. v–viii.
67. H.M. Jones, op. cit., p. 241.
68. Webster, op. cit., p. 284.
69. See *Cymru Fydd*, March 1888.
70. *Cymru Fydd*, May 1888, p. 270.
71. *Baner ac Amserau Cymru*, 12 September 1888.
72. North Wales Scholarship Association: first *Annual Report, 1880–81*, p. 3; *Caernarvon and Denbigh Herald*, 1 November 1879.
73. Twelfth *Annual Report*, 1893–4, p. 5.
74. Frances Hoggan, *Education for Girls in Wales*, p. 1.
75. Ibid., p. 11.
76. Ibid.
77. Ibid., pp. 11–28.
78. Ibid., pp. 11–16.
79. Ibid., p. 16.
80. Ibid.

81. Ibid.
82. Frances Hoggan, *Co-Education at Different Ages*, 1882.
83. Ibid.
84. Ibid.
85. Frances Hoggan, *On the Physical Education of Girls*, 1880, p. 10.
86. *Education for Girls in Wales*, p. 17.
87. Ibid., p. 18.
88. Ibid., p. 19.
89. Ibid.
90. Ibid., p. 20.
91. Ibid., p. 23.
92. Ibid., p. 27.
93. Idem. *Co-Education at Different Ages*, 1882, p. 30.
94. *Third Annual Report, National Eisteddfod Association*, 1884, p. 44.
95. Ibid.
96. Ibid., p. 51.
97. Ibid.
98. F. Hoggan, *Education for Girls in Wales*, p. 31.
99. Idem, *Co-Education at Different Ages*, 1882.
100. *Second Annual Report, National Eisteddfod Association*, 1882, p. 97.
101. Ibid., p. 89.
102. Ibid., p. 90.
103. Ibid.
104. *Sixth Annual Report, National Eisteddfod Association, 1886*, pp. 63–9.
105. Quoted in ibid., pp. 69–70.
106. Ibid., p. 64.
107. Ibid.
108. Ibid., p. 66.
109. Ibid.
110. Ibid., p. 67.
111. Ibid., p. 68.
112. Ibid.
113. Ibid., p. 69.
114. *Transactions of The Liverpool Welsh National Society 1886–7*, pp. 59–70.
115. See below.
116. *Seventh Annual Report, National Eisteddfod Association 1887*, pp. 93–6.
117. Sara A. Burstall, *Retrospect and Prospect* (1934), p. 54, p. 96.
118. *Baner ac Amserau Cymru*, 17 March 1886; 21 April 1886.
119. *Women's Suffrage Journal*, 1 June, 1885, p. 98.
120. *Baner ac Amserau Cymru*, 9 September 1885.
121. *Seventh Annual Report, National Eisteddfod Association, 1887*, pp. 1–16.
122. Ibid., p. 1.
123. Ibid., p. 5.
124. Ibid., p. 10.
125. Ibid.
126. Ibid., p. 14.
127. Ibid., p. 15.
128. *Third Annual Report, National Eisteddfod Association 1883*, pp. 52–61.
129. Ibid., p. 56.
130. Ibid., p. 57.

131. Ibid. See also 'Llythyr Llundain', *Baner ac Amserau Cymru*, 11 June 1884. Revd J. Cynddylan Jones, speaking in the discussion following Miss Hughes's Address in *Third Annual Report, National Eisteddfod Association 1883*, p. 62.
132. *Transactions of the Liverpool National Eisteddfod, 1884*, pp. 40–62.
133. Ibid., pp. 49–50.
134. Ibid., p. 53.
135. Ibid., p. 55.
136. Ibid., p. 43.
137. Ibid., pp. 43–4.
138. Ibid., p. 47.
139. Ibid., pp. 48–9.
140. Ibid., p. 58.
141. Ibid., p. 56.
142. Ibid.
143. Ibid., pp. 56–7.
144. Ibid., p. 51.
145. Ibid., p. 59.
146. Ibid., pp. 60–1.
147. Ibid., p. 55.
148. Ibid., pp. 61.
149. Ibid., p. 62.
150. Miss E.P. Hughes, *The Education of Welsh Women*, pp. 1–7.
151. Ibid., p. 5.
152. *Seventh Annual Report, National Eisteddfod Association 1887*, pp. 86–92.
153. Ibid., p. 92.
154. Ibid., p. 91.
155. Ibid., p. 92.
156. Ibid., p. 107.
157. *South Wales Daily News*, 10 January 1887.
158. *First Annual Report*, 1888.
159. Dilys Glynne Jones Papers, UCNW. Letter dated 6 June 1886.
160. *Baner ac Amserau Cymru*, 11 August 1886.
161. Ibid., 29 September 1886.
162. Ibid.
163. *Sixth Annual Report, National Eisteddfod Association, 1886*, pp. 63–9. See also G.H. Williams, Loughborough Grammar School, in ibid., p. 71.
164. *Second Annual Report, National Eisteddfod Association 1882*, p. 99. See also H.M. Jones, 'History of The Honourable Society of Cymmrodorion', unpublished MA thesis, 1939, pp. 230–1; R.T. Jenkins and H.M. Ramage, *The History of the Honourable Society of Cymmrodorion, Y Cymmrodorion*, 1951, pp. 199–202.
165. B.L. Davies, op. cit.
166. *Third Annual Report, National Eisteddfod Association*, 1883.
167. Miss Dilys Davies, *The Problem of Girls' Education in Wales*, 1887, p. 17.
168. *Transactions of The Liverpool Welsh National Society 1886–7*, pp. 59–70. See also 45 above.
169. *The Aberystwyth Observer*, 23 April 1887.
170. *The Cambrian News*, 23 April 1887.
171. Ibid.

172. *The Cambrian News*, 23 April 1887.
173. Ibid.
174. Miss E.P. Hughes, *The Education of Welsh Women*, p. 6.
175. *The Cambrian News*, 23 April 1887.
176. *Seventh Annual Report, National Eisteddfod Association* 1887, p. 92.
177. Miss E.P. Hughes, *The Future of Welsh Education with special reference to the Education of Girls.*
178. Miss E.P. Hughes, A National Education for Wales, *Young Wales*, Vol. 1, 1895, p. 105.
179. 'The Future of Welsh Education', *Trans. Cymmrodorion Society* 1894–5, p. 36.
180. Ibid., p. 47. See also *The Cambrian News*, 14 January 1898.
181. *The Renaissance in Education in Wales*, 1901, p. 4.
182. *Second Report, National Eisteddfod Association* 1882, p. 99.
183. Miss E.P. Hughes, *The Education of Welsh Women*, p. 4.
184. Ibid., p. 7.
185. Ibid., p. 4.
186. Isambard Owen quoted in ibid., p. 4.
187. *Seventh Report, National Eisteddfod Association, 1887*, p. 86.
188. Ibid., p. 88.
189. PRO Ed. 27/6628. Petition dated 12 March 1888.
190. Ibid., Draft Scheme, June 1889.
191. Report of The Association for Promoting the Education of Girls in Wales, 1888.
192. *South Wales Daily News*, 6 January 1888.
193. *The Times*, 16 March 1888; *Y Cymmrodor*, 1889, Vol. x, pp. v–viii.
194. T.E. Ellis, *Speeches and Addresses*, pp. 205–24.
195. D.D. Williams, *Cofiant Thomas Jones Wheldon*, p. 209.
196. Third Annual Report of The Association for Promoting the Education of girls in Wales, 1890.
197. See Annual Reports of The Association for Promoting the Education of girls in Wales, 1888–99.
198. Fourth Annual Report.
199. *The Aberystwyth Observer*, 14 July 1894.
200. L. Twiston Davies, *Women of Wales*, p. 312.
201. Ibid.
202. UCNW Archives.
203. H.M. Jones, op. cit., pp. 205–6.
204. *Seventh Annual Report, National Eisteddfod Association, 1887*, p. 86.
205. L. Twiston Davies, *Women of Wales*, p. 305.
206. *South Wales Daily News*, 21 December 1925; *Western Mail*, 21 December 1925; *The Times*, 21 December 1925.
207. *South Wales Daily News*, 6 August 1897.
208. Ibid., 2 July 1896.
209. *In Memory of Margaret Maria Lady Verney, 1881–1930*, p. 69.

CHAPTER 6

1. *Baner ac Amserau Cymru*, 13 March 1889.

2. J.R. Webster, op. cit., p. 285.
3. *The Cambrian News*, 12 April 1889. See also *Baner ac Amerau Cymru*, 24 April 1889.
4. Webster, op. cit., p. 285.
5. *Hansard*, 3rd Series, 15 May 1889.
6. Howell's School: Governors' Minute Book, 4 June 1889; 2 July 1889.
7. Webster, op. cit., pp. 286–7.
8. Ibid., p. 288.
9. Thomas Gee's editorial, *Baner ac Amserau Cymru*, 3 July 1889.
10. Ibid.
11. Webster, op. cit., pp. 289–90.
12. *Baner ac Amserau Cymru*, 17 July 1889; 31 July 1889; Webster, op. cit., p. 290.
13. *Cymru Fydd*, Cyf. III, pp. 313–14.
14. Thomas Gee in *Baner ac Amserau Cymru*, 31 July 1889.
15. Second Annual Report of The Association for Promoting the Education of Girls', 1889.
16. Third Annual Report of The Association for Promoting the Education of Girls in Wales, 1890, p 30.
17. Ibid., p. 31.
18. Ibid., p. 33.
19. Ibid., p. 34.
20. Ibid.
21. Ibid.
22. T.I. Ellis, *The Development of Higher Education in Wales*, p. 77.
23. Report of Proceedings of Joint Education Committees of North Wales, 12 April 1890.
24. Ibid. View expressed by W.N. Bruce.
25. Report of the Proceedings of the Denbighshire Joint Education Committee at the Public Inquiries, March 21 — September 26, 1890.
26. Report of Proceedings of General Conference of Joint Education Committees of Wales and Monmouthshire, 1890.
27. Report of Proceedings of General Conference of Joint Education Committiees of Wales and Monmouthshire, 1891.
28. Board of Education, Educational Subjects: Special Reports, Vol. 2 (1898), p. 42.
29. Bryce Report, Vol. I, p. 285.
30. S. Fletcher, 'Co-education and the Victorian Grammar School', *History of Education*, 1982, Vol. 11, No. 2, pp. 87–98.
31. Anna Rowlands, 'Progress of Women in Wales', *Young Wales*, Vol. 2, 1896, p. 100.
32. *The Cambrian News*, 10 June 1898.
33. Pamphlet No. 16.
34. Board of Education, Educational Subjects: Special Reports, Vol. 2, p. 99.
35. The Bryce Report recommended for girls' schools the same subjects as were taught in boys' schools.
36. Carol Dyhouse, op. cit., pp. 162–9; Purvis, op. cit., pp. 148–156.
37. Ibid.
38. Fifth Annual Report, 1892.

39. Pamphlet No. 13, The Association for Promoting the Education of Girls in Wales.
40. Pamphlet No. 14, The Association for promoting the Education of Girls in Wales. p. 17.
41. Special Reports on Educational Subjects, Vol. 2, p. 42.
42. F.E. Hamer, 'The Welsh County School System: Its Merits and Defects', *Young Wales*, August 1900, p. 171.
43. Special Reports, Vol. 2, p. 42.
44. *Letters of the Right Honourable Lord Aberdare*, Volume II, p. 26.
45. *The Welshman*, 24 December 1897.
46. Charity Commission Report, 1896.
47. See G.E. Jones, *Controls and Conflicts in Welsh Secondary Education 1889–1944*.
48. CWB Reports: Inspection and Examination, 1914.
49. Ibid., 6 January 1914.
50. Bruce Report, 1920, p. 35.
51. Ibid., p. 39.
52. PRO Ed. 35/3287.
53. Ibid., Ed. 109/8162. *The Schoolmistress*, 23 January 1913.
54. *Statistics of Public Education in Wales 1912–13*, p. 65.
55. A.T. Davies (ed.), *'O.M.' — A Memoir*, p. 73.
56. 'Merched: Eu Safle mewn Cymdeithas', *Y Gymraes*, 1913, pp. 107; *The Schoolmistress*, 23 January 1913.
57. *The Schoolmistress*, 5 December 1912.
58. Ibid., 2 October 1913.
59. Ibid., 6 March 1913.
60. Ibid., 9 July 1914.
61. PRO Ed. 35/3125. Letter dated 17 June 1908.
62. Ibid., Memo.
63. Report of Special County Schjools Committee: Caernarfonshire, 5 March 1914.
64. Impey, op. cit., p. 116.
65. PRO Ed. 35/3229. Letter dated 31 January 1913.
66. PRO Ed. 109/8113.
67. Impey, op. cit., pp. 55–6.
68. PRO Ed. 35/3236. Letter dated 31 May 1906.
69. Ibid. Letters, dated 15 June 1908; 15 July 1908.
70. Impey, op. cit., pp. 116–7.
71. CWB Reports — Triennial Inspection, 1912.
72. A.E. Fletcher (ed.), *Cyclopaedia of Education*, p. 66.
73. PRO Ed. 35/3219.
74. Ibid.
75. Ibid.
76. Ibid.
77. PRO Ed. 35/3281: Memo, 1913; Ed. 35/3279: Memo, 18 March 1909.
78. C. Dyhouse, op. cit., p. 134.
79. Pamphlet, The Welsh County Schools Association, 1907, p. 7.
80. CWB Reports of Inspection and Examination, 1907.
81. Board of Education, Memorandum on Teaching and Organisation in Secondary Schools, p. 15.

82. A.T. Davies (ed.), op. cit., p. 73.
83. Ibid.
84. Board of Education (Welsh Department) Report, 1914, p. 16.
85. Board of Education (Welsh Department) Report, 1910, p. 18.
86. Board of Education (Welsh Department) Report, 1909, p. 19.
87. Presidential Address to Welsh Secondary Schools Association at Shrewsbury, 28 October 1910.
88. Statement by the Central Welsh Board, 1909, pp. 1–30.
89. Board of Education (Welsh Department) Report, 1911, p. 17.
90. Board of Education (Welsh Department) *Regulations for Secondary Schools In Wales*, 1908, p. ix.
91. Board of Education: *Report of Consultative Committee on Practical Work in Secondary Schools*, 1913.
92. PRO Ed. 109/8077, Board of Education (Welsh Department) Reports, 1912.
93. PRO Ed. 35/3101, CWB Reports of Inspection and Examination 1911.
94. CWB Report: Triennial Inspection, 1911–12.
95. Ibid.
96. Ed. 109/8400. Board of Education (Welsh Department), Report of Inspection, 1913.
97. CWB Reports of Inspection and Examination, 1910.
98. CWB General Reports, 1910.
99. Ibid., 1912.
100. Board of Education (Welsh Department), Report, 1915, pp. 9–10.
101. Ibid.
102. *Y Gymraes*, November 1909, p. 162.
103. Bruce Report, pp. 42–3.
104. Ibid.
105. *Y Gymraes*, June 1911, pp. 6–7.
106. Ibid.
107. PRO Ed. 27/6440, letter dated 6 August 1892; Minutes of Denbighshire Joint Education Committee.
108. Ibid.
109. PRO Ed. 27/6403: Memo, 4 November 1895.
110. PRO Ed. 27/6403: Memo 18 November 1895.
111. *Hansard*, 16 July 1897, pp. 267–86.
112. *Baner ac Amserau Cymru*, 28 July 1897.
113. *Hansard*, 1910, Vol. v, pp. 715–35.
114. *The Howellian*, 25 July 1910.
115. Ibid., quoting Speech Day Address, July 1910.
116. Ibid., 1913.
117. J.R. Webster, 1969, op. cit.
118. *Hansard*, 15 May 1889.
119. Webster, op. cit., p. 286.
120. Memorandum dated June 1889: NLW MSS.
121. *Baner ac Amserau Cymru*, 23 August 1882.
122. Petition of the Committee of the Most Honourable and Loyal Society of Ancient Britons, 1889, NLW MSS.
123. Webster, op. cit., p. 288; *Baner ac Amserau Cymru*, 3 July 1889.
124. *South Wales Daily News*, 6 June 1889; *Y Dysgedydd*, July 1889, p. 260.

125. *A Brief Account of The Rise, Progress and Present State of the Welsh Girls' School, Ashford* (1898 edition).
126. *Welsh Girls' School Gazette,* January 1912–14.
127. PRO Ed. 35/1823: 1914 Handbook.
128. Ibid.
129. Clerk to Trustees refused present writer access to school records.

CHAPTER 7

1. Minutes of Committee of Council on Education 1881–2, p. xxiii; 1886–7, p. xxv; 1889–90, p. xxvi.
2. *The Cambrian,* 25 April 1890.
3. *South Wales Daily News,* 2 October 1886.
4. Ibid., 5 October 1888.
5. Ibid., 17 March 1887.
6. *The Cambrian News,* 23 April 1887.
7. K.V. Jones, op. cit., pp. 167–8.
8. Ibid., p. 168.
9. Aberdare Report, Evidence, p. 346.
10. *South Wales Daily News,* 18 January 1887.
11. *The Education of Welsh Women,* p. 6.
12. *Western Mail,* 18 January 1887.
13. Ibid.
14. Second annual report, The Association for Promoting the Education of Girls in Wales, 1889.
15. Third annual report, 1890.
16. *North Wales Chronicle,* 30 April 1887.
17. K.V. Jones, op. cit., p. 172.
18. A Summary of the Final Report 1888, pp. 102–4.
19. Fourth annual report, Association for Promoting the Education of Girls in Wales, 1891, p. 6.
20. *Y Traethodydd,* XLV, 1890, pp. 356–64.
21. Ibid., XLVIII, 1892, pp. 245–56.
22. Miss E.P. Hughes, *The Educational Future of Wales,* 1894.
23. Ibid.
24. *The Cambrian,* 5 August 1898.
25. *Regulations for the Training of Teachers and for the Examination of Students in Training Colleges 1906,* Article 64.
26. Swansea Training College Report, 1885.
27. Ibid., 1880; *The Cambrian,* 8 April 1881.
28. Principal's Report, 8 April 1881. See also Principal's Report, 14 April 1882.
29. Principal's Report 1881, p. 8.
30. Revd B.J. Binns, addressing Annual Meeting 18 April 1890; *The Cambrian,* 25 April 1890.
31. See Swansea Training College Reports, 1880, 1882.
32. See Minutes of Committee of Council on Education for 1880s.
33. Dyhouse, op. cit., pp. 82–3.

34. Phillips, op. cit.
35. Minutes of Committee of Council on Education 1886-7, p. 359.
36. Minutes of Committee of Council on Education, 1889-90, pp. xxii-xxiii. See also 1885-6, 1886-7, 1887-8.
37. *South Wales Daily News*, 2 October 1886.
38. Swansea Training College Report, 1890.
39. *The Cambrian*, 9 July 1897.
40. Ibid., 3 May 1895.
41. Minutes of Committee of Council on Education 1890-1, p. 459.
42. Ibid., 1894-5, p. 188; *The Cambrian*, 3 May 1895.
43. *The Cambrian*, 24 April 1891; 15 April 1892; 5 May 1893; 13 April 1894; 3 May 1895.
44. Ibid., 3 May 1895.
45. J.G. Fitch HMI, Report on Training Colleges for Schoolmistresses, Minutes of Committee of Council on Education 1890-1, p. 455.
46. Minutes of Committee of Council on Education 1891-2, p. 475.
47. Editorial, *The Cambrian*, 9 July 1897.
48. *The Cambrian*, 3 May 1895.
49. Booklet: Swansea Training College, 1872-1913.
50. Swansea Training College Report 1907-8, pp. 4-6.
51. Ibid., 1908-9, p. 5.
52. Ibid., 1909-10.
53. *The Swan*, No. 1, 1-58, 1900-22.
54. *Western Mail*, 20 January 1909.
55. Editorial, *Western Mail*, 4 February 1909; 3 March 1909; 29 March 1909; 5 April 1909.
56. See *The Schoolmistress*, 7 November 1912.
57. *The Cambrian*, 28 July 1911.
58. Ibid.
59. Editorial, *Western Mail*, 10 October 1913.
60. Governors' Minute Book, 12 January 1893.
61. Ibid., 11 October 1892.
62. Ibid., 19 June 1896.
63. Ibid., 25 May 1895.
64. Ibid., 19 January 1896.
65. Minutes of Committee of Council on Education 1896-7, p. 322.
66. Report for 1899.
67. Report for 1902.
68. Annual Reports.
69. HMI Report, 1903.
70. Governors' Minute Book, 3 February 1914.
71. Ibid., 11 May 1911.
72. Report for 1911.
73. Reports for 1910 and 1911.
74. Report for 1911.
75. H.C. Dent, *The Training of Teachers in England and Wales* (1911), chapters 1 and 2.
76. P.H.J.H. Gosden, *The Teaching Profession* (1971).
77. Governors' Minute Book, 3 February 1914.
78. North Wales Training College Minute Book. 3 September 1914.

79. *North Wales Chronicle*, 30 October 1908.
80. Bangor Normal College Report 1906.
81. Ibid., 1908, p. 8.
82. Ibid., 1906, p. 8; See also T. Roberts (ed.), *A History of Bangor Normal College, 1858–1958*, p. 82.
83. Ibid.
84. Caernarfonshire Education Committee Minutes, 18 January 1908.
85. D. Gerwyn Lewis, *The University and the Colleges of Education in Wales, 1925–78*, pp. 26–77.
86. *A History of Bangor Normal College, 1858–1958*, p. 82.
87. PRO Ed. 87/16. Memo, 2 June 1908; *North Wales Chronicle*, 11 September 1908.
88. PRO Ed. 87/16. Memo, 11 June 1908.
89. Ibid.
90. Ibid. See also *North Wales Chronicle*, 11 September 1908.
91. PRO Ed. 87/16, letter, 17 June 1908.
92. Ibid., memo, 19 June 1908.
93. *North Wales Chronicle*, 11 September 1908.
94. Minutes of North Wales Counties Training College Committee, 27 June 1910.
95. Ibid., 15 July 1914.
96. Minutes of North Wales Counties Training College Committee, 7 July 1913.
97. Ibid., 15 July 1914.
98. Booklet; *Barry Training College: Opening of New Buildings*, 6 June 1964.
99. PRO Ed, 87/17.
100. Ibid., letter, 25 May 1908.
101. Glamorgan County Council: Minutes of Education Committee, 19 May 1908.
102. Ibid., 5 May 1908.
103. PRO Ed. 87/17, memo, 12 September 1908.
104. Glamorgan County Council: Minutes of Education Committee, 1 December 1909.
105. PRO Ed. 87/17. undated memo, 1908.
106. Ibid., memo, 25 February 1909.
107. Editorial, *Western Mail*, 3 March 1909; 3 April 1909; 5 April 1909.
108. Ibid., 3 March 1909.
109. Ibid. See also 3 April 1909.
110. *Western Mail*, 5 April 1909.
111. Ibid., 2 April 1909.
112. *Barry Herald*, 9 April 1909.
113. Editorial, *Western Mail*, 3 March 1909; 29 March 1909.
114. Ibid., 29 March 1909.
115. Editorial, *Western Mail*, 3 April 1909.
116. *Barry Herald*, 9 April 1909.
117. *Western Mail*, 2 April 1909.
118. *South Wales Gazette*, 30 April 1909.
119. PRO Ed. 87/17, memo, 23 April 1910.
120. Ibid., memo, 29 June 1909.
121. See Barry Training College Files in Glamorgan Record Office.

122. *The Schoolmistress*, 29 January 1914.
123. Ibid., 5 November 1914.

CHAPTER 8

1. Address by G. Osborne Morgan at UCNW Bangor, 30 June 1887, UCNW Archives.
2. *The Cambrian News*, 10 October 1884; *Western Mail*, 4 October 1884.
3. Ibid.
4. Ibid.
5. *Baner ac Amserau Cymru*, 8 October 1884.
6. *North Wales Observer*, 10 October 1884; *Western Mail*, 4 October 1884.
7. *Calendar*, 1885–6.
8. College Council Minutes, 20 January 1885: Appendix: Amendments to the Constitution clauses 13b/20/39. See also E.L. Ellis, op. cit., p. 92.
9. Details of struggle for Charter in E.L. Ellis, op. cit., pp. 92–3.
10. W.L.J., Notes from Cambridge, *Cymru Fydd*, April 1888, pp. 233–4.
11. K.V. Jones, op. cit., p. 148.
12. *University of Wales Charter*, 1893.
13. J.R. Ainsworth Davies in *University College of Wales Magazine*, December 1894, p. 6.
14. *South Wales Daily News*, 14 April 1894.
15. *The Cambrian News*, 28 February 1896.
16. E.P. Hughes, *The Future of Welsh Education*, p. 48.
17. *South Wales Daily News*, 7 April 1894.
18. *The Cambrian News*, 22 March 1895.
19. Ibid., 4 November 1898.
20. See Minutes of Court and Reports of Senate, NLW.
21. Raleigh Report (1909), p. 41.
22. E.L. Ellis, op. cit., pp. 71–2.
23. *Baner ac Amserau Cymru*, 31 January 1883.
24. *The Cambrian News*, 18 May 1883.
25. Ibid.
26. T.I. Ellis (ed.), T. Charles Edwards Letters, No. 360, *National Library of Wales Journal*, Vol. III, 195203.
27. Report, National Eisteddfod Association, 1883, p. 34.
28. NLW MSS 6865B, letters 8 September 1883.
29. *Baner ac Amserau Cymru*, 4 December 1883; *The Cambrian News*, 7 December 1883.
30. College Council Minutes, 7 December 1883.
31. Editorial, *The Cambrian News*, 7 December 1883. See also 4 January 1884.
32. *The Cambrian News*, 4 January 1884.
33. *Baner ac Amserau Cymru*, 16 January 1884.
34. Ibid., 19 March 1884.
35. *The Cambrian News*, 25 April 1884.
36. College reminiscences 1884–6, in Iwan Morgan (ed.), *The College by the Sea*, 1928, p. 78.
37. *The Cambrian News*, 20 October 1884.

38. *University College of Wales Magazine*, Vol. XI, 1888, No. 1, pp. 5–6.
39. *Baner ac Amserau Cymru*, 29 September 1886.
40. *The Cambrian News*, 23 January 1885. See also 30 January 1885.
41. College Council Minutes, 9 June 1885; 16 October 1885.
42. Principal's Report 1884–5, p. 25.
43. College Council Minutes, 31 May 1886.
44. Principal's Report 1884–5, p. 14.
45. Ibid., 1885–6.
46. *The Cambrian News*, 30 July 1886.
47. College Council Minutes, 15 June 1887.
48. Ibid.
49. 'Y.N.R.' Hall Reminiscences, *University College of Wales Magazine*, Vol. 18, 1895–6, pp. 195–8.
50. Principal's Report, 1886–7.
51. See E.L. Ellis, op. cit., pp. 102–3.
52. *Western Mail*, 14 October 1886.
53. See Appendix B.
54. Principal's Report 1887–8, pp. 16–18.
55. College Council Minutes, 8 June 1883; 27 November 1888.
56. Ibid., 19 December 1888.
57. Lady Principal's Report, Christmas Term 1888.
58. College Council Minutes, 1 July 1889.
59. Principal's Report 1887–8, p. 25.
60. Figures taken from University Calendars.
61. Lady Principal's Report, 1890–1.
62. Ainsworth Davies, op. cit., p. 84.
63. E.L. Ellis, op. cit., p. 84.
64. *The Cambrian News*, 4 November 1898.
65. Ibid.
66. Prospectus 1892–3: Hall of Residence for Women Students.
67. *The Cambrian News*, 29 May 1891.
68. *The Cambrian News*, 5 October 1900.
69. D.D. Williams, *Thomas Charles Edwards*, p. 38, p. 95.
70. *The Cambrian News*, 31 May 1891.
71. Ibid., 2 June 1893; 18 August 1893.
72. Appeal Circular, 1891.
73. *The Cambrian News*, 6 April 1894; Ainsworth Davies, op. cit.
74. Editorial, *The Cambrian News*, 8 June 1894.
75. Ainsworth Davies, op. cit.; *The Cambrian News*, 22 March 1895.
76. *The Cambrian News*, 22 March 1895; 5 April 1895; 17 May 1895.
77. Ibid., 17 May 1895.
78. 'Facts relating to U.C.W. and the Alexandra Hall of Residence for Women Students', December 1897, in UCW Archives. The Hall was closed in 1986. See E.L. Ellis, *Alexandra Hall 1896–1986*.
79. May 1905, pp. 221–2.
80. Letter, 27 April 1899 in Letters of Lady Stamp 1898–1900, Alexandra Hall Archives.
81. *University College of Wales Magazine*, Vol. 27, 1904–5, p. 18.
82. Ibid.
83. *The Cambrian News*, 2 June 1905.

84. H.J. Fleure, UCW Aberystwyth: 'An old student looks at the College', *Trans. Cymmrodorion Society*, 1955, p. 58.
85. E.L. Ellis, op. cit., p. 146.
86. Rendel to T.F. Roberts, 23 May 1905; quoted in Ellis, op. cit., p. 146.
87. E.L. Ellis, op. cit., pp. 147–8.
88. *The Cambrian News*, 29 November 1909.
89. Ibid.
90. *University College of Wales Magazine*, Vol. 24, 1901–2.
91. Ibid., Vol. 29, 1906–7; Vol. 33, 1910–11; Vol. 34, 1911–12; Vol. 35, 1912–13; Vol. 36, 1913–14.
92. Ibid., Vol. 29, 1906–7.
93. Ibid., Vol. 33, 1910–11.
94. Senate rule Section C, clause 10, quoted in ibid., Vol. 36, 1913–14.
95. See also similar conclusion concerning women students at Cardiff in P.A. Davies, 'The women students at University College, Cardiff, 1883–1933'. Unpublished M. Ed. thesis, University of Wales, 1983.
96. 1910 Report in Alexandra Hall Archives.
97. Lord Aberdare, *Lectures and Addresses*, p. 349.
98. *Western Mail*, 10 July 1884.
99. See *Calendar*. University College of South Wales and Monmouthshire, 1884–5.
100. *Calendars*. University College of South Wales and Monmouthshire.
101. *Carmarthen Journal*, 22 July 1887.
102. *Western Mail*, 14 October 1886.
103. S.B. Chrimes (ed.), *A Centenary History 1883–1983*, p. 102.
104. Cohen, op. cit., p. 42.
105. Principal's Report, 1883–4.
106. Cohen, op. cit., p. 42.
107. Chrimes, op. cit., p. 431.
108. *Calendar*, 1885–6.
109. Ibid.
110. Tribute to Lady Aberdare in *South Wales Daily News*, 25 April 1897.
111. *Baner ac Amserau Cymru*, 29 September 1886.
112. Ladies' Hall Committee Minutes, 10 June 1886.
113. *Cadendar, 1888–9*.
114. Aberdare Hall (1935), pp. 19–20.
115. *South Wales Daily News*, 18 January 1887.
116. Ladies' Hall Committee Minutes, 2 May 1886.
117. Ladies' Hall Committee Minutes, 29 September 1888.
118. Mrs Viriamu Jones, quoted in *South Wales Daily News*, 18 July 1887.
119. Ladies' Hall Committee Minutes, 10 October 1889.
120. Executive Committee quoted in the *Calendar* 1889–90, p. 128.
121. Chrimes, op. cit., p. 122.
122. Aberdare Hall, Minutes, 11 February 1891.
123. Ibid., 15 August 1891.
124. See Archives, Aberdare Hall.
125. *Dictionary of National Biography*, pp. 139–40.
126. See Archives, Aberdare Hall.
127. Ibid.
128. *Western Mail*, 8 October 1895.

129. Ibid.
130. Ibid.
131. Ibid.
132. Minutes of Committee of Council 1895–6, p. 226.
133. *South Wales Daily News*, 28 April 1887; 29 June 1897; Calendar 1899–1900.
134. Register in University College Archives.
135. Aberdare Hall, Minutes, 10 March 1893.
136. Ibid., 1899.
137. Ibid., 31 January 1890; 31 May 1894; 12 December 1895. 1895 Circular *re* position of 'Lady Teachers' as principals in intermediate schools.
138. College Calendars.
139. Minutes, Committee of Council on Education 1890–1, J.G. Fitch's Report, p. 455.
140. *Calendar* 1892.
141. Minutes, Committee of Council on Education 1890–1. William Williams HMI, Report on Welsh Division, p. 415.
142. Ibid., 1890–1, p. 460.
143. Ibid., 1891–2, p. 470.
144. Ibid., p. 472.
145. Aberdare Hall Minutes, 11 February 1891.
146. Minutes, Committee of Council on Education 1892–3, p. 159.
147. *Calendar*, 1894–5.
148. Minutes, Committee of Council on Education, 1897–8, p. 343.
149. Ibid., 1893–4, p. 188.
150. Miss Hester Davies, *Technical Education for Women*, 1894, p. 19.
151. Phillips, op. cit., p. 10.
152. Davies, op. cit., p. 10.
153. School of Cookery Minutes, 26 November 1890.
154. Ibid., 18 December, 1890.
155. Davies, op. cit., pp. 17–19.
156. School of Cookery Minutes, 5 July 1895.
157. *Western Mail*, 11 December 1897.
158. Examination Papers in University College Archives.
159. Calendar, 1899–1900.
160. NLW, XLD 3780–9.
161. Address at Opening Ceremony, *South Wales Daily News*, 23 April 1891.
162. *The Times*, 20 June 1902.
163. Booklet, *Aberdare Hall*, 1885–1935, p. 11.
164. Recollections of HMI 1908–14 in *Aberdare Hall* (1935).
165. Aberdare Hall Minutes, 4 February 1908.
166. Ibid., 8 November 1910.
167. Pamphlet in Aberdare Hall Archives.
168. Calendar, 1914–15.
169. Cohen, op. cit., p. 70.
170. *University College of Wales Magazine*, Vol. 29, 1906–7.
171. *Calendar*, 1914–15. See also *The Training of Women Teachers for Secondary Schools,* Board of Education Pamphlet No. 23, 1912.
172. PRO Ed. 35/3227.
173. PRO Ed. 109/8084.

174. NLW, MLD 3780–9: Address to Miss Hester Davies by Management Committee 1902.
175. Prospectuses in NLW, XLD 3780–9.
176. 1906 Document, College Archives, Llandaff.
177. *South Wales Daily News*, 8 May 1907.
178. Cookery School Committee, Minute Book, 30 June 1909.
179. Ibid., 26 April 1910.
180. Ibid., copy of letter 1 October 1909 from Miss Hester Davies to University College Council.
181. *Western Mail*, 23 November 1909.
182. Ibid. See also Cookery School Committee, Minute Book, 4 March 1907.
183. Editorial, *Western Mail*, 22 November 1909; 23 November 1909.
184. Ibid., 22 November 1909.
185. *South Wales Daily News*, 9 June 1910.
186. Report of Proceedings, 2 January 1911 in NLW, XLD *3780–9*. See also Editorial, *Western Mail*, 21 March 1911.
187. *Western Mail*, 29 May 1912.
188. Ibid., 11 June 1912.
189. *Education*, 9 February 1912.
190. Minutes of Joint Committee of Management: Training School of Domestic Arts for Wales and Monmouthshire, 20 July 1914; 28 September 1914.
191. Lewis, op. cit., p. 18.
192. *Calendar*, University College of North Wales, 1885–6.
193. UCNW Archives.
194. *North Wales Chronicle*, 25 October 1884.
195. Ibid.
196. *Calendar*, 1890–1.
197. Dilys Glynne Jones Papers, UCNW, letters, 3 April 1886, 1 July 1889. See also J. Gwynn Williams, *The University College of North Wales, 1985*, p. 78.
198. *North Wales Chronicle*, 29 June 1889.
199. Miss M.O. Davies in *Sir H.R. Reichel: A Memorial Volume*, p. 94.
200. UCNW Archives, memo. October 1884.
201. *Calendar*, 1886–7.
202. *North Wales Chronicle*, 25 October 1884.
203. Ibid.
204. Dilys Glynne Jones Papers, letter, 8 April 1886.
205. Ibid., letter 6 July 1889. See also J.G. Williams, op. cit., p. 78, p. 288.
206. *North Wales Chronicle*, 8 May 1886.
207. Ibid., 5 June 1886.
208. *Calendar*, 1886–7.
209. UCNW Archives.
210. *Caernarvon and Denbigh Herald*, 5 October 1888.
211. Dilys Glynne Jones Papers, letter, 25 July 1886.
212. Ibid., letter 3 February 1887.
213. Ibid. See also J.G. Williams, op. cit., p. 106.
214. Figures taken from College Calendars.
215. Minutes of Committee of Council on Education, 1897–8, p. 343.
216. *Calendar*, 1893–4.

217. *North Wales Guardian*, 13 May 1892.
218. University Hall for Women Students, opened 9 October 1897: Report of Proceedings, UCNW Arhives.
219. Ibid.
220. *North Wales Chronicle*, 12 February 1926.
221. H.R. Reichel, 'The Bangor Controversy: A Statement of Facts 1893, in NLW, KLD 3661; Thomas Richards, *Atgofion Cardi*, 1960, p. 147.
222. Reichel, op. cit.
223. Minutes of the Senate Enquiry laid before Council, 21 December 1892, p. 12, UCNW Archives.
224. *North Wales Chronicle*, 3 June 1893; 26 May 1893; 8 July 1893; *The Times*, 1 May 1893; *Educational Review*, June 1893.
225. See transcript of court proceedings in *Liverpool Mercury*, 26–31 July 1893.
226. *North Wales Chronicle*, 28 October 1893.
227. Richards, op. cit., pp. 149–50.
228. *North Wales Chronicle*, 18 March 1893.
229. Quoted in Richards, op. cit., p. 147.
230. Boid, pp. 158–9.
231. Ibid., p. 161.
232. Editorial, *The Cambrian News*, 2 June 1893.
233. Ibid. See also *North Wales Chronicle*, 18 March 1893; 12 February 1926.
234. See J.G. Williams, op. cit., pp. 105–11.
235. Document in UCNW Archives. See also Richards, op. cit., pp. 164–5.
236. H.R. Reichel, 'A Memoir' in *North Wales Chronicle*, 12 February 1926.
237. Richards, op. cit., pp. 127–32.
238. The magazine of the UCNW, 1891–1899.
239. Principal's Review of Work and Growth of the College in *Twenty First Anniversary Pamphlet 1905*.
240. PRO Ed. 118/91, letter, 17 February 1911.
241. *Calendar*, 1913–14.

CHAPTER 9

1. B. Simon, *Education and the Labour Movement 1870–1920*: G.E. Jones, *Controls and Conflicts in Welsh Secondary Education, 1889–1944*, p. 47, p. 70.
2. T.E. Ellis and Ellis J. Griffith, *A Manual to the Intermediate Education (Wales) Act 1889*, 1889, p. 7.
3. T.I. Ellis, *The Development of Higher Education in Wales*, 1935, pp. 70–88; Kenneth O. Morgan *Wales in British Politics, 1868–1922*, 1963, pp. 101–2; L.W. Evans *Studies in Welsh Education* 1974, p.25.
4. Presidential Address to Welsh Secondary Schools Association, *The Welsh Secondary Schools Review*, Vol. 26, No. 1, 1940, pp. 1–12.
5. G.E. Jones, op. cit., pp. 4–8.
6. R.J. Williams, 'Moelona' in Mairwen Gwynn and T Gwyn Jones (eds.) *Dewiniaid Difyr*, 1983.
7. Emyr Humphreys, *Flesh and Blood*, 1974, p. 308.
8. Frances Hoggan, *Co-education at Different Ages*, 1882.

9. A.T. Davies (ed.) *'O.M.' — A Memoir*, 1946, p. 73.

10. Davies, op. cit., p. 75.

11. *Report of the Consultative Committee of the Board of Education on the Differentiation of the Curriculum for Boys and Girls respectively in secondary Schools, 1923*, p. xiii.

12. *Report of the Departmental Committee on the Organisation of Secondary Education in Wales*, 1920.

13. *Royal Commission on University Education in Wales*, 3 Vols., 1916–18.

14. D. Gwenallt Jones, *Cofiant Idwal Jones*, 1958, pp. 75–6.

15. Board of Education (Welsh Department) Report, 1919–20, p. 36.

16. *The Times Educational Supplement*, 6 January, 1923; Olive Wheeler, 'Fiftieth Anniversary of The Welsh Intermediate Education Act', *Trans. Cymmr.* 1939, pp. 124–5.

17. J. Purvis, 'Domestic Subjects since 1870' in I. Goodson (ed.), *Social Histories of the Secondary Curriculum*, 1981, pp. 148–156; M.R. Theobald, 'The accomplished woman and the propriety of intellect: A new look at women's education in Britain and Australia, 1800–1850', *History of Education*, Special Issue, Women and Schooling, Vol. 17, No. 1, March 1988, pp. 21–37; D. Gorham, *The Victorian Girl and the Feminine Ideal*, 1982; B.M. Solomon, *In the Company of Educated Women: A History of Women and Higher Education in America*, 1985.

Bibliography

I MANUSCRIPT COLLECTIONS

(i) Public Record Office, London

Ed. 21 Elementary education: public elementary school files

Ed. 21/22315 Ystrad Higher Grade School
Ed. 21/22563 Cardiff Higher Grade School
Ed. 21/22677 Ferndale Higher Grade School
Ed. 21/22765 Blaenau Ffestiniog Higher Grade Girls' School

Other public elementary education files including material relating to higher grade schools

Ed. 16/378 Llanelli
Ed. 16/384 Merthyr Tudful: Advanced Elementary School
Ed. 16/392 Porth, Rhondda
Ed. 16/397 Swansea
Ed. 20/160 Merthyr Tudful: proposed Elementary School
Ed. 20/170 Ystrad, 1900–2

Ed. 27 Secondary education: endowment files

Ed. 27/3426 Welsh Girls' School, Ashford
Ed. 27/6283–6301 David Hughes Charity
Ed. 27/6388–6403 Howell's School, Denbigh
Ed. 27/6398 Howell's School, Llandaff
Ed. 27/6426–6435 Llanrwst Grammar School
Ed. 27/6536–7 Edward Lewis Endowment, Gelligaer
Ed. 27/6578
Ed. 27/6583–5 } Dr Williams' School, Dolgellau
Ed. 27/6628}
Ed. 27/6667 } William Jones' Charity, Monmouth
Ed. 27/6737
Ed. 27/6749–6750 }
Ed. 27/6754–6756 } Tasker's Charity, Haverfordwest

Ed. 35 Secondary education: institution files

Ed. 35/1823 Welsh Girls' School, Ashford, 1905–21

Ed. 35/3103   Beaumaris County School, 1902–22
Ed. 35/3104   Holyhead County School, 1908–22
Ed. 35/3112   Llangefni County School, 1901–23
Ed. 35/3125   Bangor County School for Girls, 1903–20
Ed. 35/3126   Bangor County School for Boys (Friars' School), 1903–20
Ed. 35/3159   Carmarthen County School for Girls, 1914–23
Ed. 35/3177   Penrhos College, 1903–12
Ed. 35/3180–4   Howell's School, Denbigh, 1903–23
Ed. 35/3201   Wrexham County School for Girls, 1901–20
Ed. 35/3219   Aberdare Girls' Intermediate School, 1902–23
Ed. 35/3221   Barry Intermediate School, 1912–23
Ed. 35/3225   Cardiff Canton Municipal School, 1907–19
Ed. 35/3227   Cardiff College School, 1909–13
Ed. 35/3229   Howard Gardens School for Girls, 1908–23
Ed. 35/3236   Cardiff Municipal School for Girls, 1905–23
Ed. 35/3240   Cowbridge High School for Girls, 1905–23
Ed. 35/3243B   Lewis' Girls School, Gelligaer, 1906–21
Ed. 35/3261–2   Howell's School, Llandaff,
Ed. 35/3266   Cyfarthfa Castle Municipal School for Girls, 1922
Ed. 35/3276   Penarth County School for Girls, 1889–1923
Ed. 35/3279   Pontypridd Girls' Intermediate School, 1909–23
Ed. 35/3281   Porth Girls' Secondary School, 1909–23
Ed. 35/3287   Swansea: De La Beche School, 1904–19
Ed. 35/3297   Swansea Intermediate School for Girls,
Ed. 35/3301   Bala County School for Girls, 1914–23
Ed. 35/3304   Dr Williams' School, 1904–22
Ed. 35/3312   Abergavenny Intermediate School for Girls, 1908–21
Ed. 35/3342   Monmouth High School for Girls, 1904–23
Ed. 35/3350   Newport Girls' Municipal Secondary School, 1901–23
Ed. 35/3376   Newtown County School,
Ed. 35/3379   Welshpool County School, 1921
Ed. 35/3381   Haverfordwest County School for Girls, 1889–1921

Ed. 53   Secondary education: local education authority files

Ed. 53/507   Anglesey 1905–22 Major File
Ed. 53/508   Caernarfonshire 1906–21 Major File
Ed. 53/509   Cardiganshire 1901–23 Major File
Ed. 53/510   Carmarthenshire 1905–21 Major File
Ed. 53/511   Denbighshire 1905–23 Major File
Ed. 53/512   Flintshire 1904–21 Major File
Ed. 53/513   Glamorgan 1907–20. Devolution of Secondary Education powers
     to Rhondda Urban District Council
Ed. 53/514   Glamorgan 1922–23 Major File
Ed. 53/515   Merionethshire 1904–22 Major File
Ed. 53/516   Monmouthshire 1906–8 Major File
Ed. 53/517   Monmouthshire 1909–22 Major File
Ed. 53/518   Monmouthshire 1923 Major File
Ed. 53/519   Monmouthshire 1924 Major File
Ed. 53/520   Montgomeryshire 1910–23 Major File

Ed. 53/521 Pembrokeshire 1904–09 Major File
Ed. 53/522 Pembrokeshire 1920–23 Major File
Ed. 53/523 Radnorshire 1909–22 Major File
Ed. 53/524 Cardiff 1904–22 Major File
Ed. 53/525 Merthyr Tudful 1907–24 Major File
Ed. 53/526 Newport 1905–21 Major File
Ed. 53/527 Swansea 1905–21 Major File
Ed. 53/699 Anglesey 1929–45 Area File
Ed. 53/700 Breconshire 1930–45 Area File
Ed. 53/701 Breconshire 1908 Joint Education Committee File
Ed. 53/702 Caernarfonshire 1925–45 Area File
Ed. 53/703 Caernarfonshire 1917–18 Joint Education Committee File
Ed. 53/704 Cardiganshire 1929–45 Area File
Ed. 53/705 Cardiganshire 1910 Joint Education Committee File
Ed. 53/706 Carmarthenshire 1925–45 Area File
Ed. 53/707 Carmarthenshire 1911–12 Joint Education Committee File
Ed. 53/708 Denbighshire 1931–43 Area File
Ed. 53/709 Denbighshire Joint Education Committee File
Ed. 53/710 Flintshire 1929–44 Area File
Ed. 53/711 Flintshire 1911 Joint Education Committee File
Ed. 53/712 Glamorgan 1929–45 Area File
Ed. 53/713 Merionethshire 1907–23 Joint Education Committee File
Ed. 53/714 Monmouthshire 1937–45 Area File
Ed. 53/715 Montgomeryshire 1942–45 Area File
Ed. 53/716 Montgomeryshire 1908 Joint Education Committee File
Ed. 53/717 Pembrokeshire 1907–16 Joint Education Committee File
Ed. 53/718 Radnorshire 1923 Joint Education Committee File
Ed. 53/719 Merthyr Tudful 1925–45 Area File
Ed. 53/720 Merthyr Tudful 1928 Joint Education Committee File
Ed. 53/725 Breconshire 1904–23 Major File
Ed. 53/726 Glamorgan 1913–21 Major File
Ed. 53/727 Swansea Compulsory Powers under the 1902 Education Act, 1912–20.

Ed. 93   Secondary education in Wales: general files

Ed. 93/6, 1912–17   Board of Education instructions and administrative arrangements
Ed. 93/7, 1918–22   Board of Education instructions and administrative arrangements
Ed. 93/9, 1912–13   Copies of Board of Education general instructions adopted for Wales
Ed. 93/10, 1914–22   Copies of Board of Education general instructions adopted for Wales
Ed. 93/14, 1918–21   Regulations for Secondary Schools in Wales (miscellaneous papers)

Ed. 109   Inspectorate: reports on secondary institutions

Ed. 109/7533 Builth Wells Intermediate School, 1921
Ed. 109/7653 Bangor County School for Girls, 1926

Ed. 109/7684   Caernarfon County School, 1920
Ed. 109/7714   St Winifred's School Llanfairfechan, 1920
Ed. 109/7750   Aberystwyth Intermediate School, 1923
Ed. 109/7819   Carmarthen High School for Girls, 1919
Ed. 109/7819   Carmarthen High School for Girls, 1923
Ed. 109/7852   Llanelly County School for Girls, 1919
Ed. 109/7885   Penrhos College, 1920
Ed. 109/7906   Howell's School, Denbigh, 1905
Ed. 109/7907   Howell's School, Denbigh, 1919
Ed. 109/7966   Hawarden County School, 1921
Ed. 109/7974   Holywell County School, 1921
Ed. 109/7982   Mold County School, 1921
Ed. 109/8011   Epworth College, 1922
Ed. 109/8076   Cardiff: Canton Municipal Secondary Girls' School, 1909
Ed. 109/8077   Cardiff: Canton Girls' School, 1912
Ed. 109/8078   Cardiff: Canton Girls' School, 1914
Ed. 109/8084   The College School, Cardiff, 1913
Ed. 109/8097   Cardiff High School for Girls, 1927
Ed. 109/8112   Howard Gardens Municipal Secondary School for Girls, 1912
Ed. 109/8117   Howell's School, Llandaff, 1911
Ed. 109/8118   Howell's School, Llandaff, 1919
Ed. 109/8136   Cowbridge High School for Girls, 1915
Ed. 109/8162   Cyfarthfa Castle Municipal School for Girls, 1913
Ed. 109/8267   Porth Girls' Secondary School, 1921
Ed. 109/8284   Swansea High School for Girls, 1922
Ed. 109/8292   Swansea High School for Girls, 1908
Ed. 109/8347   Dr Williams' School, 1928
Ed. 109/8398   Monmouth High School for Girls, 1904
Ed. 109/8401   Monmouth High School for Girls, 1922
Ed. 109/8424   Newport Municipal Secondary School, 1920
Ed. 109/8488   Newtown Intermediate School, 1923
Ed. 109/8503   Welshpool Intermediate School, 1923
Ed. 109/8526   Haverfordwest County School for Girls, 1923

Teacher training-colleges

Ed. 40/99   Swansea Training College, 1907–12
Ed. 87/16   Bangor Normal, 1906–18
Ed. 87/17   Barry Training College, 1906–16
Ed. 87/19   Swansea Training College, 1907–16
Ed. 115/96   South Wales & Monmouthshire Training School of Domestic Arts, 1921

University of Wales

Ed. 119/68–69   University College of Wales, Aberystwyth, 1883–1914
Ed. 119/70–72   University College of North Wales, Bangor
Ed. 119/74–75   University College of South Wales and Monmouthshire, Cardiff
Ed. 119/81   University of Wales, 1906–14

(ii)   National Library of Wales, Aberystwyth

Welsh Girls' School Ashford, House Committee Minutes and Miscellaneous
    Papers
Frances Power Cobbe Papers
Minutes and Correspondence of the Honourable Society of Cymmrodorion
D.R. Daniel Collection
Thomas Gee Papers
Glansevern Papers
Edward Griffiths MSS
Samuel Holland Papers
Lewis Morris Papers
National Eisteddfod of Wales MSS: Swansea Eisteddfod 1891 Essay by Miss
    Winter: 'The Education of Girls in Wales'
Nefydd MSS: an essay on the advantages of education to the working classes,
    Aberdulais Eisteddfod 1860
Rendel Papers
Thomas Stephens MSS: An address to the working classes on the benefits of
    education

(iii)   University College of North Wales, Bangor

The Bangor Controversy 1893: Miscellaneous papers including statements by
    Principal Reichel, Frances E. Hughes. Minutes of the Senate Enquiry 1892.
The Bangor Women's Hostel Co. Ltd: Miscellaneous papers
Dilys Glynne Jones Papers
Minute Books, North Wales Training College (St Mary's)
UCNW: Students' Register 1884–1892

(iv)   University College of Wales, Aberystwyth

Alexandra Hall: Miscellaneous papers, including Hall Entrance Forms 1905–6
Minutes of College Council
Letters of Lady Stamp (Olive Marsh) 1898–1900

(v)   University College of South Wales and Monmouthshire, Cardiff

Aberdare Hall: Minutes of Ladies' Hall Committee; Register of Students
    1885–6; miscellaneous papers.
Minutes of the South Wales and Monmouthshire School of Cookery (later
    Domestic Arts) and miscellaneous papers.

(vi)   The Worshipful Company of Drapers, Drapers' Hall London

Minutes, Court of Assistants
Letter Books and Minutes
Miscellaneous papers concerning Thomas Howell's Trust

(vii)   Howell's School, Llandaff

Examiners' reports, 1870 and 1880s
Finance and House Committee Minutes
Governors' Minute Books

House Surgeon's Book
J.Ll. Thompson's Reports 1879 and 1882
Miss Kendall's Report to Local Governors 1880
Letters 1859–1910

(viii) Howell's School, Denbigh

Headmistress's Report Book 1870s
Governors' Minute Book
Miscellaneous letters and papers

(ix) Gwynedd Record Office, Dolgellau

Papers of the Dr Williams' School, Dolgellau including Minute Books, Notebooks, Registers.

(x) Glamorgan County Record Office, Cardiff

Minutes of Gelligaer School Board, 1882
Minutes of Governors, Lewis' School
Minutes Glamorgan Education Committee 1906–14
Miscellaneous files concerning Barry Training College

(xi) Clwyd County Record Office, Rhuthun

Miscellaneous papers concerning Denbighshire Scheme for Intermediate Education 1890–7

(xii) Swansea Central Library

Miscellaneous papers concerning Swansea Training College

(xiii) Llanelli Public Library

Minutes and miscellaneous papers concerning the Llanelli Mechanics' Institute

(xiv) Wrexham Public Library

S. Harrison, Short Notes on Private Adventure Schools in Wrexham and District

(xv) Bishop of St David's Palace, Abergwili

Minutes of Diocesan Board of Education and miscellaneous papers concerning Carmarthen High School for Girls

(xvi) The British and Foreign School Society Archives Centre, Borough Road, Isleworth

Letters of application and admission lists

(xvii) Onfel Thomas Collection, Builth Wells

Papers concerning Dr Frances Hoggan

II PRIMARY SOURCES IN PRINT

(i) Hansard's Parliamentary Debates, Third and Fourth Series

(ii) Censuses of England and Wales, 1841–1911

(iii) Official Reports

(a) Reports of official committees:

Report of the Commissioners Appointed to Inquire into the State of Education in Wales, (Blue Books) 1847.

Report of the Commissioners on the State of Popular Education in England and Wales (Newcastle Report) 1861, including John Jenkins's Report on the State of Popular Education in the 'Welsh Specimen Districts' (1858–9) I.U.P.Vol.4.

Report of the Schools Inquiry Commission (Taunton Report), 1868.

Report of the Commission on the Employment of Children, Young Persons and Women in Agriculture, Vol. XIII, 1870.

Report of the Committee Appointed to Inquire into the Condition of Intermediate And Higher Education in Wales with Minutes of Evidence and Appendix (Aberdare Report), 1881.

Final Report of the Royal Commission Appointed to Inquire into the Working of the Elementary Education Acts, England and Wales, (Cross Report), 1888.

Report of the Royal Commission on Secondary Education (Bryce Report), 1895.

Evidence, Report and Appendices of the Royal Commission on Land in Wales and Monmouthshire, 1894–5.

Reports of the Mosely Educational Commission to the USA, October 1903–December 1904.

Report of the Committee on The University of Wales and the Welsh University Colleges (Raleigh), 1909.

Report of the Consultative Committee on Practical Work in Secondary Schools, 1913.

Report and Minutes of Evidence of the Royal Commission on the University of Wales, 1918.

Report of the Departmental Committee on the Organisation of Secondary Education in Wales (Bruce Report) 1920.

Report of the Departmental Committee on Scholarships and Free Places, 1920.

Report of the Consultative Committee on Differentiation of the Curriculum for Boys and Girls Respectively in Secondary Schools, 1923.

Report of the Departmental Committee on the Training of Teachers for Public Elementary Schools (Burnham Report), 1925.

Report of the Consultative Committee on Secondary Education with Special Reference to Grammar Schools and Technical High Schools (Spens Report), 1938.

Curriculum and Examinations in Secondary Schools. Report of the Committee of the Secondary School Examinations Council Appointed by the President of the Board of Education in 1941, 1943.

(b) Minutes and reports of the Committee of Council on Education, 1839–1898.

(c) Charity Commission Reports, 1894–1900.

(d) Education Department: *Education Subjects: Special Reports*, Vol. 1 1896–7; Vol. 2, 1898.

(e) Board of Education: reports and pamphlets:

Education Subjects: Special Reports, Vols. 10–16
Reports of the Board of Education, 1899–1925
The Training of Women Teachers for Secondary Schools, 1912, Pamphlet No. 23

(f) Welsh Department, Board of Education:

Annual Reports 1907–1925
Regulations for Secondary Schools in Wales, 1918

(g) Central Welsh Board:

CWB Reports of Inspection and Examination of County Schools, 1897–1920
CWB General Reports, 1897–1920
Today and Tomorrow in Welsh Education — What Shall it be?, 1917

(iv) Publications of local educational bodies

Minutes and Reports of Proceedings of Joint Education Committees of North Wales 1890–2.
Minutes and Reports of Proceedings of General Conferences of Joint Education Committees of Wales and Monmouthshire 1890–1.
Report of Proceedings of the Denbighshire Joint Education Committee at the Public Inquiry (March–September 1890).
Report of Proceedings at the Public Enquiry held by the Joint Education Committee at the Town Hall, Cardiff, November 1890.
Proposals for a Scheme of Intermediate Education in Cardiff, 1891.
North Wales Scholarship Association: Annual Reports, 1880–94.
Minutes, Swansea Education Committee, 1919–23.
Education Act 1918: Scheme of Rhondda LEA, 1919.
R.B. Badger, Report on Technical Education for Caernarfonshire, 1896.
J.C. Smith, Report on the Organisation of Education in Caernarfonshire, 1911.
The Education Problem in Swansea — A Report by the Director of Education in view of the Education Act, 1919.

(v) Publications of The Association for Promoting the Education of Girls in Wales

Annual Reports, 1887–1901

Pamphlets, 1887–1901:
A.H.D. Acland MP, *Welsh Education*, 1891
Mrs Bryant, *Welsh University and Local Examinations in Wales,* 1887
— — (et al.) *The Position of Women on the Governing Bodies of Educational Institutions*, 1829
E. Carpenter, *Mixed Classes in Intermediate Schools*, 1891
Dilys Lloyd Davies, *The Problem of Girls Education in Wales*, 1887
— — *The Duty of Welshwomen in relation to the Welsh Intermediate Education Act*, 1894
Elizabeth P. Hughes, *The Education of Welsh Women*, 1887
— — *Dual Schools in Wales*, 1897
D. Isambard Owen, *Race and Nationality*, 1887
H.R. Reichel, *The Future of Welsh Education*, 1887

—— *Intermediate Education for Girls in Wales*, 1889
Anna Rowlands (et al.), *Manual Training for Girls in Wales*, 1894
A.R. Vardy (et al.), *The Relationship between Elementary and Secondary Education*, 1899
K.M. Warren (et al.), *The Teaching of English Literature in our Schools*, 1898
C.T. Whitmell, *A Plea for Mixed Schools*, 1889

(vi)   Publications of other associations and societies

Publications of the National Eisteddfod Association:
Annual Reports 1882–1914
Annual Transactions of the National Eisteddfod 1860–1900

Transactions of the Liverpool Welsh National Society, 1885–1912

Transactions of the National Association for the Promotion of Social Science, 1859–75

(vii)   University of Wales

Minutes of the University of Wales Court
Reports of the University of Wales Senate
Minutes of College Council and Court of Governors, Principal's Reports, and Annual College Calendars, UCW, Aberystwyth
Minutes of College Council and Court of Governors and Annual College Calendars, UCNW, Bangor
Minutes of College Council and Court of Governors, Principal's Reports, and Annual College Calendars, University College, Cardiff
Minutes of College Council and Annual Reports, University College, Swansea
Guild of Graduates: Miscellaneous reports
Pamphlets, prospectuses and miscellaneous papers concerning Aberdare Hall, Cardiff; Alexandra Hall, Aberystwyth and The Bangor Women's Hostel.

(viii)   Teacher training-colleges

Swansea Training College: Annual Reports 1872–1925
North Wales Training College: Annual Reports 1899–1920
Bangor Normal College: miscellaneous reports

(ix)   College and school magazines

University College of Wales Magazine, 1878–1903, *The Dragon*, 1904–20
The Magazine of the UCNW, 1891–1921
The Swan, 1900–22
Under the Red Dragon (Barry), 1916–23
The Howellian (Denbigh), 1906–14
Dr Williams' School Magazine, 1897–1920
The Welsh Girls' School Gazette, (Ashford), 1912–30

III DIRECTORIES

Bennett's Business Directory, 1899, 1911–12
Cassey's Directory, 1876, 1878

Hunt's South Wales Directory, 1849
Kelly's Directory of Monmouthshire and South Wales, 1901, 1914
Pigot's National and Commercial Directory, 1835, 1844
Postal Directory of Caernarvonshire and Anglesey, 1886
Robson's Commercial Directory, 1841
Slater's Directory, 1844, 1850, 1856, 1858–9, 1868, 1880, 1883
Sutton's Directory of North Wales, 1889–90
Worrall's Directory of North Wales, 1874

IV CONTEMPORARY WORKS

Anon, *Letters of Lord Aberdare*, 2 Vols. (Oxford, 1902)
Bruce, H.A. *The present condition and future prospects of the working classes in South Wales* (London, 1851)
— — *Miscellaneous Pamphlets* (London, 1874)
Crawshay Prize Essays (Bwlch, 1892)
Davies, W.C., *The Welsh Intermediate Education Act 1889: How to Use it* (Denbigh, 1889)
Davies, W.C. and W.L. Jones, *The University of Wales* (London, 1905)
Davies, W.E., *Sir Hugh Owen, his life and life-work* (London, 1885)
Derfel, R.J., *Traethodau ac Areithiau* (Rhuthun 1864)
Edwards, Lewis, *Rhagdraeth: Yr Athrawes o Ddifrif* (Caernarfon, 1859)
— — *Traethodau Llenyddol* (Wrexham, 1867)
Ellis, T.E., *Speeches and Addresses* (Wrexham, 1912)
Ellis, T.E. and E Jones Griffith, *Intermediate and Technical Education in Wales* (London, 1889)
Evans, David, *The Sunday Schools of Wales* (London, 1883)
Evans, Owen, *Merched yr Ysgrythurau* (Dolgellau, 1886)
Falconer, Thomas, *The Charity of Thomas Howell established for the benefit of his Monmouthshire Kinfolk and others* AD *1540: The Mystery of Improvidence* (London, 1860)
Gibson, John, *The Emancipation of Women* (Aberystwyth, 1891)
Griffiths, E (Ieuan Ebblig), *Teuluyddiaeth* (Swansea, 1855)
Hall, G. Stanley, *Educational Problems* (New York, 1911)
Hughes, Joshua, *A Plea for Higher Education in Wales* (London, 1876)
Hughes, Thomas, *The Law Relating to Welsh Intermediate Schools* (Cardiff, 1898)
Jones, J.M., *Trem ar Y Ganrif* (Dolgellau, 1902)
Jones, Rhys Gwesyn, *Caru, Priodi a Byw* (Merthyr Tudful, 1866)
Jones Davies, D., *Higher Education in Wales: The Extent of its Deficiency and Suggestions for its Improvement* (London, 1880)
Lloyd, D.L., *The Missing Link in Education in Wales* (Bangor, 1876)
Nicholas, Thomas, *Middle and High Schools and a University for Wales* (London, 1863)
Phillips, Sir Thomas, *Wales: The Language, Social Condition, Moral Character and Religious Opinions of the people considered in their relation to education* (London, 1848)
Prichard, T.J. Llewelyn, *Heroines of Welsh History* (London, 1854)
Rathbone, Eleanor, *William Rathbone* (London, 1905)
Rees, R.O., *Cofiant a Gweithiau Barddonol a Rhyddiaethol Ieuan Gwynedd*

(Wrexham, 1876)

Rees, Thomas, *The Alleged Unchastity of Wales in Miscellaneous Papers on Subjects relating to Wales* (London, 1867)

Rhys, J and D.B. Jones, *The Welsh People* (London, 1906)

Richard, Henry, *Letters on the Social and Political Conditions of Wales* (London, 1867)

— — *Letters and Essays on Wales* (London, 1884)

Salmon, D., 'The Story of a Welsh Education Commission', *y Cymmrodor*, XXIV, 1913

— — *History of the Normal College for Wales* (Swansea, 1902)

Southall, J.E., *The Future of Welsh Education* (Newport, 1900)

Stanton, T. (ed.), *The Woman Question in Europe* (London, 1884)

Thomas, H.E. (Huwco Meirion), *Traethawd ar Gymru a'r Cymdeithasau Llenyddol* (Birkenhead), 1854)

— — *Mêl Myfrdod: Pregethau, Traethodau, Barddoniaeth* (Pittsburg, 1882)

Webster, W. Bullock (et al.), *The Principles of Collegiate Education Discussed and Elucidated in a Description of Gnoll College* (London, 1857)

Williams, B.T., *The Desirableness of a University for Wales* (London, 1853)

Williams, Jane (Ysgafell), *Remarks on the Reports of the Commissioners of Inquiry into the State of Education in Wales* (London, 1848)

Williams, G. Perrie, *Welsh Education in Sunlight and Shadow* (London, 1918)

Williams, T. Marchant, *The Educational Wants of Wales* (London, 1877)

Zimmern, A, *The Renaissance of Girls' Education in England*, (London, 1898)

V SECONDARY SOURCES

(i) Books and articles

Aldrich, R.E., 'Educating our mistresses', *History of Education*, Vol. 12, 1983, pp. 93–102

Banks, J.A. and O., *Feminism and Family Planning* (Liverpool, 1964)

Banks, J.A. and O., *Faces of Feminism* (Oxford, 1981)

Beddoe, Deirdre., 'Towards a Welsh Women's History', *Llafur*, Vol. 3 No. 2, 1981

— — *Discovering Women's History: A Practical Manual* (London, 1983)

— — 'The Lost Sex', *Arcade*, No. 3, 1980, p. 19

Bessborough, The Earl of (ed.) *Lady Charlotte Schreiber (formerly Lady Charlotte Guest). Extracts from her Journal, 1853–1891* (London, 1952)

Borer, M.C., *Willingly to School, A History of Women's Education* (Guildford, 1976)

Boyd, W., *The History of Western Education* (London, 1952)

Branca, P., *Silent Sisterhood: Middle Class Women in the Victorian Home* (London, 1975)

— — *Women in Europe since 1750* (London, 1978)

Bridenthal, R and C. Koong, (eds.) *Becoming Visible: Women in European History* (Boston, 1977)

Bryant, M., *The Unexpected Revolution: A Study of the Education of Women and Girls in the Nineteenth Century* (London, 1979)

Burstall, Sara, *Retrospect and Prospect: Sixty Years of Women's Education* (London, 1933)

Burstyn, J.N., 'Women's Education during the Nineteenth Century: A Review of the Literature 1970–1976', *History of Education*, 1977, Vol. 6, No. 1, pp. 11–19

— — *Victorian Education and the Ideal of Womanhood* (London, 1980)

Carr, Catherine, *The Spinning Wheel: City of Cardiff High School for Girls, 1895–1955* (Cardiff, 1955)

Chrimes, S.B. (ed.), *The University College of South Wales and Monmouthshire: A Centenary History 1883–1983* (Cardiff, 1983)

Crow, Duncan, *The Victorian Woman* (London, 1971)

Davies, Sir Alfred T., *'O.M.': A Memoir* (Cardiff, 1946)

Davies, Cassie, *Hwb i'r Galon* (Swansea, 1973)

Davies, E.T., *Monmouthshire Schools and Education to 1870* (Newport, 1957)

Davies, E and A.D. Rees (eds.), *Welsh Rural Communities* (Cardiff, 1960)

Davies, J.A., *Education in a Welsh Rural County 1870–1973* (Cardiff, 1973)

Davies, Wynford, 'The Intermediate School in Rural Wales, 1897–1907: the Problem of School Organization, National Library of Wales Journal, Vol. X, 1976

Davies, L. Twiston and Averyl Edwards, *The Women of Wales* (London 1935)

Deem, R., *Women and Schooling* (London, 1978)

Delamont, S and L. Duffin (eds.), *The Nineteenth Century Woman: Her Cultural and Physical World* (London, 1978)

Dyhouse, Carol, 'Social Darwinistic ideas and the development of women's education in England, 1880–1920', *History of Education*, Vol. 5, No. 1, 1976, pp. 44–58

— — 'Good wives and little mothers: social anxieties and the schoolgirls' curriculum', *Oxford Review of Education*, Vol. 3, No. 1, 1977, pp. 21–35

— — *Girls growing up in late Victorian and Edwardian England* (London, 1981)

Eaton, G., 'A Girls' Grammar School at the Gnoll?' *Neath Antiquarian Society Transactions* 1982–3, pp. 78–9

Edwards, Hywel Teifi, *Gŵyl Gwalia — Yr Eisteddfod Genedlaethol yn Oes Aur Victoria, 1858–1868* (Llandysul, 1980)

Edwards, O.T., *Joseph Parry 1841–1903* (Cardiff, 1970)

Ellis, E.L., *The University College of Wales, Aberystwyth 1872–1972* (Cardiff 1972)

— — *Alexandra Hall 1896–1986* (Aberystwyth, 1986)

Ellis, T.I. (ed.), 'T. Charles Edwards Letters', *National Library of Wales Journal*, 2 Vols. 1952–3

— — *The Development of Higher Education in Wales* (Wrexham, 1935)

Evans, D. Emrys, *The University of Wales* (Cardiff, 1953)

Evans, L. W., *Education in Industrial Wales, 1700–1900* (London, 1971)

— — *Studies in Welsh Education* (Cardiff, 1974)

Fletcher, S., *Feminists and Bureaucrats: A Study in the Development of girls' Education in the Nineteenth Century* (Cambridge, 1980)

— — 'Co-education and the Victorian Grammar School', *History of Education*, 1982, Vol. II, No. 2, pp. 87–98

Fleure, H.J., 'U.C.W. Aberystwyth: An Old Student looks at the College', *Trans. Cymmr.*, 1955

Gardiner, J., 'What is Women's History?' *The Times Educational Supplement*, 19 April 1985

Gorham, D., *The Victorian Girl and the Feminine Ideal* (London, 1982)

Griffiths, R., *Y Gohebydd: Cofiant* (Denbigh, 1905)

Harrison, B., 'Women's Health and the Women's Movement', in *Biology, Medicine and Society, 1840–1940* (ed.) Charles Webster (Cambridge, 1981)

Holcombe, Lee, *Victorian Ladies at Work: Middle-class Working Women in England and Wales, 1850–1914* (Newton Abbot, 1974)

Houghton, W.E., *The Victorian Frame of Mind* (Yale, 1957)

Hovey, R., *Penrhos 1880–1930* (Penrhos, 1931)

Howse, W.H., *School and Bell: Four Hundred Years of a Welsh Grammar School* (Halesowen, 1956)

Hufton, O. (et al.), 'What is Women's History?', *History Today*, Vol. 35, June 1985, pp. 38–49

James, G.D., *The History of the Haverfordwest Grammar School* (Haverfordwest, 1961)

Jenkins, D. and M. Owen, *The Welsh Law of Women* (Cardiff, 1980)

Jenkins, R.T. and H. Ramage, *The History of the Honourable Society of Cymmrodorion* (London, 1951)

John, Angela, *By the Sweat of their Brow: Women Workers at Victorian Coal-mines* (London, 1980)

Jones, Abel J., *From an Inspector's Bag* (Cardiff, 1944)

Jones, Emyr Wyn, 'Addysg Feddygol i ferched; *National Library of Wales Journal*, Vol xix, No. 3, 1976

Jones, G., *Cranogwen: Portread Newydd* (Llandysul, 1981)

Jones, Idwal, 'The Voluntary System at Work', *Trans. Cymmr. Soc.* 1931–2

Jones, G.E., *Controls and Conflicts in Welsh Secondary Education 1889–1944* (Cardiff, 1982)

Jones, K.V., *Life of John Viriamu Jones* (London, 1915)

Jones, T. Gwynn, *Cofiant Thomas Gee* (Denbigh, 1913)

Jones, R, Tudur, 'Daearu'r Angylion: Sylwadau ar Ferched mewn Llen yddiaeth'. *Ysgrifau Beirniadol*, XI, 1860–1900 (Debigh 1979)

— — *Coroni'r Fam Frenhines: Y Ferch a'r Fam yn Llenyddiaeth Oes Victoria, 1835–60* (Denbigh, 1976)

Jones-Roberts, K.W., 'Education in the Parish of Ffestiniog', *Jnl. Mer. Hist. & Record Soc.*, Vol. 11, 1953–6

Kamm, J., *Hope Deferred, Girls' Education in English History* (London, 1965)

— — *Indicative Past: A Hundred Years of the Girls' Public Day School Trust* (London, 1971)

Leighton, R., *Rise and Progress: the story of the Welsh Girls' School, Ashford* (London, 1950)

Lewis, D. Gerwyn, *The University and the Colleges of Education in Wales, 1925–1978* (Cardiff, 1980)

Lipshitz, L. (ed.), *Tearing the Veil* (London, 1978)

Lloyd, Sir J.E. (ed.), *Sir Harry Reichel* (Cardiff, 1934)

McCann, J., *Thomas Howell and the School at Llandaff* (Cowbridge, 1972)

Manton, J.G., *Elizabeth Garrett Anderson* (London, 1963)

Meredith, R., 'Early History of the North Wales Training College', *Trans. Caerns. Hist. Society*, 1946

Millward, E.G., 'Canu'r Byd i'w le', *Y Traethodydd*, Jan. 1981

Morgan, Iwan (ed.), *The College by the Sea* (Aberystwyth, 1928)

Morgan, J.V. (ed.), *Welsh Religious Leaders in the Nineteenth Century* (London, 1905)

—— *Welsh Political and Educational Leaders of the Victorian Era* (London, 1908)

—— *The Welsh Mind in Evolution* (London, 1925)

Morgan, K.O., *Wales in British Politics, 1868–1922*, 2nd. edn. (Cardiff, 1970)

—— *Rebirth of a Nation, Wales 1880–1980* (Oxford, 1981)

Neff, Wanda F., *Victorian Working Women. A Historical and Literary Study of Women in British Industries and Professions, 1832–1850* (Columbia, 1929)

Owen, G. Dyfnallt, *Ysgolion a Cholegau yr Annibynwyr* (Swansea, 1939)

Parry, R.J. (ed.), *Llanrwst Grammar School, 1610–1960* (Llanrwst, 1960)

Pederson, J.S., 'The Reform of women's secondary and higher education: institutional change and social values in mid and late Victorian England', *History of Education Quarterly*, No. 19, 1979

—— 'Victorian Headmistresses: A Conservative Tradition of Social Reform', *Victorian Studies*, Vol. 24, No. 4, 1981

Phillips, Denver (ed.), *Coleshill School Llanelli 1891–1977* (Llanelli, 1978)

Pretty, D.A., *Two Centuries of Anglesey Schools* (Llangefni, 1978)

Purvis, June, 'Towards a History of Women's Education in the Nineteenth Century', *Westminster Studies in Education*, 1981, Vol. 14, pp. 45–81

—— 'Separate Spheres and Inequality in the Education of Working Class Women 1854–1900', *History of Education*, 1981, Vol. 10, No. 4, pp. 227–43

—— 'Women and Teaching in the Nineteenth Century', in *Education and the State*, Vol. 2, ed. R. Dale, G. Esland, R. Fergusson and M. MacDonald, 1981, pp. 359–73

—— 'Domestic Subjects since 1870' in I. Goodson (ed.) *Social Histories of the Secondary Curriculum* (London, 1981), pp. 148–156

Rees, B. (ed.), *Ieuan Gwynedd: Detholiad o'i Ryddiaeth* (Cardiff, 1957)

Rees, Mati, 'O Aberhonddu i Abertawe', *Y Genhinen*, Gwanwyn, 1961

Roberts, Nesta (ed.), *St Winifred's Llanfairfechan: The Story of Fifty Years 1887–1937* (Shrewsbury, 1937)

Roberts, T. (ed.), *Bangor Normal College, 1858–1958* (Bangor, 1958)

Rowbotham, S., *Hidden from History* (London, 1973)

Semmel, B., *Imperialism and Social Reform: English Social Imperialist Thought 1895–1914* (London, 1960)

Simon, B., *Education and the Labour Movement* (London, 1965)

Spender, Dale, *Invisible Women* (London, 1982)

Stone, M.K., 'Howell's School, Denbigh', *Trans. Denbs. Hist. Soc.* Vol. VIII, 1959

Thomas, C. Tawelfryn, *Cofiant Ieuan Gwynedd* (Dolgellau, 1909)

Thomas, Onfel., *Frances Elizabeth Hoggan, 1843–1927* (Builth Wells, 1970)

Thompson, K.M., *Ruthin School: The First Seven Centuries* (Rhuthun, 1974)

Trow, A.H. and D.J.A. Brown, *A Short History of the University College of South Wales and Monmouthshire, Cardiff, 1883–1933* (Cardiff, 1933)

Turner, B., *Equality for Some: the story of girls' education* (London, 1974)

Vicinus, M. (ed.), *Suffer and Be Still: Women in the Victorian Age* (Indiana, 1977)

Webb, B. (ed.), 'The Awakening of Women', *The New Statesman*, November, 1913

Webster, J.R., 'The Welsh Intermediate Education of 1889', *The Welsh History Review*, Vol. IV, No. 3, 1969

Widdowson, F., 'Girls growing up into the Next Class: Women and Elementary

Teacher Training 1840–1914', *Explorations in Feminism* (London, 1980)

Wheeler, Olive, 'Three Addresses: Fiftieth Anniversary Welsh Intermediate Education Act', *Trans. Cymmr.* 1939, pp. 124–9

Williams, A.H., *Cymru Oes Fictoria* (Cardiff, 1973)

Williams, David, *T. Francis Roberts, 1891–1919* (Cardiff, 1961)

Williams, D.D., *Hanes Bywyd T.J. Wheldon* (Caernarfon, 1922)

— — *Hanes Dirwest ynd Ngwynedd*, (Liverpool, 1921)

Williams, Gwyn A., 'Hugh Owen' in *Pioneers of Welsh Education* (Swansea, 1962)

— — *When was Wales?* (London, 1985)

Williams, J. Gwynn, *The University College of North Wales: Foundations 1884–1927* (Cardiff, 1985)

Williams, L.J. and Dot Jones, 'Women at Work in the Nineteenth Century', *Llafur*, Vol. 3, No. 3, 1982

Williams, Sian Rh., 'Nid Siol a het uchel', *Y Faner*, 9 January, 1981

— — 'Adfer y Ferch', *Y Faner*, 29 April, 1983

— — 'Y Frythones: Portread Cyfnodolion Merched y Bedwaredd Ganrif Ar Bymtheg o Gymraes yr Oes', *Llafur*, Vol. 4, No. 1, 1984

Zeldin, Theodore, Review, E.O. Hellerstein (et al.) Victorian Women, *Observer*, 24 May, 1981.

(ii)   Unpublished theses

Cohen, E.G., 'An Investigation into the Early Development of the Training of Schoolmistresses in the late nineteenth century and early twentieth century, with special reference to the Faculty of Education at University College, Cardiff', M. Ed. Wales, 1977

Davies, B.L., 'An Assessment of the Contribution of Sir Hugh Owen to Education in 'Wales', Ph.D., Wales, 1971

Davies, P.A., 'The Women Students at University College', Cardiff, 1883–1933', M. Ed. Wales, 1983

Dykes, D.W., 'The University College of Swansea' its background and development', Ph.D., Wales, 1983

Evans, W.G., 'The Establishment of Intermediate Education in Carmarthenshire, 1889–1914', MA, Wales, 1980

Gordon, S.C., 'Demands for the Education of Girls 1780–1865', MA, London, 1950

Impey, A.C., 'The Development of State-Provided Secondary Education in Cardiff, 1870–1939', M. Ed. Wales, 1973

Jones, H.M., 'History of the Cymmrodorion Society', MA, Wales, 1939

Jones, I.M., 'Merched Llên Cymru o 1850 i 1914', MA, Wales, 1939

Jones, R.G., 'The development of secondary education in Dolgellau, 1889–1946', M. Ed., Wales, 1972

Jones, S.J., 'Ieuan Gwynedd', MA, Wales, 1931

Phillips, E.R., 'The history of the teaching of domestic subjects 1870–1944', M. Ed., Wales, 1979

Rees, Ll. M., 'The history of Bangor Normal from its inception to 1908', MA, Wales, 1955

— — 'A Critical Examination of Teacher Training in Wales, 1846–1898', Ph.D., Wales, 1968

Thomas, A.M., 'The Implementation of the Welsh Intermediate Education Act of 1889 in the Wrexham Area to 1918', M. Ed., Wales, 1980

Trott, A.L., 'A history of Elementary Education in Wales, 1847–1870', Ph.D Wales, 1966

Vart, S.R., 'The development of intermediate education for girls in Wales, 1880–1900', M. Ed., Wales, 1981

Weaver, Jean A., 'The Development of Education in Swansea, 1846–1902', MA, Wales, 1957

Webster, J.R., 'The place of Secondary Education in Welsh Society, 1800–1918', Ph.D., Wales, 1959

Index

Abbott, T.S.C., 12.
Aberdare Departmental Committee, (1880–1), 6, 16, 27, 30, 35, 38–9, 40, 104, 110–16.
Aberdare Hall, 187, 209, 220, 228–34, 239, 240, 245, 246.
Aberdare Report (1881), 36, 40, 75, 116–18, 125–6, 153, 212, 259.
Aberdare, Lady, 28, 187, 211, 229, 230, 236, 239.
Aberdare, Lord, 21, 30, 38, 91, 118, 137, 165, 23, 215, 227–8, 245.
Aberystwyth
    Alexandra Hall, 217–23, 224, 225–6.
    University College of Wales, 7, 8, 9, 30, 34, 40, 72, 73, 92, 98–9, 104–9, 112, 120, 139, 140, 208, 209, 212–27, 257.
Abergavenny
    King Henry VIII Grammar School, 75, 177.
accomplishments, in education of girls, 8, 14, 57, 60–62, 64, 76, 130, 132, 262.
Acland, A.H.D., MP, 149, 151, 247, 248, 255–6.
Adam, 27.
admissions, 73, 105, 208, 216–7, 228, 244.
Adpar Academy, 56.
advanced elementary school, 119–20.
agricultural education, 248.
American experience, 21, 36.
Yr Amserau, 48.
Anderson, Dr Elizabeth Garrett, 26, 28, 36, 101, 102, 103.

'angel in the house' 50, 51.
angelic concept, 12–13.
Anglican Church, 49–50, 64, 65, 69, 72, 117–18, 257.
Anglican schools, 40, 62, 69, 132, 153–4.
Arnold, Professor E.V., 250.
Arnold, Matthew, 21.
Ashford, Welsh Girls' School 7, 40, 112, 117, 120, 121, 122, 127, 131, 132, 153, 154, 181–3, 213, 214, 260.
Association for Promoting the Education of Girls in Wales, 7, 9, 22, 26, 32, 35, 38, 39, 40, 43, 120, 121, 124, 129, 132, 136, 141, 142–52, 159, 160–1, 165, 185, 186, 188, 189, 190, 210, 231, 247–8, 254, 256, 259

Bala, Theological College, 96, 221.
Baldwin, Emily, 70.
Baner ac Amserau Cymru, 12, 13, 15, 18, 25, 26, 41.
Bangor, Girls' School, 22, 169.
    Normal College, 9, 51, 84, 85, 192, 201–4, 257.
    St Mary's College, 8, 85, 189, 197–201, 202, 257.
    University College, 9, 139, 140, 208, 209, 244–53.
Banks Olive, 2, 9, 151.
Barry Training College, 192, 197, 204–7, 257.
Bassnett, Susan, 2.
Bastardy Laws, 42.
Beale, Dorothea, 35, 133, 150.

Beale, Dorothea, 35, 133, 150.
Beaumaris David Hughes Charity,
    6, 57, 74–5, 117.
Becker, Lydia E., 26.
Beddoe, Deirdre, 1, 2.
Bedford College for Ladies, 37.
Y Beirniad, 17, 20.
Bevan, Bridget, 1.
bilingual schools, 262.
Binns, Revd B.J., 87–8, 195.
Blackwell, Dr Elizabeth 101, 133.
Blue Books (1847), 6, 7, 15, 41, 46–
    9, 55–6, 85.
blue stocking, 17.
Board of Education, 9, 159, 166,
    169, 171, 172, 239, 253, 259.
Bompas, H.M., 58, 59, 64, 68, 69,
    70.
Bonaparte, Napoleon, 49.
Borough Road College, 20, 84.
Bostock, Eliza, 67.
Bourne, Alfred, 88–9.
Bowstead, Revd J., HMI, 82.
Branca, Patricia, 2, 16.
Brecon, Christ College, 177.
    Diocesan Ladies School, 78–9, 83.
    Training College, 45, 90.
Briggs, Lord Asa, 1.
Bright, Jacob, 21, 25, 26.
Brighton, 18, 23.
Bristol, 31.
British Association, 18, 31.
British and Foreign Schools Society,
    20, 45, 84, 88, 94.
British Medical Association, 23, 101.
Brownrigg, Dean John, 183.
Bruce Report (1920), 260.
Bryant, Margaret E., 4, 16, 28, 30.
Bryant, Dr Sophie, 7, 22, 23, 35, 39,
    133–5, 150, 151, 160–1, 162, 245,
    246, 247, 249.
Burstyn, Jean M., 4.
Burton, Decimus, 65.
Buss, Frances, 28, 35, 102, 133, 151,
    222, 245–6, 249.

Caerleon, Training College, 197,
    205, 206, 207.
Caernarfon, Training College, 84,

    85, 197, 235.
Calvinistic Methodists, 27.
The Cambrian, 88, 91, 185, 195.
The Cambrian News, 9, 41, 222.
Cambridge
    Training College, (Hughes Hall),
        143, 150–1, 190.
    University, 18, 19, 25, 36, 42, 208,
        209–10.
Cardiff
    Aberdare Hall, 217–23, 224, 225,
        226.
    Howard Gardens School, 169–70,
        238.
    Intermediate School for Girls,
        169.
    South Wales and Monmouthshire
        Training School of Cookery and
        Domestic Arts, 8, 189, 210,
        236–9, 241–2.
    University College of South Wales
        and Monmouthshire, 21, 39,
        128, 135, 139, 140, 208, 227–43.
Carmarthen
    Diocesan High School for Girls,
        8, 79, 112, 125, 184, 255.
    South Wales and Mommouthshire
        Training College, 48, 83, 85.
Carpenter, E.A., 28, 149, 151, 159,
    161, 218–19, 220, 221, 222, 223–4,
    225.
census returns, 14, 32, 57.
Central Welsh Board, 9, 150, 165,
    166–7, 171, 172, 174–5, 257.
change, agents of, 5, 6, 24–43, 110–
    152, 262.
Charity Commission, 6, 7, 19, 62,
    67, 71, 74–5, 104, 124, 147, 159,
    165, 255.
Chartism, 3, 14, 44.
Cheltenham, Training College, 84,
    185.
Children's Employment Commis-
    sion, 53.
children, guardianship of, 25, 42.
Christian legacy, 27.
Clough, Anne Jemima, 150.
Clynnog, 56.
Cobbe, Frances Power, 20, 35, 133.

co-education, 6, 39, 113–4, 126, 128, 138, 141, 149, 157, 159, 170–1, 226.
College of Preceptors, 58, 77.
Collin, Mary, 166, 170, 172.
Committee of the Privy Council on Education, 29, 55, 81.
comparative education, 126, 128, 129, 131–2, 138, 140, 141, 145–6, 147, 158, 159, 171, 185–6, 188.
conservatism, 17–18.
continuing education, 40.
Corry, William, 82.
Corwen, 52.
Court of Chancery, 62–3, 69, 153.
Cowbridge, 177.
Cowper–Temple Bill (1875), 37.
Cranogwen, *see* Rees, Sarah Jane.
Crawshay, Rose Mary, 26, 31, 89.
Cross Commission (1888), 6, 181, 187, 189, 194.
Cyfarthfa, 168.
curriculum,
  academic, 8, 9, 24, 29, 57, 60–2, 125, 161–2, 164, 174, 255.
  accomplishments, 8, 14, 57, 60–2, 64, 76, 130, 132, 262.
  differentiation, 6, 8, 9, 24, 52, 138, 141, 145, 149, 155, 158, 163–4, 173, 174, 175, 260, 263.
  domestic subjects, 9, 29, 52, 55, 162, 163, 164, 174–5, 176, 193, 135, 263.
  literature, 53.
  needlework, 29, 52, 95, 193.
  Welsh language, 38, 54, 86, 114, 134, 137, 147, 259–60, 262.
  see also, liberal education.
Cymmrodorion, Honourable Society of, 6, 7, 23, 37, 38–9, 73, 121, 122, 123, 126, 128, 141, 142, 143–4, 146, 188, 189, 214, 259.
Cymru Fydd, 146.

Darbishire, W.Q., 246, 250.
Davidoff Leonore, 2.
Davies, Dr B.L., 89.
Davies, Dilys, *see* Jones, Dilys Glynne.

Davies, Emily, 20, 26, 28, 35, 36, 67, 102, 111, 133, 150.
Davies, Hester, 163, 237, 238, 239, 242.
Davies, Principal J.H., 212.
Davies, Revd H.L., 48.
Davies, Mary, 150.
Davies, Rosina, 26.
Davies, W. Cadwaladr, 143, 155, 156, 247.
Davies, W.E., 143.
Day Training Department, 8, 187, 189, 194, 234–6, 240, 247.
Deem, Rosemary, 28.
demography, 6, 30.
Denbigh, Howell's School, 7, 8, 9, 29, 53, 62–6, 68–71, 74, 99, 177–8, 183, 255, 257.
Department of Science and Art, 192, 193.
Derfel, R.J., 7, 15, 17, 20, 50.
'Desirableness of a University for Wales', 7, 38, 96.
Dickenson, Anna, 36.
differentiation, *see* curriculum.
divorce, 25, 42.
Directories, 56, 57.
Dobell, Annie M., 161.
Dolgellau, Dr Williams' School, 6, 7, 8, 15, 19, 29, 34, 74, 75–6, 111–12, 124, 133, 146, 161, 177, 179, 254, 255, 257.
domestic ideal, 5, 11–16.
domestic service, 32, 33.
domesticity, 3, 6, 8, 14, 24, 83, 84, 87, 95, 174, 258.
Don, Isabel, 230.
Dowlais, 53.
Drapers' Company, The, 62, 63, 64, 65, 68, 75, 179.
dual schools, 6, 131–2, 133, 149, 156–8, 160, 164, 176.
Dublin, University of, 18.
Dyhouse, Carol, 5, 31, 51, 64, 163.
Y Dysgedydd, 12.

Eben Fardd, 56.
economic factors, 6, 30, 31, 72, 128, 147, 226–7, 255, 258.

Education Act (1870), 30, 36, 37, 53, 72, 90–1, 132.
Education Act (1902), 166, 196, 199, 204.
Education Department, 52, 119, 162–3, 164, 185, 198, 234–5, 238.
educational history, 1–10.
educational ideas, 125–152.
educational reform, 72–9, 110–52.
The Educational Wants of Wales, 38.
Edwards, Bishop A.G., 89, 179–81, 198, 250, 257.
Edwards, Revd Ellis, 123.
Edwards, Dean H.T., 103.
Edwards, Principal Lewis, 13, 17, 46, 86, 96.
Edwards, Owen M., 13, 166, 168, 169, 171, 172, 75, 196, 200, 201, 202, 204, 205, 240.
Edwards, Principal T. Charles, 107, 143, 144, 213, 218, 221, 244.
eisteddfod, 7, 37. *see.*, National Eisteddfod,.
elementary education, girls, 8, 11–12, 29, 44–6.
elitism, 167–8.
Ellis, T.E., 35, 143, 148, 49, 153, 180, 185, 188, 194.
Elton, Professor Sir Geoffrey, 4.
emancipation, 6, 9, 12–13, 24–8, 41–3, 156, 226, 268–9, 262.
endowed grammar schools, 18, 30, 56, 176–184.
endowed girls' schools, 7, 18, 30.
see also Howell Schools, Dr Williams' School.
Endowed Schools Act (1869), 4, 67–8, 74, 119, 120.
Endowed Schools Commission, 6, 68, 72, 74–5, 159, 255.
endowments, 40, 68, 74–5, 116, 127, 145.
English boarding schools, 58, 59, 60, 77, 132, 139.
English, influences of, 35–7.
enrolment, 9, 166–7, 217, 220, 223, 224, 233.
equality of opportunity, 8, 11–24, 25, 29, 30, 40, 52, 59, 110, 118,

122, 127, 128, 145, 148, 149, 151, 155, 157, 162, 164–6, 216, 228, 254, 255–6, 261–2, 263.
evangelical Christianity, 13.
Evans, Beriah G., 123, 134.
Evans, Principal D. Emrys, 150.
Evans, E. Keri, 249, 251.
Evans, Dr L. Wynne, 53.
Evans, Revd Principal W.J., 158.
evolution, *see* Social Darwinism.
examinations, 37–8, 133, 134, 135, 147, 262
    Oxford and Cambridge, 37, 77, 134, 135.
    University Local Examinations in Wales, 39, 43, 133, 134, 135, 147.
    see also: Central Welsh Board.
exiles, Welsh, 37.

Fairchild, Principal, 198–9, 202.
Falconer, Judge Thomas, 7, 65–6.
family, 3, 12–13, 14, 54.
Fawcett, Millicent Garrett, 22, 133.
Fearon, John, 63.
fees, 9, 60, 69, 134, 141, 145, 156, 157, 165, 167–8.
femininity, 8, 11–24, 64, 74, 76, 87, 95–6, 102.
feminism, 3, 4, 16, 27, 64, 83, 88, 125, 262, 263.
Fewings, Eliza A., 19, 121, 122, 124, 144, 145, 211, 222, 225.
Ffrwdfâl Academy, 56.
Fitch, J.G., 195, 234, 235, 236.
Fletcher, Sheila, 4.
Fleure, Professor H.J., 225.
Forsyth's Bill (1876), 30.
franchise, 18, 25, 26, 29, 30, 42. *see* parliamentary franchise.
free places, 9, 167, 168, 169.
Freemason's Tavern, 39.
Y Frythones, 7, 12, 13, 41, 74, 142.

Gardiner Juliet, 1.
Garrett, Elizabeth, *see* Anderson.
Gee, Thomas, 13, 17, 18, 25, 26, 41, 55, 58, 62, 67, 72, 92, 98, 111, 118, 120, 121, 143, 154, 158, 180, 182, 209, 212, 214, 216.

gender stereotyping, 52, 83, 258, 263.

Genesis, 229.

George, David Lloyd, 250.

Gibson, John, 15, 19, 25, 27, 28, 30, 31, 32, 34, 35, 37, 41, 42, 43, 105, 108, 111, 153, 160, 213, 215, 217, 221, 222.

Girls' Public Day School Company (later Trust), 36, 113, 115, 127, 128, 132, 136–7, 138, 156, 166, 255.

Gladstone, Helen, 248, 253.

Gladstone, W.E., 120, 215, 222, 258–9.

Gladstone, Mrs W.E., 137.

Gnoll College, 7, 96–17.

governesses, 31, 57, 60, 76.

governing bodies, 6, 62, 114, 117, 141, 149, 157, 160–1.

grading of schools, 117, 132.

Griffith, Principal E.H., 243.

Griffith, J.H., 'Y Gohebydd', 18, 25, 28, 31, 33, 34, 37, 38, 72, 105.

Guest, Lady Charlotte, 53, 64.

Guest, Sir J.J., 53.

Gurney, Russell, MP, 26, 55.

Gwynedd, Ieuan, 7, 13, 14, 28, 41, 48–50.

Y Gymraes, 7, 13, 41, 43, 49–50, 176.

Hall, Professor Stanley, 170, 171.

halls of residence, 17, 126, 139, 210, 211, 217–23, 244–53, Appendix B.

Hamer, F.E., 165.

Harper, Principal Hugh, 103.

Harris, Principal D.R., 201.

Harrison, Brian, 102–3.

Hart-Dyke, Sir William, 181.

Haverfordwest, Tasker's School, 6, 75, 117, 124, 177.

headteachers, 6, 28, 149, 160, 164, 168.

health of female students, 21, 22, 23, 94–5, 171–2.

HMI Reports, 21, 29, 52.

Higginson, Emily, 111.

high schools for girls, 125, 159, 166, 169, 255.

History Workshop, 3.

Hoggan, Dr Frances E., 5, 7, 23, 25, 28, 38, 39, 100–4, 112–6, 119, 125–9, 143, 187, 299, 259.

Holland, Samuel, MP, 15, 34, 76.

home, 12–16, 55, 57.

Howell, Thomas, 62–3, 65, Appendix A.
  endowment, 40, 75, 112, 116–7, 120, 121, 127, 132, 153, 158, 177–8, 254, 264.
  Denbigh School, 7, 8, 9, 29, 53, 62–6, 68–71, 74, 99, 177–8, 183, 255, 257.
  Llandaff School, 7, 29, 53, 62–6, 68–71, 99, 124, 177–8, 255, 257.

Hughes, Elizabeth P., 7, 28, 35, 36, 38, 39, 122, 136–42, 143, 144, 145–6, 149, 150–1, 187, 188, 190, 206, 210, 211, 222, 233, 235, 243, 246, 260.

Hughes, Frances E., 244, 247, 248–50, 251.

Hughes, Revd Hugh Price, 17, 250.

Hughes, Bishop Joshua, 7.

Humphreys, Emyr, 258.

Humphreys-Owen, A.C., 143, 158, 215, 216.

Humphreys-Owen, Mrs A.C., 161.

Hurlbatt, Ethel, 232–3.

Hurlbatt, Kate, 233, 239.

Hutchins, Frances, 231.

Industrialization, 31, 53, 57, 66.

inequality, 27, 41, 42, 68, 72–5, 86, 96–109, 128, 131, 136.

injustices, 26, 116, 136, 210.

intellectual ability, women's, 20–24, 42, 61, 130, 162, 255, 260.

intermediate education
  county schemes, 148–9, 153, 154, 157, 160.
  intermediate schools, 6, 29, 37, 38, 118–25, 153–66, 254.

immorality, 15, 16, 47–8, 54–5, 249–52.

Jenkins, John, 52, 86.
Jesus College, Oxford, 103, 104, 116, 127.
Jex-Blake, Dr Sophia, 36, 37, 101, 102, 103, 133, 222.
job opportunities, 31, 32, 35, 43, 129–30, 132.
John, Angela, 2.
Joint Education Committees, 148, 154, 157–8.
Jones, Revd Bulkeley O., 178.
Jones, Dilys Glynne (nee Davies), 7, 21, 22, 28, 35, 38, 121, 122, 129–33, 142, 143, 144, 146, 147, 149, 150, 152, 155–6, 160, 188, 210–1, 245, 246, 247.
Jones, Edgar, 173–4, 256.
Jones, Elizabeth Mary, *see* Moelona.
Jones, Revd Evan *see* Ieuan Gwynedd.
Jones, Professor Henry, 143, 148, 246.
Jones, Revd H. Longueville, HMI, 81, 84, 86.
Jones, Idwal, 261.
Jones, Iorwen Myfanwy, 2.
Jones, Principal, J. Viriamu, 32, 123, 135, 143, 144, 145, 186, 187, 189, 210, 225–9, 234, 235, 261.
Jones, Mrs J. Viriamu, 229, 238.
Jones, Revd Principal, R. Tudur, 2–3.

Kamm, Josephine, 35.
Kay-Shuttleworth, Sir James, 80.
Kendall, Maria, 124.
Kenyon, G.T., MP, 120, 121, 123.

The Lancet, 23.
law, 6, 25.
Leighton, Stanley, MP, 153, 181, 250.
length of schooling, 56, 165, 176.
Lewis, Henry, 249.
Lewis, Herbert, 158.
Lewis School, Pengam, 56, 75, 120.
liberal education, 9, 125, 131, 137–8, 161, 162, 175, 235, 263.

liberal-nonconformity, 6, 40–1, 118–25, 259.
limited schooling, 44–77.
Lingen, R.R.W., 46–7.
literacy, 53.
Liverpool, 16.
London School Board, 26, 36.
London Welshmen, 37–8.
Lords, House of, 7, 63, 180, 250, 257.
Llafur, 2, 3, 50.
Llandaff, Bishop Ollivant of, 62–3. *see also* Howell School.
Llandovery College, 46, 117, 122, 177, 260.
Llanelli, Mechanics' Institute, 100.
Llanover, Lady, 1, 28, 46, 117.
Llanrwst Grammar School, 56.
Lloyd, Revd D.L., 7, 72.
Lloyd, Professor J.E., 148.

Mackail, Professor J.W., 248.
Mackenzie, Professor H. Millicent (née Hughes), 240.
male orientation, 7, 72, 73, 83, 84, 88, 97, 98, 105.
Marshall, Professor Alfred, 19.
marriage, 3, 15, 30, 42.
Maude, Mary, 250, 252.
Maudsley, Dr Henry, 23.
Mechanics' Institutes, 99–100.
medical profession
    opposition to women, 6, 23, 25, 37.
    women's struggle, 3, 37, 100–2, 258.
menstruation, 23.
mental strain, 21, 22.
Merthyr Tudful, 26, 52, 53.
Meyrick Trust, 103, 119, 121, 154, 181.
middle class, 4, 5, 6, 11, 18–19, 30, 31, 35, 43, 55, 57, 58, 64, 67, 117, 125, 127, 128, 145, 255, 262.
Middle and High Schools and a University for Wales, 7 97.
Mill, J.S., 25, 259.
The Missing Link in Education in Wales, 7.

mixed schools, 52, 156–9, 164, 170.
Moelona, 258.
Monmouth, William Jones Foundation, 6, 75, 124, 147, 148, 177.
moral reform, 15, 49, 54–5, 66.
Morgan, G. Osborne, 120, 244.
Morgan, Revd J.M., 18.
Morgan, Robin, 2.
Morris, Sir Lewis, 16, 38, 39, 128, 208, 20, 213, 214, 215, 216, 218, 222.
Mosaic religion, 27.
Moseley Commission, the, 171.
motherhood, 3, 5, 12–16, 23, 29, 42, 43, 51.
Mundella, A.J., 119, 120, 121, 123, 53, 181, 214, 217.
Mundella Circular, 119.
municipal secondary schools, 166–7.
Music Department, Aberystwyth, 106–9.

National Eisteddfod of Wales, 6, 13, 17, 18, 20, 21, 37, 38, 39, 52, 54, 98, 121, 124, 126, 128, 129, 133, 134, 136, 140, 141, 143, 144, 151, 259.
National Society for the Promotion of Social Science, 35, 36.
nationality, 128, 133, 134, 137, 139, 140, 141, 145, 142, 146, 147, 187.
Newcastle Commission Report, 6.
'new woman', 253.
Nicholas, Dr Thomas, 7, 38, 97–8.
Nonconformist academies, 56, 96.
Nonconformity, 40, 49–50, 62, 65, 114, 116, 1544, 201.
non-endowed girls' schools *see* private schools
North London Collegiate School for Girls, 35, 37, 113, 133, 150, 162, 230, 232, 245.
North Wales Scholarship Association, 73–4, 124, 145.
North Wales Women's Temperance Movement, 16.

Oakeley, H.E., HMI, 198.
obstacles, in women's struggle, 11–24, 26, 42–3, 52, 258, 262.
occupations, for women, 31, 32, 33, 34, 35, 42, 43.
Osborn, Violet, 249–50, 251.
Owen, Sir Hugh, 38, 39, 45, 51, 73–4, 89, 107, 111–12, 143.
Owen, Sir Isambard, 22, 38, 39, 123, 124, 143, 147, 151, 225, 239.
Owen, Revd John, 122.
Owen, Owen, 122.
Oxford
   Local Examinations, 37.
   University of, 18, 25, 42, 216.

Pakington Select Committee, 6.
pamphlets, 151.
parents, 131.
parliamentary franchise, 18, 25, 26, 27, 168.
Parry, Love Jones, 120.
Parry, Dr Joseph, 9, 106, 107–9.
Patmore, Coventry, 12, 50.
patriarchy, 5, 57, 255.
Pattison, Mark, 73.
payment by results, 136.
Pedersen, Joyce Sanders, 64.
Penrhos College, 125, 184, 255.
Penrhyn, Lady, 246.
Peter, Eliza, 77, 112.
Peter, Revd John, 77, 112.
Pfeiffer, Emily Jane, 23, 222, 231–2.
Phillips, Revd John, 45.
Phillips, Sir Thomas, 48, 63.
phrenology, 20.
Pontypool, 177.
post office, 32.
Powell, Mrs Ebenezer, 217.
Powell, Professor Thomas, 144.
preaching, 27.
prejudice, against women, 18–20.
private schools, 30, 55–72, 76, 77, 78–9, 117, 125, 139, 184, 254–5, 247.
professions, entry of women, 32–3.
property rights, married women's, 25, 26, 29, 41–2.
public speaking, 27.
pupil-teacher system, 8, 52, 80–3, 99, 191, 200.

Purvis, June, 5, 64, 163.

Queen's scholarships, 186–7, 192, 234, 238.

Race and Nationality (1886), 147.
Raleigh Committee, 212.
Rathbone, Miss M.F., 246, 261.
Rathbone, William, 120, 248.
Raw, Principal Hilda M., 207.
Raymont, Professor T., 234, 240.
Rebecca riots, 3, 14, 44.
Rees, Revd David, 50.
Rees, Revd Henry, 96.
Rees, Sarah Jane, 'Cranogwen', 26, 74.
Rees, Dr Thomas, 54.
Reform Act (1867), 26.
Reichel, Principal, H.R., 22, 123, 133, 135, 143, 144, 151, 157, 171, 244, 245, 246, 247, 248, 251, 253.
religion, 5, 27.
Rendel, Stuart, 40, 120, 153, 154, 181, 216, 225.
Report of the Children's Employment Commission (1843), 45.
Report on Elementary Education in the Mining Districts of South Wales (1840), 44–5.
Report on the Employment of Children, Young People and Women in Agriculture (1870), 53.
Revised Code (1862), 29, 52, 82, 85.
Rhuthun, 168, 177, 179, 180.
Rhydowen School, Pontsian, 56.
Rhys, Mrs John, 86, 249–50.
Rhŷs, Professor John, 39, 122, 144, 149, 171.
Richard, Henry, 119, 123.
Richards, Dr Thomas, 250.
Roberts, John, MP, 137, 149, 250.
Roberts, Dr R.D., 10, 143, 145.
Roberts, Principal, T.F., 35, 41, 211, 221, 222.
Rowbotham, Sheila, 1.
Rowlands, Anna, 160.
Ruskin, John, 12, 13.

Sadler, Sir Michael, 145, 170.

Salmon, Principal David, 196.
scholarships, 69–70, 73, 115, 139, 148.
school boards, 26, 36, 42.
Schools Inquiry Commission, *see* Taunton Commission.
Scotland, 185–6.
separate spheres, 3, 5, 11–13, 14, 32, 51, 64, 83.
sexism, 168–70, 174–5, 260.
sex-role stereotyping, 8, 29, 54, 85, 88, 122, 141, 145, 174, 263.
sexual division of labour, 5, 29, 32, 83, 125.
Shrewsbury Conference (1888), 22, 39, 122–3, 148.
Shirreff, Emily, 18, 51.
Sidgwick, Mrs E.M., 232.
Social class, 3, 28–9, 47, 49, 57, 69.
Social Darwinism, 3, 5, 23, 24, 146–7.
Social factors, 30, 166, 261–2.
Social Science Congress, 20, 31.
Social Welfare, 172–3.
South Wales and Mommouthshire Training School of Cookery and Domestic
    Arts, 18, 189, 210, 236–9, 241–2.
Spencer, Herbert, 24.
Spender, Dale, 1.
Stamp, Lady Olive (née Marsh), 224.
State, the, and education
    control, 6, 9, 44–50, 66–71, 255.
    finance, 40, 80, 90–1, 94, 107, 140, 212.
Stephen, H.M., 225.
strain, 22, 23–4, 85, 130, 171–2, 260.
students, women, 83–109.
On the Subjection of Women, 25, 259.
suffrage, 43, 133, 226, 253, *see* parliamentary suffrage.
Sunday schools, 99.
Swansea
    High School for Girls, 8, 18, 19, 125, 177.
    Training College, 8, 16, 21, 28,

84, 88–94, 185, 189, 192–7, 207, 257.
Symons, J.C., 48.

Tait, R.L., 22.
'*Tarian y Gweithiwr*', 39.
Taunton Commission, 4, 6, 18, 66–7.
Taunton Report, 6, 35, 53, 58, 60, 67–71.
Tawney, R.H., 167.
teachers, 32, 33, 83–96, 115, 139, 140, 158, 160, 167, 193, 194, 240.
  salaries, 85, 168.
  training of, 8, 9, 21, 80–96, 140, 141, 148, 185–207, 210, 227, 240–1, 257–8, 260–1.
technical education, 9, 38, 115, 137–8, 140, 162, 163, 174, 175, 176, 237.
Technical Instruction Act (1889), 163, 237, 239.
temperance movement, 16.
Tennyson, Lord, 12.
Thomas, Daniel Lleufer, 16.
Thomas, Revd H.E., 'Huwco Meirion', 51.
Towyn, Rhianfa School, 77.
Traethodau ac Areithiau, 50.
Y Traethodydd, 50.
training colleges, 8, 45, 185–207.
tradition, 16–17.
Tremenheere, Hugh Seymour, HMI, 44–6, 54.
Trevelyan, C.P. 197.
Trevor, Revd J.W., 47.
Tufnell, E.C., 54.
Y Tyst, 43.
y Tywysydd, 50.

universities, 8, 42.
University of Wales, 9, 10, 38, 42, 96–9, 114–5, 122, 139, 141, 210, 223, 257.
  University of Wales Movement, 7, 98–9.
  University Colleges, 8, 9, 40, 185–92, 208–53, 261.
  see also, individual colleges.

unsectarian education, 91, 94, 141, 193.
utilitarian education, 9, 175.

Vaughan-Johnson, H. 47.
Verney, Capt. Edmund, 73–4, 213, 214–5.
Verney, Mrs Margaret, 38, 111, 122, 143, 149, 150, 152, 209, 211, 212, 245, 246.
Vicinus, Martha, 2.
Voluntaryists, 14, 48–9.
voluntary system, 44, 45, 51.

Warren, Kate, 162.
Welsh Intermediate Education Act (1889), 6, 7, 15, 19, 30, 35, 40, 63, 75, 118–25, 132, 133, 147, 148, 152, 153–66, 176–81, 231, 255–6, 260.
Welsh language, 38, 54, 86, 114, 134, 137, 147, 259–60, 262.
Welsh National Society of Liverpool, 144.
Welsh press, 15, 18, 52, 58, 66, 72, 76–7, 91.
Western Mail, 103–4.
Wheeler, Professor Olive, 240.
Wheldon, Revd, T.J., 148.
'whisky money', 163.
Whitmell, Charles T., HMI, 159, 185, 187, 237, 238.
Williams, B.T., 7, 96.
Williams, Caroline, 240.
Williams, Dr Daniel, 75–6.
Williams, Principal David, 90, 185, 195–6.
Williams, Jane (Ysgafell), 48.
Williams, Professor Gwyn A., 2.
Williams, Sir John, 38.
Williams, Lewis, 185–6, 187, 238.
Williams, Thomas Marchant, 38, 73, 123, 135–6, 143.
Williams, William, HMI, 144, 145, 194, 234.
Williams, William, MP, 45.
Winter, Miss, 18, 22, 29, 222.
Withers-Moore, Dr, 23, 24, 130.
womanhood, 6, 11–24, 48–50, 52,

54, 57, 61, 64, 76, 95, 102, 132, 142, 176, 255, 261.
women's history, 1–4, 263.
women's sphere, 31, 32, 42, 46, 55, 84, 95, 255.
Woodard schools, 255.
working class, education of, 6, 11, 29, 44–45, 69, 72, 84.

World War, First, 9, 168, 227, 253, 257, 261.
Wrexham, 57, 58, 77.
Wynne, Edith, 43.

Zeldin, Theodore, 2.
Zimmern, Alice, 68.